Oscar Wilde and Modern Ireland

By the same author

Oscar Wilde
(Gill's Irish Lives, 1983)

The Dublin Gate Theatre, 1928–1978
(1984)

**The Dandy and the Herald:
manners, mind and morals from
Brummell to Durrell**
(1988)

Brian Friel and Ireland's Drama
(1990)

Lawrence Durrell: The Mindscape
(1994)

(as editor)
**Dark Fathers into Light:
essays on the work of Brendan Kennelly**
(1994)

THE THIEF OF REASON

Oscar Wilde and Modern Ireland

Richard Pine

ST. MARTIN'S PRESS
NEW YORK

THE THIEF OF REASON: Oscar Wilde and Modern Ireland

Copyright © 1995 by Richard Pine

St. Martin's Press, Scholarly and Reference Division, 175 Fifth Avenue, New York, N.Y. 10010

First published in the United States of America in 1995

Printed in the United Kingdom

ISBN: 0–312–15813–0

Library of Congress Cataloging-in-Publication Card Number 95–36425 *for Vanessa*

Contents

Preface   ix
Abbreviations   xiii

Introduction: The Irishman as Outsider   1

PART ONE

1. **'Quite Another Thing': Nineteenth-Century Irishness**   21
   (i) 'We Irish'   21
   (ii) Strategies for survival   32
   (iii) The gay temper   38

2. **A 'Regal Republic': Cultural Nationalism in the Mid-Century**   47
   (i) The book of Ireland   47
   (ii) Public opinion   71
   (iii) Middle Ireland   82

3. **A Secret and Selected Life**   107
   (i) The child   107
   (ii) The lover   136
   (iii) The criminal   149

PART TWO

4. **Fictions**   161
   (i) The stories   161
   (ii) The poems   199
   (iii) The letters   220

5. **Dramas**   **236**

    (i) Melodrama   236
    (ii) Commentary   258
    (iii) Symbolism   271

6. **The Third Meaning**   **282**

    (i) 'Professor of Aesthetics'   282
    (ii) The editor   291
    (iii) The critic   293

                    PART THREE

7. **The Parallel Decades**   **315**

    (i) Social politics   315
    (ii) Aesthetic politics   332
    (iii) Sexual politics   343

8. **Yeats's Transitus**   **354**

    (i) Myth   354
    (ii) Symbol   367
    (iii) Rhetoric   375

9. **The First Modernists**   **381**

    (i) Joyce   383
    (ii) Borges, Barthes   388
    (iii) Genet   400

    Conclusion   **405**

    Notes and References   420

    Select Bibliography   457

    Index   462

Preface

MY interest in the work of Oscar Wilde, and in particular the themes expressed and symbolised in his work, began when I was a schoolboy. Many of my contemporaries were reading Wilde and tracing his indebtedness to Pater and Huysmans. Many of them were also detecting their own inclination to homosexuality, and the apparent distress which this caused in some of my friends encouraged me to reflect on what was obviously a sexual and moral dilemma in the London before the decriminalisation of homosexual practices, even though we were being educated, as Wilde would have put it, 'near the Houses of Parliament'. Much of the material presented in the section of this volume entitled 'Sexual politics' (which has been previously published as 'Step-Children of Nature' in *Identity*, the journal of the Irish Gay Liberation Movement) was provoked and researched at that time, because many of my friends were beginning, like Wilde, to lead a double life and to gain confidence in doing so by reading his works.

In addition, I had several quite circumstantial reasons for pursuing an interest in Wilde and his circle: in childhood I had known the widow and son of Harry Marillier, the schoolboy who was one of Wilde's first crushes and who went on to become an expert on tapestry and the work of Beardsley; later I briefly held in my hand the card—*en route* to the saleroom—which Robert Ross had sent to the Passionist Fathers in Paris asking them to attend 'a dying man'; I have frequently visited the fishing lodge, Illaunroe, on Lough Fee in Connemara, which was a home to Wilde in his childhood and adolescence, a house scarcely changed since he lived there; and for a number of years I was the custodian of a large cache of documents—now in the Bodleian Library—(among them a 'new' letter by Wilde which I had the privilege of discovering) which represents the surviving evidence of Wilde's literary estate as administered by his son Vyvyan. All these fortuitous associations—some tenuous, others more compelling—led me to discover an affinity with the mind of Wilde and to develop a curiosity about the contexts in which he lived.

There seemed, however, little justification for adding to the ever-lengthening list of Wilde biographies and critical studies: until the appearance in 1987 of Richard Ellmann's long-awaited tome, little was added to our knowledge or understanding of Wilde by the volumes of Philippe Jullian (1969), Sheridan Morley (1976), or even Rupert Croft-Cooke's provocative *The Unrecorded Life of Oscar Wilde* (1972); the exception to this generalisation being the political insight of H. Montgomery Hyde (1976) and the aesthetic perceptions of Martin Fido (1973). Even specialised studies by C. S. Nassaar (1974), J. E. Chamberlin (1977) or Philip K. Cohen (1978) seemed to pursue Wilde down unrewarding *culs-de-sac* rather than grasping the essence of his work; again, the exceptions were Epifanio San Juan's *The Art of Oscar Wilde* (1967) and Rodney Shewan's *Oscar Wilde: Art and Egotism* (1977).

In the early 1980s the appearance of a series entitled 'Gill's Irish Lives' presented for the first time an opportunity to approach Wilde from an Irish perspective, and my original *Oscar Wilde* appeared in that series in 1983. The milestones of Wilde biography by Hesketh Pearson (1946) and others were becoming out of date owing to the availability of new material, especially the *Letters* (1962); moreover, only one Irishman, St John Ervine (1951), had addressed the question of Wilde at length, and that was a fiercely hostile, homophobic treatment. No Irish publisher had previously thought it worthwhile to promote this aspect of Wilde.

Still, the difficulty remained of what form and style such a biography should assume. When I reviewed Ellmann's book in the *Irish Review* in 1987, I was hesitant in my criticism because I owed him personal gratitude and held him in professional admiration. But his treatment disappointed me, because it seemed to confuse biography with critical assessment. I said then that 'there are four ways to write a book of this kind: to depict *type* (as Sartre does with Genet, for example, to the almost total exclusion of fact); to adopt the all-embracing but unleavened factual approach of Montgomery Hyde; to accept all the circumstantial, uncorroborated evidence and paint an impression, as Hesketh Pearson (with charm and some success) or Philippe Jullian (gauchely and inaccurately) set out to do; or to explore the key biographical points in terms of character, as the great unfinished essays published by A. J. A. Symons in *Horizon* in the 1940s show'.

In our post-colonial era of sexual and social liberation (as evidenced in Camille Paglia's *Sexual Personae* (1990) and Alan Sinfield's *The Wilde Century* (1994)) it seems unreasonable not also to explore Wilde's Irishness, and in plays such as Terry Eagleton's *Saint Oscar*, whatever one may think of its dramatic potential, we are witnessing a part of the new emancipation of Wilde—and writers like him—from the proprietorial acres of British academe. The fact that my 1983 volume is now out of print has allowed me to revise it completely, not only for the purpose of incorporating new material (an additional volume of Wilde's letters appeared in 1985, for example) but also to include much more extensive consideration of Wilde's circumstances than was possible in the restricted format of a pocket biography.

Even so, to have elicited every nuance of Wilde's plays or his dialogues, in particular, for their cultural, sexual or social relevance to my thesis, would have made the present book prohibitively lengthy, and readers must therefore make up their own minds to pursue his texts in these directions.

In the course of writing this book I have enjoyed the encouragement of many friends who recognised that I had something to contribute to the understanding of Wilde as an Irishman and as an Irish mind. In particular, the editor of 'Gill's Studies in Irish Literature', Terence Brown, has been a stalwart supporter; others include the late Mícheál Mac

Liammóir, who did more than anyone to shape my understanding of Wilde's personality, the late Richard Ellmann,
Brendan Kennelly, James W. Flannery, Anthony Roche, and
someone with whom I first discussed an interest in Wilde
and Huysmans thirty years ago, my oldest friend, Sebastian
Garrett. My Introduction, 'The Irishman as Outsider', first
saw the light of day in 1987 as a lecture at the University of
Birmingham, Alabama, where Dr Kieran Quinlan gave me
the opportunity of discussing it with his Faculty, and was
later revised as the subject of a Fales Colloquium which I
delivered at New York University in 1991. Someone with
whom I did not discuss this book, but whose example as an
expert in nineteenth-century Ireland is pleasurable, if difficult,
to follow, is W. J. McCormack. His admonitory influence on
the following pages will be evident. Charles Benson, Keeper of
Older Printed Books in the Library of Trinity College, Dublin,
and his staff, provided helpful and courteous assistance. To
my assiduous copy-editor, Colm Croker, who has already rendered a similar service in respect of my previous *Oscar Wilde*,
I am deeply grateful and indebted for saving me from several
errors and for making important suggestions for the book's
improvement. I was delighted that at the penultimate stage of
writing my friend the late Éilís Dillon was able to make available a proof copy of Vivian Mercier's posthumous *Modern Irish
Literature*, which is bound to become a seminal volume on the
period.

Davis Coakley's *Oscar Wilde: The Importance of Being Irish*
and Gary Schmidgall's *The Stranger Wilde* appeared after the
present volume had gone to press, and it has therefore not
been possible to discuss their conclusions in any depth.
However, the former, in its attention to Wilde's Irishness,
and the latter, in pursuit of his gay temperament, substantively address the same themes and cover the same terrain
as the present volume, although neither appears to do so in
such depth.

Richard Pine
Dublin, 1994

Abbreviations

THE convenience of citing references to a single edition of Wilde's work is not yet available (Ian Small's edition for the Oxford University Press is in preparation). However, the vast bulk of his published work became available in a single volume, edited by G. F. Maine, and published by William Collins & Sons in 1948; after many reprintings and metamorphoses, in the course of which it acquired an introduction by Vyvyan Holland, it remains, despite its ungainly and unattractive format, a widely available and easily affordable reference. Almost all of Wilde's work to which I refer is cited parenthetically in the text as (*CW*). The exceptions to this are Wilde's letters (*Letters of Oscar Wilde*, edited by Rupert Hart-Davis, London, 1962; and *More Letters of Oscar Wilde*, edited by Rupert Hart-Davis, London, 1985), which are cited in the text as (*L*) and (*ML*) respectively; in addition, Isobel Murray's edition of *The Picture of Dorian Gray* (London, 1974) has been preferred, and this is cited in the text as (*PDG*). Two notebooks, 'Commonplace Book' and 'Notebook kept at Oxford', have been edited by Michael Smith and Philip Helfand as *Oscar Wilde's Oxford Notebooks* (Oxford, 1989), and quotations from these are cited in the text as (*CPB*). Wilde's lectures and reviews were not included in G. F. Maine's one-volume edition, and these have been cited in the text by reference to the two volumes, *Reviews* and *Miscellanies*, in the First Collected Edition, edited by Robert Ross, published in 1908: these appear in the text as (*Rev*) and (*Misc*) respectively. Finally, the original French-language version of *Salomé* published in the First Collected Edition has been preferred, and this is cited in the text as (*Salomé*). I have throughout therefore preferred to use the French spelling of *Salomé* rather than the spelling *Salome* adopted in English translation.

The Irishman as Outsider

O N 17 October 1874, the day after his twentieth birthday, Oscar Wilde matriculated at Oxford University, where he was to pass the next four years as a scholar of Magdalen College, having already held a foundation scholarship at Trinity College in his native city of Dublin. He was later to write: 'The two great turning points of my life were when my father sent me to Oxford, and when society sent me to prison.' (L 469) He claimed—not without justification—that 'I was one who stood in symbolic relations to the art and culture of my age.' (L 466) But Wilde's relations with his age were conducted as an outsider both in England and in Ireland. Joyce, seeing him in the tradition of Sheridan, Goldsmith and Shaw, called him 'court jester to the English'.[1] Once he had taken that step towards Oxford, Wilde stood irreconcilably outside both worlds, the English society which, by virtue of his difference, he was to shock, subvert and despise for the rest of his life, and the Irish world which became more a state of mind than a home.

The 'difference' became the controlling factor in his critical path: it determined that he should continue to reinvent himself—'the Oscar of the first period ... the Oscar of the second period'[2]—and it also encouraged him to invent the age. He can be analysed only as an exception, and on his own exceptional terms: 'I was a problem for which there was no solution.' (L 685) Yet the complexity of his adroit use of masks obliges us to see him as a symbol, a new standard or type of behaviour in social and aesthetic manners, and also as symbolic of that type. He sets the stage and becomes the stage himself. 'Try as we may,' he is recorded as saying in Paris shortly before his death, 'we cannot get behind the appearance of things to the reality. And the terrible reason may be that there is no reality in things apart from appearance.'[3]

This book has a twofold purpose: firstly, to examine the extent of Wilde's Irishness (and how it permitted him to survive for twenty years as an outsider in England); secondly, to indicate that the Irishman stands not only outside, and in symbolic relation to, English society and literature, but also in symbolic relation, and as a stranger, to himself. For Wilde to have fulfilled the professed ambition of his adolescence, to become the defendant in the case of *Regina v. Wilde*,[4] was to underline the fact that, at the risk of losing his identity, he had conceived himself in the third person, as the central figure in the drama of his imagination.

The implications of such an ambition, even at its most frivolous level, are complex. They involve the nature of the individual's relationship with society, with its codes and mores, its moral and aesthetic evolution, and, more compellingly, they direct us towards a consideration of the relation between the two islands which, during the half-century before Wilde's birth, had constituted *de jure* the United Kingdom of Great Britain and Ireland, an entity which, *de facto*, was anything but united. To follow that route is to ask what were the essential differences between the mindscapes of the two dominant races, the Saxon and the Celt, in order to establish why what Wilde called his 'antinomianism'—his defiance of moral law—went undetected for so long. At root, we must examine Wilde's consciousness of his Irish origins—the antiquarian and folkloric dimensions of his father's work, and the aesthetic and political intensity of his mother's essays and poetry—and what Wilde might have understood by the idea of 'a nation'.

As we shall see in Part One, the idea of being Irish (as it was understood in the mid-century) is quite different from that of being English or French. The smaller and more vulnerable cultures of Europe, especially those like Ireland, Norway or Finland, which lived in the shadow of dominant imperial powers, placed a much greater interrogation point over the notions of origin, identity and relation. For the Irishman, seen both in isolation and in terms of Ireland's experience of England, the social construction of reality is in fact 'unreal' because he cannot subscribe to its rules and its canon.

The neglect of Wilde's Irishness has served to heighten the simple dramatic tension in his life as he moved almost inexorably towards imprisonment, calumny and exile. It has permitted considerable attention to be directed in particular towards his plays (most notably the recent studies by Alan Bird[5] and Katherine Worth).[6] The most thorough study of Wilde's entire *œuvre* was published in German by Norbert Kohl in 1980[7] and appeared in a modified English translation in 1989 as *Oscar Wilde: the works of a conformist rebel*.[8] Yet Kohl's almost studied refusal to consider Irishness as a factor in Wilde's work is a serious limitation to his otherwise valuable insights into Wilde as a phenomenon in the later nineteenth century and as a forerunner of modernism. More recently a useful survey of the literature has been published by Ian Small in *Oscar Wilde Revalued: an essay on new materials and methods of research* (1993).[9]

While Kohl with justification sees Wilde as 'a symbol of conflict between the middle-class values of the nineteenth century and the artist's need for freedom', he fails to see further into the conflict between the relative values of Ireland and England at the time; although he calls for 'an account that would combine the facts with sensitive characterisation and insight into the social and historical background',[10] his own insight is limited to the English background and he eschews what he likes to call 'the biographical fallacy'.[11] He nevertheless finds it possible to discuss Wilde, along with Congreve and Sheridan, in 'the English comic tradition',[12] ignoring what has so successfully been established by Vivian Mercier as 'the *Irish* comic tradition'.[13] Others, more aware of Irish writing, have dismissed Wilde's Irishness. Roger McHugh and Maurice Harmon, for example, state unequivocally in

their *Short History of Anglo-Irish Literature* that 'the plays of
Oscar Wilde . . . and of George Bernard Shaw . . . properly
belong to English theatrical history',[14] while Alan Warner, in
his *Guide to Anglo-Irish Literature*, says of *The Importance of
Being Earnest* that 'there is nothing Irish or Anglo-Irish about
it . . . his plays have no Irish dimension',[15] adding that 'we
cannot think of Goldsmith, or of Wilde, as being moulded by
influences that were moulding Ireland'.[16]

'As far as the development of British drama is concerned,'
says Kohl, 'Wilde made two vital contributions: a new style
of language, and a new critical perspective.'[17] It will be central to my concern in this book to supply the evidence that
Wilde's rhetoric, acoustic and perspective were derived from
Irish examples before he considered English examples,
because his tradition was that of the writer commenting
from a secret and alien location. Kohl quotes with approval
Robert Merle's idea of Wilde as a *'moi autarcique* [autarchic
self]',[18] but he explores neither his Irishness nor his homosexuality as reasons for the monomaniac stance which fuelled
Wilde's trajectory. When he criticises Philip Cohen for concen-
trating on Wilde's work as 'a process of self-creation',[19] he
seems to believe that such a view inhibits us from finding
Wilde where he wrote himself, among the fallen women as
much as the fallen men. There is no Parnell in Kohl's examination of 'the social and historical background', no Speranza,
no Sir William, no Mahaffy, presumably because in addition
to rejecting a biographical approach Kohl believes that with
Ireland part of the British Empire and of the United Kingdom,
with London the focus of that kingdom and empire, we may
overlook the provincial or colonial origins of so many writers. Such an approach renders the visiting writer—Kipling
or Henry James for example—merely provincial: to see
Wilde as 'this eccentric Irish Londoner'[20] is sufficient for
Kohl. Even Terry Eagleton, usually adept at evaluating the
extraterritorial,[21] settles for a comprehensive description of
'the Irish Oxfordian socialist proto-deconstructionist'[22] as if
each element in the epithet were equal and equivalent.

Meanwhile, to speak, as does Kohl, of hunger and poverty and a 'ceaseless quest for property'[23] as the background to
Wilde's *Soul of Man under Socialism*, without looking at the
Irish Famine and Land War for a possible cause of preoccupation with land and survival, is like discussing Wordsworth
without recourse to nature. Perhaps the absurdity of Kohl's
narrow stance is epitomised in his declaration that Wilde
'was basically conservative with aristocratic ambitions, feign-
ing a republican disposition that had no emotional roots
whatsoever but was grounded in the uncommittedness of a
modish intellectualism'.[24]

Here we meet the core of the difficulty in assessing and
appreciating Wilde. Kohl suggests that 'while acting as a precursor of the modern age, he remained at heart—perhaps *mal-
gré lui*—a true Victorian';[25] he points out that 'it is almost
impossible to understand how a mind of such rich and critical
originality could so often remain trapped in the circles drawn
by his predecessors' and perceptively suggests that 'Wilde had
no direct access of his own to reality'.[26] But because his is a critical rather than a biographical study, Kohl fails to pursue this
insight into the area where that connection between apparent
discontinuities might be made: nineteenth-century Ireland.

Even the most comprehensive biography of Wilde, by
Richard Ellmann (1987),[27] adds little to our knowledge and
appreciation of the milieux of nineteenth-century Dublin
and post-Famine rural Ireland, both of which are fundamental to our understanding of Wilde's early upbringing and of
his behaviour once he had left his native city and country to
seek his fortune and to cultivate his literary and sexual
appetites, abroad.

Ellmann's earlier writings—'Wilde at Oxford',[28] 'Oscar and
Oisin'[29] (examining Wilde's influence on Yeats), 'Corydon
and Ménalque'[30] (his influence on Gide), 'Overtures to *Salome*'[31]
or 'The Critic as Artist as Wilde'[32]—were all masterly vignettes
of Wilde's life and work. Unlike his *James Joyce*, however,
Ellmann's *Oscar Wilde*, in which each of these episodes found
a place, was not executed with the unity of vision which

paints the man together with his work. On Wilde's homosexuality and its relation to his poems, he was, as I shall indicate in Part Two, decidedly adrift. When Ellmann succeeds, he does so brilliantly; to turn a corner with him and to be presented with a breathtaking elucidation of Wilde's mind is an enduring pleasure. But, given his extraordinary capacity for mining information from unexpected lodes and giving it a rich and subtle explication, it is puzzling and regrettable that he did not seem to consider it worthwhile to further explore the pre-Oxford phase of Wilde's life, or to address Irishness as a background as well as a disposition.

Nevertheless, Kohl's title—'a conformist rebel'—establishes a key factor in Wilde's Irish mindscape which can be developed in relation to every other dimension: the paradoxical notion that a writer could simultaneously conform and rebel.[33] Paradox, so difficult a concept in English letters, is almost ubiquitous, a commonplace, in discussing the Irish mind. Wilde himself was responsible, on the public plane, for advocating that 'a truth in art is that whose contradictory is also true' and that 'the truths of metaphysics are the truths of masks' (*CW* 1078). The insistence on leading a double life, on seeing with a double vision, identifies Wilde as a seminal figure in the aesthetic and dramatic theory of the mask and the notion that we can accommodate, in Joyce's terms, 'two thinks at a time'.[34]

In one of the earliest entries in his student commonplace book, Wilde noted that

> tragedy breasts the pressures of life · comedy eludes them by its irony · but the ultimate peace and assurance rests with tragedy. (*CPB* 108)

The interaction of the two, comedy and tragedy, is assured in the gay temper which the Irishman brings to bear on the issue of doom. The effect of irony is to heighten the play between the two. To seek 'the ultimate peace' is to confront life and thus suffer under it, yet there is a parallel inclination to elude it by presenting a mask to the world. Wilde's nineteenth century was the nexus by means of which he could accept, and at the same time compensate for, the workings of fate. His parents' friend Aubrey de Vere wrote that the English perceived 'our insolent content, and savage merriment in misery'.[35] De Vere's phrasing is neat in suggesting both defiance of fate and determination to make of defeat some virtue if not some reward. It is oxymoronic, as is all Wilde's apparently careless phrasing, commuting between opposites but establishing an equivocal middle ground in order to be true to neither in its search for identity and self-deception. The mask performs the function of both concealment and transformation.

An oxymoron is what is commonly, but erroneously, described as a 'mixed metaphor'. Ireland in the nineteenth century almost stereotypically illustrates how such an error can occur. As I shall show in Part One, the Irish mind is an inclusive rather than an exclusive imagination, one which does have that Joycean capacity for accommodating potential contradictions but not necessarily for resolving them. Creative contradiction, in fact, helps to explain the emergence of Anglo-Irish literature as the chief contribution of the Protestant conscience to the emergence of Ireland as a cultural and political entity. By his class, religion and education, Wilde was separated from the majority of Irishmen; but it is these very aspects of his background which make the question of his Irishness most interesting. The Anglo-Irish were travellers in their own land; their descriptions of Irish life, as distinct from English life, are those of strangers who observe the field yet can only tangentially or obliquely understand how they disturb, and participate in, it.

Samuel Ferguson, in his poem 'Mesgedra', epitomised the contending claims of possession, belonging and difference:

> No rootless colonist of an alien earth,
> Proud but of patient wings and pliant limb,

> A stranger to the land that gave him birth,
> The land a stranger to itself and him.

As we shall see, this was no simple version of alienation, but one in which a complex set of relationships and non-relationships is negotiated by the patient and the pliant.

The oxymoron encapsulates the nineteenth-century problem of resolution. In terms of emotion, Wilde expressed it as the phenomenon of 'terrible joy', and throughout his published work and his correspondence he continually employed the idea of 'a land where all things are perfect and poisonous' (*L* 185). It was a phrase which would recur throughout his writing, both public and private. Thus he called a book by Edgar Saltus on Mary Magdalene 'so pessimistic, so poisonous and so perfect',[36] while Swinburne's *Poems and Ballads* were 'very perfect and very poisonous' (*Rev* 520). The role of tragedy, of doomed innocence, is intended not merely to indicate that beauty is inevitably fated to immolation, but also to suggest that life consists in experiencing the antitheses simultaneously. As with Dorian Gray's experience— 'the living death of his own soul' (*PDG* 221)—it suggests a landscape which can be occupied only in the imagination, one which, like the 'savage merriment in misery', is contradictory and yet lived by an intensely imagistic mind. Thus when Wilde spoke, in 'The Decay of Lying', of Turgenev's 'Nihilist, that strange martyr who has no faith' (*CW* 983), he intended to achieve much more than paradox: such a figure becomes both icon and paradigm, a headline for a society which lived within the experience of contradiction and difference. The dominant expression is Hegel's: 'Ich bin der Kampf. Ich bin nicht Einer der im Kampf Begriffenen, sondern ich bin beide Kämpfende und der Kampf selbst [I am the struggle. I am neither one combatant nor the other. I am both combatants and the struggle itself].'[37]

Thus the oxymoron both jeopardises and validates the contradictions it contains, defining a third state which supersedes the two elements which gave rise to it, and which depends for its existence on its inherent instability. Wilde's complexity must be appreciated as something which was simultaneously both opposed to reality and alternative to reality. His writing shares the structural instability of the Anglo-Irish novel in its need to escape and yet remain: 'I would more readily die for what I do not believe in than for what I hold to be true.' (*L* 185) In 1864 Sir William Wilde, Oscar's father, in an address to the Young Men's Christian Association on 'Ireland Past and Present; the Land and the People', referred to Ireland as 'a truly regal republic'. Seldom was the fragility of Protestant Ireland's relations with, on one hand, England and, on another, with herself so expressly stated.

It is therefore possible to understand that when Wilde said in Reading Prison that 'to be entirely free and at the same time entirely dominated by law, is the eternal paradox of human life that we realise at every moment' (*L* 443) he was speaking not only as a self-proclaimed 'lord of language' brought down to earth for disregarding social norms: his statement takes on an extra dimension when we consider that in Irish terms the paradox was much more acute than elsewhere in nineteenth-century Europe (except possibly in Finland, Norway or Hungary). That it should have become paradigmatic in the twentieth century, where the Irish experience finds complementary echoes in many post-colonial societies, is indicative of Wilde's inherent and intuitive ability to understand the complex relationship between coloniser and colonised which almost preternaturally leads to sexual or artistic deviance—a factor which will become most telling in our discussion of modernism.

Apart from the specific circumstances of Irish society and politics in the later nineteenth century, there is a prescient insight into the interrelationship of art and society in Wilde's remark

> There is no lack of culture [in Ireland] but it is nearly all
> absorbed in politics. Had I remained there, my career
> would have been a political one.[38]

To see things differently to others is to develop a set of beliefs
about the phenomenal world which may place one at vari-
ance from social norms: prophets, political subversives and
anchorites, together with sexual deviants, vagrants and criminals, act contrariwise to most orthodoxies. In matters of aesthetics—the formulation of perceptions into a system of
beliefs—the political dimension is seldom absent.

Concretely, there is no doubt that, at the time of his trial,
Wilde represented a political rather than an aesthetic or even
a moral threat to the British establishment, because gossip
about his conduct implicated close associates of the government. There was, as one contemporary commentator—and
player—observed, an 'invisible city',[39] and Wilde had made
it visible; he had thus brought aesthetics, ethics and politics
(three elements of which he was acutely conscious) into
interaction, creating a scandal which, like the Parnell and
Dreyfus affairs, had profound social ramifications. By bringing the visible and invisible cities into the same frame of reference, Wilde had 'outed' many unsuspected ways of seeing,
and had thus stripped away masks of concealment only to
establish others such as that of the decadent martyr.

It was an age of outsiders, many of whom found their
way into *The Yellow Book*: Henry James, Yeats, Shaw, George
Moore, Whistler, Frank Harris, Henry Harland, Conrad. It
was the age prior to, but also prescient of, the post-colonial;
and these outsiders, with Wilde (despite his exclusion from
The Yellow Book) and James (probably as a result of his inclusion in it) as their leaders, in fact created a decade *parallel* to
that of the conventional Victorian 1890s. It could only have
been created by outsiders, with an oblique perspective on the
strengths and weaknesses of the earliest phases of post-
industrial society. In such an age Wilde emphasised the role of
the dandy, with his attention to self; when he characterised

the new age as 'the age of style', he was profoundly herald-
ing the age of Freud and Einstein.

In searching for himself he exposed the fact that those who
run away from home forget how to rediscover it. The domestic
hearth—so foreign to Wilde after the age of twenty—is the
focus and fount of identity, so that the question 'Who am I?',
whether uttered by an individual or a nation, a child or a sage,
becomes a retrospective journey towards meaning. Once again
paradox comes to our aid in the form of Shaw's statement that

> Though by culture Wilde was a citizen of all civilised
> capitals, he was at root a *very Irish Irishman*, and as such
> a foreigner everywhere but in Ireland.[40]

Although problematic, the statement, by the very nature of
the problem, becomes revealing: while we may not know
what constitutes the 'Irishman', nor what qualities make one
more Irish than another, it fixes a relationship of strangeness
between the notion of culture and that of home. In turn
we must note Vivian Mercier's two-edged comment: 'No
Protestant Irishman can deny Shaw's Irishness without denying his own.'[41] We are never more at home than when we are
anxious and nervous about our culture. For the Irish mind,
there was no equation between the two, no bedrock of certainty against which they could be measured and identified.

Superficially, at least, Wilde's 'difference' was evident to
his Oxford contemporaries, one of whom recalled

> the unexpected angle from which he looked at things.
> There was something foreign, too, and inconsequential
> in his modes of thought, just as there was a suspicion of
> a brogue in his pronunciation and an unfamiliar turn in
> his phrasing. His qualities were not ordinary and we,
> his intimate friends, did not judge him by the ordinary
> standards.[42]

Another recollected

> a flood of paradoxes, untenable propositions, quaint comments ... preposterous theories.... His talk charmed because it was plainly the utterance of a gay and engaging and keen spirit.[43]

The point is corroborated by Wilde's lover, Lord Alfred Douglas, who asserted:

> The most remarkable and arresting thing about Wilde was that without apparent effort he exercised a sort of enchantment which transmuted the ordinary things in life and invested them with strangeness and glamour.... He had a way of looking at life and a point of view which were magical in their effect.[44]

Douglas added that

> Unless you understand that Oscar Wilde is an Irishman through and through, you will never get an idea of what his real nature is. In many ways he is as simple and innocent as a child.[45]

Foreign ... unfamiliar ... preposterous ... gay ... magical ... simple : these were the qualities by which Wilde 'charmed' and 'transmuted' the ordinary, without, however, revealing 'his real nature'. It was his Irishness which for so long prevented all but his closest associates—even perhaps his wife—from detecting his homosexuality, because the two referential contexts were so proximate.

Two further statements by Wilde begin to illuminate the initial question of 'difference', the uneasy but symbiotic relationship between coloniser and colonised, orthodox and deviant. The first was his reaction in 1892 to the Lord Chamberlain's refusal of a licence to perform *Salomé*:

> I will not consent to call myself a citizen of a country that shows such narrowness in its artistic judgment. I am not English—I am Irish—which is quite another thing.[46]

The second statement concerned the use of the English language in Ireland, a matter which goes far beyond semantics:

> I do not know anything more wonderful or more characteristic of the Celtic genius, than the quick artistic spirit in which we adapted ourselves to the English tongue. The Saxon took our lands from us and left them desolate —we took their language and added new beauties to it.[47]

The idea of Irishness as 'quite another thing', or of the existence of a Hiberno-English literary genre, identifies Wilde not as a figure peripheral to Irish letters, but as a central and dominant influence on the development of Yeats and Joyce in particular. Like Ferguson and Le Fanu, Wilde provides a powerful index to the evolution from 1830 to 1900 of the Anglo-Irish literature which provided the impetus for political independence, and of which he was a primary conduit.

Richard Ellmann states that 'Wilde created himself at Oxford'.[48] Certainly it was the origin to which almost all Wilde's eccentricity and flamboyance would subsequently be traced. Yet in 1895, at the high point of his public collapse, the *National Observer*, edited by W. E. Henley, identified him as 'the obscene imposter, whose prominence has been a social outrage ever since he transferred from Trinity Dublin to Oxford his vices, his follies and his vanities'.[49] It might therefore be more accurate to regard his years at Oxford as the transitional period in which he not so much 'created himself' but began to create *a narrative of self* in which there would be a continual fascination with the act of baptism—and thus of naming—which culminates in his own work with the appearance of the Baptist himself. Here he could accommodate the various affective calls on his consciousness such as the relation of art to life, and the concept of 'soul' (so pervasive in the nineteenth century), with its religious and psychological connotations. At the core of the narrative is the telling of secrets. It is a dramatic point because people must pretend to be someone else before they can be discovered as they really are. But discovery, the longing of the lost child to be found, of the story to be revealed, is of the essence. The core moment is a very small moment: what Wilde said is not as important as the way in which he said it. His secrets are very small secrets, even when played out fully on the melodramatic stage with histrionic declamation and gesture.

Everything he said was very simple, and consisted of a question and a statement: Who am I? (I am lost); Where have I come from? (I am afraid of the past); Where am I going? (I cannot read the book). If these are quintessentially nineteenth-century preoccupations, they are never more clearly seen than in Ireland and its literature. Yet studies of Anglo-Irish literature in the second half of the nineteenth century, such as those by Cahalan, Fallis, Foster and Hall,[50] ignore Wilde, while comparable studies of English literature fail to allude to his Irishness. Once more Wilde is excluded from both countries. It is indeed tempting to regard his work as *sui generis*, deriving from a personality which was artificial, forged, and based on an exceptional temperament. Yet Wilde's classical training, his literary style and his interest in the past and in contemporary issues such as politics and religion all stem more from his Irish background than from any other source.

Ellmann asserts that 'Wilde writes his works out of a debate between doctrines rather than out of doctrines',[51] the source of the debate being the tension between the private, secret world and the public arena. This, however, is only partially true. While it is central to Wilde's sense of the dramatic (as it is to Yeats's) that dialogue—and essentially internal dialogue—should provide the framework of his dialectic, and while this is an intensely nineteenth-century preoccupation, the debate had its own doctrine, deriving its force from the innate life of what was transacted therein. Thus a sense of striving by the soul for fulfilment is linked inextricably to another and equal sense of original sin: a dual dialectic, of growth and of loss, is established which provides the dialogue with its creative tension. Oxford confirmed, rather than created, this tension. As Ellmann himself admits, on his American tour Wilde 'rediscovered himself as an Irishman'.[52]

If for one moment we can identify in isolation the adolescent Wilde who went on to become a successful writer (and who, in a pre-echo of Douglas, once insisted to Leon Daudet that he was simple and candid, 'just like a tiny, tiny child'),[53] then we can see that for purely personal reasons he was anxious to explore the question 'Who am I?' which so many characters in his plays address both to themselves and to people in authority. Wilde's life, as narrated through his work, was in psychological terms a triple quest for identity, for innocence and for love, portrayed in his work by the figure of the foundling which, as Ellmann suggests, 'can be best thought of as a secret that stands for all secrets'.[54]

Yet we cannot in fact leave him in isolation for long, because his own triple quest is intimately related to the genres of storytelling and drama and the discovery of secrets in the Irish imagination. His statement that

> She [my mother] and my father had bequeathed me a name they had made noble ... in the public history of my own country (*L* 458)

is both personal and impersonal in relation to family and country. It is pervaded with extraterritoriality. It intimates that Wilde had made an outward journey but was conscious of the difficulty, if not the impossibility, of effecting the homeward return. He had defined himself as a person, as an Irishman and as a writer, both in Ireland and England. But the balance between objective and subjective reality eluded him; the sense of loss was at times greater than the sense of what had been lost.

Wilde was not an artist. He was not an aesthete. He was not a poet. He was not a playwright. But because he posed, played the game of appearances, he convinced society that he was artist, aesthete, poet and playwright, and passed among poets and playwrights as one of their own. Wilde was an intellectual. He was a critic, in the sense that he perceived himself and his society to be at a critical point in their evolution, and he knew intuitively, as only an outsider can know, how to comment incisively on that condition, how to make connections between the absurdities and the realities of the situation. Wilde was never what he seemed, a position which he had deliberately engineered and yet which he craved to be otherwise. None of his works agrees internally with the superficial and provisional title which it bore—his 'plays' were not truly works for the dramatic stage; his poems did not succeed as verse; his most moral writing—*The Picture of Dorian Gray*—was branded as putrefaction, while his fables—which went to the heart of folklore—were dismissed as mere nursery material; his essays, collected under the title *Intentions*, set out his critical credo and were thoroughly Irish in their vision and argument, yet his *intention* therein went unrecognised and undiscussed. Even his letters, in which he made a conscious effort to be artificial, to construct a personality, have been regarded merely as a source-book for his life rather than an index to his attitudes.[55] His life, despite the profundity of his feelings, was not a complex pattern of behaviour but a simple, pathetic adjunct to the intense speculation and activity of his mind. He was Irish and therefore provincial; homosexual and therefore culpable; artistic without being an artist, and therefore risible.

Wilde's career involved the adoption not so much of one mask as of a series of masks, all (or none) of which might (or might not) embody a degree of 'truth'. While he may have been exceptional in the extent to which he demonstrated these problems, Wilde nevertheless provides an exaggerated example of the complexity which resides in Anglo-Irish relations. His statements regarding language and liberty may appear as egocentric assertions, but they were equally applicable to many situations in which the difference between Irish and English ways of seeing—and the way in which perception gives rise to ideas of identity and behaviour—becomes a crucial factor in reading history and predicting the future. That these situations begin with John Scotus Eriugena, are developed by Berkeley, and continue in the long history of Irish drama with Sheridan's *The Rivals*, Shaw's *John Bull's Other Island*, Thomas Kilroy's *Double Cross* and Brian Friel's *The London Vertigo* indicates the extent to which Wilde's masks serve both to conceal and to reveal what it means to be 'quite another thing'. Wilde was a diacrisis in the book of Ireland and in the book of the nineteenth century. The age to which he 'stood in symbolic relations' was the age of the outsider.

Part One

1
'Quite Another Thing': Nineteenth-Century Irishness

(i) 'WE IRISH'

WE begin to live when we have conceived life as a tragedy,' said Yeats.[1] It was a powerful resolution of Wilde's simple statement that 'Life is a very terrible thing.' (L 783) Yet these were not, in their time, uniquely artistic or provocative utterances, but lapidary ways of giving voice to the way in which the Irish mind has traditionally perceived itself. 'Irishness' can be addressed both in the active sense of the historical evolution of a nation, or in the passive sense of a state of mind. The tension between the two has often characterised discussions about Irish identity and strategies for the self-fulfilment of Irish society. It has both polarised and fused notions of what Irishness actually means, and conditioned attitudes to urban and rural ways of life, approaches to external cultural and economic forces. Yet both viewpoints betray the same fatalistic attitude. Life, to give another example of Wilde's own fatalism, is 'the tragedy in one's soul' (L 691).

Richard Ellmann and I have recently been taken to task by Ian Small for continuing 'to read Wilde's life as a "tragedy", his scandals and trials as a "fate" occasioned by the hubris of the too-successful socialite'; thus, he argues, I 'continue to utilize and therefore to endorse the Wilde "myth"'.[2] Small suggests—not without substantial justification—that recent criticism enables us to regard Wilde in a very different light,[3] most notably since contemporary criticism has expanded its scope in its ability to consider aesthetics in the light of gender studies and post-colonialism. Although he quotes with approval Fletcher and Stokes to the effect that 'in all their dealings with Wilde, the English have been wrong about practically everything',[4] Small, like Kohl, pays no attention in his own revaluation to Wilde's Irishness, and thus refuses to see him through anything other than English lenses, regarding him as writer, 'homosexual martyr', socialite, conversationist, and 'flamboyant homosexual iconoclast',[5] but not as an Irishman. In this he typifies the English difficulty in relation to the 'Irish question', in recognising that 'the contradictory'—in this case Ireland's 'English question'—is also true. If 'tragedy' and its relevance to 'the soul' was self-evident to Wilde, then it is necessary for us to know why that should have been so. Nor is it prescriptively Irish: Henry James, himself a vividly anxious outsider, both culturally and sexually, referred to 'the imagination of disaster', an observation which Ellmann neatly and correctly juxtaposes with Wilde's statement to Gide: 'I must go as far as possible. I cannot go any further.'[6]

It is certainly true that much of the 'Irish question' was created in and by England: it was the site of Parnell's entry into, and domination of, British politics in the period 1877–89; but, more seriously for our purposes, it was the principal source of the typification of Irishness and the Irish as both idleness and dreaminess incarnate. Ireland's 'difference' was first promulgated by England.

We shall therefore begin in this chapter by pursuing the notion of Irishness as a state of mind, and in particular one which can be recognised as different on substantive points from that of its geographical neighbour and longstanding political master: 'quite another thing'. In the next chapter we shall examine specific instances of what nineteenth-century Protestant Ireland understood by a 'nation', and how it appropriated and acted on that idea.

The ambivalence of Irishness, as it was described by nineteenth-century writers, consists in its powerlessness to achieve reality—to give force as well as character to the state of Ireland—while ironically it was precisely this incapacity which made it unique and unassailable. As we shall discover in the next chapter, Glorvina, the heroine of Lady Morgan's *The Wild Irish Girl*, embodies everything fragile, estimable and elusive in the Irish character. To evoke Ireland was to acquiesce in the vision of 'Glorvina' as something superior to, but dominated by, 'Britannia'. The essential strategy in apprehending that vision lay in the ability to suspend both time and space, the two elements in Irish history which had proved to be the undoing of 'mind' and the curse of 'memory'.

Within that mind and memory, however, a number of competing emotions threatened the stability of Ireland: the principal quality which gave it endurance was youth, supported by innocence; the principal activity was the progress of doom and the advent of tragedy. In order to hold the charm of one and to forestall the threat of the other, it was necessary to procrastinate, to enjoy both the threat and the threatened in terms of promise rather than fulfilment. In *The Picture of Dorian Gray* Wilde 'conceived the idea of a young man selling his soul in exchange for eternal youth—an idea that is old in the history of literature, but to which I have given new form' (*L* 263). The new form consisted, as Ellmann has said, in the fact that 'Wilde had hit upon a myth for aestheticism'[7]—that is, elucidating the very Irish debate about the relation of art to life and the place and value of art in society. In *Dorian Gray* three elements—the image, the subject and his fate—combine in a single metaphor which might stand for the unstable condition of 'eternal youth', the land known to the Irish as 'Tír na nÓg'.

One cannot *define* such a thing as 'Irishness', because it means different things at different periods and to different sections of the population in Ireland and indeed to the populations of England and those of neighbouring members of the Celtic races in Brittany, Cornwall, Scotland and Wales. It is therefore necessary for us to *divine* Irishness, not merely through nineteenth-century spectacles but specifically through those of people in circumstances comparable to Wilde's.

The declaration contained in the gambit 'We Irish' began with Bishop Berkeley, 'the Irish Cartesian',[8] as part of a philosophical observation rooted in difference, thus giving vigour to the notion of something identifiable as an 'Irish mind':

> There are men who say . . . the wall is not white, the fire is not hot, etc. We Irishmen cannot attain to these truths. The mathematicians think there are insensible lines. . . . We Irishmen can conceive no such lines. The mathematicians talk of what they call a point. This, they say, is not altogether nothing, nor is it downright something. Now us Irishmen are apt to think something & nothing are next neighbours.[9]

This series of assertions was appropriated by Yeats, who converted it into the expression ' "We Irish do not hold with this" or some like sentence'.[10] Berkeley's contribution to the philosophy of the Enlightenment consisted in his elaboration of 'a new theory of vision', but it was his opposition, as Yeats saw it, to 'the mechanical philosophy of Newton, Locke and Hobbes, the philosophy of England in his day, and I think of England up to our own day'[11] that made him extra-important to nineteenth-century Ireland. The expression 'We Irish', as a mark of difference, was without doubt current in the minds of the Anglo-Irish ascendancy as they attempted to create at least the idea of an Irish nation. Yeats called it 'the birth of the national intellect',[12] and Wilde himself used it to great effect in directing the mind of Yeats: 'We Irish', he told him, 'are too poetical to be poets; we are a nation of brilliant failures, but we are the greatest talkers since the Greeks.'[13] The deliberate analogy with ancient Greece was a salutary insight into the nineteenth-century mind, and a powerful use of metaphor. With Yeats it becomes a method of eliding the reality of political failure and of making common cause with the eighteenth century and in particular with Berkeley, Swift, Burke and Goldsmith:

When Pearse summoned Cuchulain to his side,
What stalked through the Post Office? What intellect,
What calculation, number, measurement, replied?
We Irish, born into that ancient sect,
But thrown upon this filthy modern tide,
And by its formless, spawning, fury wrecked,
Climb to our proper dark, that we may trace
The lineaments of a plummet-measured face.[14]

In this remarkable series of sleights of hand Yeats fuses several elements of what Denis Donoghue has called 'the complex fate of being Irish':[15] the inchoate nature of the primeval mind, the clarity of intellectual achievement in the eighteenth century, the need for the modern political will to validate itself by reference to ancient heroism, the rejection of order as understood by the logocentric mind and its replacement by a visionary culture; the ultimate irony being that Yeats invokes 'lineaments', a word much loved by the visionary Englishman Blake, as the means by which the face of Ireland may be known. 'In Berkeley and Burke we have a philosophy on which it is possible to base the whole life of a nation,' Yeats insists.[16] What 'our proper dark' might be is, by intention, unclear, but it is suggested that it is a place where the iconic face of Irish mythology, from which all its imaginative energy is derived, can be ascertained but perhaps not yet graven. Yeats's finer and higher point is that there is no necessary connection, no philosophical link, between the mythological age, the eighteenth century, and the transitional nineteenth, but that 'a great mind' and 'a great memory' inhered in anyone capable of evoking them 'by symbols'.[17]

The common factor in these statements about Irishness is two-edged: they are assertions of identity and at the same time an apologia for the way in which that identity is lived. 'Difference' is both a virtue and a vice; it creates paradox, which is of necessity baffling and provocative, because it denies the existence of a shared referential context, yet it thus also denies the possibility of the irony necessary to leaven and excuse that paradox. The disavowal of logic becomes a special pleading for an innate and unique form of reason; a race 'too poetical to be poets' becomes an oxymoronic 'brilliant failure' by attaining the highest form of speech and song. The explanation of a difference which one might expect to be self-evident is like the 'savage merriment in misery' so baffling to the English mind: something which makes perfect sense in one hemisphere of the brain but is incomprehensible in the other. Yet the contradiction is superseded by the combination of the two factors to form a third, the concept of heroic failure. The concept of the hero as paradigm of suffering and fulfilment is central to Irish mythology[18]—so much so that myths recounting the exploits of Cuchulain, so powerfully evoked by Yeats, continue to resonate within the Irish imagination and to provide it with models of modern behaviour.[19] Furthermore, the fact that some of the greatest Irish mythological literature is concerned with such commonplace events as the stealing of cattle emphasises the Irish capacity for endowing the quotidian with heroic properties. Its seems, indeed, as if two senses of the term 'myth' are present simultaneously: the myth—or the unreality—of the Irish nation, and the myth—or legend—of real events transmuted into a commanding literature. Both are transmitted by means of an oral culture which they help to fashion simply by being articulated.

As the hero is overcome by fate, so the defeat of heroism takes on its own meaning. The song cannot be sung unless the hero is overwhelmed and his heroism enhanced thereby. Triumph consists in tragedy. It is not exclusively or uniquely Irish, this 'awareness of one's fall' (as Genet calls it), 'the reality of supreme happiness in despair'.[20] Wilde's mother attached it to Irish life as an inevitable characteristic: 'Life is agony and hope, illusion and despair all commingled, but despair outlasts all.'[21] ('Hope', which was the motto of Lady Wilde—'Speranza'—ran through the Protestant community as an aspiration in its own right.) The intensity of this experience makes it an epicurean moment, a point indefinitely locked between past and future. Living thus outside history,

in parentheses, the Irish mind, perceiving both its uniqueness and its helplessness, gives itself to the cultivation of difference, and becomes the thief of reason.

Out of antitheses, the Irish mind creates a new synthesis,
'a profane life in which everything is permissible'.[22] Feminine
intuition is opposed to masculine knowledge, dreaming gayness to materialism and utilitarianism, myth and mythopoeism to logic and logocentrism, deviance to orthodoxy,
introspection to expansionism. The result is what Walter
Pater, in a phrase powerfully transmitted to his pupil, Oscar
Wilde, called 'a multiplied consciousness',[23] and the mind
and senses enter a different order, an otherworld with its
alternative language and codes, its own images, its own
internal rhyme and rhythm.

Recently the Anglo-Irish writer Lawrence Durrell has
given a name to this condition: *dromomania*, the need to 'live
out a life of secret repudiation', to invent 'a real country of
your own', 'a crucible of dissent' populated by 'scamps and
contemplatives and dissenters'.[24] It is a condition in which
things happen to people, yet those same people are incapable
of initiating their own actions. It encourages tribal rather than
individual consciousness, and it was markedly present in
Wilde's early reading: in his Oxford notebook he remarked,
apropos the 'moral chemistry' of W. K. Clifford, that the

> preservation of *self* is not the individual self but ... the
> 'Tribal self': individualism, private property, and a pri-
> vate conscience, as well as the nom. case of the personal
> pronoun, do not appear till later in all civilizations: it is
> the Tribal self wh. is the first mainspring of action, and
> canon of right and wrong: a savage is not only hurt
> when a man treads on his own foot, but when the foot
> of the tribe is trodden on. (*CPB* 129)

When, therefore, Wilde says that 'the one duty we owe to
history is to rewrite it' (*CW* 1023), and that 'life is a failure'
(*CW* 1035), he intends us to see that wishful—or wistful—

thinking is a legitimate activity and state of mind and that Utopia is its natural goal. When he says: 'It is because Humanity has never known where it was going that it has been able to find its way' (CW 1023), he means that the critical path of the dreamer is more important, more vital and compelling, than that of the planner. 'A map of the world that does not include Utopia is not worth glancing at, for it leaves out the one country at which Humanity is always landing.' (CW 1089) This land is Tír na nÓg, an integral part of the Celtic mindscape whose absurdity made it credible.

When, in his essay on 'The Study of Celtic Literature' (1867), Matthew Arnold wrote that '*sentiment* is ... the word which marks where the Celtic races really touch and are one; sentimental, if the Celtic nature is to be characterised by a single term',[25] he was subverting the true sense of the word 'sentiment' and lapsing into his own sentimentality. It was in fact the industrialised nineteenth century of the middle classes which needed Ireland as a focus for sentiment, as the repository of a residual culture which had been exhausted in the evolution of its own system. Marginalised and diminished, the 'poetry' or 'magic' or 'charm' of the western edge became a last reservoir for the conscience of Europe, its 'soul'. It required the continual deferring of paradise so that it might always be hoped for rather than achieved, a secret garden or 'never-never land' as it would become in the literature of Lewis Carroll and J. M. Barrie.[26] In Wilde's novels the image becomes a method of examining 'soul'—the facet of Irishness most evident to the Irish and least accessible to the English reader.

The notion of the Celtic soul permitted Ernest Renan, another seminal commentator on the Celtic temperament, to say that 'The Celtic race ... is an essentially feminine race. No human family ... has conceived with more delicacy the ideal of woman, or been more fully dominated by it. It is a sort of intoxication, a madness, a vertigo.'[27] If we were to read this in one of Wilde's dialogues, we should most likely regard it as a deliberate inversion, an absurd attempt at paradox. David Cairns and Shaun Richards comment on the fact that the effect of Arnold's critique was to turn 'a particularly disabling set of Celtic "virtues". . . an image of a race almost congenitally incapable of engaging with the material world' into a condition requiring inclusion within the 'masculine morality and discourse' of that materialism.[28] Paradoxically, therefore, Ireland permitted itself to be defined as elusive and yet submissive. Even today that paradox continues to reverberate in the negative and suggestive silences of Beckett's work, the sphinx-like enigma recently described as 'mute, emblematic, unreal, a state in which the most dangerous things prove themselves over and over by remaining unuttered'.[29] Again, the unspoken chronicle of unspecified non-events in *Dorian Gray* is an example of a secret history, a book written, and only legible, within.

As Arnold explained, the 'Celtic power . . . once was everywhere, but has long since, in the race of civilisation, fallen out of sight'.[30] Thus 'a great nation' relinquishes its spatial occupation in order to demonstrate, in retreat, a role inaccessible to 'civilisation'. Arnold hereby establishes a dual relationship between Celt and civilisation, suggesting that the Celt is simultaneously in retreat from a superior power and in possession of a superior mind, while civilisation rewards its promoters by allowing them to pursue a gratifying life which is nevertheless insufficient in its inevitability: 'It is not in the outward and visible world of material life, that the Celtic genius of Wales or Ireland can at this day hope to count for much; it is in the inward world of thought and science.'[31] Arnold went on to identify *expression* as the chief characteristic of this difference ('by the forms of its language a nation expresses its very self'),[32] and again in doing so he raised a dual standard by which to interpret the idea of 'nation', since it is clear that one kind of nation (the inward world) achieves its greatness by 'saying' (or 'being'), while another (the outward) does so by 'doing', by living its 'material life'.

It has been suggested that Arnold recognised and celebrated the Celtic 'soul' at the expense of a Celtic mind,[33] but in the light of his reference to 'thought and science' it seems at least as if he acknowledged the capacity for *knowing*, even though its processes of thought might be non-rational. He characterised the Celtic sentiment as 'keenly sensitive to joy and to sorrow', 'in passionate, penetrating melancholy' but nevertheless aspiring 'ardently after life, light, and emotion, to be expansive, adventurous, and gay. Our word *gay* [possibly from *gáire*, laughter], it is said, is itself Celtic.'[34]

Arnold was responsible for reproducing the view of Henri Martin (in his *Histoire de France*) that the Celtic sentiment consisted of being 'always ready to react against the despotism of fact',[35] a position subsequently adopted by Wilde and Yeats. Arnold's comment, that this sentimentality explained the 'habitual want of success', has helped to create a view of Irishness as enjoying a compensatory or alternative success in a world removed from the 'real' world, judging its greatness by standards different from those of the modern civilisation which, by the operation of logic and mercantilism, had marginalised the Celtic genius. The industrial revolution had passed Ireland by; thus the particular concern of the nineteenth century for the nature of 'soul', as religious beliefs changed with the increasing materialism of the age and the new theories of evolution, was more naturally suited to Irish discussion. To the Irish mind, 'soul' was additionally and inversely important because it appeared to be free from domination and accessible to discourse. Instead of mastering the world, and giving 'an adequate interpretation of it', the Celt compensates by means of the force of style, 'by bending language to its will, and expressing the ideas it has with unsurpassable intensity, elevation, and effect'[36] and thus 'rendering with wonderful felicity the magical charm of nature'.[37] The Celt lacked effective means of expression, Arnold believed, because he missed 'balance, measure, patience...steadiness, sanity',[38] and this made him incapable of sustained poetic achievement, even though he could realise moments of 'singular beauty and power'.[39] In political terms, he failed because he had lost his grip on the world. Instead Arnold, like Renan, identified a feminine sensibility: 'he is not far from its secret'.[40] The Celt is 'undisciplinable, anarchical, and turbulent by nature' but 'prepared to devote himself to a leader'—he is thus 'just the opposite of the Anglo-Saxon temperament', and his ambition is 'to be a bard, [which] freed a man'.[41] To consolidate this view, Arnold even asserts that 'rhyme itself . . . comes into our poetry from the Celts',[42] a point which Wilde appropriated in his American lecture tour, proclaiming: 'Rhyme, the basis of modern poetry, is entirely of Irish invention.'[43]

In his slightly earlier essay, *The Poetry of the Celtic Races* (1859), Ernest Renan expounded 'the legend of St Brandon [*sic*]' as 'the most singular product' of a 'combination of Celtic naturalism with Christian spiritualism . . . one of the most extraordinary creations of the human mind, and perhaps the completest expression of the Celtic ideal',[44] detailing Brendan's voyage to 'the *Land of Promise* that God keeps for his saints' where 'all is lovely, pure, and innocent . . . the world seen through the crystal of a stainless conscience'.[45] Renan posited this as a 'fantastical nature created expressly for another humanity, this strange topography at once glowing with fiction and speaking of truth'.[46] Renan identified 'the essential element in the Celt's poetic life' as 'the *adventive* . . . the pursuit of the unknown, an endless quest after an object ever flying from desire' coupled with 'an invincible need for illusion' by which it achieved 'the vision of the invisible world'.[47]

To anyone familiar with Wilde's lifetime yearning for a land of youth where conscience, if not stainless, is at least suspended indefinitely, a land where forgiveness is unnecessary because sin does not exist, this topography will be self-evident:

> the perfection of those to whom sin is impossible because they can do everything they wish without hurt to the soul. (CW 1058)

Wilde knew that this state was more than elusive, that it was an impossibility in two senses: impossible of achievement and impossible if achieved because of the inevitability of sin:

> I look forward to the time when aesthetics will take the place of ethics, when the sense of beauty will be the dominant law of life. It will never be so, and so I look forward to it. (*L* 265)

(ii) STRATEGIES FOR SURVIVAL

Tribal society is feral, divisive and punitive. However sophisticated its customs and manners, it is based on death, rape and the killing instinct, and its songs will reflect all the inner fears, as well as the joys, of family life and the penalties and courtesies paid to weakness and beauty. Irish mythology obeyed tribal laws and continues today, in sports and in politics, to observe the foundations of tribal rather than national forms. Christianity provided a new dimension to this mythology, enabling Irish monks to explain the relationship of God to man which had previously been mediated by the figure of the hero.

As Brendan Kennelly has observed, one of the qualities of the Irish epic is the heightened effect of the verse episodes, as if hyperbole were a necessary part of description, whether of failure or achievement. Everything is sung in heroic terms, thereby giving a dramatic dimension to the prose saga.[48] It thus acquires 'its majestic power of vigorous narrative . . . its fantastic exaggerations, inflated descriptions and frequent repetitions'[49] as innate and inalienable features of the story being told. 'The essence of the mythological cycle', Kennelly says, is 'a wild wonder, a panorama of unearthly beings and events, an occasional harsh starkness of thought, emotion and expression, a world where the impossible, the excessive and the exaggerated are the norm'.[50] Within the feral world, man fashions methods of making sense of the received signs, because otherwise he is nothing. Within this formula are contained the ingredients of romance, imagination and paradox, the regular presence of the supernatural and the consequent confusion of reality and unreality, a poetry unconfined by any metrical rules or any syntactical niceties, whose characters observe no orthodoxies.

The centre of the mythological cycle is the personality of the hero, and his relation with this world and the otherworld. Youth and innocence are constantly embattled; 'extraordinary prowess' seems inseparable from 'vulnerability'.[51] 'At the very height of his heroic defence of Ulster', Kennelly says of Cuchulain, 'he breaks down, weeps, and lies for days in a state of paralysed grief.'[52] The role of the hero is messianic: he 'achieves immortal personal fame [and] fulfils in so doing a vital social duty towards his own people'.[53] That he should prove to be so vulnerable was perhaps an innate wisdom in the society which produced the notion of the hero. It is another essential trait that he should be capable of standing outside his society in order to be perceived and appreciated.[54] One reason for this apartness is to make it clear that the sense of a fateful doom, attached to the hero, is a personal and not a social attribute—that by dying he saves the whole community. A further reason is the need for irony, since a society and its heroes can only appreciate the notion of fate if there is a shared referential context in which that difference between hero and society is negotiated. This also facilitates the observation by society of its own spiritual growth and thus its notion of freedom. By fulfilling 'the essence of heroic art' in 'being true to oneself',[55] the hero also enables society to achieve its own freedom. Furthermore, to *see* something differently became a passport to behaving differently, and to see something which others could not see brought into existence an imaginative realm inaccessible to others.

Those who suffer from a perceived disability (illegitimacy, physical deformity, homosexuality, racial inferiority) in relation to the norms of the host or dominant culture develop strategies for survival, in order to compensate themselves for the stigmatisation imposed by that culture, or in order to escape its strictures by leading an alternative life. Such a person, as Erving Goffmann observes, 'is . . . reduced in our minds from a whole and usual person to a tainted, discounted one'[56]—this, of course, is the perception in 'our' minds, but not that in the mind of the discounted person. This dual perspective accounts for what Goffmann terms 'a special discrepancy between virtual and actual social identity'.[57] It leads, on the part of the discounted person, to such strategies as schizophrenia. Thus, Goffmann says, the person (or group) 'can break with what is called reality, and obstinately attempt to employ an unconventional interpretation of the character of his social identity'.[58] The *discrepancy* will be evident to both the normative society and the deviant, yet the grounds on which the deviance is perceived will differ fundamentally.

In the case of a stigmatised, or discounted, person, knowing who one is takes on an extra burden of understanding what it is which makes one different and of coming to terms with that difference. If that difference is located at the 'core of his being',[59] the individual will find himself confronting two difficulties: the difficulty of recognising himself as different from others, and that of accepting that the difference in some ways makes him a stranger to himself, that he can never be truly 'at home' with himself.

Much of the insistence of critics like Renan that 'the Gaelic genius . . . had its own original manner of thinking and feeling'[60] depended on the Celtic race maintaining its homogeneity and purity: 'confined by conquest within forgotten islands and peninsulas, it has reared an impassable barrier against external influences; it has drawn all from itself; it has lived solely on its own capital'.[61] But this has led the Celtic race to wear itself out 'in resistance to its time, and in the defence of desperate causes. . . . Thence ensues its sadness.'[62] Yet an imagination which defines and determines itself within such conditions is likely not only to be enervated by such sadness but also to be energised by it into behaviour reactionary to those conditions.

In Wilde's case, his preoccupation with identity, his determination to conduct a crusade which was partly nationalistic, partly aesthetic and partly sexual, and his gayness as a social player complicate this discrepancy. Acceptance is craved, yet disclosure is still feared, unless both can be achieved on the deviant's terms rather than those of society. The London of the 1890s, with two Irish scandals, Wilde's and Parnell's, was a place in which such discrepancies could be easily overlooked until its equilibrium was upset by the revelation of what had been invisible and therefore unknown.

In a case of stigmatisation, insecurity, anxiety and jealousy are frequent experiences of the deviant.[63] Despite their loneliness, however, outcasts can identify one another and thus establish a rapport which they locate in opposition to the society which excludes them. Like his mother, who emphasised that the Irish 'gift of natural eloquence' of 'the fluent, passionate Celtic race'[64] was a major factor in the success of Irish-America, Wilde in his late adolescence emphasised America as the place where deviancy could resolve its differences with society—the Irish made a success there, while Thoreau made a virtue of civil disobedience and Whitman's homosexuality was no obstacle to his success and esteem as a poet. 'The Saxon basis is the rough block of the nation,' Speranza asserted, 'but it is the Celtic influence that gives it all its artistic value and finish.'[65] America was a place of assimilation, Britain of alienation.

In another sense, Wilde's career closely parallels the Irish situation in Britain in the late nineteenth century, and in particular the evolution of parliamentary tactics by the Home Rule Party under Isaac Butt and Parnell. As Goffmann points out, the stigmatised individual

> can voluntarily disclose himself, thereby radically transforming his situation from that of an individual with information to manage to that of an individual with uneasy social situations to manage, from that of a discreditable person to that of a discredited one.[66]

In particular, the Phoenix Park assassinations in Dublin in 1882, which led to the Pigott forgery case of 1887–8 (with which Wilde's brother Willie was concerned as a leader-writer for the *Daily Telegraph*), had a political dimension which embraced Wilde himself as an onlooker and, briefly, commentator. They highlighted the bluntness with which a marginalised, discredited group could draw attention to itself by subverting social norms. Wilde's own conduct, condoned or at least ignored while it appeared to be a mere pose, confined to artistic society, or a trans-class indulgence with messenger-boys, was excoriated when it became an ardent and determined pursuit of the established class.

The act of what we would today call 'coming out' may be a small one—Wilde was certainly the author of many minor indiscretions which caused him to be lampooned as effeminate, transvestite and even of criminal tendency—but, as Goffmann says, the consequence of actions which are 'small in particular contacts' may be 'immense', not least because there is a difference between 'the visibility of a stigma' and 'its "known-about-ness"'.[67] London clubland, court society, bohemia, Ireland-in-London and the boy-houses which Wilde frequented may all have maintained discreet, hermetic consciousnesses, but the visibility of actions in one became 'known about' in others until there could be no further ignorance, or denial, of the gesture. At a certain point the Establishment which went to the theatre and tolerated its artistic excesses came into conflict with the public opinion manipulated on its behalf in the society magazines, and with the reaction of the political and artistic circles which were its manifestations. At that point Wilde's paederasty became as offensive, and as offensively Irish, as Parnell's adultery. Neither was more or less serious than the other—both were punishably deviant. And in both cases Ireland made of the martyr a saint and a pillar of shame.

Wilde himself certainly subscribed to the notion of invisible imaginary worlds, not only for those made fragile and vulnerable by the materialism of civilisation, but also because life is a mirror of which art is the reality. Thus he declared in 'The Decay of Lying': 'The nineteenth century, as we know it, is largely an invention of Balzac' (*CW* 983), while 'The whole of Japan is a pure invention. There is no such country, there are no such people.' (*CW* 988) In the first statement he was asserting the imaginative superiority of an individual who creates the conditions by which both he and the work of art are to be judged,[68] while in the second he was agreeing that the work of art could in fact be an imaginary place which the artists themselves could inhabit.

'So that I can hear things that the ear cannot hear and see invisible things'—so Wilde wrote when renting a seaside house in the hope of finding inspiration (*L* 322). The capacity of Irish folk to 'see invisible things' was vigorously attested in Yeats's *The Celtic Twilight*, and to the rational mind a commerce with the invisible world stands next to the classical 'love of the impossible' which Wilde frequently discussed in moral terms—'the poison of unlimited desire . . . the infinite pursuit of what they may not obtain' (*CW* 1030). This unknown land is both the imaginative and the contemplative life, a secret place which is both within us and beyond our grasp. Reading *Salomé*, William Archer, a champion of Ibsen and a leading critic, said that it spoke to 'that life within our life, which alone . . . is really worth living—the life of the imagination'.[69] Wilde himself had anticipated this in 'The Critic as Artist' when he said:

> Do you think that it is the imagination that enables us to live these countless lives? Yes: it is the imagination; and the imagination is the result of heredity. It is simply concentrated race-experience. (*CW* 1041)

Here Wilde seems to be confirming the English perception of Ireland as an unreal place—the otherworld where there is nothing but appearance. As we have already noted, 'rhyme' was believed by Arnold, and later by Wilde, to be distinctively Celtic, so that by opposing it to 'reason' Wilde seems to be placing the Irish world as the antithesis to the English, the 'love of the impossible' against the known, possible, real world. That the impossible should remain impossible adds to its strangeness, glamour and attraction. Similarly, the invisibility of the 'soul' becomes the central ploy in several Irish folk-tales, not least Wilde's own 'The Fisherman and his Soul' and his mother's 'The Priest's Soul'. Gide called this 'the deep central emotion' at the heart of all Wilde's stories,[70] a point borne out by Lady Wilde: speaking of 'the fantastic creed of the Irish respecting the invisible world', she asserted that 'the mythology of a people reveals their relation to a spiritual and invisible world' and affirmed 'the instinctive belief in the existence of certain unseen agencies that influence all human life'.[71] And when, in 'The Critic as Artist', her son developed the role of criticism in society, we can see that he had not abandoned the invisible life, but had in fact made it central to the critical function which he placed above all other forms of art:

> The culture that this transmission of racial experiences makes possible can be made perfect by the critical spirit alone, and indeed may be said to be one with it. For who is the true critic but he who bears within himself the dreams, and ideas, and feelings of myriad generations, and to whom no form of thought is alien, no emotional impulse obscure. (*CW* 1041)

Wilde might have had in mind the folkloric researches of his parents (principally of his father), the translations of the Gaelic epics by Ferguson, or the collections of Irish folk- and fairy-tales by the young W. B. Yeats, when he identified 'the critic' as the bearer of dreams.

(iii) THE GAY TEMPER

The Irish, especially from the sixteenth to the nineteenth centuries, lived in the silhouette of identity, the negative side of

existence, imagining life rather than living it, pursuing what
might have been, and what might still be, rather than devis-
ing tactics for achieving it. Longing and absence are the chief
features of their song, together with the vertigo which we
associate with decadence. Renan said that 'the apparent
reserve of the Celtic peoples' was due to the belief 'that a
feeling loses half its value if it be expressed; and that the
heart ought to have no other spectator than itself'.[72] To be
alone with one's own fears, hopes and sorrows is clearly the
alternative to confronting them. To approach and retreat from
action, from committing oneself to a statement, a punishable
comment or a frangible ambition, is all implicit in the fact, as
Wilde put it, that 'each man kills the thing he loves'—whether
it be by means of betrayal, failure, or the famine of faith.
Hence Wilde's belief that 'the soul is never liberated except
by drunkenness in one form or another'—the freedom is
vertiginous because it has no grounding in reality. In what
seems like a prescient deflation of Yeats's cosmogony, Wilde
talked frivolously of drunkenness opening the door to 'the
Great Silence. . . . A waiter with a tray will always find it for
you. Knock, and the door will always open, the door of *le
paradis artificiel*.'[73]

Thus 'Irishness' in the nineteenth century was more likely
to be addressed in terms of difference, otherness and absence
than in terms of vital, continuous traditions. Even the identification of the 'nation' in ideological terms by means of the
powerful and widely read organ of that name, was animated
by the liberal Protestantism of Thomas Davis, the founder of
Young Ireland. The elements present in nineteenth-century
Ireland constitute the factors which eventually liberated the
modern state.

They consist of a series of preferences, where preference is
expressed for one possible choice without excluding the possibility of the alternative. Thus Frank O'Connor said that the
Irish choose 'the imagination over the intellect',[74] but it
should be clear that this predisposition towards the creative
vagueness of the imagination, as opposed to the rational

definition of the intellect, is not an exclusive polarisation. It is a predisposition encouraged by the uncertainty of the status of Ireland in terms of the master-and-servant political and fiscal relationship with England and the mother-and-child spiritual relationship with Rome. The first element of 'the Irish mind', the tendency towards *vagueness*, is therefore one which suggests the power to subvert the logocentric method which we usually associate with the notion of 'mind'.

The second element derives from the first: the 'evolution' of Irish society into nationhood has been fuelled by the idea of *discontinuity*, by the experience that the power of Irishness failed and was defeated at the hands of a force superior in ways of doing but inferior in ways of seeing. Thus there are no perduring traditions in Irish society, except the tradition of interruption and fragmentation symbolised by historical events such as the Flight of the Earls in 1607, the Battle of the Boyne in 1690 and the continuing partition of the island into two states; and by cultural events such as the erosion of poetry as a source of learning, which is the cardinal experience of bardic society in the seventeenth century.[75]

The predominant 'way of seeing' is expressed by the third element of nineteenth-century Ireland, the *icon* or mythopoeic *image*. The distress of King Sweeney in the medieval saga[76] is echoed in the history books by the hunted life of Hugh O'Neill;[77] the city of Derry during the siege of 1689 is echoed by the Dublin GPO during the Easter Rising of 1916; the crystallisation of Irish lineaments in social portraits such as Lady Morgan's *The Wild Irish Girl* is echoed in the portrait of Lady Lavery which continues to feature in modern Irish currency; the elucidation of unities of thought by Berkeley in the eighteenth century is followed by Yeats in the nineteenth and Joyce in the twentieth. These all depend on the image as an acronym of experience and aspiration. Joyce's 'epiphany' and 'invultuation' sum up the series of images by means of which, Janus-like, Irish artists have imagined both the past and the future. Yeats endowed Davis with this gift when he evoked Young Ireland as an iconic crusade:

> A country which has no national institutions must show its young men *images for the affections*, although they be but diagrams of what it should be or may be. He and his school *imagined* the Soldier, the Orator, the Patriot, the Poet, the Chieftain, and, above all, the Peasant'.[78] [*my emphasis*]

It was succeeded by Joyce's 'portrait of the artist'—a conception which he cannot have appropriated without consciously acknowledging the appearance of the phrase in Wilde's *The Picture of Dorian Gray*[79]—which is both a way of telling the story of an individual's spiritual evolution and a designation of every Irishman as an artist.

Every image requires an explication, a satisfactory way of reading the legend within the picture, a spelling out of the acronym back into rational consciousness. Thus the *fable* is the fourth element in the history of Irish evolution. The particular way in which it was employed—in intimate relation to the image—underpins the fact that symbol, myth and fable are the resident qualities of the Irish view of both space and time, of personality both active and passive. The telling of stories and the recounting of history share this imagistic, profoundly existential use of the imagination, creating a tradition, *ex nihilo*, a presence out of absence. In this way, as Declan Kiberd has suggested, 'history becomes a form of science fiction',[80] a rearrangement of segments of real time in order to create a vision which, however unreal, will have the appearance of truth, and within which contradictions can be accommodated.[81]

That Irishmen should continue to believe that there is 'an irresoluble tension at the heart of our national condition'[82] is a legacy of the ubiquitous nineteenth-century binary mind, heightened in Ireland by an inherent belief that things can never be other than what they are, yet can only be expressed in terms of that impossible otherness. Irish consciousness has always been fuelled by this tension: King Sweeney flies like a bird in order to regain his sanity, yet since he is defined by his madness his achievement of sanity would cancel out his *raison d'être*. Irish nationalism was founded on the one criterion which would cause the Irish state to disintegrate once it was satisfied: that it should once more assume the non-existent prediluvian condition of 'a nation once again'.[83] This is intensified by the fact that the debate takes place within one mind rather than between two minds: as Wilde would put it in a love-poem addressed to Lillie Langtry, there are separate and opposing chambers within the one frame of reference:

> But strange that I was not told
> That the brain can hold
> In a tiny ivory cell,
> God's heaven and hell. (*CW* 811)

The monologue is in fact a form of interior dialogue—in Yeats's title 'of self and soul'[84]—where public and private aspects of the same persona discuss how the conscience should be positioned, and thus identified, in the world. This mind favours an inclusive, rather than an Aristotelian, exclusive, culture, 'showing that meaning is not only determined by a logic that centralises and censors but also by a logic which disseminates: a structured dispersal exploring what is *other*, what is irreducibly diverse'.[85]

By means of this inclusive dialectic, the Irish mind has succeeded in making a fruitful connection between opposing ideas, since this has proved a more attractive and successful strategy for survival than the confrontational resolution of opposites. This, as Mark Patrick Hederman has said, is a 'supralogical use of words'.[86] In this way the oxymoron gives rise to a 'supralogical' third element which contains and supersedes the first two. Between two opposing ideas, the rational and the irrational, the Irish mind elevates a third idea, the non-rational; between two codes of conduct, the moral and the immoral, it posits an amoral way of seeing and being, which Wilde ultimately formulates as 'There is no such thing as a moral or an immoral book. Books are well written, or badly written. That is all.' (*PDG* xxxiii) The recurrence of 'That is all' throughout his work is not as dismissive, peremptory, as it might seem: it is, like Keats's 'Beauty is truth, truth beauty, that is all ...',[87] a studied conclusion to the resolution and deconstruction of opposites in favour of the range of possibilities which lie between them.

The two worlds—of reality and materialism, of art and imagination—are nevertheless polarised in life and stand in antithetical relation to each other, each captivated by the charm and difficulty of passing from one to the other which constitutes the relation of every drama to its audience, of every poem to its reader, and which characterised in the nineteenth century, and still characterises today, the mutual fascination of Ireland and England. To say, as Wilde noted, that 'the impossible in art is anything that has happened in real life'[88] is to express that fascination.

Occasionally this incompatibility between art and life was made explicit: 'With the coming of the English, art in Ireland came to an end, and it has had no existence for seven hundred years. I am glad it has not, for art could not live and flourish under a tyrant,'[89] Wilde told an audience in St Paul, Minnesota, on St Patrick's Day 1882, simultaneously asserting that Irish artists were latently awaiting independence in order to flourish again. Later Wilde would say (in 'The Decay of Lying') that decadence consisted in the polarisation of life and art:

> Life gets the upper hand, and drives Art out into the wilderness. This is the true decadence. (*CW* 978)

Originally drama was 'abstract, decorative, and mythological', but with the appearance of 'Life' it became 'vulgar, exaggerated, fantastic, obscene even' (*CW* 978). The decadent drama of his own time (*Salomé* included) can therefore be seen as an attempt to strip itself of imitation and to reclaim simplicity.

Wilde is beginning to see decadence as a perverse curiosity which can only be appreciated when it impinges on the consciousness, thereby running the risk of discovery. Thus while 'art never expresses anything but itself' and 'all fine imaginative work is self-conscious and deliberate' (*CW* 991), it can only become important if its self-consciousness is noticed and commented upon by an external audience. This Wilde expressed in the paradox 'Life is the only thing that is never real.'[90]

Irishness can thus be seen as a decadent frame of mind, one which has been defined as 'afterthought, of reflection . . . the virtue of meditation upon life, its emotions and incidents; the vice of over-subtilty and of affectation'. Certainly Irishmen, without the stimulation of political crisis, reflect more upon their variable identity than Englishmen upon their secure suppositions. This introspection is the height of decadence because, to the observer, it seems perverse; its outcome is, to the observer, paradoxical because it relies on something accessible only to the eye within. As Ernest Newman said, 'We rise from the perusal of [Wilde's paradoxes] with a self-conscious wisdom that we had not before. We become wise, and know it.'[91] This wisdom is cognate with that of the secret society, of which the most acute form is the fellowship of prisoners with their code of silence and their role as outcasts in society—those of whom Sir William Wilde wrote in *Irish Popular Superstitions* as

> labouring under the smart of a real or supposed grievance . . . obliged, for crimes of his own, to be 'on the run', and seek shelter in a different country . . . to assume certain nickname . . . to have certain signs and passwords . . . a freemasonry—a craft and a mystery . . . which, quite independent of other objects, possesses a charm for the human mind . . . a sort of melo-dramatic exhibition.[92]

Perhaps Ireland's own English grievance made it a nation 'on the run' from itself, reinhabiting an imagined country which fed off mystery rather than reality; Sir William's son, who was to bring melodrama to a high art before imprisonment as 'C.3.3.' and exile as 'Sebastian Melmoth', became an adept at the manipulation of 'a different country', the freemasonry of the homosexual and the artist.

Oscar Wilde not only insisted that 'a truth in art is that whose contradictory is also true' but also that 'the truths of metaphysics are the truths of masks', thus associating, if not closely identifying, thought with pretence. When, in *The Ballad of Reading Gaol*, he declared the *leitmotif* 'each man kills the thing he loves', he was, in Ellmann's phrase, revealing 'this sudden perception of a truth opposed to the home truth'[93]—one which is subsidiary, and yet also equivalent, to the greater truth. On another occasion, when challenged that he had confused (rather than conflated) two historical Salomés in creating his drama, Wilde retorted that this represented 'the truth of a professor at the Institute. I prefer the other truth, my own, which is that of the dream. Between two truths, the falser is the truer.'[94] This is an inverted position, but none the less moral for that, as he would show in the figure of Sir Robert Chiltern in *An Ideal Husband*, who says that it is not weakness but courage which yields to temptation.

In the collision between two truths, however, the secret truth becomes the victim because it is thereby discovered. Wilde expressed this in conversation with Commandant Esterhazy, the man responsible for the incrimination of Alfred Dreyfus in 1895: 'The innocent always suffer...it is their *métier*. Besides, we are all innocent until we are found out'[95]—a gambit which, we are told, provoked Esterhazy into confessing—or asserting—his own guilt and Dreyfus's innocence. Of this incident Wilde recorded that 'Esterhazy est bien plus intéressant que Dreyfus qui est innocent. On a toujours tort d'être innocent. Pour être criminel, il faut de l'imagination et du courage.' (L 727)

There is an organic relationship between guilt and innocence, not because they are opposite but because they represent different ends of an infinitely variable degree of responsibility. That which is secret because it is an occasion of sin, or shame, and ultimately, perhaps, of guilt, is like a wound which disfigures. Thus, in Yeats's word, Hamlet and Lear, estranged and exasperated by their foolishness, become 'gay'.[96] By subtlety, stealth and pretence their mind will seek to subvert the author of its sadness and inferiority, thus giving form and meaning to its gaiety.

2
A 'Regal Republic': Cultural Nationalism in the Mid-Century

(i) THE BOOK OF IRELAND

IN his copy of Aristotle's *Nicomachean Ethics* Wilde wrote:

> Man makes his end for himself out of himself: no end is imposed by external considerations, he must realise his true nature, must be what nature orders, so must discover what his nature is.[1]

This inscription could be read as a commentary on Ireland in the mid-nineteenth century as it attempted to obey Emmet's injunction to take its place among the nations of the world. The project of *knowing* oneself, of answering the question 'Who am I?', precedes the act of *being* oneself. Within nineteenth-century Ireland there was a running embarrassment between different types of conscience, of allegiance and of ambition. Conscious that it must find its end within itself, Ireland was equally conscious that its condition was largely due to the 'external considerations' of its geographical location, its domination by Britain, and its predominantly Roman Catholic population; the true nature of Ireland had yet to be described and determined in either imaginary or real terms.

Although Matthew Arnold had said that 'by the forms of its language a nation expresses its very self', it was by no means clear what 'language', what mode of expression, would be chosen for Gaelic and Anglo-Irish Ireland to address each other. The age itself and the condition of Ireland, in particular, were twin sources of anxiety, out of which a language and a culture must be devised and a book written. The century needed a literature and the country needed a leadership.

In romance terms, it was a quest in the classic stages, as Northrop Frye states it, of 'perilous journey... crucial struggle... and the exaltation of the hero.'[2] As such, it would involve the Celtic hero and the bardic poetry which enshrined him, as a means of uniting a bifurcated country outside that embarrassment. Intellectual traditions in Ireland have—as if by common agreement—been honed as much by debate and dissent as by the desire for unity. Moreover, the nodal points of imaginative cohesion were, with the exception of Catholic Emancipation in 1829 (which in itself alarmed and disquieted the Protestant population), those of failure and disintegration, such as the rising of the United Irishmen in 1798 and the Famine of 1845–9. In this Wilde, therefore, despite his own downfall, would, as a resolutely self-defining figure, ultimately appeal to Irishmen as a symbol of such an autogenous book no less than Parnell or Pearse. The crucial factor—to continue Frye's terminology—was the capacity of the writers of this book to create a narrative of sufficient intellectual and imaginative vigour that it would underpin cognate activities in politics and in social reform. As Terence Brown has suggested, much of its success rested on 'whether a distinctive Irish identity might be forged in the English language',[3] and thus became a quest of *translation* both from one language to another and from one set of cultural values to another. The transactions between Catholic and Protestant Irelands in the mid-century, and between antiquity and modernity, bear a striking resemblance to the crisis of conscience in Victorian Britain which threw up such charismatic figures as William Morris and Cardinals Newman and Manning. Again, Wilde's highly visible role in this latter crisis replicates his less discernible place in the Irish Renaissance. It is the thesis of later chapters that Wilde's work can indeed be read as a translation of Ireland's cultural resources onto the plane of international aesthetics.

In this chapter, however, we shall consider, firstly, the development of the Anglo-Irish novel in the first half of the nineteenth century, in the work of Lady Morgan (Sydney Owenson), Maria Edgeworth, Sheridan Le Fanu and Charles Maturin, and the role of Samuel Ferguson as translator, in early attempts at the compilation of a book of Ireland; secondly, the character of two seminal journals, the *Dublin University Magazine* and *The Nation*; and thirdly, the writings of William Wilde and his wife, Jane Elgee, as a type of what I shall call 'middle Ireland'.

When, in 1839, Thomas Davis declared to the Trinity College Historical Society: 'Gentlemen, you have a country!'[4] he made little more than a rhetorical gesture. Davis, author of the irresponsible and unrealistic slogan, 'A Nation Once Again', died before the Famine—the great historical event and the central irony of Irish experience—began to bring those disparate and divergent cultures into a semblance of uniformity. That Ireland was perceived as a separate country, with qualities quite distinct from those of England and similar to those of Scotland, was never in doubt. 'Race', as Renan put it, 'is ... something that makes and unmakes itself' and 'language invites reunion; it does not force it'.[5] Despite some earnest sentiment in favour of complete integration of Ireland and England on the part of Matthew Arnold and an ultra-conservative section of Irish Protestant opinion, the issue was never a real one: the Union of 1800 had joined the Irish and English crowns, as that of 1707 had previously joined those of England and Scotland, and had extinguished the Irish parliament, but it had, if anything, exacerbated the difference between the administration of the two countries: fiscal affairs, poor relief and church denomination were the chief areas of concern. By the time when William Wilde and Jane Elgee married in 1851 the Famine had distinguished Ireland's problems as unique in Europe—unmatched even by the cultural and political dependency of Hungary and Belgium, with which it was most closely compared.

Despite the success in 1829 of Daniel O'Connell's campaign for Catholic Emancipation and his subsequent establishment of the Repeal Association (directed at the rupture of the Union), Irish political leadership slipped from influence and power in the 1830s and 1840s. One of the main consequences of this collapse was the growth in the notion that the Irish were unfit for self-government. (Indeed, in 1847, when Mazzini founded the People's International League with the principal purpose of listing the nations of the future, Ireland did not feature in the list.)[6] In the development of such an opinion 'the Irish' would be taken as native, Catholic Irish, while the so-called 'Protestant ascendancy' (a term which became current in the 1790s)[7] saw itself adopting the role of leadership which would include education and encouragement in matters cultural, agricultural and of conscience, and which implicitly (and increasingly explicitly) meant taking a constructive but confrontational attitude towards England. It is this mindset which characterised the birth of both the *Dublin University Magazine* (from 1833) and *The Nation* (from 1842), which sought to mobilise the public opinion which in Ireland always had a higher value and a more distinct nature than elsewhere in the British Isles.[8]

Where, throughout Europe, the year 1848 was one of liberty, in Ireland it proved yet again that the Irish were great in failure. Like Oscar Wilde's 'Remarkable Rocket', the Ballingarry uprising of 1848 and similar attempted revolts in 1867 expected to 'create a great sensation' and to 'set the whole world on fire', but in the event no one took any notice (*CW* 318).

Irish political initiatives consisted of nothing more significant than half-hearted parliamentary manoeuvres and ineffectual expressions of revolt.[9] Other means were therefore required to give form and direction to the undeniable energy —a loquacious energy—which existed in all parts of society, but perhaps most in the comfortably situated Protestant middle class. The notion that activity on a cultural front might help to establish a sense of both identity and identification for Irish people—action in the 'common name of

Irishman' and an understanding of the common nature of Irishness—was easily articulated, even if what was said concealed, or glossed over, much that was left unsaid.

Dublin as a capital was one of the three great cities of the British Empire, yet Ireland as a whole was a backwater and a desert. Access to a viceregal court gave its leading families and professions a means of participating in the affairs of that empire, yet their domestic economy rested on rural poverty and ignorance. Where, therefore, the nexus between gentry and peasantry in most of Europe was based on a progressive form of feudalism, no such relation existed in Ireland; possibly only Russia offered a comparable situation. For the landlord conscience to be at all comfortable, relief work in both physical and cultural conditions became mandatory, and an almost hysterical emphasis was put on the importance of popular customs and vernacular, unlettered poetry. Probably only in Finland, where Elias Lonnrött and others consciously constructed a national literature in the *Kalevala* (published between 1835 and 1849) in order to re-create both the poetry and the Finnish language, was there a cognate contemporary sense of urgency about national survival. That the personality of the peasant should be deliberately intruded into polite literature such as the novels of Edgeworth and Carleton is the distinctive irony of the period.

In order to find a place in the new Ireland, Protestants used their position to seek continuity with the Gaelic past, since its antiquity (and thus its superiority to the neighbouring culture and its equality with the senior cultures of Greece and Rome) was not in question.

This cultural curiosity took the form of folkloric research, archaeology and antiquarianism, and the translation of the Gaelic epic myths into modern poetry. The Gaelic Society of Dublin had announced such ambitions as early as 1808, when it declared that it offered an objective—similar in cultural terms to Emmet's political template—'to the Learned of Ireland, to retrieve their Character among the Nations of Europe'.[10] At the same time George Petrie (1790–1866) began his examination of antiquities which, along with many other initiatives, such as the Ordnance Survey of Ireland, gathered momentum in the 1830s. Many of the participants in these initiatives were members of the Dublin professions and almost exclusively Protestant.[11]

Samuel Ferguson gave this movement a further impetus, urging 'the recovery of the mislaid, but not lost, records of the acts and opinions and conditions of our ancestors' in order that 'the people of Ireland will be able to live back in the land they live in'.[12] The subtlety of such a proprietorial attitude on the part of a northern Protestant is considerable: establishing a common ground by the simple statement 'the people of Ireland', he appropriates the culture of 'our ancestors', which he alleges has been not lost but 'mislaid'. The degree or location of blame for such displacement is not explored, nor is the rhetorical question of whether the speaker identifies himself with 'the people of Ireland' on behalf of whom he speaks. The search for this common heritage is to be an act of repatriation, making the Celtic or Gaelic way of life the basis for conducting contemporary life. It must not be overlooked that Ferguson's own preoccupation with strangeness, with not being at home, and the way in which the landscape itself contributes to, and shares in, this sense of disorder, forms the basis of his ambition that others, not necessarily sharing his own unease, might be restored ('live back') to equanimity with their environment. It was still an attempt to reinhabit a place of the imagination rather than to build a recognisable modern polity. Members of Oscar Wilde's own family, not least in the person of his grand-uncle C. R. Maturin, played a significant role in this project, while Sir William Wilde himself was central to the antiquarian work.

W. J. McCormack makes a telling point: 'those who cleave to the theory that history tells us what actually happened are hampered by such theory when the critical questions revolve round the issue of what palpably does not happen'.[13]

Nowhere is this more evident than in the way the Irish mind, which is concerned largely with absence and longing, engages with society by means of literature. Here the work of Oscar Wilde has significant points of comparison with the novels of the early nineteenth century.

At the time of the Act of Union prevailing literary taste, especially novelistic, was a mixture of gothic and romantic. In Ireland this took the form of sentiment and mystery which very often—and we are entitled to think deliberately so—avoided the central question posed by the book. A book is a history not only of external events but also of how it itself came to be written. Neither of these facilities was available to nineteenth-century Irishmen, because history was discontinuous and therefore not history at all. History moves by certainty; Irish history (like that of Scotland portrayed in the gothic novels of Scott) by mystery and folk memory: lore rather than law. Many political figures became writers (not least John Mitchel in his *Jail Journal*)[14] because a book would represent a form of history which, since history itself was discontinuous, would otherwise be inaccessible. Thus an indigenous past might be established and a future imagined. The dilemma of the mid-century was summed up by Davis: 'I wish to heaven someone would attempt Irish historical fiction.'[15]

However, as McCormack points out, there were indeed 'intimate connections between notions of separatism . . . at the end of the 1830s and the cult of historical fiction which flourished in and around the *Dublin University Magazine* at the same period'. McCormack is insistent that this was an organic initiative among the personalities concerned: 'it is not enough to point to the influence of Sir Walter Scott or Maria Edgeworth as an explanation of this phenomenon; there is a positive dynamic in the social dilemma of the Protestant middle classes which generated this interrelationship betwen politics and literature'.[16]

When, in Jane Austen's *Northanger Abbey* (1818), Catherine Moorhead sets out in pursuit of the supernatural, the pursuit takes her into another land, where the terrain is securely unfamiliar. When, by contrast, the narrator of Sydney Owenson's *The Wild Irish Girl* (1806) pursues the heroine, the elusive Glorvina, the other land is Ireland itself, presented as an experience quite inaccessible to the English mind or temperament. The pursuit, the place of pursuit and the subject/object pursued become one. Such congruence would continue problematic for the dominant, English, forms of prose. When she compares the two countries, Glorvina gratifies Wilde's notion of nature imitating art by saying that the Irish landscape, like a painting by Salvator Rosa, is superior to the Lorraine-like England.[17] The landscape of Ireland is created before our eyes and becomes the representation of its mind— a point reiterated in 'The Decay of Lying'.

The epistolary *Wild Irish Girl* achieves its effect by means of descriptions of the images which consume the narrator's sensibility. In a passage heavily indebted to Burke's kinetic vision of the Queen of France, the narrator admonishes us:

> Surely, Fancy, in her boldest flight, never gave to the fairy vision of poetic dreams, a combination of images more poetically fine, more strikingly picturesque, or more impressively touching.[18]

As he creates the spectacle of a half-ruined chapel where at sunset an historic family service is enacted, the scene and the vocabulary which describe it combine to become a single powerful self-validating medium which embodies the emotion to be mediated: 'What a picture! ... What a captivating, what a *picturesque*, faith!' And immediately the chief danger to its fragile and temporal existence is identified: 'Who could not become its proselyte, were it not for the stern opposition of reason—the cold suggestions of Philosophy!'[19]

We may hear Wilde discussing his attraction to the Roman Catholic faith in terms of its opposition to reason: 'I confess not to be a worshipper at the Temple of Reason.' (*L* 20) Later he would enforce his espousal of a non-existent paradise by reference to the metaphysical properties of the real world: 'Reason does not help me. It tells me that the laws under which I am convicted are wrong and unjust laws.' (L 468)

Moreover, *The Wild Irish Girl* proposes the belief, which Mahaffy would later inculcate in Wilde, that the Irish genius as expressed in poetry was directly related to the Greek, if not to an antecedent and higher source, and exhibits the intangibility of the genius:

> No adequate version of an Irish poem can be given; for the peculiar construction of the Irish language, the felicity of its epithets, and the force of its expressions, bid defiance to all translation[20]

—a characteristic which would be noted in the translation of Irish ballads resulting in new forms of Hiberno-English poetry which may be found in the work of Lady Wilde and of her son.

From this extravagant précis of another land we thus receive a multiple metaphor of an Irishness which is antique, fragile, elusive and noble, and which is to be found equally in the landscape and the language, each of which, jointly and severally, embodies its history and emotions: at its heart is the oxymoron, the myth which is unbelievable but in which we must believe in order to partake, if only briefly, of the story:

> Mountain rising over mountain, swelled like an amphitheatre. . . . All was silent and solitary—a tranquillity tinged with terror, a sort of *'delightful horror'*, breathed on every side. I was alone, and felt like the presiding genius of desolation![21] [*my emphasis*]

* * *

In intention, but not in detail, Maria Edgeworth's novels attempt a wider purpose—to depict the shortcomings as well as the strengths of contemporary Irish society and rural administration. But in many of her scenes—in *Castle Rackrent* (1800), *Ennui* (1809) and *The Absentee* (1812)—she reinforces, rather than disturbs, the imagistic and seigneurial temper of Owenson/Morgan. Many commentators have argued that it is by discovering and understanding difference that assimilation can be achieved, and it is certainly true that by addressing her accounts of Irish society to a English readership Edgeworth was aiming to do more than merely depict the quaint haplessness of her subject. It was Scott who said that 'she may be surely said to have done more towards completing the Union than perhaps all the legislative enactments by which it has been followed up'.[22]

The endeavour is to reintroduce England and Ireland to one another so that each understands the other's problem. If, as the Englishman Haines says at the opening of *Ulysses*, 'history is to blame',[23] then history must be set aside so that larger and longer questions may be addressed. The novel, if it is faithfully to express the landscape, vocabulary and syntax of Irish life, must become both a quest and a question.

It may thus engage in the ancient form of discussion, the colloquy or verbal contest[24] which Wilde employs in 'The Decay of Lying' and 'The Critic as Artist' and, subliminally, in 'The Portrait of Mr W.H.', and which Joyce brings to a high point in *A Portrait of the Artist as a Young Man* and *Ulysses*.

Ultimately this involves dialogue with the self who haunts us internally, of whose existence we are aware without realising its power to determine our fate; with the idea of neighbour, both within our own society and the weak or powerful neighbouring cultures; and with the contrasting or complementary aspects of one's own nature, with the musculature of male and female genes, with one's inclinations towards the sacred and the profane.[25]

Moreover, the parabolic nature of the folk-tale—so ubiquitous as a presence in nineteenth-century Irish fiction—focuses the attention of any listener on the nature of self and self's relation to home, both as a voyager outwards and as a participant in nostalgia, the pain of the homeward journey.

The telling, or 'relation', of the tale is the means whereby the self, the home and the two journeys are articulated; in Irish storytelling an extra dimension is added in the ancient self of previous existences, while another dimension is lost in the impossibility of completing the journey. The controlling emotion is tragic, because the tragedy of the broken integer is carried over into the experience of the next journey and the next telling of it. It places a question-mark over the unsatisfactory conclusion to each story, as paradox takes the place of fulfilment. 'Relation' is to be constantly renegotiated in both storytelling and the modes of affiliation.

We should not neglect the decadent nature of much Irish narrative: while concerned with the idea of a noble vigour, it is permeated with the presence of ruin. Both *Ennui* and *Castle Rackrent*, like Huysmans' *À Rebours*, Pater's *Marius the Epicurean* and, much later, Yeats's *Purgatory*, involve the fate of an almost extinct aristocracy, while the symbiotic captivity of coloniser and colonised, city and country, man and woman, Protestant and Catholic, master and servant, points to the rapid convergence of political and social issues which characterise the imminent end of an epoch and the manumission of new forces which would provide the energies for the evolution of a new age.

By means of its very title, *Ennui* sums up Voltaire and predicts Laforgue.[26] Borrowing from Thiebauld the idea that 'we pass our lives conjugating the verb "je m'ennuie, tu t'ennuies ..."',[27] Edgeworth gave new currency to the decadent, introspective tedium of everyday life in a cultural backwater which can become galvanised by the timeless strategy of mistaken identity, used here as the key to a discussion of the value of place and the role of the traveller—'I felt only as if I were travelling incognito'.[28] The relativity of truth— Edgeworth adapts Boileau to suggest that 'le vrai n'est pas toujours vraisemblable'[29]—not only underpins the uncertainty of our own history (that we can become other than we seem because of an accident not *of* birth, but *at* birth) but also suggests that he who begins in decadence ('I had an utter abhorrence and an incapacity of voluntary exertion')[30] may end in renaissance: 'Glenthorn Castle is now rebuilding.'[31]

In *The Absentee* the mother as the author, embodiment and discloser of secrets is as pronounced as in *Ennui*. The possession of land, which depends on the telling of secrets, is a state permanently deferred: 'Everybody who comes from Ireland *will* have a fine estate when somebody dies.'[32] To be absent from the place where that secret can be told is the tragedy of modern life—a life created by conditions adverse to oneself. As such, the absentee is 'one of those enemies to Ireland';[33] lost in the vertigo of English manners and their lack of consequence, he 'know[s] nothing of the future'.[34] In danger of being lost even when at home, Lord Colambre is berated for wanting to go to Ireland 'merely because it's your native country'[35]—the pre-echo of Wilde's Algernon needing to be in London to miss an appointment because the appointment is in London (*CW* 343) is ominous. He knows his native country by being in another place; when he is in his native country, he no longer knows it.

Sheridan Le Fanu's writings continue the attempt of Maria Edgeworth to engage with the matter of Ireland, and at the same time to confront what it may be that haunts us within. He is thus concerned with continuity and isolation on both the personal and public planes, and in this respect he can best be regarded as an Irish writer who, because of his singular placing as a Protestant, can comment most insightfully not only on the nineteenth century in Ireland but also more widely on that self-conscious period which was the first to locate itself numerically,[36] conscious that it was the child of the eighteenth and would be the parent of the twentieth.

As with his predecessor C. R. Maturin and his successors Somerville and Ross (and to a certain extent Yeats), Le Fanu's material was the *house*, and its affective life in the consciousness of successive generations—its ability to shock, to curse, to belittle, but above all to project its own persona and its own mind: we do not inhabit the house—*it* inhabits *us*. The dominant presence once again is the *image*—family portraits, ghosts, memories framed as mental visions, even intense intellectual abstractions—taking shape as pictorial construct, and the pursuit is *la recherche du temps perdu* in order to recover some lost integer, some factor not forgotten but no longer understood, which might help to reorder time past as a continuous rather than a disconnected series of intelligible events.

The present is an intolerable experience of vertigo; as Le Fanu's Richard Marston says:

> To me the past is intolerably repulsive—one boundless, barren, and hideous golgotha of dead hopes and murdered opportunities—the future still blacker and more furious, peopled with dreadful features of horror and menace. . . . Between such a past, and such a future, I stand upon this miserable present.[37]

This psychic difficulty has both aesthetic and political aspects: neither people nor the groups and societies to which they belong can escape a present so enthralled by the past and so intimidated by the future. To be rid of the past, one must understand it, and to do that one must know the landscape both physical and metaphysical; as W. J. McCormack says, 'the difference between the living and the dead, as far as [Le Fanu] describes it, always refers to a topographical dimension',[38] and it is instructive that, like Edgeworth, Maturin, William Wilde, Jane Elgee, Yeats and Hyde, Le Fanu had intimate acquaintance with the rectory—the 'house'—and the church and graveyard which adjoin it.[39] Life as 'transitional stasis', 'an interlude between journeys',[40] is not merely unbearable, but impossible. In such circumstances, behaviour becomes psychotic and, as McCormack suggests, 'feelings which the personality cannot admit as its own' are projected 'on to another figure, real or imagined'[41]—in *Uncle Silas* the house of symbols separates the sufferer from her real self, from her experience, and makes her the spectator of her own history and her fate. In such a world, the common denominator of the 'lost' or 'stolen' child is more readily comprehended as the narration of a *life* stolen or misplaced.

At the outset of *Uncle Silas* (1864) Le Fanu warns the reader against 'the promiscuous application of the term "sensation"',[42] yet affirms that 'death, crime, and, in some form, mystery . . . the vision . . . the duel, the horrible secret . . . the doomed fisherman . . . the suspicion of insanity, and the catastrophe of suicide' are all aspects of a genre of writing which has 'the same moral aims'.[43]

Le Fanu takes this to such an extent that we are entitled, very early in our reading of *Uncle Silas*, to wonder whether there was ever a 'real' Uncle Silas, or indeed a father to the child, or whether all the events and discussions take place within the nursery of the child's imagination, not least because of the improbability of what is transacted in the 'real' waking world. The predominant mood is one of recollection, but a recollection which in its turn is triggered by anticipation. 'That mysterious relative whom I had never seen—who was, it had in old times been very darkly hinted to me, unspeakably unfortunate or unspeakably vicious'[44]— the syntax is deftly ambiguous, the age of the child withheld, the nature of the mystery is oracular, 'hinted'.

> Round the slender portrait . . . guttered many-coloured circles of mystery, and the handsome features seemed to smile down on my baffled curiosity with a prevailing significance.
>
> Why is it that this form of ambition—curiosity— which entered into the temptation of our first parents, is so specially hard to resist? Knowledge is power—and power of one sort or another is the secret lust of human souls.[45]

Vision, so central to the thought of Berkeley, is the organ of knowledge, and thus of satisfying a 'secret lust'. It was, perhaps, disingenuous of Le Fanu to introduce Swedenborg as the means of discussing the idea that we can in fact believe in that which we cannot see, especially since none of the arrivals or departures of 'real' people in the novel are of so much interest or relevance as the thoughts continually registering in the child's internal processes. 'We are children to the last,' says her father, as if to confirm this.[46] Meanwhile the presence within her family, her mental and intellectual universe, is the 'uncle', the father's *alter ego*, 'the vision and the problem of so many years of my short life'.[47] As her own confidante, Lady Knollys, tells her:

> Silas Ruthyn is himself alone, and I can't define him, because I don't understand him. . . . At one time of his life I am sure he was awfully wicked—eccentric indeed in his wickedness—gay, frivolous, secret, and danger-ous. . . . He always bewildered me like a shifting face, sometimes smiling but always sinister, in an unpleas-ant dream.[48]

In *Uncle Silas* Le Fanu—as would Wilde after him—takes the portrait, the visual, iconic grammar of the psyche, to an obsessive conclusion. When, in the last paragraph of the tale, he says: 'This world is a parable—the habitation of sym-bols—the phantoms of spiritual things immortal shown in material shape,' and asks: 'May the blessed second-sight be mine,'[49] he locates that world within Ireland and facilitates the transitus of the Irish folk-tale and fairy story into mod-ern literature.

While there are certainly grounds for agreeing with McCormack that there is no solid tradition of Anglo-Irish novel-writing, and that 'any enquiry into a possible homolo-gy between the structure of Irish fictional forms and the structure of Irish society'[50] is impeded by our limited know-ledge of the subject, it is not unrealistic to suggest, tentatively at least, that the novelists discussed briefly here wrote out of a common experience of dislocation or uncertainty, out of a gap between what might be and what was, which cast them in the role of early pioneers of indeterminacy, becoming, through the act of writing, actors in the field they observed.

In the case of Samuel Ferguson, whose main work was that of translating the Gaelic epic mythology into the English poetic tradition, the situation is, if anything, even more paradoxical. Ferguson himself is the key to many of the questions which we ask about the character of nineteenth-century Protestant Ireland and the way in which it perceived itself. Not only was he anxious, as Peter Denman has pointed out, 'to set up a negotiation between the ancient and the contemporary', but he was also concerned 'to assimilate . . . and to translate'[51]—to extend that negotiation to the meeting-place of Catholic Ireland and Protestant Ireland and of Gaelic and English literary idioms.

To the extent that Ireland was, in Joyce's words, 'so familiar and so foreign',[52] Ferguson also was an absentee, never at home with that which he most espoused, and thus capable of an acute yet unrewarded perspective on the subject which he pursued with missionary zeal. To the extent that this prompted him to establish a 'dialogue', he was creating a new bridgehead between cultures and historical epochs.

Like many of his class and politics, Ferguson was not impressed by the potential of the Irish for self-rule, yet even in this his natural sympathy with, and admiration for, their ancient character coloured his pessimism: 'They regard themselves, through at least three of the provinces, as a royal race. . . . I believe this proud spirit is inherent in the race, and underlies all the varying forms of their discontent.'[53]

Brendan Kennelly illuminates the fact that in making a connection between Ireland's present and its past, by making a place for that past in the polite literature of the mid-nineteenth century, Ferguson and others were creating afresh the epics which documented the heroism of the Irish mind. He quotes Eugene O'Curry's intention 'to present for the first time ... a comprehensive, and in some sort a connected account' as an attempt 'to re-create a picture of an ancient civilisation, a heroic age'.[54] In a sense, this mapping exercise echoed that of the Ordnance Survey, and in so doing it represented a way of making history. Yeats said that Ferguson was 'consumed with one absorbing purpose ... to create an Irish school of literature',[55] to which Kennelly adds that *Congal* was 'Ferguson's attempt to write a national epic'[56] concerned with the conflict between 'the evening of Paganism and the morning of Christianity'.[57] (This would become a major point of self-appraisal in the poetry of Oscar Wilde.) *Congal*, says Kennelly, 'is Ferguson's act of faith in his country's past as a source of inspiration for epic poetry'.[58]

This creation or re-creation had more than one purpose. Kennelly refers to 'Mesgedra', Ferguson's own poem on the antiquity and greatness of Dublin, in which 'Ferguson states what may be considered his vocation as an epic poet':[59]

> the Man aspires
> To link his present with his Country's past,
> And live anew in knowledge of his sires.[60]

The intention is thus not only to bring that old world into the new, but also to connect the past with himself—or, since they are not in fact *his* sires, to connect his sense of what he is now with what he might have been in a previous age, to allow himself a role in that epic. The project thus involves the creation of an acceptable image—albeit that of a hero of 'flawed greatness'[61]—into which the poet-historian may step in order to repossess himself.

On the public plane, the connection not only permits the resumption of that past, but also for the first time makes possible an imaginable future. For Ferguson and Davis, the national project was to gather for a hypothetical Ireland a construct of images which would articulate its aspirations in such a way as to provide it with the necessary freedom to rewrite the future. Irish 'history' is thus a misnomer, and gives the lie to Barthes' notion that 'there nowhere is nor has been a people without a narrative';[62] in fact it disproves this assertion while proving his further statement that the 'art of the storyteller ... is the ability to generate narratives'.[63] The distinction is crucial. The inchoate nature of the Irish nation, and its book, is expressed here. But if the epos, and the secret which it held, could be recaptured, heroism, in a modern mode, would be once more possible.

The case of Charles Robert Maturin is especially relevant, not least because he was the uncle-by-marriage of Wilde's mother—again, closely connected with the Church of Ireland: his grandfather had succeeded Swift as Dean of St Patrick's in 1745, and his great-grandfather had been Dean of Killala. He was a man of considerable mystery, not least concerning the derivation of his own name:

> Some years before the French Revolution an infant was discovered exposed in the Rue des Mathurins in Paris by a lady connected with the Court. The rich and splendid clothes of the child betokened him of no ordinary rank. She took him home and adopted him, giving him the name Maturin, after the street where he was found.[64]

The source for John Worthing, discovered by a man who in his pocket had a first-class ticket for that destination at the time, will be clear, as it was to Wilde himself, who supplied this information for the 1892 reissue of *Melmoth the Wanderer*. Since Wilde was very much aware of his grand-uncle's work, it is therefore inconceivable that *Melmoth the Wanderer* (from which he derived his final identity) and *The Wild Irish Boy* were not prominent in his appreciation of the Anglo-Irish novel. Alethea Hayter has suggested that, with Poe and Le Fanu, Maturin belongs to a 'school for which a new name perhaps needs to be invented ... whose technique is the turn of the screw, the extreme pressure of one human personality on another'.[65] But like Poe's 'William Wilson', Le Fanu's *Uncle Silas* (or indeed the story by James which gives added point to Hayter's comment), it is not so much a question of two personalities as of two tendencies—the caution and anxiety of innocence and the menace and mockery of experience— whose existence within the one frame of mind distinguishes this 'school', of which a further feature, or technique, is that of vagabondage, a commitment to the aimless yet driven road.

Melmoth the Wanderer (1820) begins with three elements which are the commonplace of decadent fiction—a ruined house, a curse, and a portrait of a past but present secret: 'you will see him again, he is alive'.[66] The 'familiarity'[67] between the undead and the innocent is the hallmark of Maturin's grotesque humour. As far as our interest in what Wilde may or may not have derived from his grand-uncle's work is concerned, we should note that he certainly took the idea of perpetual and recurrent homelessness—'I shall return an unwelcome visitant to the world that does not want me; a revenant ... as one whose face is grey with long imprisonment and crooked with pain,' as he foresaw his life after Reading (*L* 413). But much more importantly, he took from *Melmoth* the injunction that the portrait of the revenant must be destroyed:

> I enjoin my nephew and heir, John Melmoth, to renounce, destroy or cause to be destroyed, the portrait ... hanging in my closet.[68]

This, and the disclosure of secrets, of the '*odd story in the family*'[69] [*Maturin's emphasis*] becomes the central fact of *The Picture of Dorian Gray*. In the case of Melmoth, it is a secret described to the hero but left largely unspoken to the reader—'a tale so wild, so improbable, nay, so actually incredible' that it must be followed with 'interest, curiosity, and terror'.[70] It was, as Balzac noted, 'la type du Don Juan de Molière, du Faust de Goethe, du Manfred de Byron ... Grandes images tracées par les plus grands génies de l'Europe'.[71] To know the unknowable, to see fate in the face, was the ambition and the life sentence of the Irish mind.

All Maturin's work centres around the mystery of something which is both dead and undying, feeble yet powered by an unstoppable force. Chapter 3 of *Melmoth* is prefaced by the words of Pliny, '*apparebat eidolon senex* [the image of an old man appeared]'[72] (a tragi-comic ploy which would provide Yeats with plot and Synge with dénouement). Behind the quest for the original and unageing Melmoth is this spectre of agelessness expressed as antiquity, 'the curse of sanity and of memory'.[73]

> I have sought him every where.—The desire of meeting him once more, is becoming as a burning fire within me,—it is the necessary condition of my existence. I have vainly sought him at last in Ireland, of which I find he is a native.[74]

When the young Melmoth destroys his ancestor's portrait, 'its undulations gave the portrait the appearance of smiling. Melmoth felt horror indescribable at this transient and imaginary resuscitation of the figure', and even as the picture burns, its subject emerges to announce: 'Those are flames I can survive.—I am alive,—I am beside you.'[75] The rest of his career, like that of Dorian Gray, is a quest in which the incidents are immaterial and of which the dénouement is utterly singular: 'No one', says the presence, 'has ever exchanged destinies with Melmoth the Wanderer.'[76] It becomes the starting-point for Dorian.

The Wild Irish Boy (1808), despite its serious defects as a narrative, is a rare example of a text which combines the storytelling function with that of political rhetoric; as such, it may be of even greater relevance to Wilde's career than *Melmoth*. More than the work of Edgeworth, Maturin's sprawling novel explores the relationship between England and Ireland and gives a more intimate flavour of the idea of the latter, as an alternative to that of the former. The fact that he fails to fashion a unity out of the disparate elements in the text—decadence, effete nobility, intrigue, gothic horror, mistaken identity, lost children and lost parents, absenteeism—may indeed reflect the unfinished business of the society in which the book is set, and may also be due to the fact that it was intended to jump on the bandwagon of the book whose title it appropriates, *The Wild Irish Girl*, which leaves many issues equally unresolved.

It is significant that Maturin begins *The Wild Irish Boy* with a series of observations which he fails to pursue to a satisfactory conclusion in narrative terms, but which from a metaphysical point of view are all the more effective because they hang above the storyline as question-marks reminding the reader (but not the author) of characteristics of both person and landscape which remain unaffected by his long distractions. In fact Maturin barely succeeds at the end of his third volume in pulling the various threads of his story together in a welter of urgent repatriation, recognition, and the deaths of all but the righteous and the wronged.

At the opening of the novel the narrator creates the prospect of the 'wild Irish boy' whose path through life never entirely changes his character nor thoroughly explores the qualities of the initial portrait:

> I have conceived a character that I wish had never existed—a young, a very young person, almost a boy, with the form of a girl, and the feelings of a man; no, not of a man, with more modesty, more freshness, more retirement and timidity, and youthfulness of mind, than men, men in the world, *can* have ... one to whom the call to pleasure sounds like the call of friendship, who follows the invitation of vice, because he loves the friendliness of its tone; who is betrayed by the very affections that promised him happiness, because he trusted without suspicion, and loved without defect ... submitting to vice, yet aspiring after virtue.[77]

This androgynous hero, Ormsby Bethel (his first name is derived from a Maturin/Elgee family connection), after a series of misadventures involving loss of parents, dissipation, betrayal (by his close friend whom all but the hero clearly perceive to be a rotter) and love affairs, eventually discovers his true nature and his true father. None of this proceeds from an organic structure in the text but by means of the author's mismanagement of incidents which seem to take on a life of their own, only to expire episodically. These need not detain us. The chief interest in Ormsby Bethel is in 'his sensations and ideas',[78] in the frequent authorial asides on the state of Ireland and Irish education, and in the strange character of his mother. Bethel is the nephew of a Milesian chief 'who resides in a castle in the wild, western extremities of Ireland',[79] yet Bethel only approximates to the grace and distinctness of this creature from an otherworld; it is left to the reader, if he wishes, to attribute his ambivalence and his androgyny to his membership of a family and a race untouched by, and ignorant of, modern civilisation. An early admirer declares:

> I wish he would be either angel or human, and I might then have peace. But this mixture of loveliness and depravity, this beauty and brightness of a fallen angel, so rends my feelings. . . . Yes, he is depraved, and to love depravity, is to love too well. Why is vice suffered to look so lovely? why is there no mask on its brow, that all may fear and shun it?[80]

Bethel is one of life's innocents, cast parentless on the mercy of a foster-world:

> I was never taught to call any one parent or relative. . . .
> I loved to hear children talk of their parents; and I often gazed earnestly in the faces of those whom I thought might satisfy the yearnings of my soul, if they would; but the name of my father never passed my lips.[81]

In such circumstances, Bethel 'became an incurable visionary'[82] and under the influence of Ossian formulates an imagined country where he can hold sway over perfection:

> Amid the spots of quiet clouds that lay scattered over
> the evening sky, like islands on the great deep, I have
> imagined some fortunate spot, some abode peopled by
> fair forms, human in their affections, their habits, in
> every thing but vice and weakness; to these I have imag-
> ined myself giving laws, and becoming their sovereign
> and their benefactor.... [The character of the people is]
> glowing with untaught affections, and luxuriant with
> uncultivated virtue; but proud, irritable, impetuous,
> indolent, and superstitious ... disgraced by crimes which
> the moment after their commission they lamented....
> When I had conceived this character, such was its con-
> sistency, its *vraisemblance*, that I immediately concluded
> it to be ideal.... I mentioned the character I had con-
> ceived to my tutor, and ... he answered immediately
> that I had accurately described the Irish nation.... From
> that moment a firm and habitual purpose took posses-
> sion of my soul. It was my morning's meditation, it
> was the vision of my night. To be the reformer and leg-
> islator of a country I had never seen, nor with one
> native of which I was acquainted, may perhaps excite a
> smile of the most piteous contempt; yet, from the
> effects of this suggestion on my own mind, I am con-
> vinced, the source of those lonely, remote events, which
> have agitated the world, and changed the most settled
> aspects of things.[83]

As the real and the imagined become one, Bethel tells us,
'I quitted England ... and arrived in another country'.[84] At this
point events begin to overwhelm him and his author so that
the possibilities of that 'other country' are seldom exploited.
Later, however, we are given an insight into the mind of De
Lacey, the Milesian chief who lives a life apart and who

thinks of the Norman conquest of England as 'recent' because 'to a Milesian every thing is recent but his own pedigree':[85]

> It is not from a contempt . . . of jurisprudence, that its exercise is an indelible insult to a Milesian, it is from a rooted belief of native and necessary aristocracy of character and station, a belief that the conquests of the English have not reached him, that he is as yet sovereign in his own territory, and accountable only to himself for his actions. The forms of modern policy, that equal distribution of justice which extends to every part of society, he does not despise, or defy, but he does not understand, or imagine, how they can affect him. He hears of them as if they are the laws of another country.[86]

The similarity with Wilde's declarations about English laws will be obvious.

In later work Maturin, perhaps recognising more than anything the sentimentality of *Melmoth* and *The Wild Irish Boy*, said that these earlier novels 'seem to me to want *reality*, *vraisemblance*; the characters, situations, and language, are drawn merely from imagination'.[87] Yet for the modern reader it is precisely the nature of this imagination which is of value in illustrating the same means by which, in Lady Morgan's novel, nature itself coalesces, shelters, gives rise to, and is in turn impersonated by, its heroes and heroines.

The 1892 edition of *Melmoth* contains an anonymous 'Note on Charles Robert Maturin' which may have been penned by the editors, Oscar's friends Robert Ross and More Adey, but which was most likely influenced by the views of both Jane and Oscar Wilde. It reflects Maturin's own reservations about the use of imagination, but positively so:

> The works of Maturin contain *ideas* which for originality, power, and subtlety of thought place him in the highest rank. He frequently expresses opinions far in advance of his time. Certainly none of his Irish fellow-

countrymen surpass him in these intellectual gifts, not excepting the most masterly writers of English prose among them. But in choice of epithet and mode of diction Maturin commonly exaggerates the faults into which Irish writers usually fall. Like Moore he 'rouges his roses and pours perfume on his jasmine', though Maturin's flowers are rather mandrakes and night-shades too fearful and venomous to flourish in Circe's garden. ... Half the first volume of *The Wild Irish Boy* is so modern in its method of pure suggestion of character without incident, that it necessarily failed to produce any impression at all when it first appeared. In *Women* also Maturin searches the human heart so minutely as to recall one of those demonstrations in dissection conducted with such masterly skill by M. Paul Bourget.[88]

Coming shortly after the *Dorian Gray* affair, this much-neglected 'Note' is one of the most significant speculations on the fortunes of the Anglo-Irish novel and its relation with 'the analytic school now popular in France and elsewhere'.[89]

(ii) PUBLIC OPINION

The avowed intention of *The Nation* was 'to create and to foster public opinion in Ireland—to make it racy of the soil'.[90] Knowing that public opinion was a vital element in any political manoeuvre, and stating that 'a newspaper is the only conductor to the mind of Ireland',[91] the editors quickly built up what was, by the standards of the time, a mass circulation believed to have been 250,000; given the widespread nature of communal readings, its true audience may have been well in excess of this. In their prospectus of August 1842 the promoters of *The Nation* had stated:

The necessities of the country seem to demand a journal able to aid and organise the new movements going on amongst us ... and ... to direct the popular mind and the sympathies of educated men of all parties to the great end of nationality ... unshackled by sect or party; able, Irish, and independent.[92]

The purpose of fostering 'nationality' was to

not only raise our people from their poverty, by securing to them the blessings of a domestic legislature, but *influence and purify them with a lofty and heroic love of country*—a nationality of the spirit as well as the letter—a nationality which may come to be stamped upon *our manners, our literature, and our deeds*—a nationality which may embrace Protestant, Catholic, and Dissenter, Milesian and Cromwellian, the Irishman of a hundred generations and the stranger who is within our gates.[93] [*my emphasis*]

The Nation was thus a proponent of repeal of the Union and became the mouthpiece of the Repeal Association, which had the objectives not only of abrogating the Act of Union but of securing to native administration the capacity to revive Irish trade, abolish tithes, establish fixity of tenure, repeal the poor laws, with the further objective of 'purification of every branch of the Executive from the filthy taint of Orange bigotry'.[94]

It was by no means clear, however, what means were to be adopted in order to achieve this, nor indeed what form of self-government—independent republic, dual monarchy, republic with association to the Empire—was to be sought, save that the principal objective of independence in legislation was universally agreed. In 1848, five months before the affairs of *The Nation* came to a head, Charles Gavan Duffy, in a lecture on 'Ways and Means of Attaining an Independent Irish Parliament' remained equivocal:

The sudden explosion of an outraged people has sometimes given liberty to a nation; but mere turbulence, or agitation with no definite scheme of action, never.[95]

Nevertheless, it was necessary to give the lie to the myth of the Union:

> Since 1801 Ireland has not been governed as a portion of the United Kingdom, but as a conquered country... as a separate country, by separate act of parliament.... The trade between the two countries has not been carried on as between two parts of one empire, but fettered with marked restrictions, injurious in every case to this country.[96]

Predicting the future fortunes of the Irish at Westminster, he said: 'Our policy requires for its success the election of a PARLIAMENTARY PARTY.... A score of Irish members of adequate capacity and character might rule the house.'[97]

The role of those Protestants sufficiently liberal not to be overwhelmed by the rhetoric of the *Dublin University Magazine* was central to that success. An anonymous letter from 'A Protestant' in *The Nation* of 17 December 1842 asserted that

> The real interest of the vast majority of Irish Protestants is ... to have Ireland governed *by* and *for* its inhabitants, and by and for them alone.... Everything which goes in the least degree to identify them with their country... is a step towards nationality.[98]

Five years later *The Nation* had cause to criticise an article in the January 1848 issue of the *Dublin University Magazine* which 'bears all the character of the Irish Protestant—of the man who has placed himself in a false position—who refused to identify himself with the country that *naturally* claimed his allegiance, but chose to link his hopes with another land, which rejects and despises him'.[99] A week later, in an issue which included a twelve-stanza poem '"To My Brothers—Progress" by Speranza (Jane Elgee)', *The Nation* was claiming Emmet, Tone, Grattan and Davis—all Protestants—as the chief architects of nationalism.[100] In the first issue of 1848 the

editor surveyed 'five of the most tempestuous and changeful
years of our history' and noted that *The Nation* had witnessed
the 'growth of self-confidence of the masses, and the kindling
of a poetic and historic spirit of nationality'; this had spread to
the middle classes, as was exemplified by 'the foundation of
the Repeal Reading-Rooms, the publication of national books,
music and pictures'; overshadowed by the death of Davis, the
country then saw the onset of famine, but also 'the first real
growth of nationality among the higher classes'.[101]

It now seemed that 'there is no longer any Anti-Repealer
in Ireland'—surely one of the most absurd declarations of the
period, especially given the equivocation with which the journal advanced towards, and retreated from, varying degrees of
defiance and incitement in the coming months. Only a week
later it was announcing 'another new year of suffering and
struggle', with 'the aristocracy of Ireland ... ingloriously dormant and indifferent to the dreadful schemes which are
enacted in what was once *their* country'—a belated commentary on *The Absentee*. Mourning Ireland's lack of resolve and
initiative, it opined that 'from Constantinople to Washington
we are known not as a vital nation, but as a beggared community'.[102]

Two weeks later a leading article blamed indecision for
Ireland's political failures, dating from the vacillation of
O'Neill and O'Donnell between the Gaelic strongholds and
the English court[103]—this despite the fact that Irishmen
should have found resolve in apparent English indifference
to the Famine: 'It is evident to all men, that our foreign
Government is but a Club of Grave-diggers.'[104] Nevertheless,
as European events gained momentum, with the declaration
of the French Republic and growing unrest in such disparate
states as Sicily, Lombardy, Austria, Switzerland, Prussia and
Poland, *The Nation* accelerated and intensified its usually
low-key advances towards independence; it abandoned caution, and gradually relinquished its hold on moderation.
John Mitchel had parted company with the journal to pursue
a more open policy of sedition in the *United Irishman*, which he

founded in February of that year, but the temper of Gavan Duffy's journal became heated with the trials of Smith O'Brien and Thomas Meagher and of Mitchel in May. On 8 July Gavan Duffy himself was arrested on charges of felony, but continued to supply editorials to *The Nation*, that for 22 July, headed 'Casus Belli', beginning: 'The long-pending war with England has actually commenced.'[105] A second leader in that issue, 'The Hour of Destiny', written by 'Speranza', concluded: 'As you act as men, as patriots, and as Christians, so will the blessing rest upon your head when you lay it down a sacrifice for Ireland upon the red battle-field.'[106]

In the following week, on 29 July, the leading article, 'The Tocsin of Ireland', declared: 'Ireland is perhaps at this hour in arms for her rights.... It is her last resort, long evaded, long postponed.' The second leader, 'Jacta Alea Est [the die is cast]', again written by 'Speranza', by implication contradicted Davis's empty assertion of a decade earlier, but was sufficiently inflammatory to bring its author to the verge of prosecution. Its rhetoric prefigured that of the 1916 Proclamation:

> In the name of your trampled, insulted, degraded country, in the name of all heroic virtues, of all that makes life illustrious or death divine, in the name of your starved, your exiled, your *dead*.... Nothing is wanting now to complete our regeneration, to ensure our success, but to cast out those vices which have disgraced our name among the nations....You have had no country. You have never felt the pride, the dignity, the majesty of independence. You could never lift up your head to Heaven and glory in the name of Irishmen, for all Europe read the brand of *slave* upon your brow.... One bold, decisive move. One instant to take breath, and then a rising; a rush, a charge from north, south, east and west upon the English garrison, and the *land is ours*.[107]

Jane Elgee, following the precept of *The Nation* that 'each of the writers of this Journal holds himself, and himself alone, responsible publicly and privately for whatever he writes; and is fully prepared, at all times, to meet the consequences, whatever they may be',[108] admitted authorship of an article which was openly seditious and inflammatory. *The Nation* was summarily suppressed.

The *Dublin University Magazine* was founded in 1833 by Isaac Butt (its proprietor), Samuel Ferguson and Samuel Lover, a lawyer/politician, a translator/poet and a novelist. Among its first editors were Butt himself (1834–8), who was succeeded by the man to whom he sold the journal, the Dublin bookseller and publisher James McGlashan (1838–42), the novelist Charles Lever (1842–5) and later by its then proprietor, Sheridan Le Fanu (1861–9), both of the latter being friends and associates of William Wilde.

One of the most significant contributions during the first year of the journal was Ferguson's 'A Dialogue between the Head and Heart of an Irish Protestant', which appeared in the issue for November 1833. It may be viewed as an indication of the tensions between a conscience which wants to be Irish yet can only continue dependent on English examples for moral and cultural leadership. But it can also be seen as one of the first steps towards a 'middle Ireland' which became increasingly aware of the fact that, however great the denominational, territorial and class differences and difficulties, the solutions to Ireland's problems lay within Ireland itself. While, therefore, 'Heart' recognises 'the controllers of popery; the safeguards of British connection; the guarantees of the empire's integrity', and 'Head' acknowledges that *'Repeal can never take place until the Protestants of Ireland are disgusted by, and alienated from, the English Government' [original emphasis]*, there is a vigorous denial by 'Head' that the Protestants are, as 'Heart' alleges, 'strangers' in Ireland. 'Heart' says: 'I know not whence my blood may have been drawn, but . . . I feel and know that I am the heart of an Irishman.'[109] The dialogue is symptomatic not so much of tension or division within Protestantism as of the fact of its extreme confusion as to its role in modern Ireland.[110] The Famine had not yet concentrated their minds on the basic issue of survival. Between the implementation of Catholic Emancipation in 1829 (which many saw as the death-blow to the Established Church of both Ireland and England itself) and the onset of the Famine, Irish Protestantism looked with increasing frenzy for ways of curing its prejudice while maintaining its sense of intellectual superiority. The novels we have mentioned contribute little to the development of that role, if anything increasing the self-doubts of Protestant writers about their viability: one wrote in 1837 that 'the literature of a nation, and of this nation in particular, is affected by its political state and influential upon it'; on the other hand, a 'recently engrafted' literary cultivation was as yet unready to undertake the task of 'subduing and correcting or altering of old manners, prejudice, and associations, which is the actual process of civilization'. Concluding that 'our literature is *that of England*—we are substantially English, in name, laws, and prospects',[111] the writer thus established one end of the cultural spectrum, at the other end of which was a view of the Protestant 'nation' as being 'of Ireland'. In between lay a series of viewpoints which vacillated between the place of their power base and the place where that power was validated, between reality and affection, filiation and affiliation.

In 1848, as the tension between liberal Young Ireland and the conservative establishment reached its height, Le Fanu declared that 'the supremacy of British law in this country is actually maintained by, and depends upon, the loyalty of Irish Protestants'[112]—a commentary on the fact that it had been the dissension by Catholic jurors which had allowed the acquittal that month of Meagher and Smith O'Brien, and a sign that Protestant Ireland had begun to recognise the need to assert the mutuality of support: Britain needed them as much as they needed Britain. By the following year the picture had changed again, with an obituary notice of Maria Edgeworth referring to her 'truly patriotic regard for her native land', while maintaining that, like Thomas Moore, 'she was an *English writer* born in Ireland'[113]—an indication that the literary establishment was moving towards an inchoate attempt at defining what 'Anglo-Irish' literature might be, a subject on which disagreement persists to this day. The distinctive quality of Anglo-Irish writing was not merely that of having been written by Irish writers in the English language, but of having been written in a distinct form of that language, and by people whose traditions are qualitatively different from those of other writers indigenous to Ireland.

Much of this difference originates in resonance—in the different rhetorical acoustics to which the various traditions give rise and to which they continue to affiliate. If it could not be adequately addressed by novels (which were written largely for a homogeneous readership), it might be more effectively engaged by the publication of popular opinion across a wider audience. Even though the *Dublin University Magazine* had only a fraction of the circulation of *The Nation* (about 4,000 copies per monthly issue), it succeeded in speaking to most of its constituency.

Styled as 'A Literary and Political Journal', its first issue had contained 'The Present Crisis—A Dialogue', which concentrated on the contemporary domestic politics of England; but despite the anglocentricity of its politics, the *Dublin University Magazine* pursued an Irish-oriented perspective in other matters and took in a great deal of European literature. Thus the first number also contained the first part of a serialisation of Lover's *Barney O'Reirdon the Navigator*, a review of the second series of Carleton's *Traits and Stories of the Irish Peasantry* and a survey of 'The Irish Bar, as it was and as it is'. The founder-editor, Charles Stanford, introducing the journal to its readers, referred to its 'patriotism' and expressed the hope that readers were 'nationally interested in its success', sounding the warning note that 'Irish talent, like Irish valour, is valued and distinguished everywhere but at home'.[114] A further characteristic note, which would connect the name of Dublin University with a Unionist political bias, was sounded in the editor's assertion that 'Human nature, even in the cloisters of a college, cannot be divested of its attributes. . . . That very provision of the Constitution by which a representation in the legislature was given to the academic body, proves that its original founders entertained more enlightened views, and regarded learning and education but as means for the attainment of an end—as qualifications for the noble employment of taking a part in the concerns of the state.'[115]

Later issues identified the Protestant community as 'a garrison in a half-conquered and half-resisting country' and referred to Ireland as 'this doomed land, weeping with her thousand sorrows' for which 'there seems but little hope'.[116] On the other hand, while the siege mentality is pronounced, there is also a patronising, proprietorial, intention to colonise by example:

> We have no other design, but that our pages should be open to all quarters, provided they are consistent with our political principles, and the religion upon which alone they can be firmly based. We have but one object in view, THE MORAL INTELLECTUAL AND PHYSICAL IMPROVEMENT OF IRELAND.[117]

So within the apprehensive carapace of bigotry the magazine permitted many significant developments, not least of which was a lengthy and serious discussion of the nature of the Gaelic epics (in the form of a four-part review by Ferguson of Hardiman's *Irish Minstrelsy*), on the basis of which Ferguson's own opus would rest. Stories by Lever, Lover, and, most significantly, by the convert from Catholicism, William Carleton, rubbed shoulders with what we must today understand as characteristically well-intentioned 'dialogues' such as Samuel O'Sullivan's 'What is an Orangeman? A history and defence of the Orange Institution',[118] which, we have seen, was the one topic that was anathema to the concept of unity held by the editors of *The Nation*. Current affairs were noted, Isaac Butt contributing a lengthy review of Colby's first volume (relating to Londonderry) of the Ordnance Survey of Ireland.[119] Another review, by the arch-separatist O'Sullivan, of the Rev. David O'Croly's inquiry into the differences between the two main churches, wrily asserted that 'Everything indicates the speedy overthrow of the papal system in Ireland, except alone the conduct of our rulers. . . . *Let the franchise in Ireland be raised to twenty pounds, and the thing is done.* . . . Parliament has the power of rectifying every abuse by which this country suffers, if it only does its duty.'[120]

Such prejudice may seem outrageous and—even more telling—quite unrealistic; yet it was symptomatic of the fact that the English/Protestant colony in Ireland saw itself as effectively disenfranchised by the enfranchisement of Catholics. Fear mingled with impatience and frustration.

Nevertheless, the increasingly less strident tone of Protestantism, as it saw public opinion gradually moving away from entrenched positions towards a more sympathetic standpoint, made the journal, particularly in the aftermath of the Famine, more amenable to compromise. The issue for June 1849 indicates how great the impact of that catastrophe had been. An anonymous article entitled 'Experiences of Union, and Apprehension of Repeal' stated:

> We are as firmly persuaded as any man in the country, that it is desirable for the interests of every part of our great empire to maintain British connexion as established by the act of legislative union; but we have long since lost our faith in the stability of the great national compact, and we have therefore been persuaded, that, while doing our utmost to maintain a cause in which we have so deep an interest, we should not be insensible to the apprehension *that the cause may be lost.*[121]

The nature of the sea-change was radical: Irish Protestant opinion had recognised that within its own ranks were, at last, effective politicians who would lead Ireland to the end of the Union.

One of the most remarkable—but least remarked—stories to appear in the *Dublin University Magazine* was published in November 1838. Signed 'B.A.M.', its author was James Clarence Mangan, a retiring character who modelled his personal behaviour on that of Maturin and who was much influenced by Maturin's writings. The story, entitled 'The Man in the Cloak', is a pre-echo of Marie Corelli's *The Sorrows of Satan*, portraying a man who can obtain unlimited power and riches in exchange for his soul, but who must buy a soul from another before he can die. Asked if he is English, the Man in the Cloak replies: 'Your presumption is unwarrantable; I am not English . . . I am an Irishman.' The Man in the Cloak is . . . Melmoth; Mangan had deliberately chosen the name from among the literary undead. When Melmoth sells his power in exchange for a soul, he is able to die, and his identity passes to another. 'Where is he? . . . He is gone—*home*. I have taken his place. I am now *The Man in the Cloak*—in other words, I am henceforth a being of mystery— none must see me as I really am.'[122] The debate on the nature—or even the existence—of the soul (which is twice referred to as 'the ****') will reappear in both Lady Wilde's story 'The Priest's Soul' and her son's 'The Fisherman and his Soul'. Here we should note the other remarkable features of Mangan's tale: that it is concerned with a presence which is both real and unreal, with a cloak (or mask) which prevents others from seeing him 'as I really am'; and that, when relieved of his power, the creature is capable of going 'home'. Given his parents' involvement with the *Dublin University Magazine*, it is more than likely that Oscar Wilde would have found this story and determined to employ its characteristics when he came to write his own.

But perhaps for our present purposes, the most significant event in the entire history of the journal was the appearance in January 1849, six months after the suppression of *The Nation* and the publication of 'Jacta Alea Est', of a poem entitled

'Ruins'. Its author was 'Speranza'. Of all translations, that of the future Lady Wilde from insurrection to submission must be the most bizarre:

> Earnest dreamers, sooth we blame not
>   If ye failed to reach the goal—
> If the glorious real came not
>   At the strong prayer of each soul.
> By the path ye've trod to duty,
>   Blessings yet to man may flow,
> Though the proud and stately beauty
>   Of your structure lieth low.[123]

(iii) MIDDLE IRELAND

When Speranza declared: 'I express the soul of a great nation. Nothing less would content me, who am the acknowledged voice in poetry of all the people of Ireland,'[124] she was following Ferguson's lead in appropriating and mediating the intangible Irishness of 'soul' in the service of political and conceptual change. As we have seen in the case of Lady Morgan's heroine Glorvina, a merger between person and landscape was effective in emphasising the iconic nature of the translation. It was necessary to impersonate Ireland.

I want now to articulate a 'middle Ireland', a place of compromise in which many of the nineteenth-century actors—Ferguson, Davis, the Wildes—found possible ground for movement in and out of their various cultural and political positions. Without doubt, if any name could be given to this middle ground, it would incorporate the chief vehicle of Irish culture, the book, which is a place both of writing and of speaking, a place of iconography and of drama.

Ferguson found translation to be both the vehicle and the result of cultural transmission and exploration. Translation is indeed the key to the positioning of this 'middle Ireland', a transaction between possibly opposing ideas and entities.

That such a figure as Yeats could emerge as one of the architects of twentieth-century Irish consciousness; that Parnell can be seen as one of the major civilising forces in the emergence of modern Irish politics; and that Oscar Wilde is permitted a continuing role as a source of aesthetic and social stimulation and enlightenment, is in large part due to the success of such transactions.

Translation operated on many levels in nineteenth-century Ireland: in linguistic terms, between the Gaelic past and the English present, between eighteenth-century norms and nineteenth-century expectations; in social terms, between Irish peasant society and its landlord class, between Irish writers and an English readership, between politicians and intellectuals, historians and antiquarians.

There was a serious level of negotiation between the eighteenth-century concepts of revolution as achieved in America and France, and those in the post-Napoleonic, post-Vienna era. In Ireland a balance was needed between the understanding of the hero and that of a collective society. Within the discovery of the Celtic past we can, as we have already noted, detect a commerce between the hero and his community which had important lessons for the society making those discoveries. More importantly, perhaps, we can see that nineteenth-century Ireland established this middle ground as a means of being neither submerged nor seduced by either of the main available realities. Researchers such as William Wilde, George Petrie and Eugene O'Curry moved into this ground and joined themselves to the older nation. Translation was crucial to the establishment of this cultural project.

Oscar Wilde was fascinated as poet and critic by translation. Like his parents, he valued it because it enabled him to modulate influences and to filter those strengths—and weaknesses—of the native and the planter, of Catholic and Protestant, simple and complex, which he was prepared to put at the disposal of his own life.

The difference in Wilde which was perceived at Oxford was both the difference in the man himself (age, sexual interests, background) and the means by which that difference was perceived. One characteristic mentioned was his 'way of looking at things', which is intimately concerned with thought-processes and with cadence. Cadence, and the thought or emotion which it expresses, is the function and client of language, and the linguistic and stylish difference between Wilde and his Oxford contemporaries had its origins in the radical privacies of Irish and English. In 1848 *The Nation* had said that the distinctive feature of 'the Irish spirit—that principle of thought and mode of feeling which makes us Irish, not English—which constitutes our separate identity among nations' was *language*.[125] Wilde was an 'antinomian' both in relation to the imposition of public morals and in the sense that his 'Irish spirit' instinctively and inherently reacted against the dictates of fact or reason. Many of his stories would depart from the accustomed unities of literary storytelling in preference for the oral and sonorous tradition of the *seanchaí* which was more amenable to, and masterful of, the suspension of disbelief.

Ferguson had said: 'I am an Irishman and a Protestant . . . but I am an Irishman before I am a Protestant'[126] and aimed, by means of translation, to 'make Irishmen know themselves and one another':[127] 'Irish society, at the present day [1835], exhibits those anomalous features of mixed crudeness and maturity which are but the representations of two stages of society, whose antagonist principles have hitherto found no mutual means of reconcilement.'[128] Perhaps the strongest echo of that motive forty years later can be found in William Wilde's valedictory lecture of 1874, 'On the Ancient Races of Ireland', in which he said: 'It appears to me that one of our greatest difficulties in Ireland has been the want of fusion—not only of races, but of opinions and sentiments, in what may be called a "give and take" system.'[129] The best example of such a fusion, of the capacity to translate themselves and their ambitions, is the remarkable marriage of William and Jane Wilde.

Both Wilde's parents radically changed their own contexts, one with scientific, the other with artistic, fervour. Their meeting-place in the post-Famine era, when Ireland was shocked into a fundamental review of its status and relations both internal and external, is a sign of the transitus which Irish people of all backgrounds and persuasions were obliged to undertake in the face of holocaust. First-generation Dubliners, these young provincials were eager to participate in the evolution of Ireland as a nation, at a point where a country which hardly mattered in terms of national significance had almost ceased to exist in real terms. That they first met in the pages of the *Dublin University Magazine* is signal of the fact that Protestant Ireland had problems to resolve before it could attend to the problems of Ireland itself. As with the recognition of the 'absentee' problem whereby landlords were figuratively as well as physically missing from the Irish mix, the events of 1848, within the context of the Famine itself, can be said to have encouraged a 'socialist' mindset which changed the ethical, if not the political, orientation of Protestant Ireland. That Sir William and Lady Wilde (as they were to become) should have been part of the viceregal system when she had advocated marching on the seat of its authority, Dublin Castle, is a supreme, oxymoronic irony, but none the less apposite and explicable for all that. Slowly, as we have briefly noted, the *Dublin University Magazine* liberated and emancipated the Protestant conscience and directed it towards an ecumenical perspective. To have accepted 'Speranza of *The Nation*' as a convert to its cause was both a rehabilitation of a wayward prodigy and a gesture of openness and, particularly, of continuity. It lent a peculiar ambiguity to the apostrophe in 'Jacta Alea Est'—'the land is ours'.

William Wilde was born in 1815 in the village of Kilkeevin near Castlerea, County Roscommon, the son of the local doctor. In his *Irish Popular Superstitions* he referred with some pride to 'my native village of Castlerea',[130] and when he referred to 'us from beyond the Shannon',[131] he gave a Connacht voice to literature which marked his contribution with a rare and particular inflection. Educated at the Royal School in Banagher (County Offaly) and the Diocesan School, Elphin (County Roscommon), he was then sent to study medicine at two related institutions in Dublin, Dr Steevens's Hospital and the Medical School in Park Street (now Lincoln Place). For further training he went to Vienna (where he was able to observe the practices in maternity and ophthalmic hospitals) and to Moorfield's in London. With this experience, and a notable flair for innovation in surgery, Wilde went on to become one of the pioneers of otology and ophthalmology, his *Practical Observations in Aural Surgery* (1853) remaining a classic textbook for many decades.

Wilde founded St Mark's Hospital, which exists today in the form of the Royal Victoria Eye and Ear Hospital, and, on the academic level, founded the *Dublin Quarterly Journal of Medical Science*, which he edited from 1845 until 1849. He rose rapidly in his profession, in 1853 (the year before Oscar's birth) being appointed to the largely honorary position of Surgeon-Oculist in Ordinary to the Queen in Ireland, in 1864 receiving a knighthood for his work as Medical Census Commissioner, in 1862 the Order of the Polar Star from the Swedish crown, and an honorary doctorate from the University of Dublin.

The recognition of Wilde's service as Medical Census Commissioner points to another aspect of William Wilde's career: his work, from 1841, in analysing the census statistics has been described as 'a classic of great scholarship, erudition and industry',[132] and this gives us an indication of the nature of such work which, like that on the Ordnance Survey, constituted much more than a gathering of superficial data. One of the officers of the Ordnance Survey had written: 'Habits of the people. Note the general style of the cottages . . . food; fuel; dress; longevity; usual number in a family; early marriages . . . what are their amusements and recreations? . . . Nothing more indicates the state of civilisation and intercourse.'[133] This same interest in custom and behaviour characterised Wilde's census work. The changes which were confirmed—or in some cases brought to light—by the census report published in 1856 were embedded in Wilde's remarkable survey 'extending over nearly the entire range of Irish history',[134] in which Wilde summarised the history of medicine in Ireland from the earliest times, and the way in which it engaged with, and reflected, social developments. Its explicit purpose was to describe how Ireland had come into the experience of 'the most memorable period which the social state of the country has presented in modern times'.[135] Incorporating chapters on the origins of written Irish history, the chronology of the Irish Annals, a table of phenomena, meteorological records, and a specific history of potato and general crop failure, the report drew attention to the rate of emigration from Ireland, which had risen from a figure of 40,000 per annum in the 1830s to one of a quarter of a million in the year 1851. Almost two million people had emigrated—as far as these official statistics were aware—in the period 1831–51.

Wilde was especially conscious of the Irishman's passionate adherence to his hearth, and in the census report he expanded on the consequent results of starvation in relation to this attachment:

> It is scarcely possible to exaggerate in imagination what people will do, and are forced to do, before they die from absolute want of food, for not only does the body become blackened and wasted by chronic starvation, but the mind likewise becomes darkened, the feelings callous, blunted, and apathetic; and a peculiar fever is generated, which became but too well known to the medical profession in Ireland at that time, and to all those engaged in administering relief ... [a state] which may almost be called mania.[136]

Wilde was, in addition, an assiduous folklorist and topographer, conscious of the political dimension, wrily describing the disturbances of 1848 as 'almost partaking of the nature of an epidemic'.[137] In parallel with his innovations in medical

science, he was one of the foremost archaeologists and antiquarians of the nineteenth century, for which he was awarded
the Cunningham Gold Medal of the Royal Irish Academy,
whose collection (now largely to be seen in the National
Museum of Ireland) he had catalogued almost singlehandedly.
Beside the three children he shared with his wife, Sir
William is known to have fathered at least four others—the
most prominent being Henry Wilson (1838–77), who became
his assistant in St Mark's Hospital and a Fellow of the Royal
College of Surgeons in Ireland. Two daughters lived with
one of William's clerical brothers, the Rev. Ralph Wilde, and
died, aged twenty-one and twenty-two, from burns suffered
when their dresses caught fire at a dance. The mothers of
Wilson and these girls are not known. Another child, a boy,
was allegedly born to Mary Travers, a patient whose seduction
would bring about Wilde's social and professional downfall
in 1864. Owing to the existence of these half-brothers and
half-sisters, Oscar Wilde, whose plays often focus on
accidents of birth, had plentiful evidence in his own family of
unknown parentage and mysterious siblings.

Our interest in Sir William Wilde's career lies not merely
in the fact that he was the brilliant, or even the wayward,
father of a brilliant and wayward son, but in the fact that he
maintained two separate lives, never relinquishing his love
of his native Connacht which became more important to him
after the public scandal of 1864. Like his father, Oscar Wilde's
public and private interests gradually coalesced in his published works. Sir William had gained a rich first-hand knowledge of the peasantry, and his early tuition at the hands of a
local poacher, Paddy Walsh, and Dick Blake, a sportsman in
the vicinity of Cong, was affectionately recalled and acknowledged in his volumes on *Irish Popular Superstitions* (1852)
and *Lough Corrib* (1867). They introduced Wilde to many of
the 'amusements and recreations' of the Irish countryside,
stimulating his interest in both the daily life conducted on
the surface of the land and, beneath the surface, the historical evidence of the evolution of that life.

William Wilde was a member of the generation to whom the discovery of Irish history and of its literature came as a revelation. As with Ferguson, his was a didactic approach, an example to all Irish people to develop an appreciation of the past, so that they could replace the depression of years of failure, deprivation and silence with a pride in the dynamic heroism and cultural achievements of their predecessors. In *Irish Popular Superstitions* he referred to a revolution 'which has taken place, and is still going forward, in matters of belief, and popular prejudice, and national opinion, in Ireland'.[138] Noting that the 'convulsions' of famine, emigration and bankruptcy 'have broken up the very foundations of social intercourse, have swept away the established theories of political economists, and uprooted many of our long-cherished opinions',[139] Wilde saw the opportunity for recovery, renewal and rapprochement. The Famine had brought in its wake the mixed blessing that all Irishmen were for once impressed with the seriousness of their condition and the need to address their cultural, as well as their physical and economic, conditions. Wilde was capable both of clinical scientific analysis, as his census work illustrates, and of sentimental attachment to the peasantry which also inspired the analysts of the Ordnance Survey and figures of the later 'Irish Renaissance' such as Lady Gregory and W. B. Yeats: 'These matters of popular belief and folks'-lore, these rites and legends, and superstitions, were ... the poetry of the people.'[140] Wilde indicated that they could be so again, that poetry could once more have a ritual power which both elevated and enshrined the qualities which were 'racy of the soil':

> If ever there was a nation that clung to the soil, and earned patriotism by the love of the very ground they walk on, it is (or we may now write was) the Irish peasantry.[141]

The successive failures of the potato crop and the dilution of the Irish language appeared to be complementary and related factors, complicated by punitive taxation which depopulated Connacht in particular—Wilde referred specifically to the region he knew well from his place of birth and his residences in north Connemara—the Kylemore/Renvyle area bounded on the north by the Killary fjord, on the south by the mountains known as the Twelve Bens and on the east by the Maamturk mountains.[142] Wilde neatly summarised the dichotomy in the national aspiration when he referred to 'that longing for liberty—but, alas! not for independence—which made the Irish peasant rather die than quit his native hearth'.[143] This dilemma, at the heart of relations between peasant and landlord, and between landlord and government, typifies the ambivalence of the Irishman's relation to land. But the fact that 1848 had seen the formation of a Protestant Repeal Association was a primary indication that the landlord class recognised the inevitability of independence at some future stage, however tenuous and ill-conceived; while the formation in 1870 of a Home Government Association, with William Wilde among its founder members, was the second stage of that recognition. That William Wilde crossed that gap between 'Repeal' and 'Home Rule' is a signal that, however unstable such conditions might be, Young Ireland in its middle age was becoming once more a cohesive and vocal force in political life.

Wilde's friends came from 'all classes and denominations'.[144] He was a great leveller, wanting only to enjoy life to the full and to be useful in doing so. 'Westward, ho!' he began his affectionate survey of Lough Corrib, 'let us be off to the Far-West, ... to the ancient home of the aborigines—the land of the Firbolgs, the Tuatha de Danaan [*sic*], and the Milesians—the last resting-place of the Celt.'[145] Seeing an intricate relationship between the natural and the built environment, Wilde revelled—as his wife and children did during their holiday visits to Connemara—in 'the greyish-purple robe of twilight, when the shadows of the headlands sink deep into the placid waters of the lake'[146] amid battlefields, caves, cairns, raths, tumuli, monoliths, stone circles, primitive churches, holy wells, abbeys and monasteries.[147] His interests were intensely local: at Moytura, site of one of the great battles of Irish mythology, a proud reference to 'the residence of the Author' (which he had built in 1865)[148] drew the reader into an account of one of the shaping influences of William Wilde's childhood, Rev. Patrick Prendergast, 'Abbot of Cong', and to the fact that Wilde's maternal family, the Fynnes, had sheltered the monks of this abbey in penal times. Complaining that 'the chief Protestant schools of Ireland do not teach Irish history',[149] Wilde employed the topographical approach to introduce his readers to the wealth of history both for informational and for stimulative reasons. There was always a sense of responsibility, of exemplary assertiveness and encouragement, in his assurances of his personal involvement, for example, in excavating burial sites on the plain of Moytura, or in instigating a study of the Irish-speaking population, which he made a special part of the census:[150]

> The spoken Gaelic is hourly dying out; and in twenty years more the oldest tongue in north-western Europe, if we except that of the Lapps and other extreme northern tribes, will have ceased to be used. . . .
> Had the Irish language been cultivated by the upper classes as was proposed by many eminent scholars and divines, it might, perhaps, have had an influence upon many subjects connected with the interests of this country.[151]

This concern was also evident in the record of the visit (organised by Wilde as President of its Ethnological Branch) by members of the British Association to the Aran Islands in 1857, when a dinner was held within the ramparts of the prehistoric fortress of Dún Aengus. Present on that occasion were the Provost of Trinity College, Dublin; the antiquarian George Petrie; John O'Donovan, a pioneer of the Ordnance Survey; Eugene O'Curry, the philologist, who addressed the islanders in Irish in order to introduce the visiting dignitaries; Samuel Ferguson, 'who, to his valuable contributions to the science of the antiquary, has so happily blended the popular fascination of the poet';[152] John Gilbert, author of *History of the City of Dublin* and *Ancient Historical Manuscripts*; and the artist Frederick William Burton, whose 'The Aran Fisherman's Drowned Child' was drawn on this visit.

O'Curry told the islanders that their visitors 'were gentlemen...with true Irish hearts, and who loved everything that belonged to their dear old country—gentlemen of great learning, who devoted their time for many a year to study and to write about Ireland'.[153]

Addressing the assembly in his turn, with the curious islanders ranged around the walls, Wilde said:

> Why have I brought you here?...It is because...I believe I now point to the stronghold prepared as the last standing-place of the Firbolg aborigines of Ireland, here to fight their last battle if driven to the western surge, or, as I have already pointed out to you, to take a fearful and eternal departure from the rocks they had contested foot by foot. Of that race we have no written knowledge. We can but make our conjectures by such light as recorded history has afforded us, reading it, comparing, and referring it to what they have left us in these litanies of stone. Here, perhaps, the sentinel on Dún Aengus, two thousand years ago, casting his glance on a summer eve over that vast expanse of Atlantic water that now rolls between us and America, brought up in fancy on the western horizon that far-famed island of O'Brazil, the tradition of which still lingers among these peasants now grouped around us.

His reference to the 'aborigines' would find an ironic echo in a later remark by his wife, as we shall shortly discover. Admonishing the islanders for the neglect of their heritage, he continued:

It is much to be deplored that these vast buildings are so rapidly going to destruction, not by the slow hand of time, for to time they almost bid defiance. The destruction we lament has been recent, and has befallen them from the hands of those who should preserve, not destroy them, as they have done in the pursuit of rabbits. Now, let me earnestly appeal to you, Islanders—will you not after this day, when you have seen that the intense interest felt in these buildings brings so many strangers to your Island...refrain from (for the paltry advantage of catching a few rabbits) bringing these walls to the state we see so many parts of them in? In an interested view of the matter you will be the gainers—strangers, in visiting the island, cause occupation and yield profit to many of you; and do not, for your own sake, destroy the things which bring strangers to visit you. Remember, above all, that these were the works of your own kindred, long, long dead; that they tell a history of them which you should be proud of, and that there is no other history of them but these walls, which are in your keeping. You have a great right to be proud of them; they are grand monuments of the brave men your forefathers were, and of how they laboured and how they fought to defend the land they left to you and to your children. Do you defend them in peace as they defended them in war, and let your children's children see strangers coming to honour them, as we have done today.[154]

There is a remarkable mixture of respect and condescension in such remarks by both Wilde and O'Curry, which only an Anglo-Irish sensibility could effect.

All these interests met and culminated shortly after Wilde's knighthood in the lecture delivered in 1864 to the Young Men's Christian Association at the Dublin Metropolitan Hall in Abbey Street. (It was also the occasion on which the bubble of the Travers scandal burst, with streetboys distributing accusatory leaflets to those flocking to hear Sir William.)

Wilde's title was 'Ireland Past and Present; the Land and the People', and his lecture culminated in the designation of Ireland as 'a truly regal republic'. Intent on opening the eyes of his audience to 'the remote past of the land of your birth'[155] by means of 'a series of pictures of our country and its inhabitants',[156] Wilde was attesting to the power of the image as archetype. The lecture combined Wilde's practical knowledge of peasant customs with his direct experience of the Famine. It affirmed the antiquity of the Irish race, the usefulness of the objects stored in 'our great national Museum'[157] and the importance of the transmission of pre-historic culture by means of 'the bardic chronicler of unlettered days'.[158] It asserted the similarity between this form of cultural transmission and that of 'the poems of Homer ... from mouth to mouth, by those great faculties of men, speech and memory',[159] and maintained that the Irish language, the medium of transmission, was still reasonably vigorous (although elsewhere he had, like so many others, identified the Famine as the chief cause of its impending death).

There was, in everything Wilde said on this occasion, a pointed insistence on the greatness, the epic quality, of the Irish, their culture and their history:

> I can assure my auditory, from long personal acquaintance and careful examination of the battle-ground of southern Moytura, in the neighbourhood of Cong, that if a skilled and learned antiquary were now ... to visit that memorable locality, he would unhesitatingly pronounce it ... to be one of the great battle plains of Europe.[160]

Acknowledging that emigration was carrying 'Irish hardihood, bravery, and poetry, throughout the world'—in particular, to Australia, America and Canada[161]—Wilde urged:

> Let us take good care of those that remain; respect their prejudices, comfort them in their afflictions, sympa-

thize with them in their sorrows, join with them in
their mirth; above all, be just with them in their dealings, and teach them, by example as well as precept, a
love of truth, cleanliness, self-reliance, and a more perfect system of agriculture.[162]

Once again, the patronising tone, but also the recognition
(and a celebratory, if anxious, one) that 'Ireland is now in the
transition stage'.[163] Wilde's was not an apocalyptic vision,
but an evolutionary, reasoned, but none the less impassioned vision of progress towards a manageable state of
affairs. Having 'laboured not to hurt the feelings of one class
nor pander to the prejudices of another', he saw his 'duty' as
'"to point the moral", and not merely "to adorn the tale"';[164]
he wanted, 'peace and comparative plenty . . . greater security
to life and property . . . education . . . vast and rapid improvement in our metropolis . . . a perfectly free press' and that all
Irishmen should be 'living under the mildest government in
the world, a truly regal republic'.[165]

Jane Francesca Elgee, born *circa* 1822, came from a family
with many connections in the Church of Ireland: her grand-
father had been Rector of Wexford and Archdeacon of
Leighlin, and was succeeded as Rector by his son Richard
(Jane's uncle); her aunt was the mother of the explorer
Robert McClure, while on her mother's side of the family
(Kingsbury) Jane's uncle by marriage was Charles Maturin,
the novelist, playwright and curate of St Peter's in Aungier
Street, Dublin; another Kingsbury aunt married Sir Charles
Ormsby (and thus perhaps provided Maturin with the sur-
name of his hero in *The Wild Irish Boy*); her grandfather
Kingsbury had been Rector of Kildare, and her great-grand-
father President of the Royal College of Physicians in
Ireland. She was to say in old age:

> I was quite indifferent to the national movement, and if I thought about it at all, I probably had a very bad opinion of the leaders. For my family was Protestant and Conservative, and there was no social intercourse between them and the Catholics and Nationalists. But once I had caught the national spirit, all the literature of Irish songs and sufferings had an enthralling interest for me.[166]

Reviewing her *Poems* in 1865 the Fenian *Irish People* opined that 'her surroundings, we are told, were anti-Irish. She belonged to that class who were Irish only in name and whose boast it was that they garrisoned the land of their birth for a foreign country.'[167] Her conversion was thus a notable popular victory for Davis's brand of nationalism.

Jane Elgee, whose education seems to have been extensive, as she had early acquired a working knowledge of at least three European languages, came to Dublin, where her father, Charles, practised as a solicitor in Leeson Street, in the 1840s. She was full of literary and nationalistic vigour, her role-model in the latter being Thomas Davis. Indeed, her pen-name in itself, meaning 'hope', impersonated Irish ambition. 'She is fearless and original, and *vows* ... that she likes to make a sensation,'[168] her friend, the mathematician Sir William Rowan Hamilton, said of her. She redeployed her initials to write as 'John Fanshawe Ellis', as well as 'Speranza', and it was in this capacity that she achieved her greatest sensation as the author of 'Jacta Alea Est'. As her affiliations vacillated, she appeared under her most famous *nom-de-plume* as well as her married title: thus her *Poems* (1864) were authored 'by Speranza (Lady Wilde)', while her *Ancient Legends, Mystic Charms, and Superstitions of Ireland* (1888) was 'by Lady Wilde ("Speranza")'.

As a poet, Speranza's chief interest for us today is as a role-model for the more tedious and emotional aspects of her son's verse. Comfortable only when she was unfurling the national-ist flag or championing some other suppressed cause, she nevertheless deserves a minimal mention in accounts such as Seamus Deane's 'Poetry and Song, 1800–1890'[169] where she is conspicuous by her absence. Whether there is any true poetic merit in her balladry, it is inescapable that work such as hers and that of several other ladies[170] published regularly in *The Nation* had a significant contemporary effect in promoting and heightening the propagandist ambitions of Young Ireland. If for no other reason, we should take note of the fact that her *Poems*, published in 1864—that year of great significance for her family—were 'dedicated to my sons Willie and Oscar Wilde' and were prefaced with these lines:

> I made them indeed,
> Speak plain the word COUNTRY. I taught them, no doubt,
> That a country's a thing men should die for at need![171]

Didactic and imagistic, her political verse expends emotion rather than argument—indeed, conflates the two so that each carries the other along within the rhythm which, typical of Protestantism, adapts the measure of the marching-song to that of the hymnal.

Speranza was responsible for continuing the promotion of the blood-sacrifice which had fuelled the rebellion of 1798 and continued through the wastage of life in 1916 and contemporary hunger-strikes: it is noble to die for one's country—indeed, it is necessary to die in order to be noble and heroic, and better to die than to be a slave.[172] Her poem 'The Famine Year' opens with the twin dilemma:

> Weary men, what reap ye?—Golden corn for the stranger.
> What sow ye?—Human corses that wait for the avenger[173]

—the inference being that during the Famine Ireland in fact grew a surplus of export crops. It is followed by 'The Enigma', which asks:

> Pale victims, where is your Fatherland?

and, asserting 'the holiest right of an ancient land', repeats Ferguson's project of repatriation:

> we prayed, in despair, to a foreign Queen,
> For leave to live in our own fair land.[174]

Identifying herself with the downtrodden, Speranza adopts the authorial 'we' in speaking of the poor and the starving, making it clear that the hunger for land and for home is as strenuous as, and as intimately linked with, that for material well-being. 'A Supplication' (headed significantly, in view of Wilde's prison letter, 'De profundis clamavi ad te Domine') speaks of

> Miserable outcasts we,
> Pariahs of humanity,
> Shunned by all where'er we flee

and of Ireland as 'our mourning mother'.[175]

> Arise! Arise! my patriot son,
> By hearts like thine is freedom won![176]

admonishes one poem. Another, 'Man's Mission', informs us, with execrable rhyme, that

> Each must work as God has given
>   Hero head or poet soul;
> Work is duty while we live in
>   This weird world of sin and dole....
> Life is combat, life is striving,
>   Such our destiny below....
> We are struggling in the morning
>   With the spirit of the night....
> We must bend our thoughts to earnest,
>   Would we strike the idols down.[177]

Thus Speranza, impersonating Mother Ireland, bade her sons be noble, heroic, hieratic, prepared to suffer in the knowledge that life is tragic and combative. 'To love, and work, and die' is the motto of freedom.

The juxtaposition of two of her poems is telling: 'The Year of Revolutions', which presages a glorious overthrow of tyranny, or death in the attempt, is followed immediately by 'Ruins', the poem with which Speranza made her peace between *The Nation* and her future husband's associates. Published in the *Dublin University Magazine* in January 1849, it sounded the threnody for militant failure and looked for a more realistic accommodation of ambitions:

> But the stately, radiant palace,
>   We had built up in our dreams,
> With Hope's rainbow-woven trellis,
>   And Truth's glorious sunrise beams;
> Our aims of towering stature,
>   Our aspirations vain,
> And our prostrate human nature—
>   Who will raise them up again?[178]

Ireland as a peripheral and neglected vestige is evoked in several of the poems; one in particular, lamenting 'The Exodus' of mass emigration, regards Ireland as

> a Nation old,
> Fading away from History's page;
>   Outcast weeds by a desolate sea—
>   Fallen leaves of Humanity.[179]

Its relevance for Oscar Wilde can be noted in the clustered combination of imagery: the history book, the geographical location, hopelessness and drifting, decadent humanity would all be revisited in his 'Humanitad', 'E Tenebris' and 'Theoretikos'.

*   *   *

In the Preface to her *Ancient Legends of Ireland* Lady Wilde identified language, mythology and ancient monuments as the three keys to the 'shrouded part of humanity'. It was in this sense that the Anglo-Irish pursued the disclosure of the Gael. Leaving aside the native language, on which, ironically, she, as a proficient linguist in many continental languages, could hardly discourse with any skill, she spoke of mythology as revealing a people's 'relation to a spiritual and invisible world' and of their literature as expressing the 'scientific progress of a nation'.[180] (Yeats would take the same path in asserting the present reality of that unseen world to a large proportion of the peasantry.) Superstition, she said, was 'the instinctive belief in the existence of certain unseen agencies that influence all human life'.[181]

Lady Wilde subscribed to the theory that Celtic beliefs and customs were directly derived from the Ur-culture of world civilisation, and that they represented a relatively undiluted strain of that original 'creed and ... language'.[182] She believed, also, that it had come to Ireland from the Middle East.[183] Her emphasis was on the importance of the unseen life.

Lady Wilde stressed that Ireland, alone among the cultures of Europe, possessed the 'mythopoetic [*sic*] faculty'[184] which embraces a sense of beauty, 'strong, passionate emotions and heroic impulses'.[185] Speaking of fairy lore, she employed the present tense to imply that peasant beliefs and superstitions retained their validity:

> The fairies of the earth are small and beautiful. ... The fairies, with their free, joyous temperament and love of beauty and luxury, hold in great contempt the minor virtue of thrift and economy. ... Their country is the *Tir-na-oge*, the land of perpetual youth, where they live a life of joy and beauty.[186]

She thus creates a land separate from the physical reality of modern Ireland but present within, beside and beneath it, which makes Ireland itself a different, an other place.

Examining the legends, of which she gave many examples verbatim, Lady Wilde paid serious attention to the nature of the soul, to the ability of the fairies to create changelings by spiriting away new-born babies, and to the bardic element in Gaelic culture, which she called 'the first expression of the human soul'.[187] All these aspects will be of interest when we come to discuss Oscar Wilde's 'fairy' stories. Here, we should also note his mother's attention to the 'wake orgies' or 'funeral games' which took the form of folk plays and professional storytelling. 'According to all accounts,' she says,

> an immense amount of dramatic talent was displayed by the actors of these fantastic and symbolic plays. An intelligent peasant, who was brought to see the acting at the Dublin theatre, declared on his return: 'I have now seen the great English actors, and heard plays in the English tongue, but poor and dull they seemed to me after the acting of our own people at the wakes and fairs; for it is a truth, the English cannot make us weep and laugh as I have seen the crowds with us when the players played and the poets recited their stories.'

'The Celts', Lady Wilde continued, 'certainly have a strong dramatic tendency, and there are many peasant families in Ireland who have been distinguished for generations as bards and actors, and have a natural and hereditary gift for music and song.'[188]

Speranza's later distinction rests not so much on her poetry, or even on her collections of folklore, as on her essays, which were collected in two volumes, *Men, Women and Books: Selected Essays, first series* (1891) and *Social Studies* (obviously intended to be the 'second series', 1893). It is clear that not only was she well-read, with strong literary opinions, but that she held modern views on egalitarian topics such as the emancipation of women, and that her perception of the continuity of the Protestant nationalist tradition remained trenchant. Her article on Thomas Moore began:

> Strong nations fight, oppressed nations sing; and thus, not with arms and fleets, but with the passionate storm of lyric words have the Irish people kept up for centuries their ceaseless war against alien rule. For words have a mystic power over men, and with the word Liberty on their lips, and the ideal of Nationhood in their hearts, the Irish have been preserved by their poets and orators from degenerating.[189]

That on O'Connell adopted an equally artistic perspective:

> O'Connell's life truly was a wonderful drama, with Ireland for the theatre and the whole civilised world as spectators.[190]

She adopted the heroic view of O'Connell's

> long gladiatorial wrestle against oppression and bigotry in which every step was a combat and every combat a victory. . . . The life of O'Connell is, indeed, the history of Ireland for nearly a century. . . the avenger, the apostle, and the prophet of her people.[191]

Speranza also made an incisive comment about her own class and creed when she said (in 'The Poet as Teacher'):

> One of the many reasons, perhaps, of Ireland's degradations is, that her gentry were never taught to feel and act as Irishmen.[192]

Following the lead given by articles in the *Dublin University Magazine* and *The Nation* which we have noted, she, like her husband, found no difficulty in adopting a role of leadership and example:

> The list is endless of Irish genius left to struggle hopelessly against the corroding cares of life. A natural

result, when there is no kinship or sympathy between the rulers and the ruled, no pride of race, no heroic memories, no traditions of suffering common to both. Yet the word *country* should be for ever sacred, and lie at the base of all individual action and effort; for love of country is the divine force that can alone war against the degrading tendencies of mere material gain; and no mental or moral elevation can be attained by a people who do not, above all, and before all, things, uphold and reverence the holy rights of their Motherland.[193]

On Davis himself ('Irish Leaders and Martyrs') her verdict was unequivocal:

His whole public and literary career barely exceeded four years, yet, in that brief time, he created a nation with noble, definite aims, and passionate resolves to achieve success.[194]

Her retrospect on the critical year of 1848 was characteristically glowing, suggestive of the reverential yet gutsy tone which her son would adopt in speaking of Irish political verse:

Celtic fervour always finds its fullest expression in oratory and song. The Irish, especially, have a natural gift of copious and fluent speech. They are orators at all times, but under the influence of strong excitement they become poets, and in that stormy era, when every nation was reading its Rights by the flames of burning thrones, the Irish poets, mad with the magnificent illusions of youth, flashed their hymns of hope and defiance like a fiery cross over land and lake, over river and mountain, throughout Ireland, awakening souls to life that might long have lain dead but for the magic incantation of their words.[195]

The rhetoric of this rodomontade should be noted: the bracketing of oratory and song, the ubiquity of revolutionary gestures, the personality of the Irish landscape, magic, and the waking of dead souls, casts a Slavonic air of dormant power, the very nature of which defies action or proof. It was an alternative and a compensation for the fact that there was no effective communication—'no kinship or empathy between the rulers and the ruled' as she called it[196]—by means of which 'pride of race ... heroic memories'[197] could be established.

Speranza also addressed the question of 'The Bondage of Woman', a subject on which her son would commission several articles for *The Woman's World*. 'For six thousand years', she wrote, 'the history of woman has been a mournful record of helpless resignation to social prejudice and legal tyranny.'[198] Woman's love, she asserts, 'is generally aspiration—hero-worship; while man receives homage more readily than he gives it. . . . Two moral codes are framed for man and woman, one permitting the widest latitude, the other exacting the most rigid obedience.'[199] In such sentiments we find the parentage of Wilde's twice-employed remark 'A woman's life revolves in curves of emotions. It is upon lines of intellect that a man's life progresses.' (*CW* 548)

As Edward Said remarked in his 1993 Reith Lectures, it is in the nature of an emerging society to supplant those societies which then become inferior to it.[200] In view of her husband's concern for the history of the 'aborigines' of Aran, one of Speranza's essays, the lengthy 'Australia (A Plea for Emigration)', indicates the extent to which the vision of Ireland could override her characteristic compassion and display a violent prejudice against the aborigines of the antipodes, with much the same disdain which her son was to display for Australia in his plays. The essay's principal purpose was to advocate emigration by 'the poor Irish settler' to Australia as a land of hope and promise, based on the experience of successful settlement in America—'the American Irish are now a great and powerful nation'.[201] Characterising

the Irish as 'quite unsuited to the rigid bondage of manufac-
turing work', and anticipating de Valera's vision of the rural
idyll ('They need the sunlight and the open air, where the
laughter of children can be heard; their light, joyous temperament requires constant diversity, with frequent rest for
social talk, and the sense of individual freedom in the broad
rich fields and healthful air'),[202] she called for the appointment
of 'a Minister of Emigration' to encourage the development of
these aptitudes in the New World. But the side-effect of this
policy would be genocidal, since it involved the clearance of
the aborigines, who 'have no claim to interest of any kind;
they are evidently the last decaying remnant of a low pre-
Adamic race, a mere slight advance of the kangaroo towards
the human'.[203] Ignoring the ironic fact that English cartoon-
ists frequently portrayed the Irish as simian lookalikes (and
that her own husband had been described at the time of his
disgrace as 'a pithecoid person of extraordinary sensuality
and cowardice'),[204] and ignorant of the fact that the antiquity
and artistic culture of the aboriginal civilisation would eventually be established as apparently forty thousand years old,
she dismissed the indigenous Australians by advocating
ethnic cleansing:

> It is now . . . the manifest destiny of the great Adamic
> races to clear the world of these half-souled inferior types
> as a forest is cleared of its poisonous undergrowth.[205]

The Irish, evicted from Ireland by the English, were to visit
the curse of Cromwell upon those less fortunate, on whom,
in their new kingdom, they were to have no pity. The
tragedy of the lesson is that it was not learned.

By contrast, Speranza penned several feminist essays,
from which Wilde seems to have derived substantial inspiration and points of reference, both for his editorship of *The
Woman's World* and for his plays. In 'Venus Victrix' she
wrote:

> Woman lies at the base of all life, whether for good or evil.
> From Eden to Olympus, woman is the first word writ-
> ten on the page of every history and of every religion,
> and is the illuminated initial of every man's life. ... Her
> power over man, whether through beauty or love,
> through purity or sin, is the crown and the torture, the
> glory or the perdition, of almost every human career. ...
> The women gifted with this mystic charm are unfet-
> tered by chronology. They are ever young, with the
> eternal youth of the spiritual nature. To sensitive and
> clever men, they are peculiarly attractive, for they seem
> to give them a second soul, a further life. They alone
> can intensify the aspirations of a man of genius; sustain
> his noblest instincts; and appreciate and comprehend
> his divine nature, with that perfect knowledge which
> in a woman always travels along the line of sympathy
> with swift electric vitality.[206]

The mother–son relationship of Gerald and Mrs Arbuthnot
(in *A Woman of No Importance*), the husband–wife relationships of Lord and Lady Windermere (in *Lady Windermere's
Fan*) and of Sir Robert and Lady Chiltern (in *An Ideal
Husband*), the passion of Guido Ferranti for the Duchess of
Padua, of the Tsarevitch for the peasant Vera Soubaroff (in
Vera), of Salomé for Iokanaan, and the mysterious and
threatening power of Mrs Erlynne (*Lady Windermere's Fan*)
and Mrs Cheveley (*An Ideal Husband*) all obey this dictum.

These all acknowledge the image of 'woman'—or more
especially 'mother'—inscribed over the door of life. But
more importantly, the perennial spirit of woman 'unfettered
by chronology' was to pervade Wilde's consciousness of the
classical mind in modern form. When Speranza wrote:

> It is a woman that keeps watch ... for the uprising of a
> slain and buried soul[207]

she was looking back to *Antigone* and forward to her son's
Sphinx.

3

A Secret and Selected Life

'FEW races', wrote Ernest Renan, 'have had so complete a poetic childhood as the Celtic; mythology, lyric poetry, epic, romantic imagination, religious enthusiasm—none of these failed them.'[1] Born on 16 October 1854 at his parents' house at 21 Westland Row, Dublin, Oscar Wilde received as a birthright a keen awareness of all of these traits in Irish life. The hybrid fruit of a marriage between two first-generation Dubliners, he was to live most of his life exploring the mixed blessings of his unusual childhood. Despite the common denomination of their church, William and Jane Wilde epitomised both the cultural and political divisions within it, and the ways in which those divisions could be accommodated. One was a scientist, pursuing the nature of Irishness as a means of promoting national recovery; the other, a poet and a feminist, promoting a sense of Irishness as a means to freedom. Both were passionate, both learned to live with competing interests and emotions within themselves. William came to think that Irishness might further the chance of independence; Jane, that independence would increase Irishness. As he moved away from centres of influence and recognition, retreating into private research and provincial residence, she moved nearer to those centres, following her sons to London after her husband's death and accepting a small Civil List pension.

Their first child, William Charles Kingsbury (Willie, born in 1852, the year after their marriage) became a barrister, critic, journalist and unsuccessful playwright,[2] a dissipated drunkard and womaniser, and died in 1899. Oscar was their second child. Their third, Isola Francesca, died of a brain fever in 1867 at the age of eight. Many biographers have

commented on Wilde's obvious affection for his sister and
some have suggested that her death may have had a long-term
effect in impressing him with the instability of life.[3] Certainly
his poem in memory of Isola, 'Requiescat', which begins:

> Tread lightly, she is near
> Under the snow,
> Speak gently, she can hear
> The lilies grow (*CW* 724)

has a marked thematic affinity with Yeats's 'He Wishes his
Beloved were Dead' and 'He Wishes for the Cloths of
Heaven'—the latter ending 'Tread softly because you tread
on my dreams'[4]—in that both poems embody, within grief
and apprehension, a fearful longing for the transitus between
life and death.

Oscar Wilde's life was in many ways secret and selective,
and in two especial senses: firstly, we know very little of his
early life in particular, or of his private life in general; secondly, he himself contended with the competing needs of
self-advertisement and concealment on which his career
depended. Almost every aspect of his activity was, as Edmond
de Goncourt remarked of his sexuality, ambiguous.[5]

As a result, competing accounts of his life abound in many
versions. Even as thorough an archivist as Stuart Mason
[Christopher Sclater Millard] admitted a series of factual
errors into his introduction of Gide's study of Wilde: that he
was born at his parents' subsequent home at 1 Merrion Square;
that his father had been 'President of the Irish Academy' (an
honour which eluded him) and had been born in 1799
(rather than 1815); that his mother was the daughter (rather
than the grand-daughter) of an archdeacon and had been
born in 1826 (when she was born at least two years earlier).[6]
Wilde himself encouraged—and promulgated—the belief
that he himself was two years younger than he really was.
None of these except the last was a major, grievous, mistake,
but the total picture which relies on so many discrepancies

and misunderstandings encourages us to form a view of Wilde which is vague (thus complementing his own idea of himself as a dreamer) and imprecise (in turn underpinning his disregard for fact and truth). In referring to the common misapprehension as to his year of birth, I mean, of course, that in addition to providing a serious early stumbling-block to his success in his prosecution of Queensberry, it was entirely typical of what Ellmann calls his 'calculated juvenescence',[7] an increasing emphasis on the properties and conditions of youth, a regression to the innocence and irresponsiblity of the child who remains *doli incapax*. His basic characteristic in fact remained an undeveloped childishness, sometimes ingenuous, sometimes petulant, sometimes hysterical, a childishness uncontaminated by tact, discretion or inhibition. Douglas, unconsciously giving subjective support to Renan's judgment on the Celt's 'poetic childhood', insisted that 'Unless you understand that Oscar is an Irishman through and through, you will never get an idea of what his real nature is. In many ways he is as simple and innocent as a child.'[8] Conversely, these minor lacunae and interludes in his life story can be taken as indications that the child who grew into many names and disguises was at heart anxious to become, first a lover of insincerity and falseness, and then a criminal, the thief of affection, truth and meaning.

Wilde presents a puzzle in his life no less than in his works. Who was he? Why did he write such contradictory ideas into his essays and plays? Why did he allow events to overtake him, or complain at the course of events which, it seemed, he had willed to happen? Two years after his death André Gide published a 'study' which contains much valuable personal testimony, the most celebrated element of which is the remark Wilde made to him: 'I have put all my genius into my life; I have put only my talent into my works'—a remark often since misquoted, but one which Gide regarded as sufficiently important to repeat thirty pages later. His commentary is that 'It is only too true. The best of his writing is but a poor reflection of his brilliant conversation.'[9] But there is more to Wilde's ambivalence than that, for his conversation in its turn was a poor reflection of his innermost thoughts and thought-processes, which Gide rightly called 'the deep central emotion'.[10] It is this *deep central emotion*—a concatenation of moods and impulses—which concerns us: we have seen the reference by Le Fanu to 'the secret lust of human souls' which must be reconciled with 'moral aims'; we have noted his mother's comment: 'Life is one long, slow agony of death.'[11] The curiosity of the child for the purpose of life—a life which he knows instinctively to be paranormal and unusually affective, leads him to see his 'deep central emotion' as a secret, intimately concerned with the rituals of naming, discovery and relation. 'House' is both father and mother and history, and therefore man's relation to house is likely to be bisexual and atavistic. 'House' is where something unnamable has taken place. As Sartre says of Genet, 'his life is divided into two heterogeneous parts: before and after the sacred drama ... [he] carries in his heart a bygone instant'.[12] The invert is both the orphaned child of this drama and the chief celebrant. He finds himself constantly within its mysteries, yet permits only a limited vision of that hidden identity to his fellow-worshippers. They know the nature of the secret, but not the full relation. Throughout Wilde's work we find orphans, abandoned for whatever reason, who take the route chosen by Genet, that of the thief: to steal another's life, or to invent one's own, is to compensate for the loss of a life which has vanished before one can begin to live it. For those whose life is prematurely abandoned or wasted, Tír na nÓg becomes more than a vision, it becomes a reality in which we can, in Ferguson's words, 'live back'. Jack/Ernest Worthing leads a double life; Algernon Moncrieff lives by 'Bunburying'; Sir Robert Chiltern lives with a crippling secret; Mrs Cheveley and Mrs Erlynne live by trading on the power of their secret pasts; Salomé's erotic dance is also a dance of death because it brings her beyond her own experience into a place where she falls in love with the unknown; Guido Ferranti pursues the murderer of his unknown father; Vera Soubaroff dies because she finds love in the house of the oppressor; Gerald and Mrs Arbuthnot yearn for a properly constituted family relationship. These are all 'poor reflections' of the fact that their author, who was also the author of *The Sphinx*, inhabits a house of contradictions. If we look behind the mere facts of Wilde's origins and career, we will see that he was profoundly influenced by the disparate aspirations of his parents and their associates, but much more deeply by the very fact of Ireland itself—a country which, the *Dublin University Magazine* told him, was 'doomed'; a country in which it seemed his own class and creed might no longer have a place; a country which, Renan and Arnold had suggested with magisterial force, might be merely a pretext for something else. The idea of living in two countries simultaneously, one real and one imagined, becomes a life's ambition.

For every action Wilde took, every opinion he expressed, every poem or dramatic dialogue which he invented, there is an equal and opposite contention elsewhere in his life and work, and there is also a middle path to be found which is neither a compromise nor an accommodation of the two but a new element, creating a 'third meaning'[13] which was the 'deep central emotion' of his Irishness, his homosexuality and his sense of the intellectual mission of the critic.

Part of this ambition, or 'intention', was to find a middle way between his father's 'regal republic' and his mother's 'plague spot of the universe'.[14] The need to reconcile, within his own nature, these two resounding influences was a permanent one. The fact that Wilde never—as far as we know—made any explicit or specific reference to any of his parents' individual achievements, or scarcely even to the matter of Ireland, should be taken not as a disclaimer or a lack of interest but as a signal that he found it difficult to make such reference without implicating himself in the process. It is an area in which he proposes, if possible, to remain outside the field of activity. To the Irishman in England, Ireland is another country. Yet in the eyes of the English, that Irishman still represents the Ireland from which he is now estranged, and the Irish card is therefore one he must play. Becoming adept at dissimulation, at cultural and political cross-dressing, he knows that while the secret of life—its inner truth—may be tragedy, the purpose of life is to be comic. Acceptance in the adoptive home is a prerequisite to eventual return to, and acceptance in, the original home, wherever that might be. The acclaim which may be achieved in the public sphere is therefore a potential passport to the private sphere.

Much more so than with any other character of wit (Sydney Smith, for example), of artistic temperament (Whistler, perhaps), of morbid preoccupation (the case of Beardsley) or even of a double life (such as that of William Watson), there is no single life of Wilde to be told, because there was no single trajectory. Each biography is its own fiction because at best it takes a stance oblique to truth. Wilde was only half-joking when he said: 'It is usually Judas who writes the biography':[15] almost of necessity, the faithful friend initiates the betrayal, because it is his only route to a version of the story. The whole truth simply cannot be told.

Wilde extolled the achievements of his parents (in general) because it was the one point of fixity in his life; after them and his wife, all his affiliations were with homosexuals, outcasts, travellers and misfits. Thus when he wrote his autobiography (and therefore the *apologia pro vita sua*) in 'De Profundis', he was able to establish a referent for his later deviance. In that *apologia* he said:

> She and my father had bequeathed me a name they had made noble and honoured, not only in Literature, Art, Archaeology and Science, but in the public history of my own country, in its evolution as a nation. (*L* 458)

It was not an empty nor even a hyperbolic claim. As we have seen, Sir William Wilde was a man of immense distinction in medical science and in archaeology, not least when he combined the two disciplines under the rubric of the medical census. As an associate of the *Dublin University Magazine* he can be seen to have moved politically from a position of disinterested Unionism to one of, perhaps equally disinterested, Repeal and Home Rule. As the author of the expression 'regal republic', he can be said to have coined the most telling epithet for the ambivalence of nineteenth-century Protestant Ireland. His son's clear reference to the role of the Protestant community in initiating the Gaelic Revival explains for us very succinctly his sense of belonging to the Gaelic nation, of inheriting its poetry, the deep divisions of its warring tribalism, and, above all, its identity beyond, and outside, the civilisation which England had imposed in recent centuries. As far as law was concerned, Wilde saw himself as 'beyond the Pale'. There was much more than a simple desire to shock or mislead in his reference to denominational religion: 'I don't think I have any. You see, I am an Irish Protestant.'[16]

Lady Wilde's ambivalence is evident in the change from her premarital tones of insurrection to the calmer stridency of her later poetry and her essays, particularly those on women's affairs. Though a lesser figure than her husband (sometimes overshadowed by the work she undertook in completing his collection of folklore), there is no doubting her own minor distinction.

The mathematician Sir William Rowan Hamilton said of Wilde's parents that

> He is a man of great activity and considerable cultivation. . . . She is undoubtedly a genius herself . . . almost amusingly fearless and original, and *vows* . . . that she likes to make a *sensation*.[17]

Other observers were not so kindly. Katherine Everett, who knew Wilde in the late 1880s, recollected that her cousin, Lady Ardilaun (a Connemara neighbour of the Wildes) had said:

His parents were strange people, not fit to bring up boys. I never knew his father well, but he hadn't a good reputation, and his mother, who was a poetess, was pretentious and absurd.[18]

A more telling comment on the marriage is contained in a letter from the Scottish classicist J. S. Blackie to his wife while on a visit to Dublin in 1874. Of Speranza he wrote that she was

a poetess of the very fervid patriotic stamp and a giantess to boot—the biggest woman I ever saw. . . . She is a phenomenon and worth considering. . . . They say she is one of those women who love the male as a kindred animal, in whose likeness she should have been created, but failed through the mistake of Nature.[19]

The Dublin-born cartoonist Harry Furniss called her 'a walking burlesque of motherhood'[20] and caricatured her as a 'tragedy-queen'—an epithet which she earns from more than one memoirist of the time. 'Pretentious' and 'absurd' are cruel but none the less perceptive words to describe a passionate servant of poetry, while the role of 'tragedy-queen', if obvious only in relation to her eccentricities of dress, was one which fitted a soul devoted to 'love of country'.

Certainly William Wilde's lack of 'a good reputation' can be attributed to his renowned philandering, and in particular to the court case in 1864 which marked the eclipse of his public career and of his private practice, and his increased self-imposed isolation in the west of Ireland, which may have been intensified in 1867 by Isola's death. He had been pestered for some years by a former patient, Mary Travers, daughter of a Dublin medical professor, whom he had seduced and by whom he is believed to have had a child. Mary Travers manoeuvred a situation in which Lady Wilde was forced to retort in a libellous fashion. Suing for damages (in an action to which, in true Wildean vein, the real party, Sir William, was not joined), Mary Travers secured a farthing for her virtue and substantial costs which seriously embarrasssed the Wildes' finances. At the ages of ten and twelve respectively, Oscar and Willie Wilde thus witnessed the family name being brought into disrepute through a court case and a sex scandal. Oscar's sons would be ten and nine years of age when their own father's actions precipitated the same course. It was a severe example of what Maturin had called 'an odd story in the family'.

Oscar Wilde's career was equally ambivalent, sensational and 'strange': born into a strong Protestant tradition, he was fascinated from childhood to deathbed by Catholicism; a man of artistic temperament, he sought work as a translator of the classics and as the secretary of a London charity; a born homosexual, he married, fathered children and pined for their company; Irish to the core, he courted the patronage and the esteem of the highest circles in English society; a critic at heart, he made his reputation with society 'comedies'; as a poseur, he continually gave the lie to the working of his formidable intellect.

Yet there is a certain pattern of consistency within these inconsistencies. As a translator, for example, Wilde made constant returns to the Greek tragedies and the culture which contained them: his unrealised projects included the translation of Euripides' *Herakles* and *The Phoenician Women* and selections from Herodotus (*ML* 31), whom he called 'the Father of Lies' (*CW* 981), and he was always acutely conscious of the *Agamemnon* of Aeschylus, a production of which occupied his attention at Oxford and several fragments of which he had translated. As an applicant for the secretaryship of the Beaumont Trust Fund he was not entirely out of place or out of character: although he later affected a mocking tone for those who try to do good to the less well-off, the tone of the references in *The Picture of Dorian Gray* is more one of parody than of dismissal, and his ambition to extend the subject of his lectures by means of an appointment which would allow him to spread 'art-knowledge and art-appreciation among the people' (*ML* 61–2) was also part of his wider crusade to change the way people live and think. Even the ideological distinction between Protestant and Catholic becomes smudged. Although Wilde never of his own express volition crossed from one sphere of conscience to the other, he was fully capable of blurring the definitions of the two; not only did he abjure reason, the logical faculty which distinguished Protestantism from the intuitive and submissive faith of Rome, but he also demonstrated, in his obvious affection for both sides of the argument, for freedom of intellect and for poetic tragedy, for the dual nature of 'the soul of man', that he was capable of being both Protestant and Catholic at the same time. And we have his own statement of shock at the prospect of being disinherited under the testamentary wishes of his half-brother, Henry Wilson, who had stipulated that Wilde would forfeit his share in the property at Illaunroe if he became a Catholic: 'Fancy a man going before "God and the Eternal Silences" with his wretched Protestant prejudice and bigotry clinging still to him.' (*L* 43) The oscillation is part of Wilde's sense of himself as an abandoned child, one who, without the shelter and comfort and continuity of family life, and particularly of parents, is both thief and vagabond, and as such typifies the challenges to morality and ontology of the twentieth century which I shall examine in my Conclusion.

Wilde's contacts from birth to his twenty-first year were—with the exception of distinguished English visitors to his parents' home—almost exclusively with Irish people. Thereafter, although he mixed with the social and artistic worlds in America, Paris and London, the Irish attended him up to his final moments. In America he came briefly under the tutelage of Dion Boucicault, the greatest melodramatist of his day, and he also met the Fenian transportee John Boyle O'Reilly, who had become editor of the *Boston Pilot*. It was in America that he lectured on 'The Irish Poets of '48' in which, in addition to paying homage to his mother, he acknowledged William Smith O'Brien as 'the earliest hero of my childhood . . . with the dignity of one who has failed' and claimed Charles

Gavan Duffy as 'one of my friends in London';[21] and in America he championed the cause of the sculptor John Donoghue—'pure Celt is he'—whose work was to enjoy a brief flourish as a result. In the London of the 1880s and 1890s he was on intimate terms with a number of Irishmen, notably writers such as W. B. Yeats, Arthur Conan Doyle and Lionel Johnson, and the historian, memoirist and Nationalist MP, Justin McCarthy. At Wilde's prosecution of the Marquess of Queensberry, Queensberry's counsel was Wilde's exact Trinity College contemporary, Edward Carson, while the presiding judge was another Trinity man, Mr Justice Henn Collins. At his first trial an Ulsterman, Charles Gill, led for the prosecution. After his release from prison he enlisted the support of the Nationalist MP and author of *Leaves from a Prison Diary*, Michael Davitt, in raising questions in the House of Commons in relation to several matters of prison reform: 'No one knows better than yourself how terrible life in an English prison is. . . . *You* suffered for what was done by someone else' (*L* 586–7)—and he later hoped that Davitt would write a preface to a popular edition of *The Ballad of Reading Gaol*. In 1898 he wrote: 'Those who are bringing about Prison Reform in Parliament are Celtic to a man. For every Celt has inborn imagination.' (*L* 751) Even in the last months of his life his appearance had been noted in the street by J. M. Synge and Richard Best—Synge, Best recalled, was 'immensely impressed' by this epiphany.[22] On his Parisian deathbed Wilde—at the instigation of Robert Ross, who thus carried out what, he asserted, was Wilde's own wish, to be received into the Catholic Church—was baptised and given extreme unction by a Dubliner, Father Cuthbert Dunne, then attached to the Passionist Fathers in the Avenue Hoche.

Vivian Mercier has asked a most pertinent question which should be raised in discussing the Irishness of any writer, particularly from the Anglo-Irish community, writing in English: 'How [can] a writer show continuity with a tradition of whose very existence he is hardly aware, or imitate models which he has never seen[?]'[23] Mercier answers his own question firstly by reference to the predominance of oral over literary culture, and by pointing to the importance of the early environment in determining development. He also points to four 'gifts' possessed, for example, by both Yeats and Joyce:

> contact with a living folklore and thus with myth; contact with a living folk speech; a traditional sense of the professional, almost sacred prestige of poetry and learning; a traditional sense of the supreme importance of technique to a writer, coupled with the realization that technique must be learnt, by imitation, study, and practice.

This is exemplified by the corresponding facts that

> humour springs from folklore, magic, myth; wit and word play permeate folk speech; satire is inseparable from the traditional prestige of the poet; while parody grows naturally out of the Gaelic poet's obsession with technique.[24]

This resource—and the responsibilities and opportunities which accompanied it—was available to Oscar Wilde through his parents and their associates within the Protestant nation and in some cases outside it.

We have little specific statement of his parents' ambitions for Oscar Wilde. His mother's hortatory aspirations were little more than that: at his birth she told her friend Rowan Hamilton (whom she unsuccessfully asked to be a godfather to Oscar): 'He is to be called Oscar Fingal Wilde. Is not that grand, misty and Ossianic?'[25] As Lady Wilde well knew, Oscar was a major figure in the Gaelic epics, the son sometimes of Fionn MacCumhaill, sometimes of Oisín, as celebrated in the version of bardic poetry concocted by James

Macpherson as 'the lays of Ossian' and published under the titles *Fingal* (1762) and *Temora* (1763). Her own *Ancient Legends* refers to an episode in the annals of the Fianna which took place near the family's holiday home on Lough Fee:

> One day the powerful chief that lived there invited the great Finn Mc-Coul, with his son Oscar and a band of Fenian knights, to a great banquet....Oscar and his father would take no place, but stood watching, for they suspected treachery....So Oscar the Lion heart rushed forth to the encounter. And he flung his spear at the mighty horsemen, and they fought desperately till the setting of the sun. Then at last Oscar triumphed; victory was his; and he cut off the head of his adversary, and carried it on his spear all bleeding to the fort, where he let the blood drop down upon the Fenian knights that were transfixed by magic.[26]

Later Joyce would celebrate Wilde's Irishness, saying: 'His name symbolizes him: Oscar, nephew of King Fingal, and the only son of Ossian in the amorphous Celtic *Odyssey*.'[27]

Lady Wilde's ambitions were, quite naturally, for both her sons. Just after Oscar's birth she wrote: 'Willie is my kingdom....I will rear him a Hero perhaps and President of the future Irish Republic....I have not fulfilled my destiny yet.'[28] When Willie was studying at the London bar, she said he was 'ready to spring forth like another Perseus to combat evil....His hope is to enter Parliament and I wish it also'[29]— an ambition which she later extended to her younger son: 'I would like you to have a small house in London and live the literary life and teach Constance to correct proofs and eventually go into Parliament,' she told Oscar in 1883 at the time of his engagement to Constance Lloyd.[30] Half her interest in Oscar seems to have been that he should shine first at Oxford, 'the very focus of intellect',[31] and then in the 'great and mighty city—the capital of the world',[32] but she was equally anxious that he should carry into that career the spirit of the

Fianna. Yeats, himself conscious from his childhood and adolescence among the peasantry of Sligo of the power of mythology and folklore, detected this atavistic intelligence in Wilde when he commented on 'that half-civilized blood in his veins'.[33] Speranza's comment on the young Daniel O'Connell might easily sit on her son's shoulders—'destined to make a remarkable figure'.[34]

When one of his earliest poems appeared in print, Wilde's mother told him: 'The poem *looks* and reads *perfect*—musical and poetic—the evident spirit of a *poet natural* in it.'[35] Apart from Wilde's own claim to a Trinity friend, that he and his mother had established 'a Society for the Suppression of Virtue', there is little further evidence of the relationship between mother and son, and none of any real exchange between father and son.

William Wilde did, however, inculcate in Oscar a sense of the historic and the ethnic. Family holidays were spent mostly in Connemara, at the houses Sir William had built on Lough Corrib (Moytura House) and Lough Fee (Illaunroe Lodge). Other vacations took place nearer to Dublin, in County Wicklow, at the seaside resort of Bray (where Sir William was listed in the Dublin street directory as having a second residence) and in more inland places such as Glencree, which was also alive to the primitive fantastic culture which Synge was to encounter there forty years later. Oscar Wilde was aware at first hand of his father's archaeological practice, which bracketed the sense of history with that of epic achievement, of the fateful sparring between heroic figures, and of the discovery of artefacts of priceless beauty. With his father he would have encountered the Irish-speaking peasants from whom an Irish way of speaking English through translation was derived: 'I think he must be there yet'— where 'yet', as with the French *encore*, means 'still'—is such an example which Wilde used to Vincent O'Sullivan in the 1890s.[36] Other terms reminiscent of Anglo-Irish or Hiberno-English which characterise this translation from Gaelic collo-quial usage are his comment on football—'a tedious game to be always playing' (*L* 592)—or 'not to be always worrying' (*CW* 1086). His younger son recalled his singing an Irish lullaby, 'Tá mé i mo chodladh, is ná dúisigh mé', which he had no doubt learned while on a folkloric excursion with his father.[37] From his father too he derived an extra name, 'O'Flahertie', from paternal cousins to whom Sir William had referred in his *Irish Popular Superstitions*:

> The Battle of the Bog occurred in 1837, at Oughterard, between some of the 'Ferocious O'Flaherties', of H-Iar [West] Connaught, and the retainers of Ballynahinch; Thomas Martin, Esq., M.P. and J.P., the last male descendant of 'Nimble Dick', having led the van, against a friend and relative of my own.[38]

We have Wilde's own evidence for the fact that he was familiar with the terrain of ancient Irish history as well as its content:

> From my boyhood I have been accustomed, through my Father, to visiting and reporting on ancient sites, taking rubbings and measurements and all the technique of *open air* archaeologica—it is of course a subject of intense interest to me.[39]

Both his parents had testified to the affective power of the western landscape, and when Wilde himself was staying at Illaunroe during his Oxford years he wrote to a friend: 'I am sure you would like this wild mountainous country . . . it is in every way magnificent and makes me years younger than actual history records. . . . I am resting here in the mountains —great peace and quiet everywhere.' (*L* 25, 54) It was, perhaps, a terrain which reflected his interior landscape, a land of perpetual youth.

Wilde's sense of his Irishness—of the race of which he was a part and of the contribution which his parents had made to its development—was a key factor in his career, involving both something exotic and something naïve in his character as far as his chief audience, the English, was to see him. When he later claimed:

> The gods had given me almost everything. I had genius, a distinguished name, high social position, brilliancy, intellectual daring (*L* 466)

he was fully conscious that the seeds of this genius were to be found within the unlikely marriage of science and poetry. When he announced:

> I made art a philosophy, and philosophy an art: I altered the minds of men and the colour of things: there was nothing I said or did that did not make people wonder (*L* 466)

he was laying claim to the astonishing mythopoeic power of paradox and storytelling as a presence in a logocentric world. And when he made the dual claim and admission that

> I awoke the imagination of my century so that I created myth and legend around me: I became the spendthrift of my own genius, and to waste an eternal youth gave me a curious joy (*L* 466)

he was explaining how it became possible for the artist to invent his own age while at the same time destroying the inheritance which had made it possible. It was a notion probably derived from his mother's translation of Schwab's *Sicut Eritis Deus*, 'the history of an overweening aesthete who turned aesthetics into a religion of beauty and died tragically'.[40]

In such an egocentric stance, we can see that Wilde's life, like his art, was a case of 'genius wedded to insanity' to which Edgar Saltus attributed the conception of *Salomé*.[41] The creative tension between the two accounts for the apparent inconsistency of his moods and the paradoxical base of everything he said.

Wilde's schooling at Portora Royal School, near Enniskillen in the Ulster county of Fermanagh, where he joined his brother Willie in 1865, appears to have been uneventful, although he began to distinguish himself as a scholar, winning a number of prizes in competition with those who, like Louis Claude Purser, would go on to elevated positions in academe. He was noted for his imaginative, studious nature and his lack of interest in games. In 1871 he began his outstanding university career when he entered Trinity College, Dublin, having achieved second place overall in the entrance examination and an entrance scholarship which two years later he converted into a foundation scholarship. In 1874 he won the Berkeley Gold Medal for an essay on the Greek comic poets.

The main influence during his eighteenth, nineteenth and twentieth years was his tutor, John Pentland Mahaffy (1839–1919), Professor of Ancient History and later Provost of the college: 'a man of high standard and distinguished culture ... one to whom I owe so much personally ... my first and best teacher ... the scholar who showed me how to love Greek things' (*L* 338). Mahaffy drew close parallels between Greece and Ireland, for example referring to the Rock of Cashel, in County Tipperary, as 'the Irish Acropolis', just as Sir William had called the Boyne megalithic tombs a 'great Necropolis'[42] comparable to those of Mycenae and Egypt.[43] The site of the tombs, William Wilde had said, was 'one of the great wonders of the Western world', its main burial place a 'great pyramid'.[44] In his own written work Mahaffy often drew parallels between the Greek and Irish peasantry and their environment, and Oscar Wilde later criticised Mahaffy for his 'attempts to treat the Hellenic world as "Tipperary writ large"' (*Rev* 209).

Mahaffy was a socialite with a highly developed sense of the importance and effectiveness of conversational ability, particularly at table—clearly another passion which he passed to his star pupil. For Mahaffy, conversation was 'the social result of Western civilisation, beginning with the Greeks', 'a perpetual intellectual feast'.[45] It was often said that Wilde's conversation was so brilliant that it must have been written down, polished and studied intensely, rather than extempore. But Mahaffy insisted that wit must be spontaneous, that 'anyone suspected of coming out with prepared smart things is received by the company with ridicule', although he did allow that conversational skill required a good memory, perhaps aided by some shorthand notes.[46] The qualities necessary for good conversation, according to Mahaffy, were a sweet tone of voice, with absence of local accent and of tricks or catchwords; knowledge and quickness; modesty, simplicity, unselfishness, sympathy and tact. Wilde, like his tutor, lacked many of these.

Oscar Wilde, following his elder brother, joined the two main college societies, the Historical (for debating) and the Philosophical (for paper-reading)—Willie being an officer of the latter, and on two occasions joining his father (a distinguished visitor) as a discussant (on 4 December 1873, when the subject was 'Painting', and on 19 February 1874 on 'National Morality'). As recorded by Ellmann,[47] the suggestion book of the 'Phil' contains allusions by his contemporaries to Wilde's effeminacy as an 'airy-fairy'. It was in these forums that student wit was honed for future careers in politics, law and cognate professions.

At the 'Phil' Wilde may have heard Edward Dowden, Professor of English, lecture on Whitman in 1871, while a fellow-student, (later Sir) Edward Sullivan, tells us that Wilde read Symonds's *Studies of the Greek Poets*, the first volume of which appeared in 1873, and which championed the aesthetic dimension of Greek thought and behaviour, giving voice to a statement which he would incorporate into, and adapt in, 'The Critic as Artist'—'the Greeks were essentially a nation of artists'. For the artistically inclined homosexual Irishman, the pursuit of the Greek mind was especially interesting and rewarding. Superficially it allowed him to make the connections between ancient Greek and ancient Irish civilisations and ways of thought; subcutaneously it permitted him to discover an alternative moral system. By such a route Wilde was introduced—it seems almost system-atically—to the notion that 'Greek love' was widespread, noble, natural and compulsive.

Mahaffy's other sphere of influence was in teaching Wilde the value of Hellenism. In this case he was a vigorous and highly prejudiced teacher, being violently opposed to both Roman classical culture and the influence of the Roman Catholic Church. In 1874 Mahaffy published *Social Life in Greece*, acknowledging the assistance of 'my old pupil Mr Oscar Wilde' for his 'improvements and corrections all through the book'.[48] Mahaffy's was the first frank discussion in English of Greek homosexuality, 'the peculiar delight and excitement felt by the Greeks in the society of handsome youths ... the same sort of agreeable zest which young men of our time feel in the company of young ladies'. Mahaffy was a fair exponent:

> But such an entertainment as the modern ball would have appeared to the old Greek profoundly immoral and shocking, just as we are apt to regard his attach-ments as contrary to all reason and sense of propriety. There is no field of enquiry where we are so dogmatic in our social prejudices.[49]

Mahaffy based his argument on the fact that the texts under discussion

> are the writings of men of like culture with ourselves, who argue with the same logic, who reflect with kindred feelings. They have worked out social and moral prob-lems like ourselves.... They are thoroughly modern, more modern than the epochs quite proximate to our own.[50]

In a phrase which predicts Wilde, he said: 'Periclean Athens [had] life and manners strangely like our own, strangely modern.'[51]

In the second edition (1875) Mahaffy replaced this section with a discussion of the Greek response to female beauty, 'which will be suited to all classes of readers; so that the book in its present form can be made of general use for schools and family reading'.[52] Active homosexuality belonged to a social and literary underworld, defying the 'social prejudices' of mid-Victorian Britain and Ireland, and would become obvious as a literary force only in the 1880s and 1890s; in many instances it was masked by the homoeroticism of openly expressed admiration for youthful male beauty. In Wilde's case it became steadily stronger until it dominated his consciousness and his character. This was a steady process, rather than a state which suddenly materialised in middle life.

The consciousness of the classical heritage, and its potential significance for contemporary Ireland—which persists in the myth of the Kerry ploughboy with a copy of Homer in his breeches pocket—was summed up by Edmund Burke: 'If we have any priority over our neighbours, it is in no small measure owing to the early care we take with respect of a classical education. ... It diffuses its influence over the society at large.'[53] W. B. Stanford points out that from Banim to George Moore, from Darley to Shaw, Greek themes persisted as subject-matter for Irish writers. In 1896 Synge, then in Paris, was studying the affinities of Celtic and Homeric epics, while Yeats (probably unconscious of the *double entendre* which Wilde might have detected) wrote: 'Greece, would we but approach it with eyes as young as its own, might renew our youth.'[54]

Neither at Oxford nor at Trinity was the study of modern languages or literature encouraged. As early as 1808 Wilde's grand-uncle, Maturin, had criticised the Trinity system in a lengthy aside to the storyline of *The Wild Irish Boy*:

> The fellows ... are the inmates of a populous and dissi-
> pated city. ... The total neglect of the most valuable part
> of literature, modern and native literature, the study of
> the English language, its writers, its powers and its
> productions ... The students in the University of Dublin
> are not educated with any consideration for the pecu-
> liar faculties of distinct minds; all are alike compelled
> to read the same portion of the classics and the sci-
> ences.[55]

This found an almost exact echo thirty years later in Davis's
address to the college's Historical Society.[56] The focus of university education, as reflected in Wilde's college notebooks,
was classical and philosophical. Wilde's classmates at Trinity
College included William Ridgeway, a future Professor of
Archaeology at Cambridge, and Louis Claude Purser. Both
Oscar and Willie Wilde contributed to the college magazine
Kottabos, which has been described as 'the high-water mark
of academic humour in Ireland'[57] and numbered among its
contributors Edward Dowden, A. P. Graves, T. W. Rolleston,
Standish O'Grady, John Todhunter, as well as the senior figures of Mahaffy and Robert Yelverton Tyrrell, its editor. In
1875 Wilde, at twenty-one, also began to write for the *Dublin
University Magazine*, thus maintaining a family tradition
which had begun with his father, at an almost identical age,
in 1837: 'I am most anxious to continue my father's connection with the *D.U.M.*' (*L* 40)

It is from this combination of academy and agora that
Wilde conceived the ideal life of the 'scholar citizen' (*PDG*
15) (whose epitome he met at Oxford in the figure of George
Curzon). We can begin to understand what he meant by his
career in Ireland taking a political turn when we reflect that
if he had become a Fellow of Trinity College, he might have
taken one of the university's safe seats at Westminster and
combined the pursuit of learning with an engagement in his
country's political future. As it was, his gradual inclination
away from classical themes towards a modernist perspective

remained linked to an interest in the public sphere, as his 'aesthetic crusade' in London, on matters of house decoration and dress reform, his attempt 'to civilise the provinces by my remarkable lectures' (*L* 155), brought him into the same sphere of social activity as Ruskin and Morris and the same mode of artistic confrontation as Whistler and Shaw. As we shall see, Wilde's dedication to the role of the critic made him, despite his apparent frivolity, one of the most influential public figures in the evolution of modernism in late nineteenth-century England, combining the depth of the scholar's learning with the political awareness of the citizen.

Whether or not Wilde hoped to be included among the 'Souls', the intellectual and social elite among whose numbers were Curzon, Margot Tennant, A. J. Balfour, H. H. Asquith, Maurice Baring and George Meredith, we do not know, but it is certain that the notion of such a secret society, pursuing a private course in the discussion of philosophical subjects while, in the public careers of its members, achieving political power, would have been most attractive to him. He was no stranger to the notion of secret societies with cultural affinities and political aspirations, which his father had recorded in his own work, mentioning the multiform varieties of Whiteboys, Moonlighters, Peep o' Day Boys, with whom his country residence and his exploration of Irish popular superstitions had accustomed him.

He maintained a deep and flamboyant affection for Curzon himself, who went on to become Viceroy of India (1898–1905) and Foreign Secretary (1919–24). He was also on good terms with the philosopher A. J. Balfour, and would have been fascinated by the fact that this future Prime Minister (1902–5), who had been Chief Secretary for Ireland, became the author of a lecture on 'Decadence' delivered in 1907 in the course of which he said: 'All great social forces are not merely capable of perversion, they are constantly perverted' and 'We cannot regard decadence and arrested development as less normal in human communities than progress.'[58] An association with the 'Souls' would have

enabled Wilde to achieve the secret life so necessary to someone who needed to commute between two worlds, that of
social influence and that of sexual inversion. It was a dilemma which exercised Wilde from his first confrontation with
England.

At Oxford Wilde brought the Irish personality into an arena
where homosexuality, religion and aesthetics were earnestly
discussed and where he came into contact with some of the
most distinguished academics and critics of the age—Ruskin,
Pater and Jowett in particular. Among his contemporaries
were David Hunter Blair, a convert to Catholicism and a
future Abbot of Fort Augustus, the philanthropist Arnold
Toynbee, and the future ambassador to Italy, Rennell Rodd.

He was admitted into the Masonic Order (his father had
been master of a Dublin lodge in 1841–2 at the early age of
twenty-six), but he also dallied with Catholicism, attending
mass at St Aloysius' Church, where he may have met the
curate, Gerard Manley Hopkins. Catholicism attracted Wilde
for the mindlessness of its submission to a higher authority,
and it repelled him for the same reason. It also offered him a
means to assuage his feelings of (not necessarily homosexual)
sexual guilt, since he saw the Catholic Church as a woman
to whom he might submit. The attraction may have been a
very early one, since it is alleged—with perfect *bona fides*—
by one Roman Catholic priest that he christened both Willie
and Oscar in 1862 or 1863 in the chapel of St Kevin's refor-
matory in Glencree at the behest of Lady Wilde and with the
subsequent disinterested approval of Sir William.[59] Whether
or not the conversions of Newman and Hopkins were
encouraged by their latent homosexuality is unknown, but it
is definitely possible that Wilde, aware of the intense speculation in the university over the burgeoning attraction of
Rome, would have surmised as much. He may well have
recognised the homosexual strain in Hopkins, who, as we
now know, wrote that 'I always knew in my heart Walt

Whitman's mind to be more like my own than any man's living.'[60]

Wilde was closely associated with a homosexual fracas which resulted in one of his friends being sent down,[61] and his letters refer to homosexuality in a way which indicates how a morbid interest in both behaviour and attitude can develop: 'I believe Todd is extremely moral and only mentally spoons the boy.... You are the only one I would tell about it, as you have a psychological mind' (*L* 23); 'Gussy... is charming though not educated well: he is "*psychological*" and we have long chats and walks.' (*L* 32) 'Psychological' was one of several contemporary code words used to identify fellow-homosexuals.

The Oxford world brought out the strange and the exotic in Wilde, enabling him to appreciate the contrasts in society and those in his own nature. It was a metaphor for the 'love of the impossible'—

> Greek forms passing through Gothic cloisters, life playing among ruins, and, what I love best in the world, Poetry and Paradox dancing together! (*L* 181)

At Oxford Wilde proceeded to create a persona, embodying an aesthetic and a spiritual credo which embraced both certainty and doubt, and adopting a series of masks by means of which that credo could be effectively concealed or revealed at will. The 'moods' or 'phases' through which he subsequently passed may have been, as Hunter Blair observed, 'the whim of the moment',[62] but that whim was inherent and natural rather than external and foreign. Husband, father and boy-lover may have been equally valid poses of what Joyce called his 'sexless intellect',[63] while the career as poet, lecturer, reviewer, storyteller, editor, critic, novelist and ultimately playwright represented a succession of standpoints which moved from the explicit to the concealed in artistic and social intention as the public perception moved, conversely, from incomprehension to acclaim to denunciation.

In their edition of Wilde's notebooks, Philip E. Smith and Michael S. Helfand acknowledge the continuity between Wilde's Dublin education and home background and his studies at Oxford,[64] but they insist, without reference to his earlier studies, that at Oxford Wilde laid the foundations of all his future work. Whether it is in his theory of appearances or in his view of the evolution of the critic-as-artist, nothing Wilde learned at Oxford can be regarded as the origin of his aesthetic credo. It can, however, legitimately be regarded as a development of the germ of that credo.

The high point of Wilde's academic career was the final year—1879—which he spent at Oxford in preparation for the lengthy essay eventually published as 'The Rise of Historical Criticism', an unsuccessful entry for the Chancellor's Essay Prize, which was not awarded that year. That Wilde failed to achieve the prize is symptomatic both of his general lack of favour as a candidate for college fellowship and of his specific problem as a critic who wished to expand the horizons of criticism, and particularly those of art criticism.

In his commonplace book Wilde noted that 'the two Greek ideals' were

φιλοσοφειν μετ' ἐρωτος
[to philosophise with love]
φιλοκαλειν μετ' εὐτελειας
[to love beauty with frugality] (*CPB* 115)

—the first of which becomes the controlling maxim in 'The Portrait of Mr W.H.':

> I had never seen my friend, but he had been with me for many years, and it was to his influence that I owed my passion for Greek thought and art, and, indeed all my sympathy with the Hellenic spirit. Φιλοσοφειν μετ' ἐρωτος! How that phrase had stirred me in my Oxford days! I did not understand then why it was so. But I knew now. There had been a presence beside me

always. Its silver feet had trod night's shadowy mead-
ows, and the white hands had moved aside the trem-
bling curtain of the dawn. It had walked with me
through the grey cloisters, and when I sat reading in my
room, it was there also. What though I had been unconscious of it? The soul had a life of its own, and the brain
its own sphere of action. There was something within
us that knew nothing of sequence or extension, and yet,
like the philosopher of the Ideal City, was the spectator
of all time and of all existence. . . . The soul, the secret
soul, was the only reality. (*CW* 1195)

The connection between this ideal and the 'love of the
impossible' is that between conscience and poetry. The idea
that the 'secret soul' might be known, but that having been
apprehended it may then turn day to night, is the temptation and the artist's curse which Wilde intended to overcome
by the evolution of 'the critical spirit'. The motifs of the silver feet of the dawn and the artist's room pervade Wilde's
work and are particularly prominent in poems like *The
Sphinx* and 'The Harlot's House'.

In developing the critical spirit, Wilde was, as Smith and
Helfand note, 'relating [the curriculum of Literae Humaniores]
to modern controversies'. Oxford encouraged the examination of the past 'from modern analytical perspectives, after
turning it into a mirror for contemporary debates over theol-
ogy, aesthetics, politics, and philosophy'[65]—as F. M. Turner
states in *The Greek Heritage in Victorian Britain*, 'Lit. Hum.'
consisted in the application of knowledge of Greek and
Roman civilisation to history, ethics, metaphysics and political
philosophy, but avoided issues of morality and aesthetics.[66]
Mahaffy's and Symonds's work was to subvert that position
and to provide Wilde with a means of making the ancient
practices 'thoroughly modern'.

Behind the modern debates at Oxford on faith and materialism, still fuelled by the conversion of Newman, was the
longstanding examination of the nature of conscience as

evidenced in Jowett's edition of Plato, which also stood behind the question of morals most recently discussed in Mahaffy's *Social Life in Greece* and in two titles by John Addington Symonds which were given extremely restricted circulation, *A Problem in Greek Ethics* (1883) and *A Problem in Modern Ethics* (1891).[67] These provided the academic platform for a social examination of what, for many teachers and students, was also an acute personal dilemma. For the Irishman at Oxford, there was the extra dimension of loyalty —not even a straightforward one of Union *versus* Repeal, but coloured by a different perspective on all matters of perception and inclination, on, indeed, the purpose of life. Wilde espoused the βιος θεωρετικος [contemplative life] (*CW* 1041–2) not merely as an invert who preferred an ideal world to one of disappointment and imperfection, but also as a member of a race whose historical memory was full of failure and discontinuity. As Ellmann observes, Wilde's own life and career were not without their share of failure: 'his works had always had a telltale undercurrent of sorrow'.[68]

As Ruskin said in *Modern Painters*, 'The greatest thing a human soul ever does in this world is to *see* something....To see clearly is poetry, prophecy, and religion ... all in one.'[69] The juxtaposition of the words 'soul' and 'see', the assertion that poetry, prophecy and religion can be held together in the act of vision, would have provided an impetus for Wilde's already well-developed 'tendency'—as he put it in his commonplace book—'to conceive ideas always under the form of images' (*CPB* 153), a notion which he had also received from Symonds's *Studies of the Greek Poets*: 'Images are given to us clear in their plasticity like a statue bathed in visible sunlight....To the Greeks the eye and not the ear or mind was the chosen vehicle for passion.'[70] That an aesthetic problem could also be political is demonstrated by this passage from 'The Rise of Historical Criticism':

Now Polybius points out that those phenomena particularly are to be dwelt on which may serve as a παραδειγμα [paradigm] or sample, and show the character of the tendencies of the age.... This recognition of the importance of single facts, not in themselves but because of the spirit they represent, is extremely scientific. (*CW* 1138)

Again, the juxtaposition of 'paradigm', 'tendency' and 'spirit' is most telling as an indication of Wilde's willingness to submit certain areas of thought to the judgment of history, while equally asserting that above the 'facts' of history is the faculty of historical criticism by which those facts are re-created: 'Facts are the labyrinth: ideas the guiding thread.' (*CPB* 169)

The paradigm, like the plasticity of the Greek statue, is a presence palpable to the eye, one which directs the senses towards tendencies, which, by means of the highest form of activity, art criticism, is assimilated into a spirit or soul of the artist which may also be the spirit of the age. It is materialism, with its insistence on logic, which had been anathema to ancient Greece and had passed by contemporary Ireland, which dispels this spirit and deprives it of its vigour, because it replaced the metaphysician's ability to see 'a spirit dwelling in things' (*CPB* 141) with the objective view of science merely as utilitarian pursuit.

At Trinity Wilde had declared that he and his mother had founded a 'Society for the Suppression of Virtue'. Later in life he was to assert that 'Sin is an essential element in progress.' (*CW* 1023) At Oxford, in an intermediate stage, he noted that 'Progress is simply the instinct of self-preservation in humanity, the desire to affirm one's own essence' (*CPB* 110)[71] and 'Progress in thought is the assertion of individualism against authority' (*CPB* 121), a notion which he is likely to have developed from two sources—the participation of his parents in 'the public history of my own country' and, a work contemporaneous with the Irish Famine, Thoreau's *Civil Disobedience* (1849).

This was one of the foundations of his theory of art criticism which he developed throughout his life, thus defining a mode of thought and a *modus vivendi* for himself. In an Oxford notebook he copied the following from J. A. Froude:

> Poets are the original historians as well as the original men of science
>
> 1st the purely imaginative myth
> 2 the semimythic, where real persons are seen through the halo of poetry
> 3 the chronicler who translates poetry into prose.
>
> (CPB 172)

Once more we have to observe that this would not have been new to Wilde: it exactly describes the path by which 'the purely imaginative' Celtic myth had become legend, and the concept of the hero visible, and the later path by which it had been delivered by such as Ferguson to a nineteenth-century readership. Where the direct apprehension of mythology had been mediated by polite literature for centuries in England, this (apart from Charlotte Brooke's *Reliques of Irish Poetry*, 1789) was the first consistent attempt to effect the same transmission, or manumission, of Irish mythology. Nowhere more than in Ireland would it be true to say that 'to realise the nineteenth century, one must realise every century that has preceded it' (CW 1040). Equally, Wilde observes that history is both 'a work of art whose τελος [aim] or final cause is external to it and imposed on it from without' and 'an organism containing the law of its own development in itself, and working out its perfection merely by the fact of being what it is' (CW 1126). Between the two viewpoints stands the condition of Ireland.

In 'The Critic as Artist' we find this developed and perhaps resolved as follows:

> The true critic . . . bears within himself the dreams, and ideas, and feelings of myriad generations, and to [him] no form of thought is alien, no emotional impulse obscure . . . [for whom] the spirit of disinterested curios-

ity . . . is the real root, as it is the real flower, of the intellectual life. (*CW* 1041)

If there is a resolution, it is because, as Smith and Helfand
note, 'Wilde's dialectical analysis of the critic immediately
breaks down the intellectual and social distinctions between
creative and critical work, between subjective and objective
truth'.[72] The critical spirit is required not only to transcend
both art and history, but also to transform the individual
soul in a way which society itself cannot effect and should
not demand. The critic thus becomes 'the flawless type' (*CW*
1053); the important thing is to do nothing, to live the contemplative dream life so that one's autobiography will be a
pristine page. Opposed to this is the 'sordid terror of modern life' with 'a certain lack of imaginative thought, and a
certain low passion for middle-class respectability' (*CW* 1058)
which became Wilde's target in *Dorian Gray*. Because the
artist is forced to live in this materialist field, sin and
remorse become inevitable. As he noted at Oxford in his
reading of W. K. Clifford's 'On the Scientific Basis of Morals',
'Remorse . . . first appears in the following form "In the name
of the tribal self I do not approve what I have done".' (*CPB*
130) Wilde would be haunted all his life by the irreconcilable
presence of another self, the reproving conscience which
could never be seen and therefore never apprehended.

(ii) THE LOVER

Everything in Wilde's later life would be a construct of the
twin possibilities of orthodoxy and deviance. As he proceeded along the parallel lines of his life and work which
eventually merged in his trial, he made choices concerning
the degree to which he would allow them to interact. While
it might seem that everything he thought and wrote was a
record of his own deviance, the situation was at all times much
more complex: as we shall see in examining his fiction, poetry,

plays and critical essays, at every step his genius and his madness coalesced; the resulting commentary was not only an autobiography but also a statement about the age.

Yeats made an extremely perceptive comment when he saw Wilde's marriage as an artificiality, 'some deliberate artistic composition';[73] Wilde's own charm was 'acquired and systematised, a mask he wore only when it pleased him'.[74] But in the strategy of the invert and the subversive, the double life of appearance and disappearance by means of the mask is only one level of sophistication: at a deeper level is the diplomacy of negotiating a path among those whom one wishes to deceive. The balance between visible and invisible was extremely sophisticated, since it consisted in Wilde's being able to appear as a dreamer, or a charlatan, or an antinomian, when he was at his most calculating, and to be taken for a serious and profound thinker when he was in fact at his most frivolous, playing with ideas and with society. His statement 'If one tells the truth, one is sure, sooner or later, to be found out' (CW 1205) reflects the contradictions essential for such activity. There is no such thing as an inalienably private truth, because there is always more than one person present within the self. To maintain a 'regal republic' is a constant commutation between the home truth and the imagined, between the place of origin and the destination of the idea evolved.

As a lover, Wilde was not necessarily the rampant yet suppressed homosexual or paederast painted by popular comment. It is a cruel reflection on their personal fates that his wife Constance and their two sons, Cyril and Vyvyan, lost their identities in the aftermath of the scandal, and that that oblivion cast a retrospective shadow over the life which they had led before that fall. Vyvyan—with the new surname of Holland—became a distinguished writer, among many other projects translating his father's *Salomé* into a fine English version; if it were not for his poignant memoir of his childhood, *Son of Oscar Wilde*, we would have no substantive record of those years from within the Wilde household.

It is by no means true to say that Wilde was without affection for his wife, even though she was only one element in the deception which he practised on life or on himself. He was never exclusively homosexual: he was always attracted to and by women, but, while he was capable of deep and true friendships, he made love without commitment or consequence.

In the same breath where we find the adolescent Wilde—and to some extent he was always adolescent—speculating about the paederastic intentions of a fellow-undergraduate, he boasts that 'I am just going out to bring an *exceptionally pretty girl* to afternoon Service in the Cathedral.' (*L* 24) Rupert Hart-Davis surmises that this was Florence Balcombe, to whom he was quietly engaged in 1877–8 (she subsequently married his college contemporary Bram Stoker), but she may have been one of several flirtations; the mother of one girl, finding her on Wilde's knee, wrote: 'The thing was neither right nor manly nor gentlemanlike.... So low and vulgar was it, that I could not have believed anyone of refined mind capable of such a thing.... I would rather see her dead than bold, free or immodest.'[75] Wilde would find himself castigated for being 'unmanly' with girls and boys alike, encouraging all the world to be bold, free and immodest. Whether or not Wilde intended to marry, and whether or not we should read into his hyperbole as a letter-writer anything more than affectation, the fact that he wrote to Florence Balcombe on the eve of her marriage: 'Whatever happens I at least cannot be indifferent to your welfare: the current of our lives flowed too long beside one another for that' (*L* 54) rings sincere. Throughout his life, Wilde, like so many homosexuals, enjoyed and was stimulated by the company of women. Although Constance may not have entirely appreciated her husband's intentions, nor correctly interpreted his follies, she may well have divined his 'deep central emotion' more than he himself recognised.

All Wilde's infatuations were affectionate and sincere, because he was able to throw himself into a relationship—

whether sexual, intellectual or social—with an abandon which was the result of the emotional void at the centre. As a 'sexless intellect', Wilde was oblivious of whom he loved, because not only was their gender unimportant but also the loving was merely a part of his larger script. 'Love', to Wilde, was a flirtation without consequence. Yet it had its place and its prominence. A large appetite must be supplied, and in the consumption of young lives and minds Wilde was moving prodigiously towards the real object of his love, which was neither man nor woman, but himself—a point which he made with all sincerity in Arthur Goring's remark to his butler: 'The only possible society is oneself. . . . To love oneself is the beginning of a lifelong romance.' (*CW* 522)

The solitude of the lover and his dependence on mono-logue is essentially an inquisition and a review of the nature of self. In Barthes' words, 'only the Other could write my love story, my novel. . . . I cannot *write myself.*'[76] The pursuit of the image of self-as-other is the imperative of the story and its sole outcome. Barthes says 'we hear in [the lover's] voice what is "unreal", i.e. intractable. Whence the choice of a "dramatic" method which renounces examples and rests on the single notion of a primary language.'[77] Wilde's motive as a lover was to extend the idea contained in Rimbaud's '*je est un autre* ['I' is 'other']' towards the creation of another persona by means of the principle *esse est percipi.* To perceive the other, to recognise one's otherness and locate it in another place, is to bring the other to independent life. '*Je est un autre*' becomes 'I am *He*'. The purpose of love is therefore not only to describe absence and longing but also to replicate oneself under conditions which constantly redefine the absence and one's longing for the absent partner. In so doing, one can address oneself not in the mirror but in the third dimension; the relationship becomes tensive, the speech accusative. The creator of the other knows that while 'I' precedes 'me', 'me' can become nominative and thus acquire all the power and authority which resides in the capacity to engender and ablate. Everything in Wilde's poems and stories is a commentary on the fact that when we begin to think of ourself in the third person we acknowledge the difficulty of nothing except the task of being ourself. The singularity of Wilde's vision, however prismatic it may at times have appeared both to us and to him, lies in his manipulation of one storyline into many genres—poem, parable, drama, critical dialogue—all of which have the energy of monomania.

What, then, is this monomania? We have already seen that Wilde was the product of a marriage and, in the larger sense, of a society and a culture, which at its base was 'strange'. Part of his project was to rehabilitate himself within that family and within his country, to evaluate what he meant by 'its evolution as a nation' and what his own—and his parents'—true place in it might be. The role of the lover, however histrionic, was apposite. Barthes identifies 'waiting, anxiety, memory' as three characteristics of loving.[78] Within Wilde there lurked a memory of something unknown which defied reason as it defied nature. Again Barthes comes to our assistance: 'The love story ... is the tribute the lover must pay to the world in order to be reconciled with it.'[79] The Protestant dilemma—how to love Ireland?—as evinced by his father and his mother, became a way of making reparation without acknowledging guilt, and thus to restore simultaneously its leadership and its right to belong. When we look at Wilde's stories, we will see that, whatever about his sexual anxieties and sense of guilt, this was a driving ambition. Wilde makes love to Ireland, its folklore and its memory, to learning, to religion, to a gamut of artistic genres, in order to identify 'the other' which is, in Barthes' words, 'by vocation, migrant, fugitive'.[80] The truant subject of the portrait, the vagabond, is the embodiment of mystery and also of a free intellect. Within the genre of gothic literature and of Anglo-Irish literature in particular, conscience compels as it condemns. This makes the lover into an acolyte of guilt. Barthes translates this as: 'To expend oneself, to bestir oneself for an impenetrable object is pure religion. To make the

Other into an insoluble riddle on which my life depends is to consecrate the other as a god.'[81] To accept the other as a god is the orphan's strategy of connecting himself to pre-history: 'I cannot open up the other, trace back the other's origins, solve the riddle.'[82] Thus Ireland itself can be read as a lover, making of the insoluble riddle a religion and a means of abolishing time and therefore history.

The artist thus becomes a butterfly, chasing ideas from one intellectual *topos* to another. 'The true site of originality and strength is neither the other nor myself, but our relation itself,' says Barthes.[83] For Wilde, the *relation* will exist only in the expression of paradox and parable, which embodies the nature of the other and is exhausted in the moment when it is uttered. It is neither here, nor there, but *between*. It is impossible of definition, because once it is named it is dead. The act of loving is the act of naming, and 'each man kills the thing he loves'. The lover is by definition a criminal.

The appositeness of Barthes' treatise on love to Wilde's personal situation and to Ireland itself is striking: it lies in the fact of absence, the realisation that what we require in order to solve the riddle is absent and will always be so, that, in Rimbaud's words, *'la vrai vie est d'ailleurs* [life is else-where]'.[84] Wilde's luxuriant word-play typifies his anxiety about the beloved. Through over-use of language, by signifying *everything*, he wants to swallow the whole of the logo-centric world and thus capture and reclaim the beloved. There will then no longer be memory or waiting. He will understand and be understood.

It is only at the close of *A Lover's Discourse* that Barthes, like Wilde in 'De Profundis', addresses truth. Wilde had written to Douglas that 'to speak the truth is a painful thing' and that by confronting his past he can learn 'the meaning of Sorrow, and its beauty' (*L* 502, 511). His urgent assumption that with Douglas he could undertake such a project is mirrored in Barthes' expression: 'The other is my good and my knowledge: only I know him, only I make him exist in his truth. . . . Conversely, the other establishes me in truth: it is only with the other that I feel I am "myself".'[85] Wilde always needed an 'other' onto whom he could project his image of himself. The identity of the youth was irrelevant, provided that the classic age difference of approximately fifteen years was observed. His mentors, Mahaffy and Pater, were both fifteen years older than Wilde; the difference in age between Wilde and those who formed his circle was similar: John Gray being twelve years, Fred Benson thirteen, Ross and Gide fifteen, Douglas sixteen and Beerbohm eighteen years younger than Wilde.

At first he required that they be youths of beauty and intelligence. He showered them with extravagant praise for the role of scholarly aestheticism which they would play at Oxford, which became a city of the imagination. To the bisexual Harry Marillier, the stalwartly heterosexual Robert Sherard and Richard Le Gallienne (the type of 'a confirmed "*mulierast*"'—*L* 601), Douglas Ainslie, Harry Melvill, E. W. Godwin (the designer of his house) and Charles Ricketts (the illustrator of his books) he wrote letters which were works of art, creating in them an aesthetic image of friendship. With female acquaintants he was no less forward: Lillie Langtry (whom he loved), Ellen Terry, Helena Modjeska, Sarah Bernhardt, Lady Desart and the Countess of Lonsdale all attended a regular social occasion known as 'tea and beauties' in the 'untidy and romantic house' which he kept with his camp Oxford friend Frank Miles, first in rooms off the Strand and later in Tite Street, Chelsea.

Later Wilde's social and sexual tastes parted company, his artistic success bringing him into further contact with courtiers, aristocrats and the 'purple of commerce', while he indulged his physical interests with rent-boys—clerks, newspaper-sellers, guardsmen and grooms—whom he rewarded with lavish dinners and jewellery. After his release from prison he picked up cheap trade where he could find it—which included the Vatican palace—but it is striking that to the end he described these encounters in poetic terms: 'I am engaged to a fisherman of extraordinary beauty, age eighteen' (*L* 775);

Didaco—'a face chiselled for high romance' (*L* 787); Pietro—
'like a young St John. One would have followed him into the
desert' (*L* 776); Maurice Gilbert—'his upper lip is more like a
rose-leaf than any other rose-leaf I ever saw' (*L* 739); Georges
—'a most passionate faun ... eyes like the night and a scarlet
flower of a mouth' (*L* 765); 'Even at Napoule there is romance:
it comes in boats and takes the form of fisher-lads, who
draw great nets, and are bare-limbed: they are strangely perfect. I was at Nice lately: romance there is a profession plied
beneath the moon.' (*ML* 178)

But beyond these temporary crushes was a further anxiety
which could not be assuaged. Wilde hoped for respectability
in exile where he was conscious that in Paris, for example,
he was noted as a walking instance of 'pathologie pas-
sionelle', as *Le Jour* observed in 1897 (*L* 589). An Italian translation of *Dorian Gray* might cause the Italians 'to realise that
there has been more to my life than a love for Narcissus or a
passion for Sporus, fascinating though both may be' (*L* 695).
It was part of his personal tragedy that Wilde the writer was
eclipsed by the paederast and thus, having been recognised
in one aspect of his life, failed to be understood as the deep
intellectual whom he saw as his true self.

Even though he said of his marriage that 'for years I disre-
garded the tie' (*L* 516), there is a wistful air of regret in the
admission, and indeed Wilde's life was underpinned by his
marriages to Constance and to Robert Ross. Neither of these
loves excluded or threatened the other. Both—unlike the affair
with Douglas—were conducive to the work in which he
might transcend narcissism and passion and produce something of worth. His mother's motto was '*Fidanza, Constanza,
Speranza*', and it is not entirely fanciful to see his wife taking
the role embodied in her name, while Ross provided the
trust and faithfulness ('fidanza') of the 'devoted friend'.
When he came to write 'De Profundis', Wilde had decided to
identify himself with Christ, perhaps the greatest 'lover' in

history, and we can read a deliberate set of affections into the reference to 'one of the most wonderful things in the whole of recorded time: the crucifixion of the Innocent One before the eyes of his mother and of the disciple whom he loved' (*L* 478)—by which he meant Speranza and Ross.

'When I have you for my husband,' Constance had written, 'I will hold you fast with chains of love and devotion so that you will never leave me or love anyone so long as I can love and comfort you.'[86] Wilde's enthusiasm for the marriage was conventional, and his early expressions of love and physical longing for Constance were sincere. If there was a basic difference between Constance and Oscar Wilde, it existed on the artistic plane. She told him: 'I hold that there is no perfect art without perfect morality, while you say they are distinct and separate things.'[87] Later he was to say 'she could not understand me, and I was bored to death with married life' (*L* 516), but it is questionable if anyone—including Wilde himself—properly understood Wilde, and, in the age of *ennui*, he was bored by everyone and everything which did not satisfy his intellectual longings. (It was only with her second pregnancy —as in many marriages—that Constance's attractions wore thin and he expressed himself disenchanted. It was at this stage that he met Ross and—so Ross rather improbably claimed—was seduced by him into homosexual practices.)

The household was often a happy one, Wilde taking particular interest in the progress of the children. As the second, Vyvyan (1886–1967), recalled:

> He had so much of the child in his own nature that he delighted in playing our games . . . caring nothing for his usually immaculate appearance. Cyril once asked him why he had tears in his eyes when he told us the story of *The Selfish Giant* and he replied that really beautiful things always made him cry.[88]

He gave them copies of his own favourite authors: Verne's *Five Weeks in a Balloon*, Kipling's *The Jungle Book* and

Stevenson's *Treasure Island*. When they went to the seaside for holidays, he displayed his skill in building sand-castles, sailing and fishing; he could also mend the children's toys.

Constance was busy on her own behalf, editing the *Gazette* of the Rational Dress Society, contributing to *To-day*, *The World* and *Ladies' Pictorial* and (in due course) to Oscar's *Woman's World*, publishing two books of children's stories, and making public speeches to women's associations—so much so that in 1889, after hearing her address the Liberal Foundation, W. T. Stead remarked in the *Pall Mall Gazette* that 'I shall not be surprised if in a few years Mrs Wilde has become one of the most popular among "platform ladies".'[89]

Wilde's career in these years ran parallel courses between his home life, with wife and children, and his 'away' life with Ross. Up to the initial publication of *Dorian Gray* in 1890, and including the reaction to the book and Wilde's defence of it, that career had seen the steady composition of almost all Wilde's serious critical work and his fiction. After it, and resulting from his meeting with Douglas in 1891, his life became an increasing flurry of indulgence as his intoxication with 'the most beautiful young man alive'[90] brought him into conflict with the very system which he had set out to deceive. Wilde's first reaction to Douglas was to rewrite *Dorian Gray*, not only by extending its length but also by significantly adding passages and phrases which spelled out his infatuation. His second was to abandon almost all other literary endeavours in order to return to the stage with a series of sporadically composed plays which display a level of anxiety far in excess of anything in his previous work.

Although many of the overtly homosexual passages in the first edition of *Dorian Gray* were toned down in the second—a strategy attested to by all commentators, not least Isobel Murray in her excellent edition of the novel—it has scarcely been remarked that this is offset by the excessive manner in which the painter, Basil Hallward, expresses his adoration for Dorian. The revised version does not consist 'mainly of elaboration' as Hart-Davis suggests.[91] For example, the phrase 'curious artistic idolatry' creeps into Hallward's account of how Dorian has come to dominate his art, replacing the expression 'extraordinary romance' (*PDG* 10). The prophetic passage in *Lippincott's*—

> From the moment I met you, your personality had the most extraordinary influence over me. I quite admit that I adored you madly, extravagantly, absurdly

—became in the 1891 version:

> You became to me the visible incarnation of that unseen ideal, whose memory haunts us artists, like an exquisite dream. I worshipped you. (*PDG* 114)

Other expressions of admiration are added: 'He is absolutely necessary to me' (*PDG* 9); Dorian becomes 'Prince Charming! Prince of life' (*PDG* 86); 'I only know that I had seen perfection face to face and that the world had become wonderful to my eyes—too wonderful, perhaps, for in such mad worship there is peril' (*PDG* 114); 'I grew more and more absorbed in you ... it had all been what art should be, unconscious, ideal and remote' (*PDG* 114); 'You were to me such an ideal as I shall never meet again.' (*PDG* 157) If there is any doubt that Wilde was influenced by the presence of Douglas in the revision of *Dorian Gray* (and therefore that they met earlier than has been supposed), it should be dispelled by Wilde's statement:

> I knew you had feet of clay.... When I wrote among my aphorisms that it was simply the feet of clay that made the gold of the image precious, it was of you that I was thinking. (*L* 464)

The aphorism referred to appears in one of the new chapters of *Dorian Gray* (*PDG* 181).

The earliest surviving letter from Wilde referring to Douglas was ironically written to Ross in mid-1892, and was calculated to annoy Ross. It was written from the Royal Palace Hotel, Kensington, as part of Wilde's new peripatetic plan to take rooms away from home in order to work without interruption. The tone is typical of his affected effervescence:

> My dearest Bobbie, Bosie has insisted on stopping here for sandwiches. He is quite like a narcissus—so white and gold. I will come either Wednesday or Thursday to your rooms. Send me a line. Bosie is so tired: he lies like a hyacinth on the sofa, and I worship him.
>
> You dear boy. Ever yours   Oscar (*L* 314)

To Douglas, Wilde wrote his most passionate love-letters, and some of the most poetic letters extant written by an older to a younger man. Receiving a sonnet from Douglas, he replied:

> My Own Boy ... it is a marvel that those rose-leaf lips of yours should have been made no less for music of song than for madness of kisses. Your slim gilt soul walks between passion and poetry. ... Always with undying love, yours   Oscar (*L* 326)

After a lovers' tiff:

> Dearest of all Boys ... you must not make scenes with me, they wreck the loveliness of life. I cannot see you, so Greek and gracious, distorted with passion. I cannot listen to your curved lips saying hideous things to me. You are the divine thing I want, the thing of grace and beauty; but I don't know how to do it. ... Why are you not here, my dear, my wonderful boy? (*L* 336–7)

After a similar occasion (there were many in the first four years of the affair and as many when it was resumed after Wilde's release from prison):

I am happy in the knowledge that we are friends again, and that our love has passed through the shadow and the night of estrangement and sorrow and come out rose-coloured as of old. Let us always be dear to each other, as indeed we have been always. (L 347–8)

Wilde invited Douglas to his family holiday house in Worthing in terms of a desperate older man clinging to the youthful vision, yet embarrassed by his position as paterfamilias, by the meeting of the two hemispheres of his life (not least, perhaps, because Douglas had boasted to Ross that one day he would seduce Cyril Wilde):

> She [the 'horrid Swiss governess'] is quite impossible. Also children at meals are tedious. Also, you, the gilt and graceful boy, would be bored. Don't come here. I will come to you.... *I can't live without you.* You are so dear, so wonderful, I think of you all day long, and miss your grace, your boyish beauty, the bright swordplay of your wit, the delicate fancy of your genius.... I have no words for how I love you. (L 358)

> You are the atmosphere of beauty through which I see life; you are the incarnation of all lovely things.... I think of you day and night ... you honey-haired boy. (L 363)

Even during his trials, when he must have reflected on the sordid spectacle which his debauchery had created, he had not begun to doubt Douglas's motives as he did later. On the opening day of his second trial he wrote:

> I love you, I love you, my heart is a rose which your love has brought to bloom.... You have been the supreme, the perfect love of my life; there can be no other.... O Sweetest of all boys, most loved of all loves, my soul clings to your soul, and my life is your life, and in all the worlds of pain and pleasure you are my ideal of admiration and joy. (L 398)

* * *

In 'De Profundis'—probably the longest love-letter ever written—Wilde quoted Emerson's dictum that 'Nothing is more rare in any man than an act of his own.' 'It is quite true,' he commented. 'Most people are other people. Their thoughts are someone else's opinion, their life a mimicry, their passions a quotation.' (*L* 479) It was vital to Wilde that he should be both mimic and origin, a commentary on society and the source of that society's wonder, amusement, gossip and wisdom. Very often his own love-letters resemble a quotation, a parody of his own earnestness. It was difficult to 'be oneself' if he already knew himself to be many. In multiplicity he found safety, but also made it difficult to be true to the one.

It was essential that the 'soul' should avoid the recurrent sin, remorse and shame by indulging in a love which must remain unrequited, always bidding adieu. To Harry Marillier, one of his first boy-loves, he wrote: 'There is at least this beautiful mystery in life, that at the moment it feels most complete it finds some secret sacred niche in its shrine empty and waiting. Then comes a time of exquisite expectancy.' (*ML* 63) And to Ross, after the publication of 'Mr W.H.': 'Now that Willie Hughes has been revealed to the world, we must have another secret.' (*L* 247) Like Melmoth, he found himself condemned—in verse at least—to 'travel wearily/And bruise my feet, and drink wine salt with tears'. (*CW* 731) Even at the end of his life, living like a beggar penuriously in Paris, he said: 'I keep on building castles of fairy gold in the air; we Celts always do.' (*L* 666) The lover in search of himself, the wanderer is perceived as a paradox, eliciting truths which remain fabulous but never achieving his goal.

(iii) THE CRIMINAL

'You have like everyone else an evil nature and this in your case has become more corrupt by bad influences mental and moral, and by positive sin. Hence you speak as a dreamer

and sceptic with no faith in anything and no purpose in life,'
Wilde was told by a Catholic priest as an undergraduate.[92] It
was not the only reprimand which he received at Oxford:
having boasted that he found it difficult to 'live up to' his blue
china, he found himself preached against in the University
Church,[93] and at the same time was temporarily sent down
for a late arrival at the start of term—'for being the first
undergraduate to visit Olympia' (L 36). Thus calumniated
for sin, affectation and disobedience, he confirmed that the
lover and the dreamer are bound by nature to break codes
and hearts with equanimity.

There were times when Wilde's self-advertisement—and
indeed his self-concealment—were merely poses of a harmless artistic nature, yet these activities, for example his declaration as he left Oxford that he was a 'Professor of Aesthetics',
were at one end of a scale of truancy which led at the other
to criminal deviance. His stories were those of a born liar,
and every statement, however truthful it might seem, had an
alternative which identified him as a future criminal. It was
not necessary to commit, or even to contemplate, a crime for
there to be always a *mens rea*, even when he was not conscious of it. Everything he did was a travesty of manners, a
calculated commentary on public and private affairs. When,
for example, he allowed Walter Hamilton to devote a chapter in his *The Aesthetic Movement* (1882) to his activities, he
contributed to a series of misunderstandings and minor
errors which survive to this day. The 'naturally enthusiastic
temperament' which Hamilton observed[94] was the eagerness
of the young pretender to convince a new audience of an
extended past and a brilliant future. The impressions that
'he spent some months travelling in Greece and Palestine'[95]
or that 'his rooms [at Oxford] were quite the show ones of
the college, and of the university too'[96] were obviously not
ones which Wilde would be anxious to dispel.

Hamilton was, however, wise in his judgment of the
poem 'Ave Imperatrix', which, he said, showed Wilde 'to be
a Republican, not of the noisy and blatant, but of the quiet

and patient kind, content to wait till the general spread of democracy, and the absorption of governing power by the people, shall peacefully bring about the changes they desire, and remove the abuses of our present *régime*'.[97] This in itself was indicative of the extent to which Wilde, as a twenty-nine-year-old apprentice, could be identified with the aesthetic dimension of politics. It must be remembered that even the aesthetes, as cartooned in *Punch*, constituted a challenge, if not a threat, to the moral and social order. Similarly, Hamilton pointed out that Wilde's first play 'Nora, or The Nihilist' [*sic*] 'has not yet been produced, probably because of the powerful situations it contains founded on democratic ideas'. The English censorship, Hamilton observed, was conducted within 'the household of a Royal family, connected by marriage with all the despots of Europe'.[98]

Simultaneously to encourage commentators on his work to identify him as an—or as *the*—aesthetic leader and to err favourably in their use of facts became Wilde's goal as far as manipulating a public mask was concerned. Inwardly, he always knew that to allow such misunderstandings and discrepancies to continue was a form of criminality. Speaking in America, he maintained that aestheticism was a philosophy because 'it is the pursuit of the secret of life'.[99] It was essential for his purpose that the secret should ostensibly be proclaimed in poems, lectures and essays, yet reserved exclusively to the only being capable of accommodating it. If aestheticism is 'the study of the truth in art',[100] then Wilde would go to all lengths to ensure that his public would be bewildered by art and thus would never apprehend the truth.

'Oscar Wilde defies conventionality,' declared Hamilton.[101] The distinction between conventionality and convention is subtle: by rejecting conventionality one simply identifies oneself as an outsider to fashion; by rejecting convention one becomes immediately an enemy of law. To promote reform in house decoration or dress sense in the interests of beauty is to enhance society; to elevate beauty over social norms is to remake society in the image of the beautiful. Hamilton

concluded his study of Wilde by saying that the Aesthetic
school (in which he included Botticelli, Burne-Jones, Oxford,
Japan, Wagner, Sullivan, Swinburne and Wilde) was 'high in
the estimation of all true lovers of the ideal, the passionate,
and the beautiful'.[102] One can only surmise that if he had
known that love of the ideal meant, for Wilde, 'l'amour de
l'impossible' and a return to Greek love, he would have
denounced the Aesthetic movement as warmly as he had
acclaimed it.

The life of the criminal is not simply one of offences against
society or even against reason. It is much more complex: an
inversion, as well as an opposition, of values. The criminal is
the lover of, and in, society and the carrier and mistress of
his own fate. When Wilde wrote: 'There is no such thing as
changing one's life: one merely wanders round and round
within the circle of one's own personality' (L 671), he was
replicating the rhythm and the space of the prison yard which,
rather than expelling the criminal from society, emphasises
his centrality to it.

Yeats perceived this when he said that Wilde

> lived with no self-mockery at all an imaginary life; per-
> petually performed a play which was in all things the
> opposite of all that he had known in childhood and early
> youth; never put off completely his wonder at opening
> his eyes every morning on his own beautiful house

but that his 'half-civilized blood' made him 'a parvenu'.[103]
There is nothing inconsistent here with Yeats's further observation that 'the dinner-table was Wilde's event':[104] Wilde's
disillusion—or 'wonder' as Yeats calls it—stemmed from the
fact that Wilde knew himself to be the thief who had stolen
the beauty and the imagination from the world in which he
was forced to live, and that he could only make restitution
(and at the same time continue to plunder life of its trea-

sures) by amusing it and guiding it into inconsequentiality. Gide, who had the opportunity of observing Wilde closely on several occasions in the years 1891–5, not only recorded this in his study of Wilde and in his first autobiography, *Si le grain ne meurt* (1920), but also re-created Wilde as the character Ménalque, first in *Les nourritures terrestres* (1897) and later in *L'Immoraliste* (1902)—although in the latter case the title, if it is to evoke Wilde at all, should more accurately have been *L'Amoraliste*. Gide noted in 1895 a recklessness in Wilde: 'One felt that there was less tenderness in his look, that there was something harsh in his laughter and a madness in his joy.... Strangely enough, he no longer spoke in fables.'[105] The Wilde who 'would never cease from acting' was now acting the role of himself[106] which he now saw was coming to a close: Gide reported him as saying: 'I have been as far as possible along my own road ... I can't go any further. *Something* must happen now.'[107] Known quite clearly by Wilde throughout his short life—he was forty years of age at the time—was the fact that fate of a dreadful kind was not only his beckoning destiny but also his companion on the way: 'waiting, expecting, longing' is Ménalque's threefold sense of life.[108] Life is both 'the perpetual, delicious expectation of the future' and 'wonderful palingenesis'.[109] 'God is what lies ahead of us', and 'the foretaste of death' is the spur to travel;[110] yet even though he is driven by the need to escape 'homes and families and all the places where a man thinks to find rest', he also knows that 'You would search long ... for the impossible happiness of the soul.'[111] The 'crime' for which Wilde was eventually punished was not the 'gross indecency' which he practised with his gay associates, nor even the 'systematic corruption' of youth of which he was also accused, but the fact that he defied the conventions of society on all fronts. To think of oneself in the third person was to become the enemy of the increasingly vertiginous self-possession of the bourgeois male. At bay in the court-room, Wilde was levelled and all his personae came together; thus he was fulfilling his early promise that 'I am determined that the world shall understand me.' (L 146)

* * *

H. G. Wells, reviewing *An Ideal Husband*, in which Wilde stood morality on its head, thought that the author was 'working his way to innocence'.[112] The remark could not have been more acute. Although Wells could hardly have known why he had succeeded in identifying Wilde's criminal mind, he knew that he was playing with, and flouting, convention. Wilde was a criminal not because he broke the sexual codes of Victorian England but because he continually broke his own codes in order to stay ahead of himself in his personal quest for meaning. The fact that the laws on homosexual behaviour have been changed indicates the parallel fact that Wilde's offence ran in the face of perennial ideas of where the antinomian is to be located in society, and of his relation with authority. As I have indicated elsewhere,[113] the wish for another world where life might be lived differently was at the active centre of English thought and behaviour from the Romantic era at least up to the Abdication Crisis of 1936–7. It was an increasingly persistent quest for the *hortus conclusus* which became more marked with the fragmentation of a monolithic society into rebellious parts, expressing an alternative view which originated in the dandyism of Brummell and Disraeli and was augmented by the mirror-world of Dodgson and the escapism of Barrie. The bizarre epiphanies of Jarry, Yeats and Eliot in this landscape of doubt and frustration were acute commentaries upon a subliminal climate of despair at the nature of the modern world.

First Wilde talks of the 'truth of art'; then he speaks of truth in terms of contradictories; finally he abandons truth altogether—'there is no reality in things apart from appearances'. When Yeats wrote 'Away' in 1902 he cannot have known that in 'De Profundis' Wilde had said:

> The poor are wiser, more charitable, more kind, more sensitive than we are. In their eyes, prison is a tragedy in a man's life, a misfortune, a casualty, something that calls for sympathy in others. They speak of one who is

in prison as of one who is 'in trouble' simply. It is the phrase they always use, and the expression has the perfect wisdom of love in it. (*L* 465)

The connection with the Irish mind can nevertheless be suggested: the prisoner is like the 'stolen child', someone whose natural existence has been interrupted. Yeats wrote: 'Sometimes people who are "away" are thought to have, like the dead who have been "taken", that power of changing one thing into another.... It often seems as if these enchanted people had some great secret.'[114] Wilde was 'away' as a criminal and as an Irishman before he was ever accused or punished. He knew how to change 'one thing into another', perhaps because he possessed the 'great secret'.

It can be explained by the early ambition to be the defendant in the case of *Regina v. Wilde*. Wilde wanted to be in the spotlight, to have a case to answer with an alternative rather than an *apologia*. His 'speech from the dock' at his first trial may have been the factor which swayed the jury into disagreement—just as Sir Travers Humphreys, a junior counsel at all three processes, believed that they may have felt the new law of 1885 too punitive of private homosexual acts.

'The left hand is the hand of a king, but the right that of a king who will send himself into exile,' a cheiromancer told Wilde just before his downfall. Wilde knew that he had two identities, but the temptation was to adopt many. It is natural to the liar and unnatural to the lover. Erving Goffmann tells us that

> In the entertainment world it is common for a performer to change his name.... Occupations where a change in name can occur without being officially recorded, such as those of prostitute, criminal, and revolutionary, are not 'legitimate' trades.... Whenever an occupation carries with it a change of name, recorded or not, one can be sure that an important breach is involved between the individual and his old world.[115]

For Wilde, the adoption of many poses, the gradual disbursement of his many original names—Fingal, O'Flahertie, Wills—until he becomes simply 'the Oscar', and the adoption first of his cell number, C.3.3., as a pen-name and then of 'Melmoth' as his travelling identity, represented several breaches with his past. Entertainer, criminal, revolutionary, he was involved in trades both legitimate and nefarious.

To return to the difficulty which I expressed at the opening of this chapter: Goffmann insists that 'an individual can really have only one of them'—he is referring not to identities but to biographies. Wilde, however, was the author of several 'books', in each of which there is a separate Wilde. The fact that the 'real' Wilde eludes Ellmann as he had previously hidden from Symons, Pearson, Hyde and many others —including myself—is the key to these profoundly unsatisfactory attempts to write a 'life' rather than a 'mind'.

For while the sequential facts of Wilde's career may exist within his own invisible—and illegible—book, his multiplicity of selves did enable him to lead a multiplicity of lives, because in place of a home truth by which life should be lived there was an emptiness which he sent out these multiple personae to fill.

Perhaps the secret of Wilde's life and character can be best illustrated by reference to another of literature's criminals, Villiers de l'Isle Adam. In a little-known article which Wilde himself commissioned from Arthur Symons for publication in *The Woman's World*,[116] many of Wilde's own traits are revealed. Symons described Adam as

> a writer whose singular personality and work render him perhaps the most extraordinary figure in the contemporary world of letters. . . . His life has been, like his works, a paradox and an enigma.

Adam struck Symons in much the same fashion as we have so far seen Wilde:

> An immense consciousness of his own genius, a pride of race [Adam, too, was a Celt, a Breton nobleman], a contempt, artistic and aristocratic, of the common herd, and, more especially, of the *bourgeois* multitude of letters and of life.

But there was, within the enigma, a series of complications: Adam was

> a writer who seems to be made up of contradictions.... In reading him, you pass from exaltation to buffoonery with the turn of a page, and are never quite sure whether he is speaking seriously or in jest. Above all, everywhere, there is irony.

If we have characterised Wilde as a man with a singular mission, so too may we think of Adam: referring to *Contes Cruels* (1880) (which he compares to Poe's *Tales* and Hawthorne's *Twice Told Tales*), *La Revoltée* (1870) and *Le Nouveau Monde* (1876), Symons called him 'a man of one book'. It therefore comes as little surprise to find that Adam's style is highly suggestive of Wilde's. *Contes Cruels* are

> studies in modern love, supersubtle and yet perfectly finished little studies, so light in touch, manipulated with such delicate a finesse, so exquisite and unerring a tact, that the most monstrous of paradoxes, the most incredible assumptions of cynicism, become possible, become acceptable.

This might have been written of Wilde's fairy stories and social short stories. Of one of Adam's stories Symons writes:

> The mockery of the thing is elemental; cynicism touches its zenith. It becomes tender, it becomes sublime. A

> perversion simply monstrous appears, in the infantile
> simplicity of its presentment, touching, credible, heroic.
> The edge of laughter is skirted by the finest of inches,
> and, as a last charm, one perceives, through the irony
> itself—a faint and sweet perfume as of a perverted
> odour of sanctity.

Of another:

> It is with a positive physical sensation that we read it,
> an instinctive shiver of fascinated and terrified sus-
> pense.

Comparing Adam's satire with Swift's, Symons also points
to the breakthrough in style which Adam achieves through
use of language. We might imagine that Wilde's Celtic crusade on the English language and sensibility could be
described in the same tone:

> Familiar words take new meanings ... strange words
> start up from forgotten corners; words and thoughts,
> never brought together since Babel, clash and stumble
> into a protesting combination; and in the very aspect of
> the page there is something startling.

'What, in a word,' Symons asks, 'is the true Villiers? The
question', he suggests in the first instance where we might
think that Adam and Wilde part company, 'depends upon
an elementary knowledge of the nature of that perfectly
intelligible being, the cynic. The typical cynic is essentially a
tender-hearted, sensitive, idealist; his cynicism is in the first
instance a recoil, then, very often, a disguise.' As we shall
now see in Wilde's fictions, the growth of cynicism and the
development of the 'instinctive shiver' become the means by
which he brings the symbolic nature of *fin de monde* Celtic art
to a meeting-place with the *fin de siècle* symbolism of the
decadent stage.

Part Two

4
Fictions

'I *cannot* think otherwise than in stories,'[1] Wilde insisted to André Gide, who commented: 'Wilde did not converse—he told tales.'[2] As the natural *seanchaí*, he made of his life a fable and lived by its recitation. When he emphasised that *The Picture of Dorian Gray* 'is rather like my own life—all conversation and no action' (L 255), he identified the point at which his talent and his genius coalesced: the between-point where reality and art recognise one another. Wilde's stories are distinctive since in the place of action is thought: despite their simplicity, their morality and their charm, they are intensely speculative and intellectual. They are concerned with what happens when beauty meets the beast, when virtue goes unrecognised and unrewarded: they are supremely cynical.

Wilde's work was monothematic, dominated by contrasts and opposites. He continually felt the need to cross from one side of the garden to the other, not only to contrast darkness with brightness, but also to stand at the point of transition and to experience simultaneously the bitter-sweet knowledge of the twilight. The compulsion to tell the story overrides any apprehension which the teller might have for his personal fate:

> Failure, disgrace, poverty, sorrow, despair, suffering, tears even, the broken words that come from the lips of pain, remorse that makes one walk in thorns, conscience that condemns, self-abasement that punishes...all these were things of which I was afraid. (L 475)

Yet however much his fear may have tempted him to stand aside, he encountered them all in his 'real' life, the life of the fable. He identified it in 'The Happy Prince' and 'The Young King' and said: 'A great deal of it is hidden away in the note of Doom that like a purple thread runs through the gold cloth of *Dorian Gray* ... it is one of the refrains whose recurring *motifs* make *Salome* so like a piece of music and bind it together as a ballad' (*L* 475). It is particularly evident in the prose-poem 'The Artist', which combines in one submissive Celtic image 'The Sorrow that endureth for Ever' and 'The Pleasure that abideth for a Moment' (*CW* 863).

Wilde accepted that 'it could not have been otherwise. At every single moment of one's life one is what one is going to be no less than what one has been. Art is a symbol, because man is a symbol.' (*L* 476) *Otherwise* becomes the motif, syntactically and conceptually echoing Berkeley. Life is a reversal of reality because it is controlled by what one can see: Wilde saw Doom, and therefore found himself running away from it and towards it at the same time. 'You must understand that there are two worlds', he told Gide—

> the one exists and is never talked about; it is called the real world because there is no need to talk about it in order to see it. The other is the world of Art; one must talk about that because otherwise it would not exist.[3]

The world of which Wilde spoke was the 'otherwise' world which it was essential to promulgate and to elevate as more real than the real world.

As the Wild Irish Boy commuted between two countries— one a political reality and a logical base, the other a state of mind—so Wilde, in his stories, shuttles in emotional terms between three kinds of time: the imagined past, the present reality, and the doomed future. There is a powerful and rewarding sense in which his work can be seen as a bridge between the gothic intensities of Maturin's and Le Fanu's fiction (and his mother's translations of Meinhold and Schwab) and the dim landscapes, the ruined castles and the *ennui* of Yeats and Beckett. *Dorian Gray* may, like Stoker's

Dracula, represent a perennial theme of disinheritance, alienation and existence outside time, but it is essentially Irish in
its crazed and exclusive pursuit of Tír na nÓg—'Youth!
Youth! There is absolutely nothing in the world but youth!'
(*PDG* 23)—and its subtle connection between classical and
Celtic culture in its assertion that 'Nothing can cure the soul
but the senses, just as nothing can cure the senses but the
soul.' (*PDG* 20) The intellectual position adopted is akin to
Baudelaire's 'Be always drunken if you would not be the
martyred slaves of Time':[4] those who know that they are
damned or excluded or forgotten must indulge in the deepest irony if they are to enter fully into their destiny.

Vivian Mercier underlines most cogently the relation of
the fantastic and the macabre as the twin bases for Gaelic
comic literature: 'It is true that life is cruel and ugly, but the
macabre and grotesque do not become humorous until they
have portrayed life as even more cruel and ugly than it is.'[5]
And it is from the irony of this indulgence that we derive
paradox:

> In spite of the irrational element in word play, particu-
> larly common in Irish wit, a witty remark is both
> absurd and true: in other words, paradox ... lies at the
> bottom of all Irish wit; it is paradoxical truth which dis-
> tinguishes a witty remark from the mere absurdity of a
> humorous one. ... Only when we discriminate between
> the two apparent synonyms do we see its truth.[6]

The most paradoxical aspect of Wilde's writing is the deeply
moral nature of *Dorian Gray*. Most of Wilde's life was a fiction which was nevertheless true to life, and ultimately
Dorian Gray submits to the truth of life, which is the life of
the portrait. Paradox, the contrived juxtaposition of a truth
opposed to the home truth, was the essential ingredient in
everything Wilde did and in everything he said. A paradox
appears to be a fiction, but when revealed is recognised not
as a fact but as a truth. His stories, his poems and even his

letters, which we shall examine in this chapter, were a deliberate concoction of the absurd, no statement being possible
which did not contain within it a twist which at the same time
subverted and confirmed its artistry. The sitter sits always
before the portrait, in permanent regard of it and constantly
mocked and reviled by the likeness and the difference.

At the heart of life, as of art, there is a secret, and the existence of the secret is to be hinted at until the moment when it
can be told, when cognitions and recognitions can be made.
The secret must be protected and at the same time apprehended, permanently haunting the work in progress. Wilde
needed in particular to maintain the balance between being
understood and not being found out: he needed constantly
to attract an audience for his private drama, continue to offer
it something slightly beyond its grasp, and yet to deny it the
chance of seeing him complete. The elusive element in the
equation, once disclosed, becomes breathtaking not for its
novelty but for the fact that it was so clearly inherent in the
scheme, yet did not 'occur' until specially apprehended. It was
a mutual relationship, based itself on the existence of a secret
known to, but undisclosed by, both sides. Thus 'to most of
us, the real life is the life that we do not lead' (*Misc* 256). That
this should have been offered not as a comic ploy but as a
conscious, serious proposition in the course of a lecture on
the English renaissance in art is an example of how openly
Wilde was prepared to state his obfuscations. The social element on which an agreement to such a proposition depends
is that of irony.

Epifanio San Juan observes that being found out depends
'on whose truth is involved and in what context the utterance is made'[7]—paradox thus becomes the shared joke of the
two parties to irony. That everyone plays a role in life is not
an escape from life but a participation in it. The fact that he
knew, intuitively, that the two would coalesce in an act of
folly made that act all the more calculated, and although he

would subsequently blame his downfall on the selfish acts of his lover, Lord Alfred Douglas, it was a fate in which he automatically acquiesced.

Why, then, do Wilde's stories remain a mystery? Why does the reader keep pace with the narrator only in sensing their playfulness but not in discovering the residual ironies? What is there in the nature of the fairy story which strikes us as apocryphal, something existing before its composition but which is not amenable to the analysis of its construction? To answer these questions we need to turn to the essentially interior political world of the Irish recitation, and to distinguish the fairy story from the folk-tale.

A fairy story is an allegory designed to give children a picture of the real, adult, world, and to enable them, by understanding its constituent parts, to negotiate a satisfactory path in the real world. A folk-tale is more vicious, a parable: it is a tale for adults who have lost their way among the signposts and have experienced some of the disruption related in the tale. Both fairy story and folk-tale are political, in that they concern relation, but the folk-tale concentrates on experience rather than expectation, on action and sensibility rather than imagination. The fairy story deals with home; the folk-tale with the world.

Wilde's stories belong to the folk genre—they are intended not for nursery children (the point which confused many of their critics)[8]—but for adult-children. Yeats recalled that 'he made me tell him long Irish stories and compared my art of story-telling to Homer's';[9] when we consider this in the light of Yeats's observation of 1891, that 'it is, perhaps . . . by no means strange that the age of "realism" should also be the harvest-time of folk-lore'[10] and also his reference to 'our new-wakened interest in the impossible',[11] we can see Wilde's storytelling as a form of self-identification with an Homeric and primitive society, constantly weighing the known against the unknown.

* * *

The nineteenth century was greatly exercised by the notion of transfiguration which is a major element in gothic literature. In each of Wilde's stories, even the simplest, a point is reached where a change of identity takes place. Sometimes it is a semantic change, a linguistic detour into a second meaning, at others a literal exchange of minds and mindsets. In every case it is the reader's understanding of the story which is subverted, because the change is never explicitly acknowledged. It is an implicit change of focus which confuses because what is meant—signified—is not made clear. There is an *intention*, but we are not admitted to it, so greatly are we consumed by the magic of the storyline.

This idea of transfiguration is deeply rooted in the sense of doom and nemesis which Wilde early encountered in Greek tragedy, in particular in the *Agamemnon* of Aeschylus (part of which he had translated for the *Dublin University Magazine*), but it is also a fundamental, lived characteristic of the modern age, reflected in the sciences of psychology, physics and, ultimately, space exploration. Thus on one side Wilde knew from classical sources the nature of tragedy and its relation to comedy, while on another he was able to interact with what was called 'the beautiful farce of aestheticism'[12] in which the pose and the inference are as important as the substantive and the explicit. But however much the artificiality of Wilde's world rested on the firm bases of society and its literature, there is also a sense in which his secrets were those of a man deviant not only from society but also from himself. His poems display an astonishing ambivalence and equivocation, a wistfulness balanced by an epicureanism, a triumphal remorse and a remorseful triumph which suggest not so much a poet in conversation with his own age as an artist using the inevitably public medium of words to pursue the essentially private conversation with his own soul.

Wallace Stevens speaks of poetry as 'the Supreme Fiction',[13] and to the extent that poetry is the supreme art this may be true. But for Wilde, whom Pater had advised to write prose in preference to poetry because it was more difficult, the story, the prose-poem (which combined the *seanchaí's* genres of recitation and relation) and the supreme fiction was oneself. There is a sense in which anything can happen in a Wilde story—but doesn't. The course has been mapped out before the child has become the orphan—expressed in the simultaneous equations 'Art is a symbol, because man is a symbol.' In Yeats's sense, his stories are 'Ireland talking to herself';[14] in another, they are Wilde inscribing himself in the book of Ireland. The primacy of the book is paramount.

But the transference of self into legend, or book, has a consequence far more significant than its mere legibility: it requires the reader to follow the narrator into the ontological minefield of his own existence, and to imagine his own 'first misfortune'. Wilde's storytelling is ruthless because its simplicity keeps the reader on the wire; the narrator is at all times alien, yet succeeds in penetrating the reader's intellect. The absence of logic is total; each time the reader attempts to call logic to his assistance the story shifts its basis and the image slips away. Wilde is equally unrelenting in his intellectualism. The finest example is the Selfish Giant who refuses to allow children to play in the garden because it is *his* garden, not theirs. Children mean spring and summer, and by excluding them the Selfish Giant is deprived of everything except winter. The garden is empty because logic has been elevated to the level of intellect. When the Selfish Giant perceives this mistake, he dismantles his defences, and in so doing he surprises a new truth—that when one realises a truth, it ceases to be true. Like another of Wilde's 'fictions', the Star-Child, the giant's enjoyment of the truth is brief, because the paradox of two truths separated from each other has come to an end. It is only the play of paradox which keeps the story going. Once the alien in Wilde's story comes home, finds a meaning, the game is lost.

Wilde's stories, then, like the Greek tragedies, are continually faced with the difficulty of catching up with themselves. The prose-poems, particularly—and the later dramatic sketches—are caught in a time-warp which holds them somewhere between question and answer. Genet's 'the Eternal passed by in the form of a Pimp'[15] might stand for all Wilde's prose-poems, so biblical and so magdalen is the recurrent theme of the mundane in pursuit of the supernatural. The persons of his stories are a Prince, a Giant, an Infanta, a King on one level, or an actress, a harlot, a dwarf, a blind fool or a beggar on another; the locale is the palace or the peasant's hut, the gilded pavement or the dusty street. These are the opposites of life within the fable. 'When I was alive and had a human heart' is the after-life comment of the Happy Prince become miserable who stands as a reprimand, like Melmoth, to the world which he revisits permanently with his now leaden heart.

'Why do Irish novels tend to have strong narrators and weak plots?' asks James M. Cahalan.[16] The answer lies in his own explanation of the Irish historical novel, that the nineteenth-century writers 'seemed unable to face Irish history for what it was: an unresolved mess'.[17] Strongly narrated fiction in the guise of autobiography—Joyce's *Portrait* being the supreme example—identified the weakness of the inchoate plot with the development of the author's own mind and the necessary rejections, rather than accretions, which that growth entailed. Likewise Richard Fallis argued that 'the novel was not really a successful genre in Ireland during this period [1900–30], particularly not the novel as we understand it, a major narrative dealing with real people in real situations'.[18] There was, in fact, not so much a writing of Ireland as a rewriting of its oral tradition and its history. The rewriting took many forms, not least that of political rhetoric, because the narrative style was peculiar to Ireland and to Irish subjects rather than cognate with larger European styles of narration. Thus John Wilson Foster widens the net of 'imaginative prose' 'to include autobiographies and also translations, collections, adaptations, be they of folktales or ancient sagas and romances'—yet he still excludes Wilde in the pursuit of what he calls 'a changeling art'.[19]

At the same time, we must also take note of the parallel facts that, as W. J. McCormack puts it, 'the emergence of Anglo-Irish literature lies close to the heart of European romanticism', while 'the Anglo-Irish Renaissance is central to modernist literature in the English language'.[20] The passage of this literature from romanticism to modernism mirrors the emergence of modern Ireland itself from an imagined country to a political reality. Wilde's work can readily be seen as a feature of this evolution if we inspect the trajectory of his writing from the aesthetic, overwhelming and florid classicism of his poetry to the sparseness of the decadence in his plays *The Importance of Being Earnest* and *Salomé*.

The transition was possible partly because Ireland experienced no industrial revolution, nor the consequent debate on materialism, no crisis of faith between religion and utilitarianism until a different kind of revolution—that of freedom—insisted that ideological choices be made. The social and cultural issues therefore predominated, and the 'meaning' of the process was thus more accessible than its end result, which was less clear. Whether or not the ancient truths to which nineteenth-century Ireland was trying to approximate were accurately perceived and transmitted is not an issue. The 'meaning' to which the romantic antiquarians and the modernists approximated was not susceptible to any western hegemonic system of analysis, and as such it permitted the development of Ireland in relation to Europe on Irish terms.

Wilde himself (no more than Yeats) had no place in the 'Big House' tradition of Anglo-Irish writing as such, and unlike Yeats he made no attempt to imagine himself into it. His background was quite unusual—first-generation urbanite; his tradition, if he had one at all, was scientific-professional and intellectually cosmopolitan. This made him the servant of nothing other than his intellect. To Wilde, 'house' had not the same affective meaning it had for Le Fanu or Edgeworth. 'House' in his work is a place of imagination, but of perverse and morbid introspection and surrender to an internal, resident sense of doom—the 'Harlot's House', the room within the house where the Sphinx is the presiding genius, or, out of his family circumstances, the discredited house of his parents in Merrion Square, or his mother's down-at-heel bohemianism of her last years in Chelsea. His own family house, one to which he became largely a stranger, was in the forefront of a quite un-Victorian aesthetic movement. Later the hotel room was his chief experience, the café the place of his recreation.

Wilde is thus the outsider both in Ireland and in England, where he was in conflict with its materialist values and its social and sexual mores, familiar with a different political agenda and perspective; he therefore possessed yet another reason for employing the mask as both disguise and mirror. When the secret is so potentially dynamic that its disclosure could have aesthetic, political and social ramifications far beyond the significance of the mere word or act in which the secret is based, the complexity of the game of hide-and-seek, and the identity of the players in the game, becomes evident. As Erving Goffmann says:

> The possession of a discreditable secret failing takes on a deeper meaning when the persons to whom the individual has not yet revealed himself are not strangers to him but friends. Discovery prejudices not only the current social situation, but established relationships as well; not only the current image others present have of him, but also the one they will have in the future; not only appearances, but also reputation. The stigma and the effort to conceal it or remedy it become 'fixed' as part of personal identity. Hence our increased willingness to chance improper behaviour when wearing a mask, or when away from home; hence the willingness of some to publish revelatory material anonymously, or to make a public appearance before a small private audience, the

assumption being that the disclosure will not be connected to them personally by the public at large.[21]

Goffmann's entire observation is true of every aspect of
Wilde's career. The movement between Paris and London,
the use of a private dining-room in a public hotel, the speaking in code, were Wilde's necessary occlusions of a life which
was becoming increasingly audacious. It is by no means
unlikely that Wilde was, as reported, a part-author of an
explicitly homoerotic novel, *Teleny*, which, as its title suggests,
was decidedly scatological in its preoccupations. It would
have provided a method of sublimating his rampant carnal
desires in the way he knew best—in writing. To conceal himself from his friends was Wilde's consummate art, but it was
an art which relied on the same paradoxes which shielded
him from the public gaze.

We must also recall Goffmann's further viewpoint, that
'nearly all matters which are very secret are still known to
someone, and hence cast a shadow'.[22] Wilde's 'secret', his
aesthetic subversion and his sexual orientation, was known
to very few and yet was apparent to the whole world. There
was a permanent nameless shadow in his work, represented
by the figure of the Sphinx, which took the form of the remorse
which dogs the soul, or the double values which shadow the
achievement of innocent happiness, or the murderer within
each of us who treads the prison yard.

The companion is the interrogation mark, the mark of
caution, of reprise, which attended Wilde at every moment
of his social and intellectual life. It is more than simple conscience (which detects and reports the difference between
right and wrong in life's trajectory) because, as Dorian Gray
and Sir Robert Chiltern discover, you can, with varying
degrees of catastrophe, kill conscience. It is soul itself—and
this becomes the narrative.

The companion's most explicit appearance was in *The
Picture of Dorian Gray*, and his most enigmatic in the poem
'The Harlot's House'. But he/she is also present in Wilde's

letters, the wistful actor haunted by times irretrievably past, ambitions inevitably sullied by experience, passions unrequited, or loves requited in mere lust. Throughout his work Wilde made disclosures in a systematic and deliberate way, for anyone with the correct spectacles to recognise them for what they were: critical commentaries not only on the age but also on the personality of their author. The personae of poet, lecturer, critic, editor, essayist, short-story writer, novelist, socialist, epistolist, were like those of son, husband, father, lover, paederast, socialite and convict: each had its own way of being told, rehearsed before its public. The discovery of the correct story was both a means of concealment and a key to the secret. The 'strange and secret smile' of Charmides (CW 757) is the sign of the invert acknowledging the vulnerability of his secret. Detection by the world at large was both necessary and damning; and while escape from detection is in itself delicious, it serves only to postpone the ultimate satisfaction of being unmasked.

Wilde told his Sphinx:

> You wake in me each bestial sense, you make me
> what I would not be (CW 842)

—yet what he is is what he must be, and however much wistfulness there may be to proclaim:

> Ah! it was easy when the world was young
> To keep one's life free and inviolate (CW 800)

the writer knows that the world is not what he wishes, and is only what it is.

The 'Devoted Friend' and the Judas in our life are too close to be separated and too distinct to be twinned. Judas betrayed Christ with the supreme sign of love—the kiss—which is also a betrayal, and confirmation, of the relationship of teacher and pupil, master and servant.

The gothic preoccupation with the relationship of master and servant is at the heart of all Wilde's paradoxes: master and servant feed off one another's vanity; man and woman enact their traditional roles of superior decision-maker and submissive handmaiden; language is both the tool of human expression and the labile shaper of intercourse. There is thus a social, sexual and semantic dimension to our approach to authority and our construction of meaning.

Algernon Moncrieff depends on Lane for his connection with the external world; Arthur Goring depends on Phipps for the supply of trivial buttonholes which identify him as the leader of fashion. The action of *Salomé* depends implicitly on the existence of servants to die for love of Salomé and, eventually, to kill her. Dorian Gray lives in fear of his servant discovering the secret of the portrait. The identity of John/ Ernest Worthing depends on the identification of the hand-bag by Miss Prism and her revelation of the baby's fate.

A servant can be menial and at the same time menacing and mocking. No master is complete without the ready wit, wisdom and efficacy of his servant, no servant complete without the status and validation of his master; nor is their relationship whole without at least a partial exchange of roles between them. The absurdity and the common sense which accompany Quixote and Panza, Wooster and Jeeves, are present in each of Wilde's stories and plays. The Infanta (and her mincing court), juxtaposed with the triumph and disaster of the dwarf before her and before the mirror, is a collective irony with the deepest semiotic consequences. The inversion of faith between the Miller and little Hans in 'The Devoted Friend' is a cruel twist of a commonplace—the assumption of one's own goodness and the expectation of the world's obeisance. It is extended by Wilde's deliberate reference to the Judas who writes the biography.

The critical point of exchange between master and servant lies in the location of the secret self. As Genet observes, 'mythologies are full of heroes who are changed into servants'.[23] In Dostoyevsky's *The Double* (1846) it is sometimes in the physical presence of Golyadkin's lookalike, sometimes in the mirrored reflection. In Poe's 'William Wilson' (1834) it is a continual, leering companion who lures him to madness, and in Stevenson's *The Strange Case of Dr Jekyll and Mr Hyde* (1885) the companion is summoned and dismissed by chemistry. In works later than *Dorian Gray* such as Hesse's *Demian* (1919) and Nabokov's *Despair* (1922) the secret self is respectively an androgynous otherself and an exact double permanently waiting to become thief and murderer. In all these encounters between self and anti-self, one becomes the thief of the other's identity. It is the servant's function to re-create himself imaginatively as the master, to adopt his origins, status and perspectives as his own—which makes it important for us to realise that it is not always the *apparent* servant who is the *actual* servant. The foundling, the orphan, may not merely aspire to riches and titles and palaces, but may in fact achieve them by stint of pretence and impersonation. Those who are by nature dispossessed of land, family or sexuality may repossess them by an act of inversion. The mirror becomes the membrane between the 'real' world and the 'makebelieve' world, and the dispossessed live constantly within the mirror itself, both subject and portrait.

The most acute state of this liminality is the androgyne, celebrated by Shakespeare and therefore by Wilde: 'Of all the motives of dramatic curiosity used by our great playwrights, there is none more subtle or more fascinating than the ambiguity of the sexes,' he says in 'The Portrait of Mr W.H.'. 'To say that only a woman can portray the passions of a woman, and that therefore no boy can play Rosalind, is to rob the art of acting of all claim to objectivity, and to assign to the mere accident of sex what properly belongs to imaginative insight and creative energy'. (*CW* 1180)

Wilde wrote thirteen stories, the novellas *The Picture of Dorian Gray* and 'The Portrait of Mr W.H.' and a 'study in green' of the artist and poisoner Thomas Griffiths Wainewright, 'Pen, Pencil and Poison'. Of the stories, four were modern society fables ('Lord Arthur Savile's Crime', 'The Canterville

Ghost', 'The Model Millionaire' and the much shorter 'The Sphinx Without a Secret') which were published in book form in 1891 under the title *Lord Arthur Savile's Crime and other stories*; they had previously been published serially in *The World* and the *Court and Society Review*. The remainder were allegedly written for children: five—'The Happy Prince', 'The Nightingale and the Rose', 'The Selfish Giant', 'The Devoted Friend' and 'The Remarkable Rocket'—were published as *The Happy Prince and other tales* in 1888; the four others—'The Young King', 'The Birthday of the Infanta', 'The Fisherman and his Soul' and 'The Star-Child'—were published under the collective title *A House of Pomegranates* in 1891. 'The Portrait of Mr W.H.' appeared first in *Blackwood's Magazine* in July 1889; an extended version, intended for publication in 1893, eventually appeared in 1921. *The Picture of Dorian Gray* appeared first in *Lippincott's Monthly Magazine* in July 1890 and subsequently, with six additional chapters and a 'Preface', in book form in the following year. 'Pen, Pencil and Poison' was included in Wilde's volume of critical essays, *Intentions*, but is briefly considered here as a biographical fiction. Wilde also composed many 'poems in prose', six of which, including perhaps the most famous, 'The Doer of Good', were published in his *Collected Works*, and many more of which have been recalled by associates such as André Gide, Ada Leverson, Charles Ricketts, Arthur Conan Doyle, Guillot de Saix and numerous others.

We will now examine the stories, beginning with the shortest—the prose-poems—followed by the folk-tales, the society stories and the novellas.

All folk-tales have the same characteristics of leavetaking, experience and homecoming, and thus obey to a certain extent the classical unities. They posit the teller abroad and at home, at risk and at peace. Wilde's prose-poems, however, dispense with development and concentrate on an intense image of intellectual emotion. Jealousy and despair ('The

Master'), denial ('The House of Judgment'), self-absorption ('The Disciple') and impotence ('The Doer of Good') are depicted as self-evident states of mind in the prose-poems accessible in Wilde's *Collected Works* (863–70), many of which were told to André Gide.

Others, however, continue to appear from more obscure sources. One, untitled, is of particular interest for what it tells us of revelation:

> A man saw a being, which hid its face from him, and he said 'I will compel it to show its face.' It fled as he pursued, and he lost it; and his life went on. At last his pleasure drew him into a long room, where tables were spread for many, and in a mirror he saw the being whom he had pursued in youth. 'This time you shall not escape me' he said, but the being did not try to escape, and hid its face no more. 'Look' it cried 'and now you will know that we cannot see each other again, for this is the face of your own soul, and it is horrible.'[24]

As a reading of *Dorian Gray* shows us, this is a highly condensed recital of the most deeply mystical of all prayers, 'Show me your face'.[25] Another, collected by Gide but not normally reprinted in Wilde's *Works*, is concerned with belief and unbelief:

> Once upon a time there was a man who was beloved in his village because he used to tell tales. Every morning he left the village, and when he returned in the evening all the labourers of the village who had been working all the day would crowd round him and say 'Come, now, tell us a tale. What have you seen to-day?'
>
> The man said 'I have seen in the forest a Faun playing on a flute and making a band of little wood-nymphs dance.'
>
> 'Go on with your story; what did you see?' the men would say.

'When I reached the sea-shore, I saw three mermaids beside the waves, combing their green hair with golden combs.'

And the villagers loved him because he used to tell them tales.

One morning he left his village as usual, and when he reached the sea-shore he saw three mermaids at the water's edge combing their green hair with golden combs. And as he passed on his way he saw, near a wood, a Faun playing a flute to a band of wood-nymphs.

That evening when he returned to his village the people said to him as they did every evening, 'Come, tell us a tale: what have you seen?'

And the man answered, 'I have seen nothing.'[26]

The 'moral' of the story is that things are not worth the telling unless they do not exist, and cease to be true when they can be believed in.

There is a thematic link between Wilde's folk-tales and his plays which may be more significant than the verbal and contextual relationship between the plays and the society stories. This link lies in the 'supernatural' elements by means of which Wilde introduces Irish folk motifs into naturalistic drama, of which the most striking are the changelings in the stories 'The Star-Child' and 'The Young King' and the deserted soul in 'The Fisherman and his Soul'. A changeling, born to humble parents but intended for greatness, is a commonplace of folklore, but, as Yeats observed, 'the gift most valued [among the peasantry] seems to be the power of bringing back people who were in the power of "the others"'—that is, the *sídhe*.[27] The stolen child who grows up in obscurity, unaware that he is of great lineage, is restored to his true position. From that moment there is awakened in him 'that strange passion for beauty that was destined to be so great an influence over his life' (*CW* 225). Like Dorian Gray, he develops an eclectic curiosity for works of art, which combines beauty and strangeness. He dreams three great dreams in which he can travel incognito among his subjects, learning of the injustice and suffering, including famine, on which his own life and luxury depend. (In his dream he even succeeds in speaking in the pentameter favoured by Wilde in many of his poems: 'The land is free and thou art no man's slave.' (CW 227)) In the third dream he is permitted to discover the identity of the King—by looking into a mirror. The King's response is altruistic: 'On the loom of sorrow, and by the white hands of Pain, has this my robe been woven. There is Blood in the heart of the ruby, and Death in the heart of the pearl.' (CW 230) He sees, in the vestments and riches of his coronation, the palace—'Joyeuse'—turning its back on the history of famine and exploitation, to which the courtiers' dismay indicates a reversal of 'The Emperor's New Clothes':

> Surely he is mad; for what is a dream but a dream, and a vision but a vision? They are not real things that one should heed them. And what have we to do with the lives of those who toil for us? (CW 231)

The King is mocked because he is the 'dreamer of dreams ... apparelled like a beggar' (CW 233). King and beggar become one—the reconciliation of opposites is one of Wilde's keynotes as a dreamer. The closure of the story adopts the tone of some of Wilde's later parables: 'The young King came down from the high altar, and passed home through the midst of all the people. But no man dared look upon his face, for it was the face of an angel.' (CW 233) The redemptive quality of the young King's true poverty and humility might speak for all those whose degradation under the Famine had been noted by his father's coldly analytic pen and the strident sympathy of his mother's verse. It also predicts the close of Yeats's *Cathleen ni Houlihan*, where the eponymous heroine proceeds through her four green fields, transformed by an inner light: 'I saw a young girl, and she had the walk of a queen.'[28]

The analogy with Christ is deliberate in the reversal of the proposition that 'the burden of this world is too great for one man to bear, and the world's sorrow too heavy for one heart to suffer' (CW 233). The identification of all the King's subjects as 'slaves, though men call us free' is the Rousseauesque ploy by which the redemption and rehabilitation of the kingdom is achieved, just as it will be the noble means by which Lord Arthur Savile acquires the strength to commit murder: 'He had to choose between living for himself and living for others.... Sooner or later we are all called upon to decide on the same issue.' (CW 178)

'The Birthday of the Infanta' also indulges in displacement in order to bring home a moral truth to a developing consciousness. Once more mirrors are at hand to demonstrate, in this case to a dwarf who has captivated, and is captivated by, the Infanta, the cruel truth that he is not the handsome rogue he imagined, but 'a monster' whom he discovers to be himself—'misshapen and hunchbacked, foul to look at and grotesque' (CW 246)—and dies of grief and shame. '"His heart is broken"... And the Infanta frowned, and her dainty rose-leaf lips curled in disdain. "For the future let those who come to play with me have no hearts," she cried, and she ran out into the garden.' (CW 247) This too will be echoed in drama at the turn of the century, with the dual disclosures in Synge's *The Well of the Saints*, where Martin and Mary Doul, both blind beggars, lose their blindness and discover that each other's supposed beauty is in fact ugliness. It is better to live in darkness and ignorance than to suffer in the light of day; better to have no heart than to die of a broken one. The Infanta has become a cynic. Thus the story removes the blindfold from a child of a court which was 'always noted for its cultivated passion for the horrible' (CW 239)—and then replaces the blindfold. Everyone in Wilde's stories who realises the truth—whether joyful or otherwise—dies shortly after. The dwarf seeks everywhere for the Infanta—the question 'Where was she?' (CW 243) is the perennial quest of lover for beloved, of servant for mistress—and finds only rude reflections and mockery. The world of mirrors tells him that 'everything had its double' (*CW* 245) and that the double is not the beloved, but himself. In retrospect, it is instructive to note Goffmann's concern regarding what has been called 'minstrelization', 'whereby the stigmatized person ingratiatingly sets out before normals the full dance of bad qualities imputed to his kind, thereby consolidating a life situation into a clownish role'.[29] Wilde may very well have been projecting his own stigma, his own sense of being a 'court jester', onto the dwarf who does not know he is a monster.

The next distinctly Irish character in Wilde's stories is contained in 'The Fisherman and his Soul', which derives from stories in Lady Wilde's *Ancient Legends of Ireland* and Yeats's *Fairy and Folk Tales of the Irish Peasantry* but which also has obvious thematic similarities between the contemporary Andersen's 'The Little Mermaid' and the later story by Giuseppe di Lampedusa, 'The Professor and the Siren'. The notion of the ondine itself is ubiquitous in European folklore, but, as Norbert Kohl notes, 'The Fisherman and his Soul' 'is strikingly different from the other tales in its scale, its complexity and its decorative style'.[30] With the notable exception of Philip Cohen, however, most critics, including Kohl, have ignored the position of the story 'The Priest's Soul', contained in both Lady Wilde's and Yeats's collections, in the flow of Wilde's writings up to the parable 'The House of Judgment' (1893). Cohen in particular demonstrates the connection between the original story, in which the priest by denying the existence of the soul also denies the existence of heaven, hell *and* purgatory, with 'The House of Judgment', where Man denies God's power to send him to hell because 'in Hell have I always lived' (*CW* 866).[31]

The reason for the neglect of Irish folklore as an influence on Wilde's own tales is threefold: firstly, it is too easy to make comparisons between his work and that of Hans Christian Andersen and the Brothers Grimm; secondly, the tales have been too much overlooked as part and parcel of the fashionable society chatter put out by Wilde as a smoke-screen and a money-raiser; thirdly, and most importantly, because Wilde appears to have little mainstream connection with indigenous (as opposed to *émigré*) Irish writing—a situation which seems to have been largely created by the neglect of the critics—there has seemed little cause for delving into the marginalised Irish folklore when similar instances could be found in more accessible texts.

The story 'The Dead Soldier' in Lady Wilde's *Ancient Legends* is another potential source of the ondine legend, not least because it makes it clear that the belief extends to inland waters:

> There is an island in the Shannon, and if a mermaid is seen sitting in the rocks in the sunshine, the people know that a crime has been committed somewhere near; for she never appears but to announce ill-luck, and she has a spite against mortals, and rejoices at their misfortunes.
>
> One day a young fisherman was drawn by the current towards the island, and he came on a long streak of red blood, and had to sail his boat through it till he reached the rocks where the mermaid was seated; and then the boat went round and round as in a whirlpool, and sank down at last under the waves.
>
> Still he did not lose consciousness. He looked round and saw that he was in a beautiful country, with tall plants growing all over it; and the mermaid came and sang sweetly to him, and offered him wine to drink, but he would not taste it, for it was red like blood. Then he looked down and to his horror he saw a soldier lying on the floor with his throat cut; and all round him was a pool of blood, and he remembered no more till he found himself again in his boat drifting against a hurricane, and suddenly he was dashed upon a rock, where his friends who were in search of him found him, and carried him home. There he heard a strange

thing: a soldier, a deserter from the Athlone Barracks, being pursued had cut his throat and flung himself over the bridge into the river; and this was the very man the young fisher had seen lying a corpse in the mermaid's cave. After this he had no peace or comfort till he went to the priest, who exorcised him and gave him absolution; and then the wicked siren of the rocks troubled him no more, though she still haunts the islands of the Shannon and tries to lure natives to their death.[32]

That this is an Irish version of the ondine legend is obvious; that it occurs in his mother's collection, however, suggests at the least that Wilde was as much aware of this version of the legend as of any other. In Lady Wilde's *Poems*, too, two further freshwater instances of commerce between humans and merfolk are suggested:

> Couldst thou but know our joy below
> Thou wouldst leave the harsh, cold land,
> And dwell in our caves 'neath the glittering waves
> As lord of our sparkling band[33]

—an invitation which the fisherman ultimately accepts. And a long poem translated by Lady Wilde 'from the Danish' entitled 'Undiné' has the following author's note:

> These Undinés ... are gentle, beautiful, harmless creations in the form of a woman, but without a soul. They can attain this only by union with a mortal.... It is a beautiful mythus, and veils a deep and profound meaning... namely, the power of Love to create an intellect, in fact a *soul*, in woman.... Love gives soul to a woman, but takes it from a man.[34]

Another item collected by Yeats, 'The Soul Cages', also suggests the nature of life lived beneath the waves, where humans can converse with merfolk, and the souls of drowned sailors are kept in lobster-pots, and merfolk can come ashore and feast on land with men. Not only is this of a kind with Kingsley's *The Water-Babies*, but it also suggests that a subterranean existence might offer the same alternative life as the 'underground' secrecy which is often forced on the political rebel and the sexual deviant.

But it is 'The Priest's Soul' which contains the largest model for Oscar Wilde's story. The essence of the story is that a priest of enormous intelligence comes to believe that the existence of the soul could only be maintained if it could be seen—a thoroughly Berkeleian proposition. Denial of the existence of the invisible soul leads him to the brink of eternal damnation, encouraged by his pupils who, accepting his wisdom, also accept his precepts (the tale would find its own sequel in Yeats's *The Hour-Glass*). Ultimately he is confronted with a new pupil who offers him a new challenge: 'if he believed he had life to show me his life'. But, objects the priest, 'Life cannot be seen; we have it, but it is invisible.' 'Then,' retorts the pupil, 'if we have life though we may not see it, we may also have a soul, although it is invisible.' At the end of the story the pupil stabs the priest in order to liberate the now visible soul.

Everything about Wilde's future writing is contained here: the nature of the soul, its value, the way life is lived and expressed. In *Dorian Gray* he would present the opposite view—that the soul *is* visible and cannot be dispensed with; but neither pole disproves the fact that the soul is our constant companion and our least and greatest burden.

In 'The Fisherman and his Soul' the word 'soul' is hammered into the story. The mermaid says: 'If only thou wouldst send away thy Soul, then could I love thee,' to which the fisherman responds: 'Of what use is my Soul to me? I cannot see it. I may not touch it. I do not know it.' (*CW* 250) Thus the existence of the soul is called into doubt, and at the same time its extreme value is identified: that which is doubted occupies centre stage. In Wilde's story it is the priest who asseverates the existence of the invisible soul, while the merchants (in a situation which in turn would be reversed by Yeats in *The Countess Cathleen*) repeat: 'Of what use is a man's soul to us? It is not worth a clipped piece of silver.' (*CW* 251)

As in *Dorian Gray*, the story's tendency is towards the separation of self and soul, in order to make the soul visible and of value to the self. The fulcrum of the story, however, is its irony. The soul begs not to be separated, but the fisherman says: 'The world is wide, and there is Heaven also, and Hell, and that dim twilight house that lies between. Go wherever thou wilt, but trouble me not, for my love is calling to me.' (*CW* 256) The sentence is remarkable, firstly since it posits a twilight zone between heaven and hell; and secondly because it grants complete freedom of movement to the soul while binding the fisherman himself to the mermaid's underwater region of love. Subsequently it is the soul which, once a year, describes its adventures to the fisherman, in particular the Mirror of Wisdom in which everything except the looker's face is reflected. Love is superior to wisdom and riches, good and evil. 'He who receiveth back his Soul must keep it with him for ever, and this is his punishment and his reward.' (*CW* 268)

The core of Wilde's Irishness in his storytelling is in the distinction between fiction and myth. As Denis Donoghue has observed, 'fiction is a means of being conscious without further responsibility. A myth may be equally fictive, but it has these quite different qualities: we have not invented it; we have received it from its use by other people'[35]—in fact it has invented *us*. In his stories and plays Wilde receives the mythic wisdom of a previous world and makes it modern.

James Stephens remarked, after reading some of *A House of Pomegranates*, that there were more possibilities in fiction than the two themes he had been considering—philosophy and murder—and that it was admissible to write stories without consequence which can be 'wise on a minimum of thought'.[36] Such a statement, however, conceals more than it reveals: philosophy and murder, we might observe after reading Wilde, are indeed two of the few basic themes available to literature. The narrow line between fable and reality is that between a fictive life and a veristic life. As Wilde said to Gide, 'the most treacherous lies are those nearest the truth',[37] and the story which resulted from Stephens's discovery, *The Charwoman's Daughter*, while depending on 'makebelieve' for its charm, rests on the twin pillars of self-deception and poverty, on the willing suspension of disbelief which can not only make an ugly life beautiful for those 'whose whole lives were tricks'[38] but also reveals the violence of a 'grave and debasing vice'.[39] Throughout Stephens's writing, and nowhere more so than in *The Charwoman's Daughter* and *The Demi-Gods*, philosophy and murder are evident either in person or through their antonyms. Stephens, who wrote extensively in folk idioms, was incapable of departing from the twilight between this world and the otherworld; the word 'unnatural' is always applicable, and his characters, like Wilde himself—Patsy MacCann in *The Demi-Gods* is the chief example—spend most of their time on the margins of society and its conventions. Stephens may very well have had the recently released text of 'De Profundis' in mind in 1914 when he wrote of Patsy MacCann:

> For forty-two years he had existed on the edges of a society which did not recognize him in any way. . . . Laws were for other people, but they were not for him. . . . Religion and morality . . . were not for him either. . . . Between himself and a query he interposed a distance. . . . He stood outside of every social relation, and within an organized humanity he might almost have been reckoned as a different species. . . . In this gigantic underworld he moved with almost absolute freedom.[40]

Stephens goes to the heart of the folk-tale also when he announces: 'Every man from the beginning has one enemy from whom he can never escape, and the story of his lives is the story of his battles with that enemy whom he must draw into his own being before he can himself attain to real being, for an enemy can never be crushed, but every enemy can be won.'[41]

The longest of the society stories is 'Lord Arthur Savile's Crime—A Study of Duty', yet, like the others, it is remarkably thin in plot. Like all his fictions, including *The Picture of Dorian Gray*, which runs to over 80,000 words, it is a parable decorated with social insight and criticism, designed to carry a single moral point from its conception to its conclusion. In this case the 'study of duty' is Wilde's jocular, or perhaps cynical, way of saying that, in order to become happily married, Lord Arthur is obliged to commit a murder, that he is told of his inevitable crime by a chiromantist, and that the seer neatly fits the bill of classical typology ('kill the messenger') by becoming Lord Arthur's victim.

Wilde immediately sets the tone of everything he would write about modern society by mocking its habits and doubting its value. His hostess, Lady Windermere, keeps more of a menagerie than a salon—'All my lions . . . are performing lions, and jump through hoops whenever I ask them' (CW 171)—and sentiments which would abound in his later work originate here: 'The proper basis for marriage is a mutual misunderstanding. No, I am not cynical, I have merely got experience, which, however, is very much the same thing.' (CW 172) Indeed, cynicism, the depiction of a host of characters subordinate to the solitary central protagonist, and a preoccupation with portraits are also features of Wilde's poetry, underlining the fact that identity and discovery were the driving forces of his imagination. It was one prolonged gesture, combining self-confidence with self-abuse.

Equally immediate was the way in which Wilde established that the tone of the story would be 'psychological' in the ambiguous sense which he also established in his letters and poems: 'She looked wonderfully beautiful with her grand ivory throat, her large blue forget-me-not eyes, and her heavy coils of golden hair...they gave her face something of the frame of a saint, with not the little fascination of a sinner. She was a curious psychological study.' (*CW* 168) Linked to this curiosity is 'the secret of remaining young' (*CW* 168).

It should be noted that Wilde himself was seriously interested in palmistry. In 1894 he was anxiously consulting the society fortune-teller Mrs Robinson, who told him: 'I see a very brilliant life for you up to a certain point. Then I see a wall. Beyond the wall I see nothing.' (*L* 358) More importantly, on the première night of *A Woman of No Importance*, 19 April 1893,[42] Wilde, with other guests at the house of the society hostess Blanche Roosevelt, showed his palms to Louis Hamon, who practised palmistry under the name 'Cheiro'. Hamon noted the discrepancy between the left hand (hereditary tendencies) and the right (acquired tendencies). The left hand

> promised the most unusual destiny of brilliancy and uninterrupted success, which was completely broken and ruined at a certain date in the right; a being who will send himself into exile. 'At what date?' he asked rather quietly. 'A few years from now...between your forty-first and forty-second year.'[43]

The discrepancy between left and right was the oxymoron at the centre of Wilde's own life, the heaven and hell in the single imagination. Wilde was extremely susceptible to such predictions, as if the 'book of the hand' could be read as a map of the soul. In 'Lord Arthur Savile's Crime' Lady Windermere says: 'Every one should have their hands told once a month so as to know what not to do.' (*CW* 169) The ambiguity between the avoidance of sin and the evasion of responsibility is crucial.

When he reads Lord Arthur's palm, the chiromantist is circumspect about announcing what he has found. Lord Arthur waits with a 'feeling of dread', a 'sickening sense of coming evil.... His reason revolted against it, and yet he felt that some tragedy was hanging over him, and that he had been suddenly called upon to bear an intolerable burden.' (CW 173–4) When he discovers what he has been fated to do, he wanders through London, insensible of direction, as will Dorian Gray under his own increasing burden of guilt. He sees 'the crooked-back forms of poverty and eld. A strange pity came over him. Were these children of sin and misery predestined to their end, as he to his? Were they, like him, merely the puppets of a monstrous show?' (CW 176) When, however, Lord Arthur discovers the simplicity of murder by tipping the unaware chiromantist into the Thames, the notion of 'tragedy' is reversed. At the conclusion of the tale he attributes his happiness to the fact that the murder has enabled him to live happily ever after. The burden of tragedy, as of prophecy itself, is to live with a knowledge denied by, and to, the rest of the world.

In 'Lord Arthur Savile's Crime', as in all Wilde's society writing, the tone is distinctly laboured, as if the author were fatigued by describing in anything other than elaborate, heavily doom-laden phrases, the tedium of pretence suffered by those living in 'the native land of the hypocrite' (PDG 151). Indeed, there is often a naïveté or even a gauche character to his narrative. By contrast, the tone of the stories for children has a cleverness which is belied by its simplicity: Wilde is much more sympathetic to the supernatural figures of mermaids, moving statues, animals and inanimate objects to which he has given the power of speech, than he is to 'Royal Academicians, disguised as artists' (CW 168) and other luminaries of London society. The natural sympathy, always expressed in supernatural ways, is with the poor in spirit, the marginalised, the misunderstood, or the unbelievable.

In other cases Wilde subverted the moral within his story: thus in 'The Model Millionaire' the reward of virtue by which a gift of a sovereign to a beggar reaps a return gift of £10,000 from the beggar, who is really an eccentric millionaire. But the story, subtitled 'a note of admiration', revolves around the portrait for which the rich man has posed as a beggar, the point being that, because both the model and the picture are so convincing, a transfer is effected by means of which the 'millionaire model' becomes a 'model millionaire'. The incidence of 'word play', as alluded to by Mercier, should not be overlooked. It was more important to Wilde that a society portrait should contain a curious secret than that a simple story should be simply told. It was at all times essential to him to introduce elements which would indicate, if only to himself, his anxieties, motifs such as the washing away of blood in 'The Canterville Ghost' (*CW* 195) or the recurrent theme of a sinful soul and the purity by means of which it can be rescued:

> When a golden girl can win
> Prayer from out the lips of sin,
> When the barren almond bears,
> And a little child gives away its tears,
> Then shall all the house be still,
> And peace come to Canterville. (*CW* 208)

Norbert Kohl has suggested that 'Wilde frequently equated form with "style", which was for him a *conditio sine qua non* of the work of art', and that by 'style' 'he means a linguistic style';[44] elsewhere he has pointed out that 'Wilde was continually giving shape to personal tensions and conflicts, but deliberately choosing a diction that only rarely conformed to the nature of the statement he wished to make'.[45] Although he makes these assertions in relation to Wilde's poems and criticism, they are particularly true of the fictions, since it was Wilde's natural tendency to incorporate a moral into a story which was not necessarily designed to accommodate it. We question the moral because we see only one side of it, and which side that is, is not exactly clear; meanwhile we are puzzled because the narrative form itself does not conform to the conventional unities. As politically incorrect formulations, Wilde's stories convey a morality of a different order.

They are unique because no other teller of tales has so successfully brought together a form and content which derive from such deeply unlike taxonomies.

Nowhere is this more evident than in 'Pen, Pencil and Poison', where the identity of subject and motivation of narrator are so clearly at one, and where the form of the recitation—a 'memoir' or 'study'—is never properly established. 'Pen, Pencil and Poison' makes the assertion that artists are ncessarily 'lacking in wholeness and completeness of nature'. (*CW* 993) Wilde immediately identifies himself with the subject of the 'memoir' by listing Wainewright's attributes—poet, painter, dandy, art critic, antiquarian, writer of prose, forger and 'subtle and secret poisoner'. Elevated to the status of a hero for the originality of his aesthetic and criminal schemes, Wainewright becomes the incarnation of the notions that 'a mask tells us more than a face' (*CW* 995) and that 'one can fancy an intense personality being created out of sin' (*CW* 1007)—a personification of the need for sin as an element in the progress of a nation. The story, like most of Wilde's longer poems, revolves around, and refuses to develop, the theme of Wainewright's irresponsibility as artist and the corresponding need for novelty as a criminal. It lacks the dénouement of the folk-tales in that no final morality is adduced—Wainewright, having been transported to Australia, 'died of apoplexy, his sole living companion being a cat for which he had evinced an extraordinary affection' (*CW* 1007).

Wilde himself referred to 'The Portrait of Mr W.H.' as a 'story...on the subject of Shakespeare's sonnets' (*L* 244, 245), which clearly merges the idea of a fiction with that of history. The literary reconstruction of W.H.'s identity is thus based on fictional biography of which the centrepiece is the portrait itself. Unlike the portrait of Dorian Gray, it is painted not from a real subject but in order to re-present a subject who never existed. Belief in the existence of W.H. depends on prior belief in the authenticity of what one knows to be false. Wilde asserts this at the beginning of the story when the narrator—one of three participants who first reject and then accept the evidence within the sonnets—says that 'we had no right to quarrel with an artist for the conditions under which he chooses to present his work' and that 'to censure an artist for forgery was to confuse an ethical with an aesthetical problem' (*CW* 1150). The inference is clear: art is illusion, and therefore any method is permissible which will enable the artist to achieve a magical effect. Where the allegory of the fairy story or the folk-tale re-presents a subject through the speech of animals (as in 'The Star-Child') or of fireworks ('The Remarkable Rocket'), the ploy in this story is to allegorise the components of the sonnets by means of the portrait as a focus. In *Dorian Gray* and in 'Mr W.H.' the narration continually returns the reader to a covert, illicit picture as the source of the story's energy, just as, in 'Pen, Pencil and Poison', the speaker revisits the mind of Wainewright, within which the experiments in forgery and murder are taking place.

In all cases the writer is reinventing himself by means of the story: it is 'an attempt to realise one's own personality on some imaginative plane out of reach of the trammelling accidents and limitations of real life' (*CW* 1150), and with Wilde's characteristic disclaimer on reality it becomes 'quite a different matter'—out of reach of ordinary reason because it is irreducibly other, inaccessible to any value system but the narrator's own.

There are five participants: Cyril Graham, who originates the theory; Edward Merton, who paints the portrait at Graham's request; George Erskine, who relates the theory and the forgery to the anonymous narrator; the narrator; and the portrait itself. Where in *Dorian Gray* Wilde saw himself in different aspects of the three actors, here he sees himself as the total of the story—as theorist, debater, forger and portrait. It is a statement of the way in which he lived his life, and it is a commentary on the ways of religion. At one point the narrator exclaims: 'The one flaw in the theory is

192 The Thief of Reason

that it presupposes the existence of the person whose existence is the subject of dispute.' (CW 1198) This, however, is
precisely what the narrator eventually acknowledges *in order*
to believe in the theory. '*Credo quia absurdum ut intelligor*' is
Wilde's method of accepting the illogicality of his own existence, but it is also his revelation of the absurdity of believing in God. 'Who was he?' thus becomes a parable of three
pursuits—the flaw in the theory, the identity of the narrator,
and the ontology of the rational faculty. If 'thou art all my
art' and all art is illusion, then the beloved is substantively
illusion, and therefore life and love will be meaningless
unless the illusion is accepted as real. Wilde returns to his
Sphinx in discussing the lines in Sonnet LIII—

> What is your substance, whereof are you made,
> That millions of strange shadows on you tend?

—the meaning of the term 'shadow' being of vital significance, a term applied rhetorically to a portrait or to an actor
in contrast to the reality which portrait or actor represents.
What is the nature of art? What is the nature of love? How
can two 'characters' in life's mystery relate to one another?
—or, as Wilde puts it, 'How is it that you have so many personalities?', going on immediately to talk of 'the truth of acting' and later 'that strange mimicry of life by the living
which is the mode and method of theatric art' (CW 1173).
The ultimate questions are both personal and public. 'Had I
touched upon some secret that my soul desired to conceal?
Or was there no permanence in personality?' (CW 1196) The
identity of the soul itself and the multiplicity and flux of personalities are somehow interrelated. 'Were we to look in
tombs for our real life, and in art for the legend of our days?'
(CW 1196) If Wilde is correct in considering man's future
equally important as his past in determining what he is
today, then the grave as the ultimate destination of the body
is a legitimate place to find ourselves and art is a valid
method of designing a legend for reality.

* * *

Denis Donoghue quotes Yeats to the effect that 'Irish poetry and Irish stories were made to be spoken or sung, while English literature ... has all but completely shaped itself in the printing press'; on which Donoghue comments: 'The novel is the work of an isolated writer in league with a printing press.'[46] In pursuing the course of Wilde's fiction from prose-poem to novel, we have observed this qualitative difference in the modes of storytelling. An Irish story is something to be told *because* it is, literally, fabulous or fantastic; an English one, *because* it is true. If 'Pen, Pencil and Poison' shows Wilde calmly offending both compositional and philosophical reason in his admiration for an aesthetic law-breaker, *The Picture of Dorian Gray* provides us with one of the most succinct statements by Wilde of the various personae in which he envisaged himself, and the circumstances in which they became possible for his essentially fictive imagination. Reacting to adverse criticism of the story, he replied by way of explanation:

> Basil Hallward is what I think I am: Lord Henry what the world thinks of me: Dorian what I would like to be—in other ages, perhaps. (*L* 352)

On the same day he had written to W. E. Henley: 'Work never seems to me a reality, but a way of getting rid of reality.' (*L* 352) Taken together, the two statements reveal a great deal about the way Wilde understood the practicalities of life and also of how they might be combined. As with the balance in the story 'The Fisherman and his Soul', there is a fulcrum, here represented by the word 'perhaps'. It is this difference which distinguishes *Dorian Gray* from James's *The Princess Casamassima*, the only novel of the period with which it might otherwise be measured.

The Picture of Dorian Gray is a simple story of a man and his soul, converted into a portrait of complexity, in which four personae—the artist, the sitter, the sitter as reflected in the portrait, and the *eminence grise* in the life of the sitter—

become one. Wilde saw himself as Basil Hallward, the artist who, because he idolises the sitter, creates his portrait and thus makes possible the parallel development of self and soul in which the picture—the soul—becomes the mirror of imperfection while the self continues to reflect nothing but beauty. He thought that the world saw him as Lord Henry Wotton, the dominant figure in Dorian's dawning self-consciousness, the messenger of a hedonistic philosophy which is both tired and hungry, whose influence—partly through his own words and partly by means of an unspecified book, generally thought to have been Huysmans' *À Rebours*[47]— sends Dorian on his headlong search for sensation and the neglect of his internal equilibrium. Dorian Gray, the beautiful boy whose wilful conduct owes its apparent stability to the compact between himself and the soul which has been transferred to the dimensions of the portrait, would have been Wilde's choice if such conduct had been as morally and ethically possible as it was aesthetically imperative.

Wilde's work in developing the moral dimension of the folk-tale (as we have seen in relation to 'The Fisherman and his Soul') intimately related the historical European folk memory to its new situation in an age of utilitarianism and 'progress'. If a new Hellenistic society could have been achieved, Wilde would have liked to live in its permissive embrace, even though he knew that Hellenism had its own morality and psychology. The idea that it was achievable only 'in other ages' indicates that, in his experience, it could exist only in the mind, not in the vanished past nor in the materialist future; it could exist only in the extra-spatial, extra-temporal, imagined present. This is the meaning of the additional word 'perhaps', which introduces the fact that such a present is entirely conditional; it predicts Beckett's statement: 'Where we have *both* darkness *and* light, there we also have the inexplicable. The key word of my work is *perhaps*.'[48]

Each time Dorian Gray regards his portrait an exchange takes place which seems to intensify the beauty of the one and the moral turpitude of the other, yet their symbiosis means that it is in fact the vileness of Dorian Gray himself which is increased, leaving us to suppose that the portrait suffers from this transfer. As in the case of 'The Fisherman and his Soul', it is the soul which turns to the bad, but while in that story the fisherman is captivated by love, here the soul—or its likeness—is imprisoned in the hidden picture, while the freedom to sin is granted to the outer man. The criticism levelled by the *Daily Chronicle*, that the book emitted 'the mephitic odours of moral and spiritual putrefaction',[49] suggested that the odours were the author's own, whereas the opposite is the case: *Dorian Gray* is an essentially—perhaps excessively—moral tale, a claim, or admission, made by Wilde himself: 'Dorian Gray, having led a life of mere sensation and pleasure, tries to kill conscience, and at that moment kills himself.' (*L* 259) He doubted if he had been able 'to keep the moral in its proper secondary place' (*L* 263), and the idea that *Dorian Gray* is a moral book may be surprising to readers who have accepted the popular view of Wilde as a decadent—and therefore necessarily a corruptive—influence. The notion that 'creation is doomed' is central to Wilde's conception of the portrait in *Dorian Gray*. It suggests that art is pointless, since it continues to circle the inward-looking question *of* personality rather than the outward-looking reasons *for* personality. This is stated in the first pages of *Dorian Gray* where, before the entry of Gray himself, Lord Henry says to Hallward: 'In the wild struggle for existence, we want to have something that endures, and so we fill our minds with rubbish and facts, in the silly hope of keeping our place.' (*PDG* 12) The fact that Lord Henry is normally taken to be speaking facetiously should not obscure the equally interesting fact that within his facetiousness is more than a grain of truth, irresponsible though it may be.

There is no action in the novel. Like Wilde's essays and dialogues, it is an internalised dialogue between the three or four constituent elements of the portrait. When Wilde said in its defence that 'each man sees his own sin in Dorian Gray' (*L* 266), he was pointing out that the book was an *apologia pro*

vita sua for the age at large, that there is an outlawed noble-
man and a perverted telegraph-boy in each of us. As he says
in 'The Critic as Artist', 'The soul [is] the protagonist of life's
tragedy' (CW 1042), and Dorian Gray, as Everyman, leads
with his soul.[50] It was a book for its time, coming three years
after the serialisation of Pater's unfinished *Gaston de Latour*,
five years after his *Marius the Epicurean* and six years after *À
Rebours*, but it also has something in common with *The Wild
Irish Boy* as a record of mental and spiritual evolution.

Certainly Wilde owed much to Pater; yet to the Irish mind
the equivocal status and power of the *word* and of the *book*
were paramount. The dual capacity of the word to traduce
or to transfer culture, the fact that it is indispensable in for-
mulating concepts, and yet is so prone to falsity and unreality, underlines every negotiation between the Irish mind and
the outer world. To the Irish, the notion that 'in the beginning was the Word and the Word was God' might be amended and amplified: 'and the Word was the Book and the Book
was God'; it has a curious resonance within the Irish experience, because it was the logocentric mind of Western imperialism which eroded the heartland of Celtic 'genius' or 'soul'
and imposed its own words and books. The idea that Lord
Henry had 'poisoned' Dorian with a *book* has its parallel in
the fact that Pater had deeply influenced Wilde and his generation with a book, *The Renaissance*. The novel which 'fasci-
nates' and captivates Dorian is 'a novel without a plot . . .
simply a psychological study' (*PDG* 125). Wilde saves the portrait from morbidity in his Preface: 'No artist is ever morbid.
The artist can express everything. Thought and language are
to the artist instruments of an art.' (*PDG* xxxiii) Thus he puts
'thought and language' at the service of art, subjecting them
to a higher purpose and authority, which is (in Paterian terms)
the achievement of the condition of music and, in terms of the
Celtic genius, the mode of poetry. The 'psychological study'
takes the form of a portrait not so much of oils on canvas as of
words on paper which create a dominant and evolving image.
The transfer between the portrait and the subject not only

allows Dorian to view his own sinful progress, but also permits an exchange between Basil Hallward and Lord Henry long after either has ceased to have any material presence in the story; part—perhaps all—of Basil Hallward is in the work of art he has created, and much of Lord Henry is in the mind of the living Dorian. But the negotiations between these elements in the overall 'portrait' or 'image' also serve to highlight the fact that when one 'become[s] the spectator of one's own life' (*PDG* 110) one becomes aware of the discrepancy and the distance between the self and the image.

Dorian Gray declares himself to be in love with his portrait, and that 'it is part of myself' (*PDG* 27), just as Wilde identified himself with his stories; yet two pages later Basil tells him that the portrait is 'the real Dorian' which causes Dorian to ask: 'Am I really like that?' (*PDG* 29) As soon as Dorian detects the first change in the appearance of the portrait, he becomes aware that 'It was certainly strange. . . . It held the secret of life, and told his story.' (*PDG* 90–91) He thus becomes estranged from his 'soul' and decides that 'the portrait was to bear the burden of his shame' (*PDG* 105). It thus becomes possible (in a reversal of the situation in 'The Fisherman and his Soul') to step outside the shadow of his conscience and to observe himself staggering under the burden of a shame which he himself cannot feel. In such clinical fashion he continues until in the final moment of the book he is reunited with his soul and as he 'tries to kill conscience, at that moment kills himself' (*L* 259).

As soon as we realise this discrepancy we find it possible, as Dorian Gray says, to take part in a Greek tragedy, but not to be wounded by it (*PDG* 100); but, as Lord Henry says in deepening the argument, 'we find that we are no longer the actors, but the spectators of the play. Or rather we are both.' (*PDG* 101) The portrait is thus not a mere spectacle, but 'the most magical of mirrors' (*PDG* 106) through which one is called to judgment (*PDG* 119).

It is distinctly possible to suppose that subconsciously Wilde, who had an acute perception of the nature of history, wrote *Dorian Gray* not as a parable simply of 'Everyman' but more specifically as a commentary on the Irish race experience and on what had been lost in that experience. In this he was also profoundly European, in the same stylistic sense as Knut Hamsun, Pádraic Ó Conaire or Brinsley MacNamara. The same 'philosophy and murder' is evident in these writers' brutal reaction to life: stories such as Ó Conaire's 'The Woman at the Window', 'Disillusioned' and 'The Woman on Whom God Laid His Hand' are outstanding for the lyricism which they bring to the themes of revenge and insanity. Here too a fable as pungent as MacNamara's *The Valley of the Squinting Windows* is notable for the *agon* between a young man and the 'enemy' who turns out to be his brother. 'It is reason that has ruined our lives,' cries one victim of reality in Ó Conaire's 'The Woman on Whom God Laid His Hand',[51] and it might stand as the motto for all these works (which might have been Wilde's) which, together, represent a lost generation of Irish fiction.

Wilde was at pains to give plentiful expression throughout his writing to two notions—that 'sin is an essential element in progress' and that 'by its curiosity Sin increases the experience of the race.... The imagination is simply concentrated race-experience.' (CW 1023, 1042) His essay on 'The Rise of Historical Criticism' begins with the idea that progress is part of 'that complex working towards freedom ... the revolt against authority' (CW 1105). It is implicit in his *schema* that the future should build on past denials and nay-saying to all but the experience and aspirations of the race. In *Dorian Gray* Dorian sees this in both public and personal terms:

> As he looked back upon man moving through History, he was haunted by a feeling of loss. So much had been surrendered! and to such little purpose! There had been mad wilful rejections, monstrous forms of self-torture and self-denial, whose origin was fear, and whose result was a degradation infinitely more terrible than that fancied degradation from which, in their igno-

rance, they had sought to escape, Nature, in her wonderful irony, driving out the anchorite to feed with the
wild animals of the desert and giving to the hermit the
beasts of the field as his companions. . . . There were
times when it appeared to Dorian Gray that the whole
of history was merely the record of his own life, not as
he had lived it in act or circumstance, but as his imagination had created it for him, as it had been in his brain
and in his passions. He felt that he had known them all,
those strange terrible figures that had passed across the
stage of the world and made sin so marvellous and art
so full of subtlety. It seemed to him that in some mysterious way their lives had been his own. (*PDG* 130, 144)

As in 'De Profundis' he would identify Christ with the sins
of the world, and himself with Christ, so here Wilde makes
Dorian into the conscience of downtrodden generations
whose great famine and great injustice had marginalised and
degraded his imagination:

> To him, man was a being with myriad lives and myriad
> sensations, a complex multiform creature that bore
> within itself strange legacies of thought and passion,
> and whose very flesh was tainted with the monstrous
> maladies of the dead. (*PDG* 143)

Pushed to the edge of the landmass and to the edge of
endurance, the Celt was reasserting the primacy of imagination, of mythopoeism, against the despotism of fact.

(ii) THE POEMS

The poem with which Wilde chose to open his early, and
only, collection of *Poems* (1881) is 'Hélas!', which he regarded as his most significant:[52]

> To drift with every passion till my soul
> Is a stringed lute on which all winds can play,
> Is it for this that I have given away
> Mine ancient wisdom and austere control?
> Methinks my life is a twice written scroll,
> Scrawled over on some boyish holiday
> With idle songs for pipe and virelay,
> Which do but mar the secret of the whole.
> Surely there was a time I might have trod
> The sunlit heights, and from life's dissonance
> Struck one clear chord to reach the ears of God:
> Is that time dead? lo! with a little rod
> I did but touch the honey of romance—
> And must I lose a soul's inheritance? (CW 709)

Whatever it is that the poet regrets, it is clear that he regards the loss as irreparable and as having a fundamental bearing on his future development. Potential is no longer a future possibility but a past liability, and thus he is condemned to long for a future which is already pluperfect. Henceforth life can only be described in terms of narrative images of the past. As San Juan remarks, 'Wilde, unlike the gallery of live masks that constituted his personality, could not divorce himself from the speaking voice of his poems.'[53] Thus, as San Juan goes on to explain in an important perception,

> throughout his career Wilde persistently sought to com-
> pose a verbal artifice that would be absolute in itself....
> He strove to present a complex exercise in a mode of
> lyrical intensity that would successfully unify multiple
> ways of feeling and thinking in a meaningful totality.[54]

Nevertheless, the temporal disturbance inheres in a corre-sponding semantic disturbance which destabilises the poet. This henceforth was to be his voice, its trope, timbre and tra-jectory defined by both a hesitancy in embarking on an active life of pleasure and a yearning for the passive, con-templative state. Unity was particularly the quest of later Irish writers, most notably Yeats and Joyce. The striving towards what has been called 'a single, unified record of ontogenesis'[55] was a strategy for dealing with an otherwise unlivable situation which consisted of the twin tensions: 'Out of ourselves we can never pass, nor can there be in creation what in the creator was not.' (*CW* 1045)

Wilde's strategy was to turn this mixture of competing elements—the 'deep central emotion'—to creative purpose. It was in many ways an act of translation—the art in which he had first demonstrated his literary prowess—and one in which it was possible for him not only to transmute the literary material into a greater thing by means of its transfer from one language, one ontological construct, to another, but also to effect a change in himself, a heightening of his own awareness of the way in which he was perceived by others. This grounding of the work in the personality of the artist as an autochthonous entity leads in every case to the poet being essential to the creation of poetic meaning. In this sense all Wilde's work—especially that which surprised or perplexed the critics—is extra-canonic in its source, its style and method of composition, and its effect.

'Hélas!' in itself typifies what Douglas Bush has noted as a common feature of Wilde's poems, 'all the traditional elements of romantic Hellenism in all the refinement and purity of decadence'.[56] It also proceeds beyond the dilemma by suggesting that life might become a palimpsest, 'a twice written scroll', and that if the poet could overcome his boyish fears and longings, he might inaugurate a third age of poetry. Wilde had this in mind when he said, in the Preface to *Dorian Gray*: 'All art is at once surface and symbol' and where he also expressed the antithetical nature of the portrait: 'The nineteenth century dislike of Realism is the rage of Caliban seeing his own face in a glass. The nineteenth century dislike of Romanticism is the rage of Caliban not seeing his own face in a glass.' (*PDG* xxxiii) These options—the self-awareness and the self-confusion—are the different sides of the strategies of concealment and disclosure which Wilde would employ throughout his poetry and which would also baffle and infuriate the Victorian establishment in tracking down his real intentions.

The 'farce of aestheticism' was in one sense the continuing revolt of the artist against materialism, of the individual genius against collective mediocrity, but in another sense it was a growing awareness of something more cyclic than perennial, a *fin de siècle* progression towards a showdown between totalitarian forms of authority and microcosmic forces and forms of art. The elements which will suggest, in the one sense romanticism, and in the other decadence, are both present with equal vigour in Wilde's poems. Contemporary reviewers commented on this without realising quite how much potential lay in the equivocation, the commuting between the ancient springs and the modern pit-heads. This is partly because Wilde exploited the uranian strategy of concealment, a poetic genre which consists in veiling the expression of homosexual emotions, and in particular the celebration of the relationship of older men with boys. It aimed at the timelessness which is achieved in Auden's ambiguous 'Lullaby': 'Lay your sleeping head, my love, / Human on my faithless arm'.[57]

Classical and pastoral subjects were the particular territory of the uranians. Thus in Wilde's 'Endymion':

> You cannot choose but know my love
> For he a shepherd's crook doth bear,
> And he is soft as any dove
> And brown and curly is his hair....
> Where is my own true lover gone.
> Where are the lips vermilion? [...]
> Ah! Thou hast young Endymion,
> Thou hast the lips that should be kissed! (CW 750)

'Charmides' (CW 753–70), a morbid account of a young man's love for a statue, also explores the theme of narcissism, the disillusioned self-love which encourages 'a strange and secret smile':

> It is Narcissus, his own paramour,
>> Those are the fond and crimson lips no woman
>>> can allure.

Another uranian method of evasion was substitution, writing a piece about a boy and then making the subject into a girl. Wilde's most obvious substitution was a poem originally entitled 'Wasted Days', first published in *Kottabos* in 1877:

> A fair slim boy not made for this world's pain,
>> With hair of gold thick clustering round his ears,
>> And longing eyes half veiled by foolish tears
> Like bluest water seen through mists of rain,
> Pale cheeks whereon no kiss has left a stain,
>> Red under-lip drawn in for fear of Love,
>> And white throat whiter than the breast of dove—
> Alas! alas! if all should be in vain [...]
>> The boy still dreams, nor knows that night is night,
>> And in the night-time no man gathers fruit.
>>> (*CW* 732)

In *Poems* the verse is retitled 'Madonna Mia', the 'fair slim boy' becomes a 'lily-girl', and the suggestion of impossible seduction is turned into one of hopeless worship:

> A lily-girl, not made for this world's pain,
>> With brown soft hair close braided by her ears,
>> And longing eyes half veiled by slumberous tears
> Like bluest water seen through mists of rain:
> Pale cheeks whereon no line hath left its stain,
>> Red underlip drawn in for fear of love,
>> And white throat, whiter than the silvered dove,
> Through whose wan marble creeps one purple vein.
> Yet, though my lips shall praise her without cease,
>> Even to kiss her feet I am not bold,
>> Being o'ershadowed by the wings of awe,
> Like Dante when he stood with Beatrice
>> Beneath the flaming lion's breast, and saw
>> The seventh Crystal, and the Stair of Gold. (*CW* 732)

As a result of most uranian passion being unrequited—at least in verse—the poet often expresses his inability to find a refuge. Wilde, like Melmoth, found himself condemned to 'travel wearily / And bruise my feet, and drink wine salt with tears' (CW 731)—the typical fate of the outcast, condemned to guilt and shame.

The sense of 'sin', which was most acute in uranian writers, appears often in *Poems* ('My white soul / First kissed the mouth of sin'), and in 'San Miniato' Wilde writes:

> O listen ere the searching sun
> Show to the world my sin and shame (CW 725)

—an extremely early use in this context of 'shame'. 'Shame', in uranian verse, was accompanied by 'anguish' and 'remorse'. Timothy d'Arch Smith has suggested that André Raffalovich's use in 1885 of the word 'shame' 'may very well be the first use of the word . . . to imply homosexual love':[58]

> The first is Beauty clad in Love's proud weeds,
> And Love the second with the badge of grief,
> A thorny wreath rose-red, a breast that bleeds
> The third is Sorrow: but men call her Shame.[59]

As we see from 'San Miniato', however, Wilde used the word in contexts which at least imply, and, we might construe, make explicit, the feeling of remorse to which his love of young men gives rise.

In his very thorough account of uranian verse in late-Victorian and Edwardian England, d'Arch Smith explores its 'themes and philosophies': the fleeting days of boyhood; guilt; the angelic vision; the superiority of uranian love (which John Gray called 'passing the love of women');[60] methods of concealment; and the frequent social contrasts between lover and beloved.[61] On sexual love, he quotes from Montague Summers's 1907 *Antinous and other poems* (which epitomises the use of classical allusions to such figures as Adonis, Hyacinth, Narcissus and Hylas):

We worship love, adore him,
Low in the dust before him
We bow down, and implore him,
Give thanks for our sweet Shame.[62]

The loss of youth, both in oneself and the beloved, is of paramount regret; next is the remorse felt for what the conscience tells the poet is an unnatural act; and finally the leitmotif for homosexual love between man and boy, and its passing, is 'bitter-sweet', called by the Greeks γλυκυπικρος ἐρως, a title which Wilde gave to his final piece in *Poems* (thus, in company with 'Hélas!', framing the book's contents) —a poem which discusses the aspirations and failure of uranian love and its consequences:

Sweet, I blame you not, for mine the fault is, had I not
been made of common clay
I had climbed the higher heights unclimbed yet, seen
the fuller air, the larger day. (*CW* 802)

In 'The Burden of Itys' Wilde unequivocally expresses the torture of homosexual love:

... memories of Salmacis

Who is not boy nor girl and yet is both,
Fed by two fires and unsatisfied
Through their excess, each passion being loth
For love's own sake to leave the other's side
Yet killing love by staying ... (*CW* 739)

Salmacis was a fountain which made effeminate all who drank of it: Hermaphrodite changed his sex there. The final poem, as we have seen, is called in Greek 'bitter-sweet love'—the oxymoron at the basis of 'not boy nor girl yet both', but evasively muted in its English title, 'Flower of Love'. It suggests that Wilde may have had at least one 'platonic' affair at Oxford: in an amplification of 'Hélas!' he tells his beloved:

From the wildness of my wasted passion I had struck a
                                        better, clearer song [...]
I have made my choice, have loved my poems, and though
                            my youth is gone in wasted days,
I have found the lover's crown of myrtle better than the
                            poet's crown of bays. (*CW* 802–3)

In addition to the sexual concealment there is a hitherto
unperceived political form of uranianism in Wilde's verse,
whereby he acts as a republican while claiming to be part of
empire. Within the republican vigour of 'Ave Imperatrix'
there is nevertheless a strong whiff of Englishness:

> What profit now that we have bound
>   The whole world round with nets of gold,
> If hidden in our heart is found
>   The care that groweth never old?
>
> What profit that our galleys ride,
>   Pine-forest-like, on every main?
> Ruin and wreck are at our side,
>   Grim warders of the House of Pain.
>
> Where are the brave, the strong, the fleet?
>   Where is our English chivalry?
> Wild grasses are their burial-sheet,
>   And sobbing waves their threnody. (*CW* 712)

It can, of course, be argued that in the nineteenth century
Irishmen regarded London as the centre of the Empire of
which they were members, and that 'the whole world' was
their oyster. It can also be argued that for an Oxford-educated,
London-domiciled writer, associated with Ruskin and other
literary prophets, it would have been quite normal to look
for a reform of a society which had (as we are reminded in
'To Milton') already experienced a form of republicanism. It
is certainly true that the editor of the *Irish Monthly* objected
to Wilde's expression 'O poet-painter of our English Land' in

the poem 'The Grave of Keats', and that Wilde defended it by saying: 'It is a noble privilege to count oneself of the same race as Keats or Shakespeare' (*L* 40), but the identification was not with a nationality but with the race of poets.

To the son of the 'regal republic', there was a more insidious and ambivalent reason for using the possessive 'our', the identification 'we', just as he had attempted to identify himself with the heterosexual poets. Many others of these poems, 'Sonnet to Liberty', 'Libertatis Sacra Fames' and 'Theoretikos', for example, reveal that Wilde the Irishman saw England as a target, a place where action reaped reaction, a source of great poetry but also of great woe for his own race. Writing to Gladstone to present these very *Poems*, he acknowledged 'the one English statesman who has understood us, who has sympathised with us, whom we now claim as our leader, and who, we know well, will lead us to the grandest and justest political victory of this age' (*L* 231)— this was in 1888 at the height of the Home Rule controversy and on the eve of the fall of Parnell—'one whom I, and all who have Celtic blood in their veins, must ever honour and revere, and to whom my country is so deeply indebted' (*L* 218). To a Scotsman, James Nicol Dunn, managing editor of the *Scots Observer*, he wrote: 'I hear your paper is anti-Home Rule, and I am a most recalcitrant patriot.' (*L* 232)

It is thus possible to read the word 'our' as representative of a Celtic world of the imagination which might also have a political role to play in what most Irishmen at the time would have regarded as the likely outcome of events—an Ireland autonomous but within the Empire. It is also possible that Wilde genuinely vacillated between open revolt in the face of English hegemony and the secret sustenance of the spirit of that revolt. The lines in 'Sonnet to Liberty'

These Christs that die upon the barricades,
God knows it I am with them, in some things (*CW* 709)

are consummately equivocal.

As with *Dorian Gray*, where it is easy not to know the nature of Dorian's offences, Wilde's sexual and political ambivalence was expressive of what was hinted at no less than of what was concealed. There is considerable scope for a separate investigation of how Wilde may have employed language ancient and modern to construct a personal semiotic system which would carry his private burdens in a meaningful and yet surreptitious way: I have in mind particularly Steiner's observation that

> We know absurdly little about the vital congruence of eros and language. Oscar Wilde's bilingualism may be an expressive enactment of sexual duality, a speech-symbol for the new rights of experiment and instability he claimed for the life of the artist. Here, as at other important points, Wilde is one of the true sources of the modern tone.[63]

The translation involved in such linguistic manoeuvres is intensely concerned with secrecy, with the approach to and the retreat from a veiled statue. This, as we shall see, took the form in Wilde's poetry of a massive act of displacement and dissembling in relation to the Sphinx which reverses the proposition that a translation should be faithful.

I have been severely criticised by Patricia Flanagan Behrendt in her *Oscar Wilde: Eros and Aesthetics* for reading more into the poems, particularly 'Hélas!', than their verbal content will bear:

> The specifically homoerotic connotations which critics like Pine attach to the 'little rod' that touched 'the honey of romance' derive less from the actual lines themselves, which are simply erotically suggestive in the context of the entire poem, than from a complex set of associations often inferred and assumed rather than defined

and explained. In other words, knowledge of Wilde's homosexuality which the critic brings to the work seems often to be the primary—perhaps the only—justification for reading certain imagery as homoerotic, especially since authors like Pine, for example, do not provide the reader with a full literary analysis in support of their claims; they do not focus on the work itself as Wilde would have preferred.... For Pine and others, Wilde's known homosexuality merely illuminates the 'remorse' of Wilde's poems; explains Wilde's 'dilemma'; and echoes what Pine already knows: that Wilde was a homosexual.[64]

Behrendt particularly objects to my use of the fact that lines from the Book of Samuel—'I did but taste a little honey with the end of the rod that was in my hand, and lo, I must die'— which spring directly from the relationship of Saul and Jonathan, had previously been quoted by Pater in a homosexual context in his essay on Wincklemann. I have already stated my grounds for treating both Wilde's Irishness and his homosexuality as the source of his alienation from normative society and from himself. In respect of the specific criticism that I display posterior knowledge to illuminate texts, I should state further that the 'complex associations' to which Behrendt alludes are not in fact as complex as she imagines. As I pointed out in my original *Oscar Wilde*, the honey-rod association is a clear one. A virgin reading of 'Hélas!' would, as Behrendt asserts, certainly indicate an anxiety and an erotic suggestiveness on the poet's part. And if we read 'Ave Imperatrix' as an English poem, then we derive certain knowledge of the author's political disquiet. But if we read a work in translation—and it is clearly my thesis that all Wilde's work is in some sense a translation— we are bereft of the markers necessary to 'focus on the work itself'. How might we approach a non-specific text published in a language other than the original—Proust's *Swann's Way*, for example? How are we to interpret the frequent expression of 'remorse' in Wilde's poems? It is undoubtedly true that Wilde functioned (as Behrendt implies) in a literary climate where sexual and aesthetic politics were a prime concern, and there is a certain tendency in the face of such criticism as Behrendt's to suspect that one's partial and sectoral approach might be too strict. Yet if we divest William Morris's decorative art of his socialism, or John Clare's lack of centre of his madness, what is left? The merely beautiful; a 'stylistic arrangement', to anticipate Yeats, but of what order of experience? If we do not join Wilde's Irishness and his homosexuality—or indeed his social status or his pre-eminent intellect —to his written work, we will be left with an aesthetic crusade which will be largely without direction. From whom or what was Wilde concealing his intentions, and what were those intentions? What is meant by 'ancient wisdom' or 'austere control'? Control over what? Are we not to question the long shadow of identity which pervades the Irish novel, the significance of the portrait or the 'odd story in the family'? Text without context may well reward analysis in certain situations—the clinical identification of ideological or stylistic indebtedness or aspirations, the arid dissection of Ruskin's or Arnold's litanies—but it cannot properly recognise the reasons for either Pater's hesitancy or his stumbling enthusiasms, nor can it repay in due coin the tenderness of Auden's ambiguity.

The dismissive tone of most contemporary critics of *Poems* was due to the almost ubiquitous appearance of 'remorse' as a concomitant of the discovery of the soul, and gave a sorry down-turn to the expression of aestheticism. In Wilde's case, not only do his poems frequently carry expressions of 'remorse', but also the popular perception of him, however lightheartedly, as a poseur, carried an undertone of at the best mischief and at the worst something far more sinister. The continual admonition to the soul to depart into happier realms is linked both to artistic revolt against materialism

and to the transition from classical paganism to modern
Christianity:

> Come out of it, my Soul, thou art not fit
> For this vile traffic-house, where day by day
> Wisdom and reverence are sold at mart.
> > (CW 716: 'Theoretikos')

> For Pan is dead, and all the wantoning
> > By secret glade and devious haunt is o'er:
> > Young Hylas seeks the water-springs no more;
> Great Pan is dead, and Mary's son is King.
> > (CW 716: 'Santa Decca')

It would appear that the soul has nowhere to go: the past is
irrecoverable and the present is impossible. It remains for
the soul to re-create that irredeemable past in isolation, to construct an autonomous universe where it can rest in peace, a
'Garden of Eros' where one can contemplate the ideal by the
strategy of 'philosophizing with love'.

In the poem 'The Garden of Eros' Keats, Byron and
Swinburne are evoked as poets capable of summoning such
a condition into existence, while Morris is intimated as the
one living poet who has made 'an earthly paradise' (CW 721)
with Rossetti as the painter who can depict it in images. The
poet characterises himself as 'the last Endymion' (CW 722)—
Endymion being the young man to whom Jupiter granted
everlasting youth and who enjoyed the favours of Diana and
thus of the moon. He is trapped by 'the age of Clay' (CW 722),
whereas

> > I was nurtured otherwise, my soul
> Passes from higher heights of life to a more supreme goal.
> > (CW 723)

The idea of a young man blessed with, and at the same time
condemned to, everlasting life, striving to retain control of a
soul which is put upon by the difference between his

'supreme goal' and his present realities, is the encounter at the centre of *The Picture of Dorian Gray*. The tensions set up between the Self and the Soul throughout Wilde's poems, from the earliest pseudo-love lyrics to *The Ballad of Reading Gaol*, are never resolved. The chief penalty for the soul attempting to live in the gap between the two is the sense of 'wasted days' —the expression undulates across the poems with that of remorse:

> Or our high Gods have sick and wearied grown
> Of all our endless sins, our vain endeavour
> For wasted days of youth to make atone
> (CW 780: 'Panthea')

> Is it thy will that I should wax and wane,
> Barter my cloth of gold for hodden grey,
> And at thy pleasure weave that web of pain
> Whose brightest threads are each a wasted day?
> (CW 785: 'Apologia')

Thus while the soul may be imprisoned in poetry, the poet himself is liberated by the experience of love, the intensity of which is epicurean by Pater's standards, if the derivative stanza in 'Humanitad' can be relied on:

> To burn with one clear flame, to stand erect
> In natural honour, not to bend the knee
> In profitless prostrations whose effect
> Is by itself condemned, what alchemy
> Can teach me this? (CW 793)

The questioning tone indicates that he is unsure of his pathway; the need to be free and unfettered has never been more clearly professed. As in his essay *The Soul of Man under Socialism*, Wilde was concerned with both collective and individual freedom—the latter was usually called 'Liberty' in the poems. Both are equivocal, since each depends for its achievement on extraneous factors, but the poet's own freedom predominates. As a classical scholar, Wilde would have known that the Greek word for freedom, ἐλευθερια, derived from the concept of movement—freedom to go as I wish (ἐλευθειν ὁπος ἐρω)—and this stands behind the opening aspiration of 'Hélas!': 'To drift with every passion'. As songs of freedom, therefore, Wilde's poems are unequivocal in their lust, yet tempered by their experience of love: 'lo, with a little rod / I did but touch the honey of romance'. It is not that he *knows* he will lose his inheritance, but that it has been clearly intimated to him that he *may* lose it.

Wilde was, in Genet's phrase, *un captif amoureux*,[65] at once the author and the victim of a consuming passion as demanding as any political imperative. It was an invisible passion, which evaporated as soon as it was articulated, evanescent *en plein air* yet permanently resident in, and in conflict with, his conscience.

The ambivalence of Wilde's early poems is also demonstrated in his attitude to the idea of a house as a home for his soul. In 'Apologia' he asked:

> Is it thy will—Love that I love so well—
>   That my Soul's House should be a tortured spot
> Wherein, like evil paramours, must dwell
>   The quenchless flame, the worm that dieth not?
>
> (CW 785)

The questioner and the respondent are one, since the dominant love is self-engendered; in 'Taedium Vitae' [weariness of life] the traveller says:

>   better the lowliest roof
> Fit for the meanest kind to sojourn in,
> Than to go back to that hoarse cave of strife
> Where my white soul first kissed the mouth of sin.
>
> (CW 788)

The most extreme example of this ambivalence in the early poems is 'The Harlot's House', where the poet and his love (his soul) watch in fascination a dance of death performed by 'clockwork puppet[s]', 'phantom lover[s]' and 'horrible marionette[s]':

> But she—she heard the violin,
> And left my side, and entered in:
> Love passed into the house of lust. (CW 789)

Wilde seemed to associate the evaporation of love with the arrival of the dawn:

> Then suddenly the tune went false,
> The dancers wearied of the waltz,
> The shadows ceased to wheel and whirl.
>
> And down the long and silent street,
> The dawn, with silver-sandalled feet,
> Crept like a frightened girl. (CW 790)

It is an image frequently encountered in Wilde's poetry and prose, and demonstrates his capacity to encapsulate, in a particular *tableau vivant*, a single verbal image. Here the opposing tensions of endogamy/exogamy are expressed in terms of love/lust, man/woman, darkness/light. Elsewhere the contrasts incorporate the Ireland/England axis and that of imagination/reason. The dawn, in particular, has this affective property of eliciting fear and yet appearing as an innocent girl—

> I waked at last, and saw the timorous dawn
> Peer with gray face into my darkened room
> (CW 824: 'Artist's Dream')
>
> across the silent lawn
> In sea-green vest the morning steals
> And to love's frightened eyes reveals
> The long white fingers of the dawn
> (CW 726: 'By the Arno')

—and has the capacity to transform the subject of beauty into an object of mere lust. It is a peculiarly Irish phenomenon, which Wilde shared with Yeats, who would write at the opening of *The Only Jealousy of Emer*:

> A woman's beauty is like a white
> Frail bird, a white sea-bird alone . . . A strange
> unserviceable thing.[66]

In 'Impression du Matin' the dawn perverts Keats's 'La Belle Dame Sans Merci':

> But one pale woman all alone,
> The daylight kissing her wan hair,
> Loitered beneath the gas lamps' flare,
> With lips of flame and heart of stone. (CW 745)

It is a sentiment which we also encounter in Wilde's final poem, *The Ballad of Reading Gaol*, which employs the same narrative technique of much of the earlier verse, by portraying a man, or a conscience, on the move, in this case trudging the regular rhythm of the prison yard. Here love has entered the house of lust in the person of the brave man who has killed because it is inevitable that we kill the object of our love, thus losing whatever freedom we had enjoyed up to that point, and submitting to the harsh routine of the place of sin. The poet identifies with the murderer as prisoners actually bond together in defiance, and acceptance, of the law; the murderer's death becomes his own—

> I groped my way
> Into my numbered tomb (CW 849)

—and their fate as outcasts is sealed:

> A prison wall was round us both,
> Two outcast men we were:

> The world had thrust us from its heart,
> And God from out His care:
> And the iron gin that waits for Sin
> Had caught us in its snare. (CW 847)

(The trap for Wilde's soul which Father Bowden identified may well have recurred as Wilde wrote this.) As with the earlier poems, the notion of 'Shame' is revisited, in echoes of 'The Harlot's House': here 'marionettes' taunt the inmates:

> 'Oho!' they cried 'The world is wide,
> But fettered limbs go lame!
> And once, or twice, to throw the dice
> Is a gentlemanly game,
> But he does not win who plays with Sin
> In the secret House of Shame.' (CW 851)

It becomes clear, as Wilde himself, the prisoner of Reading, accompanies his *alter ego* around the yard, that the rhythm is serving to inculcate the fact that all our lives are spent within these walls, that the 'house of shame' is ever present in our thoughts and actions. Although his own experience of prison life, and the fact of the execution of Charles Wooldridge, the trooper in the Royal Horse Guards, for the murder of his wife, had deepened Wilde's sense of his personal tragedy, the recurrent vocabulary is that of the poems written up to twenty years earlier, because the emotions are the same. Wilde's imprisonment and subsequent suffering merely confirmed what he had known as a college student and indicates that his life had been lived in the full consciousness that a progression from joy to horror, from loving to sinning, was inevitable once one put thought into action.[67]

In all Wilde's long poems the singularity of the imagery is striking. 'Humanitad', consisting of seventy-three six-line stanzas, like the even longer 'Charmides', reads like a Victorian novel rather than a neo-classical poem. All human, superhuman and vegetable life is there. Just as he had said that Browning was pre-eminently a writer of fiction who 'used poetry as a medium for writing in prose' (*CW* 1013), so Wilde flaunts vocabulary, pushing syntax and scansion to the limits in painting vast canvases—and yet the experience gained by the reader is minimal, and, one feels, intentionally so. Running through all the longer poems is the theme of shame after illicit love, love stolen or misaddressed. Within every bud of nature is a worm, 'some evil thing' (*CW* 793), and this panoramic account of a humanity already mortally diseased by its own innate badness ironically contemplates the impossible prospect of man reconciled to nature, of body reintegrated once more with soul.

Little attention has been paid to *The Sphinx*, the single poem which, with 'Hélas!', runs as a commentary and connecting thread through all Wilde's work, and which represents the past, woman, poetry and his own homosexual nature. Wilde allegedly began it at Oxford and continued to revisit it for twenty years until its eventual publication in 1894. In his Oxford commonplace book he signposted the poem when he wrote of the Sphinx: 'Those who do not try to answer her questions are annihilated—and often he who solves her riddle comes to no good end.' (*CPB* 140–41) The note is thoroughly classical in its realism: it acknowledges the necessity of the dilemma, it submits to the exercise of fate, and it recognises that both to ignore and to obey the Sphinx is to suffer. The poet's temptation is to lie somewhere between silence and an answer, but the poem itself equivocates throughout its 174 lines by piling rhyme upon unlikely rhyme and adjective on encrusted adjective—a strategy to compensate for the poet's failure to come to the point.

The Sphinx is oxymoronic—'exquisite grotesque! half woman and half animal!' (*CW* 835), the element which connects the possible with the impossible. An obvious source for the Sphinx as a resident terror and torment of the conscience is 'The Raven' by 'le grand poète celtique' (*L* 288), Edgar Allan Poe:

> suddenly there came a tapping,
> As of some one gently rapping, rapping
> at my chamber door.[68]

It becomes

> the fowl whose fiery eyes now burned
> into my bosom's core

and when asked its name gives only the ambiguous reply 'Nevermore'.

But although such an emblematic presence is evocative, there is only the merest indication of what is evoked, of what it is the emblem. Much of the Sphinx's fascination will have been suggested by Lady Wilde's account of cats: mentioning the venerability of the Egyptian cat, she observed:

> The Irish have always looked on cats as evil and mysteriously connected with some demoniacal influence. . . .
> It is believed that the devil often assumes the form of these animals. . . . [Black cats] are endowed with reason
> . . . . Their temperament is exceedingly unamiable, they are artful, malignant, and skilled in deception. . . . Cats
> have truly something awful in them. According to the popular belief they know everything that is said, and
> can take various shapes through their demoniac power.[69]

The inhabitant of Wilde's study has all these properties, but it is clear that he evoked the Sphinx itself as the emblem of his enigmatic soul, in order to signify—to himself more than to the reader of this intensely private poem—that the only possible ploy is to find space between question and answer. The most obvious allusion in the classical world is that of the oracle—'it neither tells nor conceals, but hints'. Wilde would have been fully conscious that from the original Greek, σημαινει [*semanei*], descends the entire history and future of human meaning, *semantics*. That which is signed, that which is indicated but neither uttered nor falsified, is the answer between, the only ontological course possible for the language-animal, yet the course most open to misunderstanding and violence. Wilde's was thus both a supremely personal and a uniquely public statement.

Here too the traitorous dawn has been at work:

> What songless tongueless ghost of sin crept through
> the curtains of the night,
> And saw my taper turning bright, and knocked, and
> bade you enter in? (CW 841)

As between Salomé and Iokanaan, there is a mutual fascination and antipathy. The poet tells his Sphinx:

> Your eyes are like fantastic moons that shiver in
> some stagnant lake,
> Your tongue is like a scarlet snake that dances to
> fantastic tunes (CW 841)

and he is both enamoured of, and repulsed by, the silent reproach which this resident conscience exercises before him:

> Get hence, you loathsome mystery! Hideous animal,
> get hence!
> You wake in me each bestial sense, you make me
> what I would not be. (CW 842)

The same difficulty will be encountered in Yeats's 'Anima Hominis': 'I think it was Heraclitus who said: the Daimon is our destiny. When I think of life as a struggle with the Daimon... I understand why there is a deep enmity between a man and his destiny, and why a man loves nothing but his destiny.'[70] Elsewhere, in 'Anima Mundi', he says: 'I am in the place where the Daimon is, but I do not think he is with me until I begin to make a new personality.'[71] Yeats sees the Daimon as male; Wilde sees the Sphinx as 'that "sweet marble monster" of both sexes' (*CW* 996). Both, however, recognise that it is unnatural and unworldly yet intimately related to the self. In the Sphinx he sees both monster and himself and knows that his days will henceforth be spent as liar and thief, a murderer in the service of a monster driven by the irreconcilable personalities of male and female. Not only does the Sphinx contain the poet's secret, but that of all history. The presence or non-presence, within the poet, of the two participants in history and family life, is *the* question. Henceforth, having looked in the face of this most fundamental of dilemmas, he will, like Genet, 'engage in a dialogue with himself through the intermediary of things'.[72]

(iii) THE LETTERS

It has frequently been said, since their appearance in one collection in 1962, that Wilde's *Letters* are a major source-book for his life. But what characteristics do they disclose? Cynicism, deceit, candour, hysteria, elegance, charm, but seldom real wit or more than a superficial intelligence. As an index to Wilde's personality, they suggest that he was an astonishingly artificial person by nature rather than by construct, a heterodox composition of types and styles. They were the method of his self-dramatisation, of self-creation and, indeed, of self-discovery.

'All trials are trials for one's life, just as all sentences are sentences of death,' Wilde wrote in his longest letter, 'De Profundis', written in Reading Prison to Lord Alfred Douglas (*L* 409–10). It was a method of reshaping and restyling his life, but we do not have to go so far into his short career to find him writing in such fateful terms. As a gauge of his poses, all his letters, from the affectionate and dutiful, even ingratiating, tone of his adolescence, to the submissive yet hopeful timbre of his Parisian débâcle, suggest a careful composition, an arrangement of moods and choice ideas. Even a card accepting or refusing an invitation can take on the character of a deliberate affectation, yet nowhere did Wilde give away the fact: despite the intention, the effect is achieved without apparent artifice.

In Reading he had time to bring these moods to a more schematic form, but 'De Profundis' ranks as no more than an *apologia* for a life which had proceeded as he had conceived it *ab initio* as a critical path to doom. 'The trivial in thought and action is charming. I had made it the keystone of a very brilliant philosophy,' he said in 'De Profundis' (*L* 432), yet it sums up the play which he had made of his first fictions—moreover, it was a part of those fictions.

Wilde had always known what he expressed in Reading, that 'Modern life is complex and relative. . . . To render the first we require atmosphere with its subtlety of *nuances*, of suggestion, of strange perspectives: as for the second we require background.' (*L* 460) In his two novellas, to which in length 'De Profundis' is comparable, Wilde had brought the suggestive to a high art, while in his poems he had introduced 'strange perspectives' on every subject he addressed; his shorter stories and parables had emanated from, and were permeated by, the 'background' of the Irish bardic tradition which made them stranger than those of Andersen or Grimm by virtue of the access to the unseen world.

His greatest achievement in 'De Profundis' was to make a fiction of his own life: his *apologia* was not an account of what he had done or how he had lived, but of what he had set out to do and how he now saw that achievement, unaware of any discrepancy between what he saw and the way he was perceived as saying it. Making claims for his unique contribution to, and conquest of, all art form, he said:

> I awoke the imagination of my century so that it created myth and legend around me: I summed up all systems in a phrase, and all existence in an epigram.
>
> Along with these things, I had things that were different. I let myself be lured into long spells of senseless and sensual ease. I amused myself with being a *flâneur*,

a dandy, a man of fashion. I surrounded myself with
the smaller natures and the meaner minds. I became
the spendthrift of my own genius, and to waste an eternal youth gave me a curious joy. Tired of being on the
heights I deliberately went to the depths in the search
for new sensations. What the paradox was to me in the
sphere of thought, perversity became to me in the
sphere of passion. (*L* 466)

The most striking aspect of this abject confession / prodi-
gious claim is that at first sight it appears to be a monstrous
confection of egoism and self-deception, an audacity of monomaniac proportions. Yet on further inspection it becomes
clear that although it never ceases to be preposterous, it is
nevertheless *true*: Wilde *did* succeed in persuading people
that he could sum up 'all existence in a paradox', and he had
made the reversal of the functions of life and art the centrepiece of his dialogues. Whether or not he believed in what
he was doing is immaterial. In flattening the distinctions
between art forms, and in introducing to each art form the
strangeness of his perspectives, he subjectivised everything
he wrote so that it became entirely personal, yet so extraordinary was he that he persuaded readers and listeners of its
universality. The *apologia* is an exceptionally Irish reading of
his own book, claiming difference and inversion as the centre-
points around which the mere subject-matter was taught to
revolve. Even in describing his own lifestyle, difference
became the distinguishing feature as he made life a fiction
and fiction a life. He lived the unbelief of his own constructs.
In becoming the dandy he was merely laying claim to the
future which, he had persuaded playgoers, was the absolutely modern thing to do. To marry art and philosophy was both
the ancient pursuit which he had learned from his classical
reading and the new trick which metamorphosed the stage
and the library. 'Truth in Art is the unity of a thing with itself'
(*L* 473) is one way of describing the identity of the symbol and
the symbolised, the existence of nothing but the mask.

* * *

For a biographical note prefacing a French newspaper feature on himself in 1891 Wilde had suggested, in a letter to the writer, that he should be described as the son of Sir William Wilde, celebrated archaeologist and man of letters, and as a descendant of the author of *Melmoth*. At first sight, it seems strange that he should refer neither to his father's world-renowned medical achievements nor to his mother's work. Yet it was, as always, a deliberate artificiality, designed to make a connection between the titled parent involved in one form of historical study and 'l'étrange romancier Maturin, l'ami de Goethe, de Byron, et de Scott' (*ML* 103): it was an archaeology of the gothic, an exercise in atmospherics. Wilde lived by reference, in relation to cardinal points of the affection which constantly recur in his correspondence. Just as 'De Profundis' continually invokes Christ as a role-model for the artist, so Wilde was recruiting Christ as early as 1876 in a letter to an Oxford friend in which he discusses a crisis of faith: 'Since Christ the dead world has woke up from sleep. Since him we have lived. I think the greatest proof of the Incarnation aspect of Christianity is its whole career of noble men and thoughts and not the mere narration of unauthenticated histories'. (*L* 20) Thus the concept of the hero supersedes that of time. This is a vital element in Wilde's mythology for two main reasons: firstly, it enables him, like his parents' friends such as Ferguson and Petrie, to connect pre-history with modernism; secondly, and as a consequence, it made it possible to reintroduce the idea of fate, without which one would be aimless in one's quest for meaning. If one is doomed to failure, and if there can be a redemptive figure in the hero, and if one can become that hero, the identification of man and fate is secure, even in defeat, since one can redeem oneself. It is autobiography masquerading as biography, and, moreover, written before the life is lived.

Wilde's letters, like all his writing, are morbidly concerned with sin, death and love. Many employ the oxymoron of 'perfect and poisonous' to describe the critical path, and accept sin as the consequence of love, and death as the end of sin.

Wilde describes Moranzone, the catalyst of revenge in *The Duchess of Padua*, as 'the black spectre of the past moving like Destiny through the scene' (*L* 137). 'Death and Love seem to walk on either hand as I go through life: they are the only things I think of, their wings shadow me,' he wrote at the height of his powers (*L* 358). The note of apprehension struck in melodrama at the entrance, or even the mere mention, of the villain is never far from his pen, and is always in his imagination. The sense of doom experienced by Lord Arthur Savile as an inescapable burden was inalienably Wilde's. As with the Canterville Ghost, there was a spirit waiting always to be appeased and laid to rest. 'My romance is a tragedy of course, but it is none the less a romance,' he wrote after imprisonment (*L* 648), but it is present in some of his earliest letters. Again, discussing *The Duchess of Padua*, he said that 'sympathy [of the audience for a character] must not be merely artificial, it must have its intellectual basis'—thus romance actually depends on tragedy for its proper effect: 'Above all, it must be summed up for them briefly in the form of thought: audiences are well meaning but very stupid.' (*L* 139) This was Wilde's method of underpinning the romantic with the classical, by means of which, in *Salomé*, he created a truly decadent spectacle because it depends only on the twin internal dynamics of lust and fate, of innocence and cruelty, for its melodramatic effect. 'Emotion is momentary, ceases with the fall of the curtain, and cannot be remembered, or if remembered is thought a weakness, but intellect is eternal.' (*L* 140) Behind these words Wilde would have had in mind the dénouement of his parable 'The Artist', that Joy lives only a moment but Sorrow lasts for ever. 'Art is the mathematical result of the emotional desire for beauty. If it is not thought out, it is nothing.' (*L* 143) At base, the playwright must learn the classical rules, that the tragic is also comic and is intensified by comic relief: some lines in *Salomé* are farcical and would be utterly risible were it not for the fact that Herod hears the beating of the wings of the angel of death, as Wilde in his own life sensed the presence of 'Doom that walks always swiftly, because she goes to the shedding of blood' (*L* 440). 'The artistic life is a long and lovely suicide, and I am glad that it is so.' (*L* 185)

The coincidence of love and death is not merely a commonplace of what Mario Praz has called 'the romantic agony';[73] it is at the core of Celtic mythology, and in particular in the legend of Tristan and Iseult, played out on the shores of Ireland, Cornwall and Brittany. Despite Wilde's homosexuality and his socialising, there is a sense in which the doom motif, the love or friendship under sentence of betrayal or death, is a modern restatement of the perennial love-theme.

When E. W. Godwin was designing the 'house beautiful', of which Constance Wilde was to be the châtelaine, Wilde wrote to him that 'the house *must* be a success' (*L* 166). His private life and his public career were both deliberate constructs: he was busy 'civilising the provinces with my remarkable lectures', and from a provincial centre such as Bristol, Leeds or Edinburgh he was writing to Godwin on close details of the house decoration, while also writing to Constance: 'Dear and Beloved, Here am I, and you at the Antipodes. O execrable fates, which keep our lips from kissing, though our souls are one.' (*L* 165) It is a remarkable achievement on Wilde's part that such a letter should appear simultaneously to be cynical, effusive and yet sincere.

But while a certain amount of affectation was permissible as beauty, the full extent of Wilde's effeminacy and alternative existence could only be enjoyed in ambiguous communication. As he baffled and exasperated his critics in veiled texts such as *The Picture of Dorian Gray* and *The Sphinx*, so he wrote letters which, as the transcripts of his trials establish, almost succeeded in escaping detection. Yet what was there to detect? Let us consider the following letter of 1893 to Richard Le Gallienne in response to the latter's review of *Salomé*:

My dear Richard, I have just read the *Star*, and write to tell you how pleased I am that you, with your fluid artistic temperament, should have glided into the secret soul of my poem, swiftly, surely, just as years ago you glided into my heart.... You have got into the secret chamber of the house in which *Salomé* was fashioned, and I rejoice to think that to you has my secret been revealed, for you are the lover of beauty, and by her much—perhaps over-much—loved and worshipped. Ever yours

Oscar (*ML* 120–21)

That Wilde was prepared to admit the existence of his secret, but not to acknowledge what that secret might be, was something to be shared only between himself and Le Gallienne. It is clear to us, however, that the 'secret chamber of the house' is that occupied by the Sphinx, and into which the beloved had entered in 'The Harlot's House'. As with the letter to Lord Alfred Douglas which eventually became a sonnet under the hand of Pierre Louÿs and was published in *The Spirit Lamp*, the ambiguity is intense: nothing is admitted, everything is suggested under the rubric of tragic reason. It is as 'uranian' as any of his poems, and as plausible/implausible as any of his stories.

This ambiguity entered into every aspect of his correspondence, as of other compartments in his life. Thus he placed on language itself a dual burden: 'There really must be two derivations for every word, one for the poet and one for the scientist.' (*L* 173) If by 'poet' we understand 'Irishman' and, by contrast, 'Englishman' for 'scientist', then we have a classic distinction between what is intended and interpreted by one sensibility as compared with and contrasted by another. When, for example, he defended *The Picture of Dorian Gray* in the columns of the *St James's Gazette*, he succeeded in dissembling simply by being straightforward. He spoke of the moral of the book 'which the prurient will not be able to find in it'. But he also made it clear why that moral was inaccessible:

> Romantic art deals with the exception and with the
> individual. Good people, belonging as they do to the nor-
> mal, and so, commonplace, type, are artistically unin-
> teresting. Bad people are, from the point of view of art,
> fascinating studies. They represent colour, variety and
> strangeness. Good people exasperate one's reason; bad
> people stir one's imagination. . . . Life by its realism is
> always spoiling the subject-matter of art. The supreme
> pleasure in literature is to realise the non-existent.
>
> (*L* 259)

'Good people' are clearly English, and the norm from which
'bad people' deviate is Englishness. The bad are therefore
Irish, homosexual, nihilist. Bad people excite the imagination, which, *pace* Arnold, is a distinctly if not uniquely Irish
property: thus bad and Irish make common cause. It therefore follows that a realistic life is an English one, and that in
order for there to be any pleasure in art it must be inspired
by a vision of an alternative life. Conversely, he wrote a cou-
ple of years later what must at first sight seem to contradict
this: 'It is only shallow people who do not judge by appearances. The mystery of the world is the visible, not the invisible.' (*L* 324) Read literally, this certainly seems to disavow
the unseen life. But read as a commentary on English ways
of seeing and believing, it further illustrates Wilde's point
that to be someone 'pour qui le monde visible existe' was, by
virtue of Irish 'reason', something else. That which is invisible—the alternative life—is where the artistic spirit abides,
and thus is known and natural; conversely, the visible world
becomes the world of magic because it is the world with
which the artistic spirit has to contend. Shallow people look
for the life behind the appearance, because it is their methodi-
cal, realistic way of finding out what is inherently accessible
to the deeper nature.

Thus about a year before his climax and his downfall
Wilde could write:

> To the world I seem, by intention on my part, a dilet-
> tante and dandy merely—it is not wise to show one's
> heart to the world—and as seriousness of manner is the
> disguise of the fool, folly in its exquisite modes of trivi-
> ality and indifference and lack of care is the robe of the
> wise man. (*L* 353)

Here we see Wilde moving behind the pose of shallowness:
'the world' has become once more the flat, tedious world of
appearances, and in that world Wilde's own 'appearance' or
'disguise' draws the accusation of triviality; he appears to be
careless or reckless because it is in his deeper nature to be
'wise'—the term which homosexuals would later employ to
distinguish one who is adept at distinguishing *them*.[74] 'I
invented that magnificent flower,' he said of the green carnation (*L* 373), a claim which was manifestly untrue, but which
was clever enough to make people think it was true, thus
diminishing the real significance of the flower to all but
those who wore it.

Once Wilde had been levelled by his court appearances,
there was no further need of the pretence which he had
manipulated with such dexterity, but an even greater need
to reconstruct his personality along lines of contrition. 'I am
determined not to revolt but to accept every outrage through
devotion to love, to let my body be dishonoured so long as
my soul may always keep the image of you,' he wrote to
Douglas while awaiting his sentence (*L* 397–8). Thus penitent, the artist was ready for martyrdom, to assume the robe
of an Irish Christ. After prison, he wrote that 'My life was
one quite unworthy of an artist in its deliberate and studied
materialism.' (*ML* 147) The experience of prison thus revealed
to Wilde that his own pose of dilettantism had in fact become
his sole course, that he had abandoned the artistic intention
which lay beneath it. Simultaneously he told Laurence
Housman that he was writing *The Ballad of Reading Gaol*—
'terribly realistic for me, and drawn from actual experience,
a sort of denial of my own philosophy of art in many ways'

(*ML* 153). But both statements also indicate that nothing had fundamentally changed in Wilde. The *Ballad* was 'a sort of denial', but not a complete rejection of that philosophy: it was another disguise, so that within the insistent rhythm of the poem, which of itself re-creates the circularity of the prison yard, the subversion of the prison system takes place. Similarly, when he petitioned the Home Secretary for leniency after he had served half his sentence, he admitted that he suffered from sexual madness, referring with secret pride to the fact that Max Nordau's book on degeneration 'devoted an entire chapter to the petitioner as a specially typical example' of 'the intimate connection between madness and the literary and artistic temperament' (*L* 402). It would have been sufficient to refer to himself as 'a typical example', but to add 'specially' was the hyperbole of an irrepressible egoism. In that same petition Wilde wrote:

> The petitioner is now…conscious of the fact that while the three years preceding his arrest were from the intellectual point of view the most brilliant years of his life …during the entire time he was suffering from the most horrible form of erotomania, which made him forget his wife and children, his high social position in London and Paris, his European distinction as an artist, the honour of his name and family, his very humanity itself.
>
> (*L* 402)

Wilde does nothing to deny the accuracy of Nordau's diagnosis (absurd though Nordau's thesis was); he allows the parallel facts of intellectual brilliance and insanity, of 'monstrous sexual perversion' to stand. They are neither mutually inconsistent nor necessarily dependent. Madness did not undermine, or deprive him of, his humanity, but led him to 'forget' it. While living lives of brilliance and depravity he put out of his mind those parts of his life which a normal, sane person would regard as the bedrock of respectable behaviour. There is no doubt that in one sense Wilde was

genuinely remorseful for the ills which had befallen his wife
and children and his parents' good name. In one sense, too,
'he knows only too well that his career as a dramatist and
writer is ended . . . and that an obscure life in some remote
country is in store for him' (L 404), but the fact that he was
not to write again with any fluency or sustained power
should not blind us to the fact that for Wilde to live in obscurity could only bring out the ostentation of the Irishman and
the homosexual who no longer had anything to hide. Having
failed in everything except his success at martyrdom, there
remained to him only the opportunity to come out on sexual
and social matters as a critic of British standards. When an
old boy-friend, Harry Melvill, cut him in a Paris street—as
so many English acquaintances did—he wrote to Ross: 'For
people whom one has had, to give themselves moral or
social airs is childish.' (L 760)

When we read (in a further petition): 'Of all modes of
insanity . . . the insanity of perverted sensual instinct is the
one most dominant in its action on the brain. It taints the
intellect as well as the emotional energies' (L 411), we might
legitimately substitute 'Irishness' for perversion. Wilde was
an outcast from Ireland—'all my friends have vanished'
(L 211)—and a stranger in England until he was cast out
from there to 'some remote country'. When he wrote to Ross:
'My entire tragedy sometimes seems to me grotesque and
nothing else' (L 414), he may have been writing more truth-
fully than at any other time. Life had always been a tragedy,
and thus the role which he had chosen to play—whether
Hamlet, Lear or Othello—was immaterial. What mattered
was whether it would be a brilliant tragedy or merely
'grotesque'—the choice of epithet is in itself telling: Wilde
was still capable of seeing himself by means of a critical, and
melodramatic, idiom.

'De Profundis', although ostensibly a private communication to Douglas, was promulgated by Wilde in a letter which

suggests that publication of at least part of the text was always envisaged:

> If the copying [of the manuscript] is done at Hornton Street the lady type-writer might be fed through a lattice in the door like the Cardinals when they elect a Pope, till she comes out on the balcony and can say to the world '*Habet Mundus Epistolam*' for indeed it is an Encyclical Letter, and as the Bulls of the Holy Father are named from their opening words, it may be spoken of as the *Epistola: In Carcere et Vinculis*. (*L* 513)

The letter serves three purposes: Wilde's autobiography, it is also the biography of the addressee—'you see that I have to write your life to you' (*L* 448)—and a justification, or *apologia*, of the spirit of refusal, the search for another life. The vision of Christ is central to the letter: 'It is the imaginative quality of Christ's own nature that makes him this palpitating centre of romance. . . . Out of his own imagination entirely did Jesus of Nazareth create himself.' (*L* 482) Christ, it seems, was the first dandy, the first artist and the first oxymoron: 'He was the denial as well as the affirmation of prophecy. For every expectation that he fulfilled, there was another that he destroyed.' He was responsible for Hugo's *Les Misérables*, Baudelaire's *Les Fleurs du Mal*, 'the note of pity in Russian novels, the stained glass and tapestries and quattrocento work of Burne-Jones and Morris, Verlaine and Verlaine's poems . . . the troubled romantic marbles of Michael Angelo, pointed architecture, and the love of children and flowers' (*L* 482). Elsewhere we have found Wilde saying that sin is essential to progress. Here Christ becomes the patron saint of sinners, and it is clear that sin is as important to Christ as Christ is to the sinner. Like Wilde, he is essentially an intellectual: 'The great sins of the world take place in the brain, but it is in the brain that everything takes place.' (*L* 483)

Wilde also intensifies the spirit of Celtic vision by saying that 'Suffering . . . is the means by which we exist, because it is the only means by which we become conscious of existing; and the remembrance of suffering in the past is necesary to us as the warrant, the evidence, of our continued identity. . . . Suffering is one long moment. . . . The secret of life is suffering. It is what is hidden behind everything.' (L 435, 457, 473) Yet 'the gods are strange. It is not of our vices only they make instruments to scourge us. They bring us to ruin through what in us is good, gentle, humane, loving. But for my pity and affection for you and yours,' he tells Douglas, 'I would not now be weeping in this terrible place.' (L 440)

As with Christ, so with Wilde there must be a 'false friend . . . to betray him with a kiss' (L 478). Wilde now realises—and here is the compelling reason for this reconstruction of his shattered life—that 'I thought life was going to be a brilliant comedy, and that you were going to be one of the many graceful figures in it. I found it to be a revolting and repellent tragedy.' (L 444) Douglas, he decides, was the cause of this illusion. If Douglas had not worn a 'mask of joy and pleasure', Wilde would not have been deceived. Yet we have already heard him say to Ross that life is a tragedy, a fact from which he seems to have been 'led astray' only by the epiphany of Douglas in 1891. All his other attachments brought with them the sense of doom: the relationship with Douglas challenged it. Wilde explains this as follows: 'The fatal errors of life are not due to man's being unreasonable: an unreasonable moment may be one's finest moment. They are due to man's being logical. There is a wide difference.' (L 446) To be logical is to be English, to be unreasonable is to be Irish. Wilde was misled because for a moment he allowed himself to be different from his real self and to act logically. He had not judged things by their appearances, and thus, for a moment, had become shallow, which, he told Douglas, was the supreme vice (L 469, 508), adding that lack of imagination was 'the one really fatal defect in your character' (L 447).

In order to re-create his life—'a *Vita Nuova*' (L 467)—he must discover the meaning of sorrow. We find him deceiving himself in prison, as he had deceived himself with Douglas:

I used to live entirely for pleasure. I shunned sorrow and suffering of every kind. I hated both. I resolved to ignore them as far as possible, to treat them, that is to say, as modes of imperfection. They were not part of my scheme of life. They had no place in my philosophy.

He says that he refused to accept his mother's advice when she often quoted to him Goethe's lines:

> Who never ate his bread in sorrow,
>   Who never spent the midnight hours
> Weeping and wailing for the morrow,
>   He knows you not, ye Heavenly Powers. (*L* 472)

Now prison has shown him

that sorrow, being the supreme emotion of which man is capable, is at once the type and test of all great Art.... There is no truth comparable to Sorrow. There are times when Sorrow seems to me to be the only truth.... Out of Sorrow have the worlds been built, and at the birth of a child or a star there is pain. (*L* 473)

Wilde says that 'I wanted to eat of the fruit of all the trees in the garden of the world' and that 'My only mistake was that I confined myself so exclusively to the trees of what seemed to me the sun-gilt side of the garden, and shunned the other side for its shadow and its gloom.' (*L* 475) Yet the existence of that side was never in doubt, and Wilde could not have claimed that he was unaware of it. He always knew that there was a 'grotesque' side to life, and he was, in his own words, 'afraid' of the fruit of the shadows: 'failure, disgrace, poverty, sorrow, despair, suffering, tears even, the broken words that come from the lips of pain, remorse . . . conscience . . . self-abasement that punishes . . . misery . . . anguish' (*L* 475)—many of which, we have noted, he had amply acknowledged and experienced, at least in verse. They were prospects of which he had been particularly aware in his mother's 'above all, despair'. In fact Wilde's chagrin was due to his confrontation not with failure, sorrow, despair or suffering, not even remorse or anguish, but with poverty and disgrace. It had never been part of his plan, or 'philosophy', to be treated so ignominiously for his failure, but failure itself had been intended in some form. Reading Prison was the outcome of his desired fate—the case of *Regina v. Wilde*—but, whether an acquittal or a conviction had been contemplated, Wilde's fate was to be the defendant not solely of his actions but of his nature. It was to have been a trial of individualism, as was the judgment of Christ, but an individualism which came from the philosophy of love, 'that beautiful unreal world of Art, where once I was King' (*L* 463).

Only the spiritual quality will enable Wilde to re-create himself, because it is superior to morality, religion and reason (cf. *L* 468). It is the one quality which, because it is innate, is inaccessible to law. Christ too had been an antinomian: 'For him, there were no laws: there were exceptions merely.' (*L* 485) By its means, Wilde would always be able to transcend the ignominy of prison. Although physically broken, he was supremely unaffected by it, however much pain it may have caused him. 'When first I was put in prison some people advised me to try and forget who I was. It was ruinous advice. It is only by realising what I am that I have found comfort of any kind.' (*L* 469)

In prison, therefore, the essential intensification of personality continued until, like Christ's, his life, however execrable, became 'an idyll' (*L* 478). Once more the oxymoron is the central pivot of the life: 'It was of course my soul in its ultimate essence that I had reached. In many ways I had been its enemy, but I found it waiting for me as a friend.' (*L* 479) Wilde goes further than denying the existence of law; he also proves to his own satisfaction that history is a form of fiction: 'Of course the sinner must repent.... The moment of repentance is the moment of initiation. More than that. It is the means by which one alters one's past.' (*L* 487) He maintains that by means of repentance one can make the most 'revolting and repellent' aspects of one's past into 'beautiful and holy incidents'. This revisionism is the ultimate, and some might say the most creative, form of historiography.

This is the final outcome of the Irishman's supreme dialogue with himself, the thrust of mythology which culminated for Wilde in the story 'The Fisherman and his Soul'. It enabled him to answer the question 'Who am I?' When he said: 'Every single human being should be the fulfilment of a prophecy' (*L* 481), he gave full force to that mythology: the 'continual assertion of the imagination as the basis of all spiritual and material life. . . . The final mystery is oneself.' (*L* 484, 488)

In *Reading* Wilde had already fulfilled one part of his own autobiographical prophecy: 'If I ever write again ... there are just two subjects on which and through which I desire to express myself: one is "Christ, as the precursor of the Romantic movement in life": the other is "the Artistic life considered in its relation to Conduct".' (*L* 484) Both ambitions, however, were accomplished in the letter which contained them.

5
Dramas

(i) MELODRAMA

'WOULD you kindly inform me who I am?' With this question the dénouement of Wilde's most famous play, and only true comedy, commences (*CW* 380). The process of disclosure had begun with his first play, a melodrama of Russian revolution, written in 1882 and first performed in New York in 1883. *Vera, or The Nihilists* set a declamatory tone for Wilde's career as a dramatist, which included seven dramas (four of them the society plays which capped his reputation) and several more abandoned fragments. 'Melodrama' might be written across the top of Wilde's entire opus. The heightened dimensions of his life, the background music towards which he tried to progress, the easy achievement of sensation, the occurrence of incidents which all share the characteristics of a single previous incident, all point to an artificiality which seems to spring from an unknown nature. To the extent that Wilde's own life was dramatic, from his rendition of the lessons in Magdalen College Chapel to his speech from the dock at the Old Bailey and his dead voice in 'De Profundis', it was natural that he should begin early with attempts at stage work. He did not entirely succeed until he had adopted and—at least temporarily—abandoned verse drama (which he attempted in his second play, *The Duchess of Padua*) as a medium and the histrionic as a style, and proceeded instead to the more subtle ironies of social commentary. Yet there are exceptions to this generalisation: in *Salomé*, for example, he raised macabre incident and painted stage to the highest level of decadence, thereby creating the first act of the Irish Renaissance[1] and capturing the European imagination, while in *The Importance of Being Earnest* he restored the histrionic touch with the peacock cadences of Lady Bracknell.

In this chapter we shall trace the emergence of the play-wright whose children-in-waiting are hiding in order to be found—from Vera Soubaroff, who rises from provincial obscurity to become the saviour of Mother Russia, to Iokanaan, the Christian protomartyr. If drama is the last repository of truth, it is on the stage that Wilde eventually found himself, and enabled audiences to witness revelations which, because their truths are 'away' from direct experience, become valid for their own lives. Wilde as storyteller lived a fictive life which was capable of travelling imaginatively between the Greek tragedies of emotion and the Restoration comedy of manners and producing from their forms and forces a hybrid drama encompassing melodrama, social commentary and symbolism with equal success and disregard.

The search for identity runs through Wilde's plays as through his fiction. Where the poems, for example, are concerned also with liberty, the growth of consciousness, and the nature of sin and goodness, the plays develop the theme of identity in the pursuit of sexual and social guilt, and the juxtaposition of antitheses. Drama is concerned with naming, with the conferring of identity. It is also concerned with the named person being able to find home. 'Play', says Sartre, 'is at the origin of the world.'[2] Only a child who is secure in his identity and in the source of love can, with any comfort, *play*. A name carries with it a portrait of its owner. To be nameless is to be without a visible identity. To have one's 'good name' removed by society is to be deprived of one's currency in everyday life, and compels one inward to a secret, untouchable life where one invents one's own life.

Secrecy was natural to Wilde. The greatest secret of all is that kept from the child—the truth about his parents, about what social, intellectual and racial elements combined to make him what he may discover himself to be. The genre of *embarrassment* runs like an ore-bearing lode through the Irish imagination. It is a commonplace of Irish fiction that it can sustain these inquiries until such a melodramatic declaration as 'Stop, Gerald, stop! He is your own father' (CW 469) or, as Wilde has it in the same play, 'The Book of Life begins with a man and a woman in a garden.' 'It ends with Revelations.' (CW 443) Wilde was acutely conscious that he carried within him what Steiner, referring to the antigonal conflict, calls 'the seed of all drama . . . the meeting of a man and a woman'.[3]

The single most powerful antithesis is that of man and woman, whether in love or in hate. Between them is a route of compromise, a place where secrets are told; when the dominant secret, which is the story's motto, is disclosed, and all the sub-dominant anxieties are released, it becomes possible for son and mother to recognise one another and to be reconciled, for lovers to be united, for Salomé and Iokanaan to assuage their passion in death. Throughout his dramas Wilde was emphasising the Hegelian notion that the narrator's identity lies not in either participant but in the struggle itself, in the working out of antinomies.

Despite the fact that Wilde scored his successes with plays such as *Lady Windermere's Fan* and *The Importance of Being Earnest*, he never entirely abandoned his interest in quasi-religious themes, in fact switching his attention alternately from one genre to another in the 1890s. Thus after the early *Vera* and *The Duchess of Padua* (1883) Wilde resumed play-writing with *Lady Windermere's Fan* (1891), and realising the potential for this strain of theatre he set out to write *A Woman of No Importance*, but not before he had conceived and executed the *Salomé* project; he next attempted a second biblical drama, 'La Sainte Courtisane', also referred to as 'The Woman Covered with Jewels', while also beginning work on a blank-verse drama, *A Florentine Tragedy*; he put this aside to work on the more lucrative prospect of *An Ideal Husband*, taking it up and abandoning it once more when the cistern had filled for *The Importance of Being Earnest*. Three further projects were begun before his imprisonment: after writing most of *Earnest* in 1894, Wilde jotted down the scenario of another 'good woman' play, which he intended to call

Constance, subsequently staged under Frank Harris's name as *Mr and Mrs Daventry*; and sketches exist, also from 1894, for another mediaeval drama, *The Cardinal of Avignon*, and another 'good woman' subject, *A Woman's Tragedy*.

There is a continuity of theme running through all these plays: from the aesthetic farce of *Vera* to the crisp definition of *Earnest*, Wilde's ideas of man and woman are caught in, and shaped by, the balance between sentimentality and dandyism,[4] one libertarian in bearing, the other libertinist. With free-thinking at the core of all his writing, Wilde explored the question of whether man can ever be truly good, or woman anything else. Sentiment informed Irish nationalism; dandyism, the continual invention of an antinomian future, accounts for the gay timbre of his central ideas. *Vera* flaunts the 'libertatis sacra fames' in unfurling the anti-imperialist flag, while in *Earnest* Wilde provocatively displayed his homosexuality—his côterie had worn the green carnation, the badge of the Paris homosexual, at the première of *Lady Windermere's Fan*, and now he employed 'earnest', a code-word for 'homosexual', in the title of the play. Another term which Wilde appropriated as a 'between' term for homosexuality was 'bimetallism', which appears both in *A Woman of No Importance*—'Bimetallism! Is that quite a nice subject? However, I know people discuss everything very freely nowadays' (CW 463)—and in *Earnest*: 'When one has thoroughly mastered the principles of Bimetallism one has the right to lead an introspective life.' (CW 355) The fact that in each case an innocent commentator unconsciously makes a knowing remark is a real and cruel twist of his humour. (Linda Gertner Zatlin further suggests that Wilde was ostentatiously flaunting sexual innuendo by naming his unseen character 'Bunbury', which, she says, was a current term for a homosexual pickup,[5] but I can find no other evidence for this; indeed, Wilde had a friend of the name (which also occurs in *The Princess Casamassima*).[6] It may be, however, that as a result of its occurrence in the play the name for a spurious alibi was adopted by homosexuals—a case of life imitating art.) Between *Lady Windermere's Fan* and *Earnest*, both *Salomé* and *An Ideal Husband* give a mannered and fully developed voice to the dandyism in both woman and man. At all times Wilde was anxious that the question of trust—or faith—between man and woman, of negotiation between sacred and profane, should infuse the drama, as it had his stories, as a spirit almost inaccessible to the actors or the characters they represented.

There was a devotional side to Wilde's continued pursuit of 'goodness'. *Vera* and *The Duchess of Padua* have a passionate sense of imperilled goodness; among the other projected titles, 'La Sainte Courtisane' embodies a paradox which runs through all his thinking—the idea that goodness and evil contain each other, that within condemnation can be found forgiveness. Similarly, *A Florentine Tragedy*, conceived before his imprisonment and subsequently worked into a brief fragment, is more a black comedy on the theme of transformation; here too is a possible source for the force of unveiling and recognition in Synge's *The Well of the Saints*:

> BIANCA: Why
> Did you not tell me you were so strong?
> SIMONE: Why
> Did you not tell me you were so beautiful? (*CW* 700)

Wilde had a relentless passion for inversion as a necessary part of discovering oneself: to reverse moral poles in order to experience 'both sides of the garden', and to reinvent oneself imaginatively as a woman, were steps on the way to the integration of the full artistic—and social—personality. It is this quality which distinguishes him as a pioneer of modern drama and explains what was regarded, but not understood, at the time as his unique talent.

The essence of melodrama, like that of the *commedia dell' arte*, is its deployment of stock characters whose gestures and vocabulary stand 'in symbolic relation' to one another, and who are therefore capable of representing, and eliciting, stock emotions. Wilde also appropriated this simple fact and disguised it by clothing his gallery of puppets in society suits and civilised manners. At heart, however, he unremittingly sustained the argument of *The Duchess of Padua* that 'they do not sin at all who sin for love' (*CW* 645) as the core of the story to be told.

This seriousness is evident despite—or perhaps because of—the melodrama of *Vera*. Melodrama, familiar to Wilde not least through his friendship with the Irishman Dion Boucicault, depends for its effect on capturing the sympathy of the audience for the spectacle of endangered innocence. In doing so, it requires a defensiveness which puts goodness in a corner, besieged by monsters and betrayed by misunderstandings. Boucicault's *Arrah-na-Pogue, The Shaughraun* and *The Colleen Bawn*, in particular, were at the core of the nineteenth-century genre, which had pantomime, or *opéra comique*, at one extreme, and Wagner's and Richard Strauss's *musikdrama* at the other. Shaw, Synge, and O'Casey acknowledged Boucicault's influence and incorporated some of his effects into their own works. One of the keynotes of melodrama as it appears in these writers is its macabre humour, its symbolism shot with pathos. The stage elements of 'exile, the loveless marriage...the endless vigil of mothers'[7] are present in many of Wilde's plays. Comedy is more a relief than a structural feature in plays which replace the happy ending with poignant submission to the mixed blessings of fate.

Melodrama, as a transition between romanticism and modernism, allowed *The Importance of Being Earnest* to become, in Katherine Worth's words, 'an existential farce' and its author a 'revolutionary moralist'.[8] When in *Vera* Vera Soubaroff dies, exclaiming: 'I have saved Russia,' she allows other potential heroes and heroines (among whom Lady Wilde might have seen herself) to exclaim: 'I have saved Ireland.' Melodrama was a regular—almost the only—feature of the Dublin stage in the mid-nineteenth century. Wilde as a schoolboy or undergraduate may very well have seen Boucicault's *The Corsican Brothers* (as Shaw certainly did)[9] in 1868 at the

Theatre Royal, or, in 1869, T. J. Williams's *Who Is Who, or All in a Fog*, or, after the opening in 1871 of the Gaiety Theatre (where he himself was to lecture in 1883 and 1885), more serious fare such as *She Stoops to Conquer*.

Like Shaw, Wilde was attracted to melodrama for its philosophical possibilities and its focus on the perilous.[10] It was an extension of his single-minded ploy as a storyteller, that the inner life of the drama should be populated by persons each representative of one aspect of their author, and that their revelations and discussions were philosophic meeting-places where that personality might be negotiated and reconstituted. The question 'Why?' at the end of *A Florentine Tragedy* is intimately related to 'Who am I?' in its further pursuit of recognition after blindness, ignorance and confusion. It is a misjudgment on Martin Meisel's part to suggest that 'the rhetorical drama of the eighteenth and nineteenth centuries was a drama of passion and sentiments, not ideas'.[11] There was always an 'idea' at the heart of melodrama, however much it became sentimental and served the display of passion. This is demonstrated not least by the fact that Wilde based the incidents of *Vera* on real life,[12] which caused the permanent deferral of its London production. Contemporary disturbances in Russia, including the phenomenon of nihilism itself and the assassination of Tsar Alexander II in 1881, made Wilde's play (which predicts such an incident)[13] dangerously topical; furthermore, in the following year the murder in Dublin's Phoenix Park of the Chief Secretary and Under-Secretary for Ireland put assassination onto a dangerously high dramatic plane. At the extremities of Europe famine was the experience, and nihilism the form of resistance, of a peasantry melodramatically suppressed by aristocratic disdain. On the artistic plane, *Vera* is in the same politically inspired genre as Verdi's *Un ballo in maschera*; in the longer term, however, it had a further purpose, to achieve, as Auden said of *Earnest*, the status of 'the only pure verbal opera in English'.[14]

But we also have the spectacle of the dandy in *Vera*: Prince Paul anticipates Lord Goring in *An Ideal Husband* in such epigrams as 'Experience, the name men give to their mistakes' (CW 663) and 'Indifference is the revenge the world takes on mediocrities' (CW 664), and in identifying *ennui* as 'the *maladie du siècle*' (CW 665). And melodrama retains its place in Wilde's work both in the immediacy of its revelations and in the plangency of its emotional appeal: 'Go back to that child who even now, in pain or in joy, may be calling you' (CW 413) and in its emphasis on the artificiality of social constructs. Everything is contrived, because nothing can be allowed to be itself, to be 'real'.

Vera was a form of artistic and social manifesto. We should be aware that it succeeded—even if unwittingly so—in combining an Irish spirit of defiance, a dandiacal posturing, and an artistic interest in nihilism (in wiping the slate clean) and a private, psychic fascination with disguise, into a solitary statement—not yet unified or achieving satisfactory dramatic form, but giving voice to a thematic singularity. As with all his later stage works, the interrelationship of the elements is striking.

Prince Paul's idea that 'one is sure to be disappointed if one tries to get romance out of modern life' (CW 677) is echoed, viciously, in Michael's rejection of Vera:

> You left your father that night, and three weeks after he died of a broken heart. You wrote to me to follow you here. I did so; first because I loved you; but you soon cured me of that; whatever gentle feeling, whatever pity, whatever love, and whatever humanity, was in my heart you withered up and destroyed, as the canker worm eats the corn. You bade me cast out love from my breast as a vile thing, you turned my hand to iron, and my heart to stone; you told me to live for freedom and revenge. (CW 680)

These replace, and kill, romance and love.

Wilde's 'unique' talent as a playwright was acknowledged by such critics as William Archer and G. B. Shaw;[15] it was attributed to the fact that he was not a playwright at all, but 'a thinker and a writer',[16] bringing his critical views into the theatre and playing with the idea of that theatre rather than submit to its disciplines. Together with Shaw himself, and to a lesser extent mainstream playwrights like Pinero, Jones and Gilbert, Wilde created an Ibsenesque theatre of modern life, which he intended not only in *Vera* but also *The Duchess of Padua*. His early intention, until he found his métier with *Lady Windermere's Fan*, was 'to produce the modern idea under an antique form' (*L* 137); this, he said, was 'the essence of art', the high point of which was *Salomé*, of which Katherine Worth has said: 'Herod has a modern self-consciousness, and Herodias would be quite at home among the tart dowagers of Lady Windermere's society.'[17] Influenced, as Worth has also shown,[18] by Maeterlinck's *La Princesse Maleine*, Wilde developed his interest in doom as it occurs inevitably in the lives of three characters—Salomé herself, Herod, who fears the moon and slips in blood, and Iokanaan. Passion and death are inextricable. But beyond this, Wilde was obeying Baudelaire's exhortation to be 'absolutely modern', firstly in expanding the theme of the tragedy of woman to an extent not encompassed outside the legend of Phèdre, of which Racine's is the only comparable modern example. (Wilde himself contemplated a 'Pharaoh' which may or may not have been based on the legend of Joseph and thus, presumably, of Potiphar, which gave rise to the legend of Phèdre, and which, like *Salomé*, was eventually put to music by Richard Strauss.)[19] Secondly, Wilde was modern in the absurd words he gave to Herod: 'Il ressuscite les morts? Je ne veux pas qu'il fasse cela. Je lui défends de faire cela. Je ne permets pas qu'on ressuscite les morts.' (*Salomé* 49)

With *Lady Windermere's Fan*, however, Wilde was ready to announce: 'Time: the Present'. It is a present which reverses the formula of *Salomé* and presents the antique idea under a modern form: it is all comedy of manners, Sheridan *redivivus*.

It is all play, but Wilde demonstrates that within play all the viciousness, fragility and susceptibility of human nature is present. In order to do so, he establishes antitheses: between town and country, between young and old, innocence and experience, purity and corruption, man and woman; these create a dramatic, dynamic tension within which individuals must create themselves.

'Much of the interest in Wilde's drama', says Worth, 'springs from the sensitivity and realism of his exploration into the different kinds of love and need involved in trying to be oneself and at the same time think of others.'[20] Yet while he often appears to draw a character with compassion—Mabel Chiltern in *An Ideal Husband* would be a prime example—it is clear from 'De Profundis' that principally Wilde was trying to solve the problem of how 'to be oneself' in an impossible world: he was able to 'think of others' provided that at the same time, and preferentially, he could think of himself—and in this way he became someone else. To conceive of others as simple, monodimensional characters was comparatively easy, while to conceive of oneself under conditions at best strange and more likely menacing, to steer a course which would permit his artistic persona its fullest expression and yet conceal other aspects of the persona from a suspicious world, required a complexity which permeates his more difficult characters.

In this he also has something in common with W. S. Gilbert, whose 'never-never land' of fantasy and concealed origins is seldom far removed from the Victorian realities; Martin Meisel observes that 'Gilbert used the Otherworld formula' in the pursuit of political satire in *Iolanthe*, *The Gondoliers* and *Utopia, Limited* and, furthermore, that Shaw acknowledged it, in Gilbertian vein, in *Back to Methuselah*.[21] Wilde's dramatic intentions not only serve two purposes—to tell his own story and that of his imagined homeland—but also illustrate the schizophrenia of a writer living, in R. D. Laing's terms, 'an unlivable situation',[22] one in which multiple personae are adopted and multiple scenarios are enacted.

Wilde's characters, like his own situation, occupy two categories, the simple and the difficult; and as such his dramas fall naturally into the mannered stage from the Restoration to the Act of Union and the melodramatic stage which went on to develop the accident of birth in *The Corsican Brothers* and that of idleness and prudery in Boucicault's *A Lover by Proxy*, a forerunner of *The Importance of Being Earnest*.[23] Studied symmetry, within which one could observe the reasons for this standing apart, was the seedbed of Wilde's unique insight into human nature, and the idea of a 'school for scandal' was merely the screen from behind which a more developed philosophy could emerge.

When the suitor in Lady Morgan's *The Wild Irish Girl* said that

> My gay young mistress seems already to consider me as her husband, and treats me accordingly with indifference. In short, she finds that love in the solitude of the country, and amidst the pleasures of the town, is a very different sentiment [24]

he was laying the foundations of one of Lady Bracknell's most inverted paradoxes:

> A girl with a simple, unspoiled nature, like Gwendolen, could hardly be expected to reside in the country.
>
> (CW 333)

Are we witnessing the artifice of nature, or the naturalness of artifice? Wilde is developing the 'truth of masks', which is that we all have a mask which may conceal nothing more or less than another mask, with no 'real' personality to be discovered at the end of the inquiry. It suits the characters who use it to evade discovery, as much as those who wish to be discovered. Gwendolen's 'If you are not too long, I will wait here for you all my life' (CW 379) is both exquisitely touching as a sentiment and a grim reminder that she is the daughter of Lady Bracknell, and a participant in a grotesque farce.

It creates situations of sublime absurdity, such as Miss Prism's eventual reply to the question with which this chapter commenced: 'Any inconvenience I may have caused you in your infancy through placing you inadvertently in this handbag, I sincerely apologise for.' (CW 380)

When A. B. Walkley described the author of *Earnest* as 'an artist in sheer nonsense',[25] he was very close indeed to unveiling Wilde's 'intentions'. The interplay between sense and non-sense, between an English and an Irish temperament and perspective, was the tinder on which his wit was laid. Walkley was correct to surmise that in this play Wilde had 'found himself', even though he had already achieved this in *An Ideal Husband*. But he believed that the achievement lay solely in the playwright's capacity to excite laughter 'absolutely free from bitter afterthought'. Nothing could be further from the true aesthetic position. 'To a modern,' said Walkley, 'the laughter of the antique stage is cruel, or stupid, or simply incomprehensible. What a gulf there is between ancient and modern ideas on this subject may be seen from the significant little fact that ... Aristotle ... makes the ridiculous a sub-division of the ugly.'[26] The really significant fact is the one overlooked by Walkley, an oversight in which the superficial comedy of *Earnest* encouraged him, that Wilde was returning comedy to the sub-category not only of ugliness but of cruelty.

Wilde's dramas—all of them, from the naïveté of *Vera* to the mannerism of *Salomé* and the black gayness of *Earnest*—are exercises in inversion, and as such they anticipate not only the 'absurd' and 'grotesque' theatres of the twentieth century but also the entire surrealist movement. 'Ceci n'est pas un pipe,' Lady Bracknell might say as she produced one and began to smoke it. 'This is not a play,' might say Wilde, who wrote across the top of *Earnest*: 'a trivial comedy for serious people', while omitting to inform us whether the 'serious people' were those on the stage or those in the stalls.

Irish playwrights from Farquhar to Shaw have vacillated between providing the English public with trivial comedies for serious people and serious comedies for trivial people. Provided that the end result is an artistic success, that it obeys the dictum *ars est celare artem*, then what is presented in the guise of comedy will successfully conceal the severe commentary of the undertone. Perhaps, for the Irish writer in a strange land, writing with an adopted pen, the need for an enabling fiction[27] is more urgent than that for artistic or monetary success. It is not, of course, exclusively an Irish phenomenon: Tom Stoppard, of Czech origin, is one of the few playwrights in the contemporary British theatre providing work of any vigour, writing plays which look behind the scenes, at what happens in the interstices between people and events, trying to put meaning and value on words themselves. One might say that for the external writer, with distinct cultural baggage, being in England but not entirely of it imposes certain strategies to both enable and compensate for physical and linguistic displacement. One of these strategies is the creation of characters who are not, and never can be, real, wholly rounded and filled out; behind this dexterous approach to artifice is what we might call the sinister approach, which Walkley identified when he said of *Earnest*: 'The conduct of the people in itself is rational enough; it is exquisitely irrational in the circumstances.'[28] 'They laugh angrily at his epigrams,' said Shaw of the audience for *An Ideal Husband*,[29] but it required an Irishman to appreciate the grounds for that anger. When Sir Robert Chiltern in that play declares: 'Freedom is everything' (CW 505), his audience cannot have known quite how vital that notion of freedom was to his author, more vital indeed than the mere freedom itself. From within the imperial strength of contemporary England the notion of freedom would have been of a qualitatively different order—paternalistic, custodial, directive—whereas for the Irishman, regardless of apparent similarities in dress, behaviour, language and domicile, it meant the vision of something which was not, and could not be, experienced or possessed.

The natural suitability of melodrama to the modern stage is clear from a comparison of Boucicault's *A Lover by Proxy*, a one-act 'comedietta' (1842) and *The Importance of Being Earnest*. Two men-about-town, Lawless and Blushington, who delight in high-jinks excursions into the country, become enamoured of two sisters in the care of a killjoy aunt/governess, Penelope Prude, who advocates the study of 'Zimmermann on Solitude' and asserts: 'You will never understand the sweetness of liberty until you have lost it.'[30] Both Lawless and Blushington have difficulty in proposing, the title of the play deriving from Lawless undertaking to propose on Blushington's behalf. After much confusion of identity, as to who loves (and is loved by) whom, and considerable knock-about over the question of carriages and other conveyances, in which menservants play an important part and in the course of which Miss Prude narrowly escapes matrimony, the two pairs of lovers are united.

By contrast, *Earnest* sees a lesser role for the menservants, retains the significance of the carriage, increases the importance of the governess, and extends the confusion and flappery surrounding the pursuit of two ladies by two young gentlemen.

Boucicault's play is, of course, no more 'Irish' than is *Earnest*. But it utilises the stock properties of the servant concealed under a sofa or behind a screen which supplied the needs of Sheridan's *School for Scandal*, and here we may see that the Irish contribution to the English stage was vital to its continued health in the eighteenth and nineteenth centuries: if it was not Irish subjects or Irish expressions which made it distinct and allowed it to engage so successfully with the expectations of English audiences, what was it that endowed it with such relevance? One could argue, naturally, that dramatists such as Macklin, Congreve, Sheridan, Kelly, Murphy and Boucicault had no domestic audience, and that, while Irish theatres consumed third-rate touring productions of second-rate English farces, London's playgoers thronged to hear the work of those who had sought the natural centre of the English-speaking world. This—and the argument applies equally to the migration of lawyers, journalists and businessmen—is, however, to make the fundamental mistake of assuming that Britain and Ireland were one island. When an Irishman crosses water, whether it be from Dublin to Holyhead, from Cóbh to New York or from Galway to Aran, he becomes a different person, he lands in another place. He becomes, in Steiner's view of Wilde, Joyce and Beckett, 'extraterritorial'. Leavetaking—and the perpetual deferral of homecoming—creates a constant state of exile in which language changes with perspective.

At the centre of this experience is the ubiquity of the secret, which, in the midst of cultural discontinuities, remains the only certainty, the only continuity. Whether it is a servant or a lover concealed behind a screen (Wilde takes up this tactic too in Mrs Cheveley's hiding-place in Lord Goring's dining-room), a secret agent in disguise (as in *Vera*), or a man's paternity hidden behind the silence of his mother, the secret is supreme. Until he came into direct conflict with this aspect of English life Wilde was largely untouched by the dramas enacted daily in parliament, the law-courts or even the pageantry of the royal family. His imagination was populated by issues common to Irishness and Englishness—the lacuna in the argument, the secret, the master–servant relationship, ways of seeing—and it was to these issues that he attended when writing his dramas. The blood relationships between Mrs Erlynne and Lady Windermere (in *Lady Windermere's Fan*) and between Gerald Arbuthnot and Lord Illingworth (in *A Woman of No Importance*) are a vital secret, and the impact of their respective revelations is of less importance than the fact that—in the former case—the characters themselves *never* discover the truth. 'Had I intended to let out the secret, which is the element of suspense and curiosity, a quality so essentially dramatic, I would have written the play on entirely different lines,' Wilde told George Alexander, the producer of *Lady Windermere's Fan*. 'I would have made Mrs Erlynne a vulgar horrid woman. . . . The audience must not know till the last act that the woman Lady Windermere proposed to strike with her fan was her own mother. The note would be too harsh, too horrible. ...If they knew Mrs Erlynne was the mother, there would be no surprise in her sacrifice—it would be expected. But in my play, the sacrifice is dramatic and unexpected.' (*L* 308) After capitulating to Alexander's wishes, however, he continued to assert: 'As to those of us who do not look on a play as a mere question of pantomime and clowning, psychological interest is everything.' (*L* 313) The point is critical: expectation is dependent on psychology, and the moment of revelation will be quite different from one audience to another.

The distinctive intrusion into the space of the English stage by Irish dramatists—and their residence there—followed by the arrival of Ibsen, Strindberg and Chekhov, was first and foremost a linguistic disturbance which became a cultural one. *Salomé*, *The Devil's Disciple* and *Ghosts* are wedded as much to the past as to the present. The contemporary success in Britain of epics such as Tom Murphy's *Bailegangaire*, Frank McGuinness's *Carthaginians* or Brian Friel's *Dancing at Lughnasa* is due no less to the ancient history which is excavated in each performance than to the language which displaces the ordinary expectations created by a televisual culture. English society has never been comfortable with its past, despite the emphasis on tradition and continuity which runs through its history books and the drama from Shakespeare onwards. Severe disruptions in that tradition throughout the fifteenth, sixteenth, seventeenth and eighteenth centuries were at the back of all minds as Victoria's long reign attempted to consolidate a domestic harmony and to sustain a newly shod Empire. Such a culture would by its very nature suspect plays with titles like *An Enemy of the People* or *Vera, or The Nihilists* as easily as they would welcome (in prospect at least) *An Ideal Husband* or *The Importance of Being Earnest*. It would be ill-at-ease with the melodramatic notion of what Maeterlinck called 'man face to face with the universe' or of 'people face to face with each other, seeking to look into the depths of personality'.[31]

In Wilde's case this encouraged him to create 'difficult' characters, which in turn clearly creates difficulty for critics and audiences—all those who 'laugh angrily'. Seamus Deane adverts to this difficulty in the preface to his *Short History of Irish Literature* when he refers to 'naming of the territory ... the frailty of the assumptions which underlie any working system of civilization' and the 'extraordinarily interrogative' nature of Irish writing. 'The conviction that the matter of Ireland is, *in parvo*, the matter of civilization itself'[32] is a remarkably egocentric viewpoint, where the ego concerned is unlike anything else to which it relates or on which it comments. It leads, in the case of Irish engagement with the larger matter of England, to what Deane calls 'a critique of the idea of authority'.[33] We find its continuity (in itself a critique of its own experience of discontinuity) in Burke's view of the French monarchy on the eve of the Revolution as modified by Lady Bracknell's premonition of 'acts of violence in Grosvenor Square'. Wilde, in *The Soul of Man under Socialism*, took up this point, saying: 'The error of Louis XIV was that he thought human nature would always be the same. The result of his error was the French Revolution. It was an admirable result.' (CW 1100) As the originator of the proposition that progress depends on sin, he was a cruel commentator on authority and, as such, thoroughly Irish.

The ability to set a distance between oneself and social convention makes one both an insider and an outsider. In *Vera* it is the provincial Siberians, Vera and Michael, who precipitate the action at the heart of the empire. There is (if one excepts the butler, Farquhar, in *A Woman of No Importance*) no Irishman in any of Wilde's plays, and this is the closest that he came to presenting the inferior provincial as the catalyst of cosmopolitan action. In the case of the principal characters in *An Ideal Husband*, it is the 'woman with a past', a woman from a far country, who is set against the paradoxical Sir Robert Chiltern and the 'absolutely modern' dandy, Lord Goring. In the case of *Earnest*, the movement both in body and mind between town and country presents the provincial, invisible, alternative existence of Ernest-in-town/ Jack-in-the-country and of Algernon's 'Bunburying'. In *Salomé* the welter of Syrians, Jews, Nazarenes, Nubians and Cappadocians attempt to define their status between the distant but dominant empire of Rome and that proclaimed by Iokanaan: 'the palace of Herod' is provincial in location but cosmopolitan in focus. The *agon*, although it is of a different order, remains one of attracted polarities, from which the commerce and commutation between them derives its vigour.

The characteristic of both centuries—the eighteenth and the twentieth—is thus summed up by the theory of the mask, the capacity to dissemble, which was elaborated in the mind of nineteenth-century Ireland: putting itself at the disposal of a centripetal, metropolitan audience, this alternative, peripheral phenomenon enabled the unspoken but evident secret at the heart of the play to engage with the secret in the heart of the playgoer, and thereby to allow an exchange, a transformation, to take place, and truths to be both universally, if subliminally, acknowledged and tacitly reinterred.

Wilde's own transitus, so essential that, as we have seen, generations of writers have failed to detect (or have chosen to overlook) the Irishness resident in all his work, took him not only from a minor capital to a major one, from the barrenness of the Irish bog to the niceties of Hampshire, but also from one side of an equation to the other, inverting his value system and poisoning his role as 'court jester'. Within the confines and security of a self-confident system, misunderstandings, displacements, reversals of roles and fortunes, even cross-dressing, can be taken merely as tropes of fun; but for the enemy within that system they are weapons which begin in farce and end in warfare. 'In the native land of the hypocrite' the actor, the subversive, goes long unnoticed; for Wilde the classical scholar, the literal meaning of *hypocrisia* —acting a part—would have provided a delicious irony.

This is evident not least in the exchanges in Wilde's plays between masters and servants. Lord Goring's views— 'Vulgarity is simply the conduct of other people. . . . The only possible society is oneself' (*CW* 522)—are met by the near-silence of his valet, Phipps, which is elegant in its reserve. Phipps, who enjoys a close bond with Lane in the Worthing household, is permitted only one comment:

> GORING: Extraordinary thing about the lower classes in England—they are always losing their relations.
> PHIPPS: Yes, my lord! They are extremely fortunate in that respect. (*CW* 523)

Lane, by contrast, is nicely verbose:

> ALGERNON: I see from your book that on Thursday night, when Lord Shoreman and Mr Worthing were dining with me, eight bottles of champagne are entered as having been consumed.
> LANE: Yes, sir; eight bottles and a pint.
> ALGERNON: Why is it that at a bachelor's establishment the servants invariably drink the champagne? I ask merely for information.
> LANE: I attribute it to the superior quality of the wine, sir. I have often observed that in married households the champagne is rarely of a first-rate brand.
> ALGERNON: Good heavens! Is marriage so demoralising as all that?
> LANE: I believe it is a very pleasant state, sir. I have had very little experience of it myself up to the present. I have only been married once. That was in consequence of a misunderstanding between myself and a young person.
> ALGERNON (*languidly*): I don't know that I am much interested in your family life, Lane.
> LANE: No, sir; it is not a very interesting subject. I never think of it myself. (*CW* 321–2)

In *Salomé* the demarcation between the principal characters and their servants is less strict: the latter supplement the

social dialogue more pointedly because here Wilde was trying to create a total focus of humanity rather than the partial
focus by means of which simple and complex characters are
distinguished in his society plays. (This makes *Salomé* no less
comic, or absurd, of course, than it makes the society plays
tragic of their own kind.) The opening patter of *Salomé* is
indicative in that it is sustained and involves not principals
but supposed servants. It is here that we are told of the
strangeness of the moon in terms that leave an Irish reader
in no doubt that the moon is the symbol of death. In Lady
Wilde's *Ancient Legends* we read:

> In some parts of Ireland the people, it is said, on first
> seeing the new moon, fall on their knees and address
> her in a loud voice with the prayer: 'O moon; leave us
> well as thou hast found us'.[34]

Wilde stressed the presence of the moon throughout the
play—'cinquantes lunes enchainés dans un filet d'or'
(*Salomé* 73)—and was himself caricatured as the moon in
Beardsley's illustrations for the play.

> JEUNE SYRIEN: Elle a l'air très étrange. Elle rassemble à
> une princesse qui porte un voile jaune et a des pieds
> d'argent. Elle rassemble à une princesse qui a des
> pieds comme des petites colombes blanches.
> (*Salomé* 5)

Death, in fact, is evoked throughout the opening scene, so
that by the time the principals enter there is only one dominant character who subsumes every other. Salomé herself
'rassemble au reflet d'une rose blanche dans un miroir d'ar-
gent' (*Salomé* 7). Ireland is also evoked in the Arnoldian
migration of the gods to remote regions:

> Dans mon pays il n'y a pas de dieux à présent, les
> Romains les ont chassés. Il y en a qui disent qu'ils se

sont refugiés dans les montagnes, mais je ne le crois pas.... Je pense qu'ils sont morts. (*Salomé* 9)

The voice of Iokanaan is the first principal to be heard, but the response is a continued commentary by the slaves. One begins to see that if we were permitted to observe Phipps, Lane and the other minor players on Wilde's social stage in their own context, we might discover a commentary as acid and as damning as that in *Salomé*.

'The gap between moral conduct and social behaviour is narrow in Sheridan,' comments Deane.[35] In Wilde the gap is not so much closed as obfuscated: morality and behaviour overlap to a confusing degree. Wilde's plays are at their most moral when the characters invert social values in order to voice paradoxical truths. One reason for this inversion was Wilde's attempt, as with his poetry, to reconcile the pagan concept of 'sin' with the new Christian idea of 'love'. 'Love' is necessary, and only necessary, where there is sin and, consequently, where remorse is experienced and the prospect of 'paradise' is jeopardised. Because we now witness a separation of love between *eros* and *agape*, the virtues of pagan society break down and sin, hitherto accepted but uncomprehended, becomes a fact of consciousness. It is the confrontation between the lust-driven paganism of Salomé and the new light of passionate *agape* embodied in the disturbing image of Iokanaan which gives *Salomé* its dramatic tension. Everything in the play—even the babel of decadent voices from the lost people clamouring around Herod—contributes to piling up the contrasts between the two.

Revelation was an essential ingredient in a dramatic climate which had *The Lost Child* as a staple diet. The flat melodramatic strategy which Wilde had employed in his stories— for example the declaration 'I am thy mother' in 'The Star-Child' (*CW* 277)—is only slightly amended in the methods by which relationship is revealed in *A Woman of No Importance* or concealed in *Lady Windermere's Fan*. The stock elements in melodrama—spectacle, romance and flamboyance—survived the break-up of form and of theatrical convention. Characters required a clouded past, an uncertain, turbulent present and the prospect of a future, and the unity which produced a transformative experience in the playhouse greeted the introduction of new themes with equanimity. Thus the tug-of-war between innocence and experience, or the tug-of-love between the sexes, survived the arrival of such 'larger' dramatic issues as religion, sex and politics. Wilde (and Shaw) greatly expanded what Martin Meisel calls 'the duel of sex'[36] and introduced the theme of judgment by a daughter of her mother and by a son of his father. But although the setting of such dramas moved largely from the rural to the metropolitan, from the tavern to the drawing-room, the basic instruments of the theatre—suspense, identification with hero or heroine, the master–servant relationship, the holding of the mirror up to nature—were still in play.

Wilde's particular triumph was that, unlike Pinero in *The Profligate* (1889), for example, he clothed these social commentaries with humour, thus giving rise to the assumption by audiences and critics that they were 'social comedies'. With the possible exception of *Earnest*, they were nothing of the sort. The inclusion of funny lines does not of itself constitute a comedy. *Vera* reads (and would probably play) today as an absurdly histrionic confection, but it remains a tragedy despite the occurrence of some of Wilde's funniest lines; *Salomé* is none the less a death-devoted play for all Herod's daftly unconscious *drôleries*. There was, in fact, little place for comedy pure and simple in an age which required a mirror for its own social and intellectual ferment. H. A. Jones in 1895 said that drama should not fear 'to keep bold and reverent hands on the deepest things of the human life of today and freely expose them'.[37] It was not necessary for Wilde or Shaw to abandon the melodramatic form in order to belong to the theatrical movement which included Ibsen and Maeterlinck as writers, Antoine and Grein as directors. The serious depiction of social life on the stage was, indeed, moving, as Boucicault's own genre was moving, into the streets.

During this crucial period Shaw, Wilde and, later, Yeats provided a new thrust to British theatre which was still powered by the ramshackle energy and emotive vigour of the peasant play. In Wilde's case, and to a lesser extent Yeats's, this was also tied into a deep understanding of the Greek tragedies. Henry James was perplexed in 1880 by 'the infatuation of a public which passes from the drawing room to the theatre only to look at an attempt, at best very imperfect, to reproduce the accidents and limitations of the drawing room'.[38] His question was characteristic: James was incapable of appreciating the need for spunk on the stage, and he could not understand the poor fate of his own *Guy Domville* while *An Ideal Husband* was triumphant in London—'The thing seemed to me to be so helpless, so crude, so bad, so clumsy, feeble and vulgar. How *can* my piece do anything with a public with which *that* is a success?'[39] But it was the uniqueness of the vulgarity and crudity, and the seriousness of his intent, which enabled Wilde to take the town by storm while quietly mocking its structures and its heroes.

(ii) COMMENTARY

It was in creating images of confusion rather than simplicity that Wilde excelled both as a playwright and as a schemer. His most complex characters are, like the oxymoron, impossibilities. In Lord Goring, the dandy at the centre of *An Ideal Husband*, Wilde created a pivotal character around whom the 'good' and 'bad' characters revolve and through whom the moralities of the play are mediated. Goring, described as 'a mask with a manner... the first well-dressed philosopher in the history of thought', 'stands in immediate relation to modern life, makes it indeed, and so masters it' (CW 522)— the role which, as we have seen, Wilde accorded himself in 'De Profundis'. It is Goring's function to act the dandy and yet to broker the ambitions of Sir Robert Chiltern and Mrs Cheveley—the one his best friend, the other a former fiancée. When his father, Lord Caversham, describes him on two occasions as 'heartless, sir, quite heartless' (*CW* 490, 524), he provides a pre-echo of Shaw's criticism of *Earnest*. Yet heartlessness—the mark of the cynic—is not the entire dandy, who balances the masculine and feminine temperaments, rational and irrational, public and private. It is because the men and women in the play, those who live different lives in public and in private, recognise this in Goring that they appeal to, and submit to, his mediation.

Lady Markby's observation, in *An Ideal Husband*, that 'As a rule, everybody turns out to be somebody else' (*CW* 486) is not merely a way of saying that by adopting a mask we eventually catch up with our origins, but a commentary on the fact that such masks are necessary in order for us to conduct our everyday lives. Goring is the supreme example of this liminal person, through whom others can discover and lose themselves, a Janus of complete indifference and intense caring.

There is a sense, detected by the actors preparing for the first production of *Earnest*, in which the play 'would prove too subtle for the public'.[40] Little of the commentary within the lines of Wilde's society plays is evident to the urbane playgoer. The motion by which, in *An Ideal Husband*, Mrs Cheveley steps into the next room has profoundly semantic consequences both for the play and its audience. It is the same intellectual ploy by which, in *The True-born Irishman* and *The London Vertigo*, Macklin, followed by Friel, shows people moving from one affective room, or field, to another, speaking relative languages and enacting different scenarios. The simultaneous rendition of these disparate modes of speaking would indeed have been too subtle for the London audiences and critics who accepted Wilde's plays as comedies.

The crucial scene at the opening of the second act of *An Ideal Husband*, for example, when Sir Robert Chiltern exposes the situation to Goring's judgment, depends for its success on Goring, hitherto and hereafter an intelligent popinjay, convincing the audience that he is man enough to facilitate the rescue of his friend, and woman enough to effect it. Both sincerity and the apparent lack of sincerity are the prerequisites. When Goring announces: 'All reasons are absurd' (*CW* 489), he does not deny the existence of reason, but affirms it and makes the critical connection between reason and absurdity on which ontology depends—*credo quia absurdum*. When he adds to it: 'A man who allows himself to be convinced by an argument is a thoroughly unreasonable person' (*CW* 490), he is asserting the primacy of the individual mind over the rational standards of others: reason is the quality which resides in oneself when all other qualities and categories have been dispensed with. During their conversation Chiltern makes an assertion to Goring which is breathtaking in its personal logic and in the way in which that logic stands conventional morality on its head:

> Do you really think, Arthur, that it is weakness that yields to temptation? I tell you that there are terrible temptations that it requires strength, strength and courage, to yield to. To stake all one's life on a single moment, to risk everything on one throw, whether the stake be power or pleasure, I care not—there is no weakness in that. There is a horrible, a terrible courage.
> (*CW* 506)

The role of Goring in facilitating this is acknowledged in Chiltern's 'You have enabled me to tell the truth.... The truth has always stifled me.' (*CW* 510) It also echoes Eteocles in Euripides' *The Phoenician Women*: 'If one must do a wrong, it were best done in the pursuit of power—otherwise, let's have virtue.'[41]

The motility of ideas is crudely represented in *An Ideal Husband* by the naïve transfer between Goring and Lady Chiltern of the lines 'A woman's life revolves in curves of emotions. It is upon lines of intellect that a man's life progresses' (*CW* 548, 549), which, as we have seen, acknowledges

Lady Wilde's view of woman's submission to, and power over, man. Alan Bird comments that in *An Ideal Husband* Wilde demonstrates 'that the great secret of public success is simply never to be found out' and that this represents 'the basic hypocrisy of English life'.[42] It is certainly a play which has cynicism—and thus, as Bird argues, dramatic irony—at its heart; yet it also has a simple faith which is no less significant for feeding off, and contributing to, that same melodramatic irony. The lack of action in most of his plays underlines this intense capacity in Wilde for pursuing ideas. The fact that his dramatic work culminated effectively in the assertion of 'the importance of being gay' adds to, rather than detracts from, this achievement: Wilde was stating that a point is reached in life on which a stand, however perverted it may seem to others, must be taken, when we must stop being 'somebody else' and discover who we ourselves are. At that point we will indeed seem, by discarding the mask we have been wearing, to have become somebody else, but that self is the home self towards whom we have been proceeding. Wilde thus becomes the conduit by means of which the stylised symmetry of Farquhar and Sheridan could be passed to Shaw and ultimately Beckett: it was a restatement of the aesthetic and political question of the Restoration—'how define the network of social relations that condition and ultimately determine my public image?'[43]—in modern terms.

In relation to *A Woman of No Importance*, Alan Bird observes that 'the real problem of the play is not that set out on the stage but one inherent in Wilde the man as distinct from Wilde the dramatist',[44] and this is true partly because Wilde was a playwright merely by necessity. He derived a satisfaction from seeing his ideas exploited to mercenary advantage, yet he perhaps derived a greater satisfaction from the fact that he could do so without detection. By pretending to be 'Wilde the dramatist' he could promote both the acid view of English hypocrisy—'a lot of damned nobodies talking about nothing' (*CW* 490)—and the idea that this wasteground could become the seedbed of a new society. To deconstruct society by exposing its insubstantiality is to posit the need for amorality: 'It is indeed a burning shame that there should be one law for men and another law for women....I think that there should be no law for anybody.'[45]

That this went undetected was part of Wilde's personal, singular play. On the morning after the première of *An Ideal Husband* Wilde said that the critics had missed 'its entire psychology....They really thought it was a play about a bracelet. ...The critics subordinate the psychological interest of a play to its mere technique. As soon as a dramatist invents an ingenious situation, they compare him with Sardou.'[46] This has, in fact, become a substantial part of the analysis of Wilde's plays; their origins, like Shakespeare's, often seem more important to commentators than what Wilde himself intended to do with his raw material. But, as Wilde himself said, he had shown in *An Ideal Husband* the difference between the way men and women think, and therefore love and live:

> the difference in the way in which a man loves a woman from that in which a woman loves a man; the passion that women have for making ideals (which is their weakness) and the weakness of a man who dares not show his imperfections to the thing he loves.[47]

Whether or not it was in Wilde's interests to make such an assertion is difficult to judge. His self-revelation in interview may have been as deliberate as his self-occlusion in his plays. It is as if he was determined to come out in real life and yet to insist by means of his plays that he was someone else. While there is no evidence for Hesketh Pearson's assertion that *Earnest* was originally set 'in the period of Sheridan', it is easy to see why Pearson should have said that 'the moment Wilde gave rein to his native genius, it burst through the style and costume of the eighteenth century and rioted in its own dimension'.[48] It would have been more accurate to say that *Earnest* subsumed the eighteenth-century conceits and amplified their gayness.

A glance at Sheridan will indicate precisely how far Wilde was prepared to subsume or openly adopt both the genre and the thrust of Restoration drama. In *The Rivals* Mrs Malaprop stands as the 'old tough aunt in the way' of love and marriage[49] and thus precedes both Boucicault's Penelope Prude and Wilde's Lady Bracknell. Her malapropisms were a profound influence on Miss Prism; there is much to be said for her confusion of 'parallax' and 'paradox',[50] while the discontinuities of time which we have noted in the Irish historical experience are fully expressed in her 'We will not anticipate the past.... Our retrospection will be all to the future.'[51] Sheridan's characters are called by one name in town and another in the country,[52] while Sir Anthony Absolute's questions, 'Who the d[evi]l are you?', 'Are you my son or not?—answer for your mother, you dog, if you won't for me,' and his son's answer 'Faith, Sir, I am not quite clear myself,'[53] is the same part-burlesque, part-tragedy which runs throughout Wilde.

Meanwhile in *The School for Scandal* the remark of the servant, Snake, to Lady Sneer—''Tis very true.... She wants that delicacy of Hint and mellifluousness of sneer which distinguish your Ladyship's Scandal'[54]—anticipates Phipps's observation on the buttonhole, while the backbiting remark 'Her Face resembles a Table d'hôte at Spaw where no two guests are of a nation'[55] would become a stage direction in *An Ideal Husband*: '*In all her movements she is extremely graceful. A work of art, on the whole, but showing the influence of too many schools.*' (*CW* 484) Lady Sneer's distinction between the capacities of men and women for scandal would weigh significantly with Wilde in his own drawing of the sexes: 'We have Pride, envy, Rivalship, and a Thousand motives to depreciate each other—but the male-Slanderer—must have the cowardice of a woman before He can traduce one.'[56]

The relationship of men to women was important to Wilde because he was deeply concerned both with his own marriage to Constance and with his 'marriages' to Ross, Douglas and other young men. In *A Woman of No Importance* one character rejects the idea that there could be such a thing as 'an ideal husband' which ostensibly became the subject of his next play. Equally important to Wilde was the existence of the 'good woman', and beyond that was the image of the woman as artist, the dark side of which was significantly expressed in the dance of Salomé. Wilde very early abandoned the sentiment of Guido in *The Duchess of Padua*:

> Women are the best artists of the world,
> For they can take the common lives of men
> Soiled with the money-getting of our age,
> And with love make them beautiful. (*CW* 598)

Wilde wanted to reverse—or at least to equalise—the idea expressed in *A Woman of No Importance*, that 'The woman suffers. The man goes free.' (*CW* 473) Freedom, in an amoral, asexual society, would be for everyone, to compensate for the fact that everyone also suffers. 'Let us call things by their proper names,' says Chiltern to Mrs Cheveley, an admonition she returns to him as their positions are reversed. It becomes possible to give correct names to things when their properties are recognised. Mrs Cheveley, like Lady Bracknell, must be seen as a man in a man's world, capable of daring acts because she combines flair with strength. Until that point is reached the masks, codes and other disguises which first entered Wilde's secret stage in *Vera* remain necessary and in place; ambivalence, which resonates in the iconography of the *fin de siècle*— both in the decadence of Moreau and Klimt and in the baroque genius of portraitists such as Sargent and Orpen—remains the leitmotif of an age of vacillation between opposites.

All Wilde's plays, with the possible exception of *Salomé*, address the issue of parentage and the obscurity or uncertainty of origins. Relations between fathers and sons, mothers and sons, mothers and daughters (and this, of course, does include *Salomé*) are determined by the degree to which they know and recognise one another. At the centre of the relation is the question of honour and the activity of conscience:

some children, like Jack Worthing, have been 'lost' and inhabit a world of makebelieve—a world which they try to make credible; others, like Gerald Arbuthnot, have been forsaken or abandoned by one parent and spend their time innocently sheltered from the truth by the other; all of them come to realise that some cloud darkens their origin, that there is an air of dishonour from not knowing sufficiently clearly who one is. (Here Euripides' *Ion*, with its plot of concealed parentage and a cradle reappearing at the dénouement, must be considered as a forerunner of the handbag in *Earnest*.) To become the elusive person, to be reintegrated with the missing parent and with the missing part of oneself, to effect a family reunion, is the storyboard of the individual quest. It exercises conscience because it places an onus on the child not only to discover the truth but also to grant forgiveness and acceptance to the wayward parent.

Within the unfulfilled world of the child the possibilities for action are wide. In the discovery of oneself one is able to invent relations and to adapt the given situation to one's needs. In *Earnest* Jack Worthing invents a brother, Ernest, while the man revealed in the play's final scene as his actual brother, Algernon Moncrieff, invents an invalid friend called Bunbury; both of them do so in order to be somewhere else at inconvenient moments. Jack's ward, Cecily Cardew, whom Jack at one point suggests is his aunt, has fallen in love with, and written extensively to and about, her guardian's brother whom (because he does not exist) she has no real hope of ever meeting. The fact that she does, in fact, meet 'Ernest', who is none other than Algernon on a 'Bunburying' exercise, should not be allowed to obscure this reality. At the moment of discovery, when the outcome of the entire mystery seems to depend on ascertaining the first name of General Moncrieff, none of the participants, not even his own son Algernon, is able to recall the vital detail. The fact that his name was Ernest John, thus doubly ratifying Jack's own invention, or that the child is called Worthing because that was the destination of the man who found him, seems as fortuitous as the

fact that Wilde himself called him Worthing because that
was where the play was written.

Within the plays concerned with missing origins, friendship becomes very important: that between Chiltern and
Goring is the rock on which the standards of the play are
based; the bantering friendship between Jack and Algernon
permits the double deception to blossom into true brother-
hood; even in the 'revenge tragedy' of *The Duchess of Padua*
Guido Ferranti is brought into existence by means of a letter
signed 'Your Father's Friend'. Trust of a kind otherwise
unavailable to the protagonist is the order of the day.

This, in many senses, set the pace for his later stage
works. They are less dramas of passion than exercises in personality, portraits of goodness and badness juxtaposed within the social distances of the English family and its politics.
As in his verse, the author's own conscience travels along an
axis between the polarities which he establishes, sometimes
expressing remorse, at others calling for pity. The differences
between men and women are explored exhaustively, so
much so that it emerges that Wilde was less interested in
what distinguished the sexes—rational thought *versus* intuition, natural grace *versus* artifice, guilt *versus* innocence—
than in the way in which these opposites are present in us
all. Man and woman are accomplices in the subversion, perversion and inversion of the social graces, in their replacement
by the invention of paradox and irony, and in the elevation
of the concept of play, in which passion runs unchecked.

Behind this stalks another presence, that of the conscience
which is born of doubt and which polices the vacillating dialogue between 'self' and 'soul'. In *The Duchess of Padua* the
Duke, subverting Hamlet, discusses conscience as 'but the
name which cowardice/Fleeing from battle scrawls upon its
shield' (*CW* 584). Dorian Gray pays the ultimate price of self-
destruction in his attempt to kill conscience, but in *An Ideal
Husband* the relation between cowardice and conscience has
been turned around so that the strength necessary to embrace
cowardly actions is acknowledged and elevated to a virtue,
while in sixteenth-century Padua a citizen declares:

I like no law at all:
Were there no law there'd be no law-breakers,
So all men would be virtuous. (*CW* 630)

The last reason for the uniqueness of Wilde's drama lies in the fact that the outcome of each play depends not only on a dénouement but also on a further concealment. At the conclusion of *Earnest* Jack declares that precise principle: he regains his patrimony because his name is Ernest, but as he embarks on his new life of marriage he also practises a further deception by simultaneously declaring, in the same words, his homosexuality. In order to do so, Wilde has employed two parallel sets of codes and thus of meanings both disclosed and dissembled.

A Woman of No Importance is Wilde's most formless and inchoate drama and, as such, offers more explicit, less subtly crafted, examples of the way he combined social and artistic ideas, finding a *via media* to the apparently autochthonous quality of *Earnest* and *Salomé*. It is important to stress that the uniqueness of his work was multiple rather than singular. Although many influences can be traced in his work, Wilde's eclecticism was transcended by the power of his intention and the nature of his imagination; whatever came into his mind was made subservient to that originality—the seedbed of his Irish mind, which looked on the rules and formats imposed by others as foreign and unnatural. His work was thus not only autochthonous but also autonomous, making distinct amendments and metamorphoses to any received wisdom. It was nihilistic in that it accepted nothing conventional, recognised nothing which could be put into a form of words unless it was *sui generis* and thus, by definition, was a form engendered by himself. It was anarchic in that it refused to submit to any discipline and denied the validity of power structures.

'Nothing is serious except passion,' Wilde said in *A Woman of No Importance*. 'The intellect is not a serious thing, and never has been. It is an instrument on which one plays, that is all.' (*CW* 438) This echo of 'Hélas!' is interesting in that it combines the idea of soul and intellect, suggesting that in an 'ideal' climate one might dispense with such distractions. The notion that the distinction has entered modern consciousness as a result of a development in ways of seeing and thinking is compelling; it recalls Yeats's observation that 'Until the battle of the Boyne, Ireland belonged to Asia.'[57] The mythopoeic life being superseded by the logocentric is the beginning of modernism and the end of poetry. 'Nothing should be out of the reach of hope. Life is a hope,' says the American heiress, Hesther Worsley (*CW* 433)—a perfectly Irish aspiration, coming from the son of 'Speranza'. Wilde followed the statement immediately with a seminal distinction between men and women:

> LADY STUTFIELD: The world was made for men and not for women.
> MRS ALLONBY: Oh, don't say that, Lady Stutfield. We have a much better time than they have. There are far more things forbidden to us than are forbidden to them.   (*CW* 434)

He suggests that the feminine type continues to enjoy greater access to the imaginative life, while the masculine has the entrée to the public life. Later he confuses this with Lord Illingworth's declaration that 'Society is a necessary thing ... and women rule society' (*CW* 460), but if one understands that it is due to their ability to resort to an affective life beyond clubland that women exercise power over men, the statement becomes much clearer: women remind men of their mothers, of their origins, of a power beyond the grasp of high finance and politics. In *A Woman of No Importance* we see Wilde's first clumsy attempt to express the commerce between the sexes which can take place in a single imagination. Women are 'sphinxes without secrets' (*CW* 441)—in other words, a disappointment because they offer no mystery.

* * *

A play of manners—or conceits—requires persons of a certain class and disposition. A play of commentary, however, looks beneath class and disposition in order to discover truths not about individuals but about their society; it need not therefore concern itself with their personal niceties. Wilde's characters are not characters in their own right, but counters signifying 'man', 'woman', 'son', 'mother'. But more than that, they are also transsexual: his strong women—Mrs Cheveley, Mrs Erlynne, Lady Bracknell—are not really women but men, dandies shaping the world of fashionable ideas and action. Where, in Sheridan, home truths are elicited by chorus agreement, in Wilde they have more of a tragic note. It is the sign of Wilde's nonchalance that it matters not whether the injured are innocent or guilty. People are hurt because they live. Women in Wilde's plays—no less than in Ibsen's—are cut adrift from society, while men succeed in disguising their guilt. The men, however, are weak, despite their ostensible privilege, while the women, because they are sinister, are also strong.

In three plays Speranza's son establishes the paradoxical nature of the 'bondage of women'. As we have seen, in *An Ideal Husband* Lady Chiltern adopts Goring's view: 'A man's life is of more value than a woman's.' In *Lady Windermere's Fan* Mrs Erlynne replies to her own daughter's 'You are bought and sold':

> You don't know what it is to fall into the pit, to be despised, mocked, abandoned, sneered at—to be an outcast! to find the door shut against one, to have to creep in by hideous byways, afraid every moment lest the mask should be stripped from one's face, and all the while to hear the laughter, the horrible laughter of the world, a thing more tragic than all the tears the world has ever shed. (*CW* 413)

And in *A Woman of No Importance* Mrs Arbuthnot says: 'The woman suffers. The man goes free.' (*CW* 473) Because by nature he was neither man nor woman, by affiliation neither Irish nor English nor French, Wilde found his sympathies to lie with the extraterritorial, the extrasexual, those who are different, separate, and yet who fail, ultimately, to be autonomous. His mockery of some women (the puppets) and his obvious sympathy for others (the strong and the wronged) stems from this. His mother had written of 'the bondage of women': 'For six thousand years the history of women has been a mournful record of helpless resignation to social prejudice and legal tyranny.'[58] It is clear from the bewilderment caused by his plays that her son, adopting her role as polemicist, was not a true dramatist. Yeats wrote of *A Woman of No Importance* that 'Despite its qualities, it is not a work of art, it has no central fire, it is not dramatic in any ancient sense of the word.'[59] In this sense, Shaw too was undramatic in his drama, rejecting the conventions of the stage not merely because he intended to introduce a new type of play but because he was neither responsible for, nor responsive to, its dominant genres. Thus, as Meisel puts it, 'he was not a man of the theatre; resisting the conventional route to dramatic excellence, he chose to adopt the nineteenth-century popular theatre'.[60] Shaw went so far as to build this disclaimer into *Fanny's First Play*, where he makes the critic (modelled on Walkley) denounce the work of a playwright, identifiable as Shaw himself, as 'exhibitions of character, perhaps: especially the character of the author. Fictions, possibly.... But plays, no. I say NO. Not plays.'[61]

Thus in 'De Profundis' we find Wilde, in boasting mood, claiming to have transformed

> the drama, the most objective form known to art, and made it as personal a mode of expression as the lyric or the sonnet, at the same time that I widened its range and enriched its characterisation. (*L* 466)

It was in this autonomous and autocratic way that Wilde succeeded in creating his decade, persuading readers and audiences of the uniqueness of his voice. In his characterisation he put on the Victorian stage people who disown or deride its values and yet are applauded for doing so. They are acid portraits of decadence, but they are not in themselves decadent because they retain at all times a vestige of their author's own preoccupations and, above all, vulnerability.

(iii) SYMBOLISM

'We write plays, I feel, in order to populate a stage,' says the contemporary Irish playwright Thomas Kilroy. 'It is this curious desire to move about actual living bodies, to give them voice and the mantle of character in a conspiracy of play, which distinguishes playwriting from all other kinds of writing.'[62] Wilde's drama was always symbolic—his puppets rarely wore more than the mere 'mantle of character'—and he remained faithful to the idea that the purpose of the stage was to provide a space for the witnessing of doom in action. Nevertheless, he obeyed the ubiquitous compulsion to 'populate a stage', thus permitting the eternal re-creation of the family to whom that doom is as natural as clothing.

'All dramatic technique begins with the first image that is imposed upon the empty stage,' says Kilroy. 'As playwrights we are defined by that first image. We are what we are by where we choose to make things happen.'[63] A Russian inn, the market-place of Padua, a series of drawing-rooms, a great terrace in the palace of Herod, a valley in the Thebaid, are the places which define Wilde's drama. Ostensibly they can be divided into two sharply contrasting locales, that of nineteenth-century London and its environs and that of the largely biblical province. But the niceties of Mayfair society should not prevent us from seeing that all Wilde's people are affected by a Fate which they do not understand. Wilde himself was the superbly undramatic dramatist because he too could not understand why he continued to put before his audiences the archetypally wounded family. 'As for living, our servants will do that for us,' declares Axël, in a drama symbolically dressed in death. Wilde's people do not so much live or die as linger in a supercharged limbo where, surrounded by their servants, they discuss the pros and cons of a life which they cannot impersonate.

Behind the façade of manners, which Wilde borrowed from his eighteenth-century Irish predecessors, lay not only the question 'Who am I?' but the further question 'What am I doing here?' In 'The Critic as Artist' he wrote:

> For Antigone even, with Death waiting for her as her bridegroom, it was easy to pass through the tainted air at noon, and climb the hill, and strew with kindly earth the wretched naked corse that had no tomb. (CW 1024)

He was intent on establishing that 'those who gave [such characters] reality, and made them live for ever' are perhaps 'greater than the men and women they sing of.... The world is made by the singer for the dreamer.' (CW 1025) Nowhere is this more true than of his own *Salomé*, where the princess, in her doom-driven focus on the figure of Iokanaan, in death as in life, bears a striking similarity with Antigone.

The fascination with death was ubiquitous in the nineteenth century. It was both a compulsive interest in the morbid nature of death as the opposite to life, and an attempt to analyse the ways by which we reach it: death as fate rather than death as the natural end of life. In the iconographies of both Salomé and Antigone, this interest revolves around questions of the relation of good to evil which are not only ethical but also ontological. The most overtly decadent of Wilde's plays is also the most modern, because it addresses the crisis which had become evident in the work of Ibsen and would be exercised in the political dimension in the First World War.

Steiner places the burden of the Antigone myth on the shoulders of language and translation—a responsibility which, as we shall see in the next chapter, Wilde placed at the centre of criticism. Its ubiquity, in Steiner's terms, derives from the concentric nature of the issues: the words which constitute the myth itself must be capable of metaphor, of translation, and yet in themselves are inherently unstable and at the same time the unique means by which the biological problem of existence can be articulated. Man, the language-animal,[64] is both empowered and devastated by this special attribute.

Steiner states the uniqueness of Sophocles' *Antigone* thus:

> It has, I believe, been given to only one literary text to express all the principal constants of conflict in the condition of man. These constants are fivefold: the confrontation of men and of women; of age and of youth; of society and of the individual; of the living and the dead; of men and of god(s). The conflicts ... are not negotiable. [The characters] define themselves in the conflictual process of defining each other. Self-definition and the agonistic recognition of 'otherness' (of *l'autre*) across the threatened boundaries of self, are indissociable.... To arrive at oneself—the primordial journey—is to come up, polemically, against 'the other'.[65]

The issue so powerfully conveyed in *Salomé* is both 'here and now' and 'then and there'—it places the individual in an acute relationship to 'the other', to society, and to history. In each case there is the imperative of an attempted homecoming,[66] in which one passes from one side of a metaphorical equation to the other, knowing oneself as an integrated entity for the first time. Antigone's imperative is ethical—the defence of friendship, of respect, of innocence which by its very exercise becomes unhesitatingly and irrecoverably involved in the world of mendacity, of autarchy—the world of experience—to which it reacts. Her trajectory towards death is fated because she stands at the cardinal points of relation to family and community. Salomé's imperative is equally ethical: she, the silver-footed beauty, must discover, within the beast of Iokanaan, the purity which she lacks in her own breeding, must acknowledge him as the 'voice crying in the wilderness', the harbinger of a new world order. At the moment of fusion between beauty and beast, of a beautiful known corruption and an apprehended purity, Salomé submits to the death which hangs above the palace of Herod.

Steiner says:

> *Men and women use words very differently*. Where their uses meet, dialogue becomes dialectic and utterance is drama. ... The original source of the dramatic lies in the paradox of conflict, of agonistic misunderstanding, in language itself.[67] [*my emphasis*]

Such a view helps us to appreciate the exchanges between Guido and the Duchess in *The Duchess of Padua*, Sir Robert Chiltern and Lady Chiltern and Mrs Cheveley in *An Ideal Husband*, Lord Darlington and Lady Darlington and Mrs Erlynne in *Lady Windermere's Fan*. It also illuminates the androgyny of the dandies, Lord Goring and Lady Bracknell. And taken at its most sophisticated level, it underlines the ritualised nature of *Salomé*.

'Agonistic misunderstanding'[68] is Steiner's method of explaining the ways of God to man. But we must remember that for the cast of the house of Atreus, of Priam, of Laius, it was no simple matter to bring the *agon* and the mis-take into such easy congruence. Behind the deaths of Oedipus, Antigone and Agamemnon is the sinister existence of the Sphinx, the monster with a human voice sent by Hera to plague the land of Thebes, where Wilde set his last play, 'La Sainte Courtisane'. We must also remember that Orestes and Oedipus became travellers in their own land, exiles from everything except the past, yet unable to touch the one thing in their past which might redeem them, the secret of their birth. 'At his birth a snare was laid for him,' it is said of Oedipus, and if we examine some of the plays with which

Wilde was thoroughly familiar—Euripides' *Herakles* and *Phoenician Women* and Aeschylus' *Agamemnon*—we will find this translated into the refrains 'I sing that I may weep'[69] and 'May he reap the crime of his own heart'.[70]

Greek drama, like Irish, continually bewails its tragedy, yet accepts it. The 'destruction of the house', the complete deconstruction of reality, is the daily fear of its participants, expected because they must atone for sins which are innate. The conflict born of ancient bitterness is not 'a thing new thought upon, but pondered deep in time'.[71] The hero must be toppled because he impersonates the fate of his family and his race. Even the ground itself, which is local, familial, tribal, and universal is 'the land that gave him birth',[72] 'the land herself who bore me',[73] and 'love of country' is supreme.[74] Like *Salomé*, *Herakles* is distinguished by its peripety, its dislocation, the 'virtuosity and violence' of its structure;[75] brutal power and tenderness go hand in hand. Wilde would have been drawn to this play because, as in the mythical Irish epics, we see here the exchange of gods and men, mediated by the figure of the hero,[76] by means of which the audience can partake of a transformative experience and thus witness not only the truth of their own tragic condition but also 'a courage founded on love'[77] and, indeed, hope (a word which, to the Greeks, embodied expectation of both good and evil). It is this duality which explains how a play—embodying its audience's capabilities—can be rooted in such concepts as Amphitryon's line, which we know to have been a favourite of Wilde:

I am in love, it seems, with what cannot be.[78]

The 'madness' which pervades the house is the madness of a man at play with fate which so disturbs the usually wise Chorus that it asks: 'What dance shall I dance for death?'[79] It is in the non-place of contradiction that the hero is caught.

'The secret chamber of the house in which *Salomé* was fashioned', Wilde had admitted. He was never more gushing than when he felt that he was being appreciated and, perhaps, found out, as if embarrassed by an artistic triumph which was as transparent as it was translucent. It is clear that his continued referral to biblical themes—Salomé, Jezebel, Joseph—like his repeated return to the Sphinx who also inhabited that 'secret chamber', revolves around his interest in strong women. He is both repelled and attracted by the fascination of the strong woman, and both admonished and driven to mockery by that of a good one. He thus exhibits a complex set of associations with ideas of womanhood which relate both to his own sexuality and to the sexual politics of the time. As we see in Beardsley's illustrations to *Salomé*, men and women naturally crossed the barriers which conventionally distinguished the sexes.

The 'secret' which Wilde had buried at the heart of *Salomé* was the importance of transsexuality, of the capacity to inhabit a space between masculinity and femininity. Naturally this was a blatant breach of sexual convention, but it was not necessarily evident to the audience, and we are helped to detect it by means of Beardsley's pictures. When Wilde said at the time of Beardsley's death that 'behind his grotesques there seemed to lurk some curious psychology' (*L* 410), he was being less than candid, since the published text of *Salomé* can be read as a collaboration in which the portrayal of androgynous figures in a variety of poses both suggestive and reflexive, including that of Wilde himself as 'The Woman in the Moon', expressed the artist's conscious decision to refute and reform Victorian attitudes to sexuality.

The identification of signifier and signified is the hallmark of symbolist drama, its sureness of the gerund. Salomé is the dance, and the dance is death. Yeats ultimately thought the play 'typical in our generation'.[80] Bernhardt's attraction for Wilde as the interpreter of the title part may well have rested on her well-proven capacity to perform male roles such as Pelléas, Hamlet, Cherubino and L'Aiglon, and thus to play 'an elfin travesty of a man' in such a way that sex was an 'accident'.[81] Once again it is the difference between appearance and reality, but intensified to the point where the mask of personality becomes the only reality. 'I am not *a* Man in *a* Cloak, but *the* Man in *the* Cloak,' Mangan insisted,[82] and the same can be read in the characters on Wilde's stage. 'The future', Wilde had announced in *A Woman of No Importance*, 'belongs to the dandy' (*CW* 459), meaning that the imaginative transfer between the sexes would create a new society as it would renew the theatre. As Barbey d'Aurevilly said of the dandiacal figure, '*Paraître*, c'est *être* pour les Dandys, comme pour les femmes':[83] the ability, not to resemble, but to become a woman. The very fact that the title of his 'La Sainte Courtisane' represents a supreme oxymoron is indicative of the theatre of transformation which Wilde secretly hoped to achieve.

Helen Grace Zagona has suggested that 'probably the most ingenious element in his translation of the eternal legend [of Salomé] into terms proper to the decadent period is Laforgue's version of Salomé's fatal, intoxicating performance. The carnal dance sequence which provided the powerful climax to the original legend now becomes an intellectual monologue.'[84] Thus Salomé, like Antigone, can confront all the elements of conflict: to her, Iokanaan is husband, brother, father and god. Wilde saw in her the most subtle method of acknowledging the coexistence of the three selves whom he had described in *Dorian Gray*: the artist (here represented by Salomé), the work of art (here, the dance), and the artist's mentor, here taking the form of Iokanaan and consumed by Salomé in the execution and the kiss.

This is the enactment of a complex passion which, as Worth has pointed out, is prefigured in 'The Harlot's House' as 'a near-scenario for a symbolist shadow play'.[85] It is probably true of that poem and *The Sphinx* that together with *Salomé* they represent the most fearful and serious aspect of

Wilde's writing. Sartre has said: 'After you have explained Racine by his environment, by the age, by his childhood, there remains *Phèdre*, which is inexplicable';[86] for Wilde, provincial, secretive, inverted, rebellious against all forms of authority, dismissive of convention, resentful of despotism and injustice, the 'inexplicable' is whatever is irreducible. Like Le Fanu's *Uncle Silas*, the text and action of *Salomé* need not be Irish in subject-matter or even in inflection in order to address, as the texts and actions of Ibsen, the preoccupations of *l'homme dominé*,[87] of the 'gay science' which seeks to express 'something else' in its depiction of a new order. By ushering in a new age the properties suppressed or inhibited by history are recognised and thus history is rewritten. The age which witnesses 'the New Woman' and describes her in one word—'man'[88]—has, however facetiously, acknowledged the overtures to the liberation of all sexuality, but it has also enabled us to see once again the significance of cross-dressing in Shakespeare's Rosalind and Viola.

For Wilde, the creation of comedies was pointless; even its inconsequentiality was uninteresting and unrewarding. Passionate to extremes, he required an intellectual challenge which would also be visceral in its impact. In this, again, he was echoing some of the intensity and apprehension of the Irish nineteenth century which was such a fertile period for the central feature which William Archer detected in *Salomé*—'the life of the imagination'.[89] For Edgar Saltus, the effect of the play was to make him shudder, to which Wilde retorted: 'It is only the shudder that counts.'[90] The remark is neither facetious nor superficial: the beating of the wings of death is experienced by Herod, but it hovers over the whole palace, over masters and servants alike; it is a strategy by means of which Wilde articulated the notion of doom which he took from the gothic imagination of his mother and her predecessors.

Salomé, in the repetition of gnomic phrases, becomes its own cliché, but Wilde has also deepened the outline in order to 'touch the minds of others' on a shared—even if only imagined—plane of experience. That he did so with the assistance of the Greek tragedies and the compelling example of Ibsen (whose *A Doll's House* had been followed in 1889 by *The Pillars of Society*, and between 1890 and 1892 by *Hedda Gabler*, *Rosmersholm* and *Ghosts*, and in the projected year of *Salomé*—1893—by *The Master Builder* and *An Enemy of the People*) was perhaps inescapable. In a masterly essay Kerry Powell has traced the influence of Ibsen on Wilde: of the 'ideal parent' in *Ghosts* on *Lady Windermere's Fan*; of *The Pillars of Society* on *An Ideal Husband*, and of *Hedda Gabler* and *A Doll's House* on *The Importance of Being Earnest*. But the simplest expression of that influence lies not so much in any transfers of ideas or gestures but in the sharing of emotions, the breeding-ground of the subtlest ironies. Of *Hedda Gabler* Wilde indeed said: 'I felt pity and terror, as though the play had been Greek' (*L* 293), and Archer described *Salomé* as 'an oriental Hedda Gabler'. 'Not even an Irishman can depict a contradiction in terms,' he said, but that is what Wilde achieved in the depths of the play. As Powell remarks, 'Hedda and Salomé—nervous, depraved women whose desperate sexual games turn murderous in the end—represent a total contradiction of the pure and noble attributes with which the Victorian male had constructed his feminine ideal.'[91]

Powell quotes a London review of *Hedda Gabler*: 'Many a man's face was expressive of disgust, but I regret to say that I did not mark such an expression upon any woman's countenance.'[92] *The Times* described *Salomé* as 'an arrangement in blood and ferocity, morbid, *bizarre*, repulsive'.[93] The two reviews speak to each other. *Salomé* is everything *The Times* pronounces it to be. That either play could put a look of disgust or repulsion on the faces of its auditors is beyond doubt. In the 1890s—a decade which, we hardly need to remind ourselves, was one of the most transitional in all modern history—the dilemma of the citizen, whether associated with the arts or not, lay in the increasingly difficult choice between tradition and the unknown. In the dance of Salomé with its 'blood and ferocity' and in *A Florentine Tragedy*, which was originally entitled 'Love and Death', the playgoer would be offered a vision of a world which took the Greek tragedies, and the Wagnerian passion which had adopted Celtic themes and personalities, and the gothic mysteries of Irish literature, and made them fascinatingly modern. In 'La Sainte Courtisane', which Wilde set in the most problematic territory of Greek drama, the environs of Thebes, the two traditions of paganism and Christianity met for the last time.

A Florentine Tragedy has the cadence and atmosphere of *The Duchess of Padua*; 'La Sainte Courtisane' that of *Salomé*. Both address the issue of reversal, the transfer from one body, one mind, to another, of understanding, value and meaning by means of which 'facts' become 'something else'. The intellectual dimension is evident in Simone's exclamation in *A Florentine Tragedy*:

> Is all this mighty world
> Narrowed into the confines of this room
> With but three souls for poor inhabitants? (CW 694)

The lines are equally worthy of Maeterlinck's *Les Aveugles* or Beckett's *Endgame*.

The location of 'La Sainte Courtisane' has already been noted. But equally significant is the fact that Honorius, the prophet of Christ who lives as a hermit in the Thebaid, is enticed by Myrrhina, a native of Alexandria, the centre of the belief which rests on gnosticism, the power of a lie. 'La Sainte Courtisane' is a prose-poem writ large, and replicates many of the dramatic idiosyncracies of *Salomé*, especially its repetitive drive towards the dénouement. Its first words are 'Who is she?', the complement to Salomé's pursuit of Iokanaan. The discussion of the nature of the gods is repeated, not least in the debate between the singularity and multiplicity of 'God' and 'the gods'. Here Myrrhina, imitating Herod, woos Honorius with the recitation of her riches and marvels, identifying herself as both princess and whore: 'He at whom I smile leaves his companions and follows me to my home' (CW 704), and asserting her power to transform men: 'I made the Prince my slave, and his slave who was a Tyrian I made my Lord for the space of a moon.' (CW 704) But Honorius rejects her promiscuous interpretations of 'love' and 'beauty' in favour of the love and beauty of the singular god. But the fragment of this play which we possess concludes abruptly with Honorius transported to her Alexandria while Myrrhina takes up residence as the servant of the Lord. Each is tempted, and each denies the basis of his/her own existence and nature in favour of the position which the other has deserted. Neither is true, because it is believed by the other. The conclusion is a summary of everything Wilde set out to express by means of writing:

> HONORIUS Why didst thou tempt me with words?
> MYRRHINA: That thou shouldst see Sin in its painted mask and look on Death in its robe of Shame.

The dichotomy between truth and belief returns us to the position in which Wilde left us in his stories—that a logical situation, but not an intellectual one, can be reversed by the adoption of the opposing argument. In discussing the plot of 'La Sainte Courtisane', Wilde repeated this notion to Beerbohm Tree: 'When you convert someone else to your own faith, you cease to believe in it yourself.'[94] As San Juan has noted, doubt, questioning and disbelief are the hallmarks of modern western culture and can all be summed up in the term 'self-consciousness'.[95] Yet the phenomenon of self-consciousness in the western imagination was the greatest legacy of symbolism and decadence. We continue to live in 'the dark castle which is Maeterlinck's house of life',[96] but we do not know how to inhabit it, nor how to wrest life from its darkness.

6
The Third Meaning

(i) 'PROFESSOR OF AESTHETICS'

The most striking fact about Wilde's critical writing is that it was not taken seriously. When *The Soul of Man under Socialism* was first published in the *Fortnightly Review* in 1891, *The Spectator* commented: 'The article, if serious, would be thoroughly unhealthy, but it leaves on us the impression of being written merely to startle and excite talk.'[1] The discrepancy between impression and intention, between pretence and pretension, was caused by a subtle manipulation on Wilde's part of the masks by which he sometimes concealed himself from the world and at other times revealed himself. Because he was often deliberately flippant in voicing social criticism, as in the contemporaneous *Dorian Gray*, Wilde's more trenchant views on ethics and aesthetics were likely to be taken by the watchdogs of Victorian society as little more than ill-mannered badinage. In this sense, he may truly have appeared as a 'conformist rebel': his work in the 1890s might be regarded as a hardening of the farceur of the 1880s into a satirist of cheeky but scarcely malevolent wit. Even the vituperation which greeted *Dorian Gray* can be seen as a reaction not so much to Wilde himself or even his less than specific subject-matter, as to his manner of presenting it.

In this chapter we shall examine Wilde's critical 'intentions' as scholar, lecturer, editor and essayist, in promoting a body of work which is marked for the way in which he identified a middle space between two contradictory but complementary points of view. In doing so we shall consider the relevance of Barthes' term 'the third meaning' to designate a 'semiotics of the text' distinguishing between the *obvious* meaning and the *obtuse* meaning which is concerned with disguise and yet with adding to the original meaning of what is signified.[2]

* * *

Wilde himself may have contributed to the confusion between reality and unreality by his own groping towards, for example, the nature of drama. When he wrote to George Alexander of *Lady Windermere's Fan* that he could not 'get his people real' (*L* 282), it is clear that he was experiencing serious difficulty in coming to terms with the purpose of satire. His previous plays, *Vera* and *The Duchess of Padua*, had been melodramas because they were two-dimensional; now, setting out to depict modern society, he would not succeed in reaching his unique standard until he made them unreal. Here Wilde reveals the thinker whose critical faculty came between him and his love of the stage, and thus gave him the opportunity to transform it beyond the expectations—and the intellects—of his audience.

From the beginning of his career Wilde had recognised criticism as the companion to poetry, and rapidly came to realise that Pater had been correct to emphasise prose as a more difficult—and more rewarding—medium than verse. As an undergraduate, he had ploughed a furrow with his essay on 'The Rise of Historical Criticism'.

Another essay on 'Hellenism', unpublished until 1979, indicates the way in which Wilde's thought would continue to vacillate between the need for racial homogeneity and that for individual freedom. In his insistence that there existed in Greece a variety of 'self-governing towns ... differing completely in general character, political and philosophical thought and schools of art',[3] Wilde identified the natural alliance of divergent types which fascinated him about modern society. It also brought him remarkably close to the idea of the Irish 'nation', embracing different traditions and composed of different tribes like his own—the O'Flaherties—and yet articulating a common name and a single voice. He established the template for a federacy of political nations when he insisted that

In spite of local differences there did exist a general Hellenic sentiment and character which counted among the cementing causes of a union apparently so little assumed. For, these elements of union, of which we have been speaking, bound the Greeks together only in common feelings and sentiment: they never produced any political union; for, one of the fundamental notions of the Greek mind was the independence of sovereignty of each city ... this worship of the πολις [city] as opposed to the πατρια [*patria*, country].[4]

The essay on 'Hellenism' is remarkable because it refers to the 'intense individuality' of the Greek mind: not least because Wilde juxtaposed it with 'the mediocre sameness of thought and feeling which seems always to exist in the cities of great empires'.[5] It was the spirit which, fourteen years later, almost at the end of his short career, he would elevate in *The Soul of Man under Socialism* of 1891. While Wilde admired the self-discipline of the Spartans, who 'tyrranized over themselves that they might be better able to tyrranize over others',[6] he more seriously craved the 'one-sided enthusiasm for ideas'[7] within which Sparta (like Anglo-Ireland, he might have thought) formed 'a hostile garrison in an enemy's country, and always regarded themselves as such'.[8]

The essay on 'The Rise of Historical Criticism' is equally remarkable for Wilde's persistence in associating freedom with authority, and novel in that it introduces, at the start of his career, the concept of criticism as an art form, necessary to the development of society.

The purpose of art, says Wilde, is to create beauty; that of history, to discover the laws of the evolution of progress (*CW* 1115). 'The two great problems' with which Greek thought concerned itself were 'the origin of society and the philosophy of history'. In suggesting that the work of the philosopher is 'to proceed from *a priori* psychological principles to discover the governing laws of the apparent chaos of political life' (*CW* 1124), Wilde was making a statement of considerable personal significance which was also essentially modern.

'The first critic is perhaps as difficult to discover as the first man' (*CW* 1106)—here, on the second page of his essay, Wilde suggests in a subtle manner that the first critic *was* the first man. In the pages following he piles up a series of interconnected ideas which build towards his formal statement that 'the Greek spirit is essentially modern' (*CW* 1148). Greek thought is 'so peculiarly rational' (*CW* 1106); its modernity derives from the moment when the 'speculative invades the domain of revealed truth' (*CW* 1106), when it becomes necessary to adopt the contemplative stance—by means of which it might address the imbalance of 'a chaos of miracles' among which might be found 'metaphors and hidden meaning' (*CW* 1107).

Wilde's assertion that 'Between a poet's deliberate creation and historical accuracy, there is a wide field of the mythopoeic faculty' (*CW* 1109) is one of the hallmarks of nineteenth-century criticism, evident in his appreciation of Arnold and Renan, and at the same time suggestive of the steps which Irish historiography would take in finding a pathway between myth and legend on one hand and between myth and fact on another, an acknowledgment that there are generically different types of truth. At the centre of the inquiry is the present moment, 'the key to the explanation of the past, as it was to the prediction of the future' (*CW* 1113). For Wilde, nothing, not even the sculptures of Phidias, was written in stone that could not be refashioned. Just as, under Pater's analysis, the Mona Lisa became 'more wonderful than it really is' (*CW* 1029), so the past and future develop a capacity to be rewritten in the light of experience. However problematic, the 'mythopoeic spirit and that tendency to look for the marvellous' (*CW* 1131–2) are at the heart of the 'chaos of miracles'. At stake for Wilde is the connection with origins. In 'The Rise of Historical Criticism' he refers to Thucydides:

'The fact' he says, 'that the people in these parts of Hellas are still living in the old way points to a time when the same mode of life was equally common to all.' (CW 1116)

In the same vein he would later (in 'The Critic as Artist') refer to Homer's designation of οἶνοψ πόντος [*oinops pontos*, the wine-dark sea] as an ontological point of reference.

It is instructive to recall George Steiner's comment, in *Antigones*, that

> The speech and expressive conventions of Heraclitus, Archilochus, or Pindar convey the authority of morning. It is by their light that we set out. It is they who first set down the similes, the metaphors, the lineaments of accord and of negation, by which we organize our inward lives [9]

and that he elsewhere says: 'The history of western drama . . . often reads like a prolonged echo of the doomed informalities . . . before gods and men in a small number of Greek households.'[10] The same informalities might attend the transference of knowledge and ideas between men and gods in Celtic mythology, as explored in a title we have previously noted, Stephens's *The Demi-Gods*. The continuation of prime figures in the imagination as ways of seeing, ways of believing, and ultimately ways of behaving, is the central ontological strategy for human survival. The fact of man as a 'language-animal' is at once his distinguishing feature and his downfall: man *as* man is at best able to communicate with other men in a limited fashion permitted by the deep structures of their common generic composition; to ensure the success of this capacity, it must be constantly deepened and enriched by what Steiner calls 'real presences'.[11] This requires successful resort to a small number of verbal images. But man *as* man cannot communicate so successfully with man *as* woman: they speak differently, because they see and think differently. Part of Wilde's intention in his essays was to merge the male and female sensibilities in order to produce an androgynous type which would be 'absolutely modern' and at the same time embody the mythopoeic and intuitive, the rational and harmonic, sides of the Greek mind. When Steiner says:

> 'Initial' and determinant Greek myths *are myths in and of language*, and in which, in turn, Greek grammar and rhetoric interchange, formalize, certain mythical configurations. Thus the 'figure of speech' will, at its inception, have been the literal persona in the mythological construct[12]

he explains Wilde's use of the oxymoron as an expression, and embodiment, of myth.

As a lecturer—another 'career' which he began brilliantly and allowed to fade into mediocrity—Wilde brought his critical theories to the fore at an early stage. He spoke throughout North America in 1882, principally on 'The English Renaissance' and also on 'The House Beautiful' and 'The Decorative Arts'; later, in the six months from October 1884 to March 1885, under the new financial pressure of marriage, he lectured the length and breadth of the British Isles, on 'Impressions of America', 'Dress Reform', 'The Value of Art in Modern Life' and similar topics. During his American tour all Wilde's early poses—scholar, poet, apostle—crystallised as he concentrated his thoughts into an intellectual *schema* which would at the same time be artistically and rhetorically convincing.

Wilde ambitiously described the 'English Renaissance'—of which he claimed the leadership—as

> a sort of new birth of the spirit of man, like the great Italian Renaissance of the fifteenth century, in its desire for a more gracious and comely way of life, its passion for physical beauty, its exclusive attention to form, its seeking for new subjects in poetry, new forms of art, new intellectual and imaginative enjoyments. (*Misc* 243)

Tracing its origins to the spirit of Hellenism and individualism, he again planted the seeds of what would eventually become *The Soul of Man under Socialism*. Its simplicity is evident in the statement 'Art has only one sentence to utter.' (*Misc* 244) Wilde's most lapidary statements were often succinct and regularly punctuated by the final and dismissive coda 'That is all'. The idea that all art could be summed up in one sentence is characteristic: Wilde clearly believed that art could be reduced to a single epithet (just as he would condense a narrative into a terse prose-poem) because he would have regarded that epithet as in itself irreducible—a statement which was self-evident and bore no necessary relation to any other: 'I summed up all existence in a phrase.' Nevertheless, he knew that the society to which he made such a pronouncement was not easily persuaded of the singularity of art. Acknowledging the 'intricacy and complexity and experience of modern life . . . the mystery of its vision' (*Misc* 244), Wilde spoke of

> that strained self-consciousness of our age which, as it is the key-note of all our romantic art, must be the source of nearly all our culture. I mean that intellectual curiosity of the nineteenth century which is always looking for the secret of life that still lingers round old and long gone forms of culture. (*Misc* 269–70)

Clearly the self-absorption of the century in its decadent introspection was an obstacle to the new birth, because materialism and utilitarianism had pushed the contemplative capacity into an unhealthy relation with science and belief. Return to first base was a necessity:

> For what, as Goethe said, is the study of the ancients but a return to the real world (for that is what they did); and what, said Mazzini, is mediaevalism, but individuality? (*Misc* 244)

(Here too we see Wilde accepting the dualism under which classicism was regarded in the nineteenth century.) Attributing the momentum of the English Renaissance to the French Revolution (that same initiative which had caught the imagination of modern Ireland) and seeing its continuation in the work of Keats, as the supreme romantic, succeeded by the Pre-Raphaelites as both poets and painters (Dante Gabriel Rossetti and Swinburne foremost) and by the critical work of Ruskin, Wilde said:

> In the work produced under the modern romantic spirit it is no longer the permanent, the essential truths of life that are treated of; it is the momentary situation of the one, the momentary aspect of the other that art seeks to render. (*Misc* 244)

This passage is important for three reasons: firstly, it is the prelude to Wilde's appropriation of the Conclusion to Pater's *Renaissance* ('Art comes to one professing primarily to give nothing but the highest quality to one's moments, and for those moments' sake' (*Misc* 274));[13] secondly, it indicates that he was conscious of the separation of 'situation' and 'aspect', of 'the one' from 'the other', that each could be contained in, and possess, the moment without necessarily reaching an accommodation; thirdly, the movement away from permanence and essence towards the momentary is designed not to abandon the former, but to indicate that by means of the momentary the root can be apprehended. This is further suggested by the statement

> He who seems to stand most remote from his age is he who mirrors it best, because he has stripped life of what is accidental and transitory. (*Misc* 258)

In what might seem an argument for the continuing validity of a stance and perspective from the western isle, Wilde thus claims that the modern spirit requires the presence of the critic for its true formulation, and that the momentary is not 'accidental' or 'transitory' but a reflection of the perduring, because it brings the artist or art critic into an intimate relation with time.

In two further *ex cathedra* statements in this lecture Wilde, no doubt under the influence of Walt Whitman, whom he had met soon after his arrival in America, said that 'Whatever spiritual message an artist brings to his aid is a matter for his own soul' (*Misc* 259) and—in a formula which he would reiterate constantly—'One should never talk of a moral or an immoral poem—poems are either well written or badly written, that is all.' (*Misc* 267) The first statement makes the claim that the artist's referents are entirely a matter for himself, without recourse to any prevailing contemporary standards; it echoes words written by Wilde during his visit to Boston in direct reference to Whitman: 'the spirit who living blamelessly but dared to kiss the smitten mouth of his own century'.[14] The second statement extends that claim, arguing that the effect of that spiritual message is entirely a matter for the chemistry which takes place in the artist's own mind, thus establishing not only the amorality but also the total independence and individualism of art.

Even in his journalism (which became his principal source of income after he abandoned the lecture circuit) Wilde made small but telling points which were largely overlooked at the time because of the ephemeral nature of their appearance. It is evident, however, that Wilde was consciously forging and extending an aesthetic credo with political ramifications, which had three main points: that the critic was central to the artistic process, which was itself central to society; that modern society was in danger of extinction because of its insistence on material values to the exclusion of the spiritual and imaginative dimensions of existence; and that it could be liberated from this fate by means of an artistic process which would establish an amoral zone secured by mutual respect between the individual and society.

(ii) THE EDITOR

Wilde's journalistic career took two forms: firstly, as a literary critic he contributed reviews to London dailies and weeklies, mainly the *Pall Mall Gazette*, where a series of anonymous articles appeared almost weekly between 1886 and 1888. Beginning with a notice of the Grosvenor Gallery in the *Dublin University Magazine* in 1877, Wilde's association as a critic with journals such as the *Dramatic Review*, the *Court and Society Review* and the *Pall Mall Gazette* lasted until 1894. In addition, his essays first appeared in Frank Harris's *Fortnightly Review* and in *The Nineteenth Century*. Secondly, as an editor, Wilde took charge of *The Lady's World* in November 1887, immediately changing its title to *The Woman's World*. At first he was an enthusiastic editor and contributor, although as his other interests developed his direction lost its momentum and his association with the magazine lapsed at the end of 1889.

Under Wilde's editorship, *The Woman's World* pursued three major strands of inquiry and reportage, designed to appeal to a broad range of social and intellectual interests. Firstly, articles on woman's role in modern society—with particular relation to suffrage and women's ability to take their place in a male-dominated society—frequently provoked trenchant argument. For example, the first number under Wilde's control contained 'The Position of Women' by Eveline, Countess of Portsmouth, which asked:

> May not the time be come when the strength of woman is imperative to make men stronger—when it is necessary for him that she should be his fitting companion— loyal but not servile? May not the hour have struck when her own elevation is absolutely necessary to prevent his deterioration?[15]

The distinct editorial style pursued by Wilde in such articles is both reminiscent of his own mother's feminist writing

(Lady Wilde did in fact contribute a poem entitled 'Historic Women' to the third number)[16] and a signal of the 'good woman' theme of his plays where the sentiment expressed here by Lady Portsmouth might be taken to represent the approach to several of his female characters.

In the issue of November 1888 the militant campaigner Millicent Garrett Fawcett wrote on the current Women's Suffrage Bill[17]—another indication of Wilde's interest in making the magazine attractive to the broad spectrum of potential women readers, and of his own support for social reform. In retrospect, it is instructive that he should have succeeded in obtaining contributions from as wide a range of women as he did: in terms of prestige, it was equally impressive to have published a campaigner such as Millicent Garrett Fawcett as society leaders such as the Countess of Shrewsbury,[18] Lady Jersey,[19] Lady Dorothy Nevill,[20] the Countess of Cork and Orrery,[21] the Countess of Munster[22] and Viscountess Herberton.[23] Linking the social and artistic worlds was the Queen of Romania (the poetess, librettist and illuminator who published under the name 'Carmen Sylva'), who was the subject of one article on her work and the author of four contributions to *The Woman's World*.[24] Among leading women writers, Wilde published the last piece written by Mrs Craik (best known as 'the author of *John Halifax, Gentleman*'),[25] four contributions from 'Ouida',[26] two by Olive Schreiner[27] and one each from 'Violet Fane'[28] and Marie Corelli.[29] Lady Gregory, along with several eminent members of English society, such as Queen Victoria herself and the wife of the Conservative Prime Minister, the Marquess of Salisbury, was canvassed unsuccessfully for a contribution.

The second strand in *The Woman's World* was a series of articles on professions for women, ranging from medicine and nursing to elementary schoolteaching, music, typewriting and shorthand. The third was a detailed account, in each issue, of current fashions, amply illustrated and not only announcing the latest designs from London and Paris but also describing the costumes of leading figures in society and the arts such as Bernhardt's appearance in *La Tosca* and Patti's in *Lucia di Lammermoor*.

In addition to these features, Wilde included many articles on Irish topics. Prominent among these was the particular attention he paid to discussion of Irish manufacture: lace-making, weaving and knitting were extensively covered, with other articles on Alexandra College, Dublin; the town of Youghal, County Cork; the valley of Glendalough and its association with St Kevin; and Dublin Castle (with four engravings by Walter Osborne). Wilde himself reviewed the pathetic novel of Irish rural poverty *Ismay's Children* and contributed two reviews of work by the young W. B. Yeats.

Few men contributed to *The Woman's World*, the chief exceptions being Arthur Symons[30] and Oscar Browning,[31] and few male subjects were addressed, the exceptions here being Guy de Maupassant (by Blanche Roosevelt),[32] Georges Ohnet (by Gabriel Sarrazin),[33] Pierre Loti[34] and Symons's article on Villiers de l'Isle Adam. On the other hand, three articles on androgynous themes should be noted: the first issue carried an article on three productions by E. W. Godwin which focused on the figure of Orlando in *As You Like It*;[35] the second, a discussion of images in vase painting of the Lesbian poetess Sappho;[36] and the third, an article on 'Women Wearers of Men's Clothes' which concentrated on Joan of Arc.[37]

(iii) THE CRITIC

Wilde's critical credo was firmly stated in an anonymous article in the *Pall Mall Gazette* in 1887, 'The Poets and the People, by one of the latter':

> Never was there a time in our national history when there was more need than there is now for the creation of a spirit of enthusiasm among all classes of society, inspiring men and women with that social zeal and the spirit of self-sacrifice which alone can save a great people in the throes of national misfortune.[38]

For Wilde, once again dissembling by pretending to '*our national history*' which in other circumstances he would emphatically reject as not being his, the impetus was to come from poetry, but he found that contemporary poets— Tennyson, Swinburne and Browning in particular—were lacking in the requisite spirit to achieve 'a higher, a holier, and a more useful life', 'to rouse the nation to a sense of duty and inspire the people with hope'.[39] (In 'The Rise of Historical Criticism' he had pointed to Aristotle's delineation of a society where 'utility is not the sole motive, but that there is something spiritual in it if, at least, spiritual will bring out the memory of that complex expression of το καλον [the good/the beautiful]' (*CW* 1120).)

It was impossible for Wilde to stray far from the question of self-discovery. For him, as for any paranoiac, his private situation was one which could satisfactorily be projected onto the wider world, precisely because he could not see that world in terms other than his own. This accounts not only for the foundlings, the misunderstandings and the *double entendre* of his plays, but also for the way in which he would say of Dickens:

> That Dickens should have felt bitterly about his father and mother is quite explicable, but that, while feeling so bitterly, he should have caricatured them for the amusement of the public, with an evident delight in his own humour, has always seemed to us a most curious psychological problem. (*Rev* 141)

The 'psychological' dimension of society in all its aspects dominated Wilde's thought. As we have seen, in 'De Profundis' he took it to its limit by identifying the antinomian, the paranoid and the artist in a triple alliance or yardstick, against which all human endeavour should be measured, as if he himself constituted an Everyman, a remote figure to mirror society's ills. As a reviewer, he used the same yardstick. Thus the heroine of Dostoyevsky's *The Insulted and the Injured*,

Natasha, 'mean and ordinary though the surroundings of the story may seem . . . is like one of the noble victims of Greek tragedy, she is Antigone with the passion of Phaedra', while Aleosha, 'the beautiful young lad whom Natasha follows to her doom' is,

> from a psychological point of view. . . one of the most interesting characters of modern fiction, as from an artistic standpoint he is one of the most attractive. An we grow to know him, he stirs strange questions for us, and makes us feel that it is not the wicked only who do wrong, nor the bad alone who work evil. (*Rev* 157)

Wilde was an iconoclast who delighted in promoting social reform because it reflected his own need to both defy and remake society. Thus, in discussing contemporary women poets, he promoted Elisabeth Barrett Browning as the leader of 'the really remarkable awakening of women's song that characterises the latter half of our century in England' (*Misc* 110). In the same review he declared that 'English prose is detestable', excepting Carlyle, Pater, Froude, Arnold, Meredith, Lang, Stevenson and Ruskin, all of them with condescension.

> Possibly some day our women of letters will apply themselves more definitely to prose. Their light touch, and exquisite ear, and delicate sense of balance and proportion would be of no small service to us. I can fancy women bringing a new manner into our literature.

Here is a clear echo of his statement in 'The Rise of Historical Criticism' that 'The new age is the age of style' and a prediction of the fact, asserted in *A Woman of No Importance* and embodied in *An Ideal Husband*, that the future belongs to the dandy. In his reviews he also unnervingly predicted his own fate, saying in 1889 that 'Prison has had an admirable effect on Mr Wilfrid Blunt.' (*Rev* 393) Blunt had been imprisoned for championing the cause of Irish tenants and Wilde commented: 'Like a sickness or a spiritual retreat it purifies and ennobles; and the soul emerges from it stronger and more self-contained.' The sonnets of Blunt's volume, *In Vinculis* (a name with which he would toy as the title of his own letter to Douglas from Reading) 'are, of course, intensely personal'. Since Blunt identified himself with the causes for which he fought, this enabled him, in Wilde's view, to write 'The Canon of Aughrim' as 'a most masterly and dramatic description of the tragic life of the Irish peasant'. Prison meant that one became the mirror of society's ills, its outcasts and its deviants. Thus anything written about Ireland, for example Froude's *The Two Chiefs of Dunboy*, becomes 'a record of one of the great tragedies of modern Europe' (*Rev* 476). Wilde wrily noted that England ruled Ireland 'with a stupidity that is aggravated by good intentions', thus emphasising the fact that, as a leader of aesthetic opinion within England, his own intellectual fifth column was motivated by 'intentions' which were other than good. At the same time, he asserted that Irish social development had recommenced as a result of the emergence of Irish-America: 'At home it had but learned the pathetic weakness of nationality; in a strange land it realized what indomitable forces nationality possesses. What captivity was to the Jews, exile has been to the Irish.' To go outside oneself and one's history thus presents the opportunity to see oneself as one really is, and thus to become a mirror for oneself. A nationality which stays at home becomes inert; a nation which leaves home is better able to repossess home. It is not until one becomes 'other' that one recognises 'self'.

This is particularly evident in a seminal review of Confucius which Wilde published in the newly founded *Speaker* (later *The Nation*) in 1890. Characterising his subject as the author of 'the most caustic criticism of modern life I have met with for some time', Wilde said: 'It is clear that Chuang Tsu [Confucius] is a very dangerous writer', promoting the view that 'the ideal of self-culture and self-development, which is the aim of his scheme of life, and the basis of his scheme of philosophy, is an ideal somewhat needed by an age like ours.... But would it be wise to say so?' Clearly Confucius struck Wilde as possessing the qualities of the dandy while living the life of the sage and the ascetic, and he was fascinated by the fact that even living two thousand years ago Confucius 'looked back with a sigh of regret to a certain Golden Age'. The destruction of that age Wilde, like Lady Bracknell, lays at the door of education and of the philanthropist who thinks it necessary:

> In an evil moment the Philanthropist made his appearance, and brought with him the mischievous idea of Government. 'There is such a thing, says Chuang Tsu, as leaving mankind alone: there has never been such a thing as governing mankind.' (*Rev* 528)

But it is left to Wilde himself to say that 'all modes of government are wrong', thus leading us back to the nihilists and the anarchists of his first play and his current allegiances. This is a natural orientation for someone who believes that 'the world [has] lost its equilibrium'—a position which Wilde, conscious of his own lack of status and relation, could easily project onto his century.

Confucius was 'dangerous' because his writing pointed to the reorientation of society along amoral, non-judgmental lines by means of which the artist-as-thinker could give it new direction. Similarly, Whitman was dangerous because he portrayed 'the drama of a human soul' in such a way that he intended to elevate 'a *Person*' above society. By assenting to Whitman's notion of literature having a social aim (*Rev* 396–401) Wilde was advocating the notion that the slogan 'Know thyself' should be superseded by the slogan 'Be thyself'. It was an argument to which he would not give such explicit statement again until he published *The Soul of Man under Socialism*. Here we can see that Wilde was clearly at one with Thoreau, who, in his 'Essay on the Duty of Civil

Disobedience' (1849), had argued that the motto 'That government is best which governs least' has as its logical conclusion 'That government is best which governs not at all'.[40]

In Wilde's own case, the need to understand oneself, to resolve the dilemmas which he exposed in *Salomé*, of one's *relation to* the world and one's *relation of* it, could not be achieved merely by means of poetry or drama. All his life he cultivated, principally, the critical faculty because he recognised criticism as the superior art—a position which he eventually expressed in 'The Critic as Artist', first published in two parts in *The Nineteenth Century* in 1890 and subsequently in book form as the centrepiece of *Intentions* in the following year:

> Out of ourselves we can never pass, nor can there be in creation what in the artist was not. (CW 1045)

This resolutely personal assertion of the fact that we are locked into ourselves, yet suffer from the need to metamorphose, was summed up in 'The Critic as Artist' a few sentences later:

> Man is least himself when he talks in his own person. Give him a mask, and he will tell you the truth.
>
> (CW 1045)

The paradox arises because the lapse of criteria, on which the life of the paradox itself depends, leads us to overlook the fact that there may be a truth away from the home truths of real/unreal. It was Wilde's intention to inhabit that other truth.

Twice he tried to express this paradox in a way which heightened its dichotomous nature rather than resolving it. In *Salomé* Herod, terrified by the consequences of his lust for the princess, his step-daughter, declares:

> Je vous ai trop regardée. Mais je ne le ferais plus. Il ne
> faut regarder ni les choses ni les personnes. Il ne faut
> regarder que dans les miroirs, car les miroirs ne nous
> montrent que des masques. (*Salomé* 70)

This dramatises and gives a new dimension to the passage
in 'The Critic as Artist' in which Gilbert speaks of doom:

> We may not watch it, for it is within us. We may not see
> it, save in a mirror that mirrors the soul. It is Nemesis
> without her mask. It is the last of the fates and the most
> terrible. It is the only one of the Gods whose real name
> we know. (*CW* 1040)

The essence of the critical faculty is simultaneously to deal
with mask and mirror, in order to discover, in the interstice
between them, the area of 'truth' which Wilde was afraid to
articulate because it represented the final discovery, the act
of homecoming.

The need of the uranian to be detected lies not in the disclosure of the poet's adoration of the 'fair slim boy' or the
'lily-girl' but in the apprehension simultaneously of *both*.
Similarly, the Irish fifth-columnist, hailing the English Empress
and her Prime Minister as 'ours', wished to be seen neither
as a Fenian nor a Great Briton but as a citizen of a 'regal
republic'. The orphan demands to know, and to be held by,
his parent, but wishes to retain the personal mysteries born
of his uncertainty. In critical terms, Wilde put this as follows:

> The difference between objective and subjective work
> is one of external form merely.... All artistic creation is
> absolutely subjective.... The objective form is the most
> subjective in matter. (*CW* 1045)

To put the burden of discovery on the relation of form to
content, or 'matter', on a merger between them so that content becomes form, and form content, was a daringly modern stance evident in playwrights such as the contemporary

Chekhov and the older Ibsen. By designating the mind and imagination of the artist/critic as the place where the work of art essentially resides, Wilde effected a merger between mind and imagination and established art criticism not as a subsidiary activity but as a type of art superior to the plastic arts themselves. It was totally personal because 'the highest art . . . is the record of one's own soul' (CW 1027), and thus ultimately the outer work of art was subordinate to what occurred between the heaven and hell of the bifurcated mind.

As I observed in my chapter on 'Irishness', this has all the hallmarks of a reaction to Aristotle's 'excluded middle', which asserts that a matter must be either 'A' or 'not-A'; instead the Irish mind, in a position recently adopted by Derrida, leans toward an *included* middle, which allows that there may be matter which is both 'A' *and* 'not-A', which allows the resolution of polarities rather than their continued opposition. In this the case of the see-saw is apposite: its fulcrum is the point at which these extremes meet and balance. It is more often a possibility than a likelihood, and it is something to be striven for, but Wilde was, as we have already seen from his letters, a wistful person. Ernest, in 'The Critic as Artist', says: 'There is much virtue in that If' (CW 1010), shortly afterwards following it with a highly conditional argument:

> What is the use of art-criticism? Why cannot the artist be left alone, to create a new world if he wishes it, or, if not, to shadow forth the world which we already know, and of which, I fancy, we would each one of us be wearied if Art, with her fine spirit of choice and delicate instinct of selection, did not, as it were, purify it for us, and give us a momentary perfection. (CW 1011)

It is the deeply subjunctive nature of the question which betrays its Irishness, its capacity to balance 'two thinks at a time' on the head of the moment.

Another signpost to this multiple singularity comes when Gilbert yearns for 'the divine μονοχρονος ἡδονη [*monochronos hedone*, undivided pleasure] of another cigarette' (CW 1019). Monochronicity—the oneness of the moment—is naturally an echo of Pater's epicureanism; as such, it might be taken as a mere frivolity. Yet the ability to live all the time in one moment of time is an intensely Einsteinian achievement[41] which demonstrates the capacity to summon past and future into one's conception of time present and is thus a particularly constructive method of addressing their problems: 'if' becomes, as it did for Beckett, 'perhaps'.

Furthermore, it helps us to appreciate why there is so little variation, so little character development, in Wilde's two-dimensional characters, in their monochromatic acting out of their parts in contrasting shades of the same colour. The explanation lies in the fact that, as with most of his work, 'The Critic as Artist' has an extremely simple argument. When Wilde prepared his periodical essays for publication in book form, he amplified them, but he seldom extended their argument, preferring simply to add to the ornateness of the language and the conceits of his imaginative flights. This in itself emphasises the narrow bases on which the essays are placed: in 'Pen, Pencil and Poison' the validity of murder as an artistic pursuit; in 'The Truth of Masks' the necessity for disguise as a method of acknowledging lies. It is, as Declan Kiberd has stated, a strong source for Synge's Christy Mahon, who becomes a strong man 'by the power of a lie'.[42]

Intentions puts forward the views that the liar is an essential part of society, that the place where the work of art takes form is inside the head of the artist, and that art criticism is the highest form of art. Despite the presence of two dialogists, Wilde at no point attempts to defend these monstrous assertions by Gilbert: Ernest's purpose is to act as a subsidiary foil, urging Gilbert to further outrages of reason by means of which he can internalise the dialogue in his own mind. The daring fact which was not perceived by the reading public, despite the evidence of his own career up to 1891, is that these were Wilde's own beliefs. In viewing Greece as the place where criticism was natural and not subversive,

Wilde was making a further claim for the anaesthetic zone where aesthetics was judged higher than ethics. In positing the βιος θεωρετικος [contemplative life] as 'the true ideal', a 'tower of Thought' which makes us 'calm, and self-centred, and complete' (CW 1042), Wilde was drawing philosophy and literature into one frame of reference. This is of extreme importance because it enables us to see that he was at one with the classical tragedies in understanding the confluence of myth and metaphor, what Steiner calls 'the underlying pattern of the economy of myth in western thought'.[43] Wilde's essays read as myths because their monochrome and monochronic qualities are a deliberate attempt to translate what he saw as the simple thought of classical life.

The self-centred nature of such contemplation is inevitable:

> That is what the highest criticism really is, the record of one's own soul. It is more fascinating than history, as it is concerned simply with oneself. It is more delightful than philosophy, as its subject is concrete and not abstract, real and not vague. It is the only civilized form of autobiography, as it deals not with the events, but with the thoughts, of one's life; not with life's physical accidents of deed or circumstance, but with the spiritual moods and imaginative passions of the mind.
>
> (CW 1027)

This is the 'mind', or 'soul', which, in ideal terms, would enjoy the freedom to 'drift', and it is in such circumstances that the impossible indeed becomes possible.

'What is a fine lie?' Vivian asks of his friend Cyril in 'The Decay of Lying'; 'simply that which is its own evidence'. The liar makes 'frank, fearless statements' and enjoys 'superb irresponsibility' (CW 971). Lying, like poetry, is an art opposed to the 'morbid and unhealthy faculty of truth-telling' (CW 973); 'the cultured and fascinating liar' is the 'lost leader' of modern society (CW 981)—does the phrase presage the fall of Parnell? Echoing Arnold's characterisation of Celtic society as rejecting the despotism of fact, Vivian says that 'Facts ... are usurping the domain of Fancy, and have invaded the kingdom of Romance.' (CW 980) In so far as it goes, this is reasonably harmless, reinforcing the idea of an increasingly remote region where the exercise of reason is suspended. But Wilde goes further, in suggesting that 'facts' and 'the truth' are not necessarily the same thing. Vivian tells Cyril (the names are those of his own sons) that 'Lying for the sake of the improvement of the young ... is the basis of home education' (CW 990) and cites Plato's *Republic* as his authority, setting it beside 'lying with a moral purpose' as another pursuit of 'the antique world' (CW 989).

Lying, Vivian tells Cyril, reaches its highest point in art (CW 990). Gilbert tells Ernest that all art is, in its essence, immoral, and that all thought is dangerous (CW 1044). Naturally the inference is that such a view was tenable in the amoral Greek society, but that it becomes problematic in modern society. Behind this easily accessible distinction is the fact that, in spite of it, Wilde viewed it as necessary that art should continue to persist in being immoral, not merely on a scheme of internal reference, but outwardly, on a collision course with modern manners. To implicate Arnold in the argument by reference to Arnold's elevation of the critical faculty as the essential element in creation (CW 1020) and to his view that criticism 'creates the intellectual atmosphere of the age' (CW 1055) was a daring move in that by sleight of hand it introduced the foremost conscience of the age as a supporter of Wilde's crusade to undermine materialist society and reform the republic of letters.

Arnold's definition of literature as 'a criticism of life' becomes Wilde's announcement—in a deliberate echo of his earlier statement in 'The Poets and the People'—that 'There was never a time when Criticism was more needed than it is now. It is only by its means that Humanity can become conscious of the point at which it has arrived.' (CW 1055) In terms of Wilde's agenda, 'The Critic as Artist' marked the point at which he wished to reveal his plan for the reinstatement of art as the superior force in life, and of criticism as the superior form of art.

When, in 'Pen, Pencil and Poison', Wilde stipulated that 'the fact of a man being a poisoner is nothing against his prose', he intended a quite different suggestion than the apparently liberal proposition that art and motive might be distinct, one excusable, the other culpable. He not only intended the inversion of the statement as read—that the condition of a man's prose is nothing against his being a poisoner—but also that there was a necessary connection between them: 'His crimes seem to have had an important effect upon his art. They gave a strong personality to his style.' (CW 1007) From the man who put himself so far into his art as to publicly and systematically proclaim his homosexuality—even if only in a widely available code—this is a clear indication that Wilde saw the necessity in the modern world of establishing the nexus between the cognate functions of social and literary comment, of art and mendacity, of play as both deception and portrayal.

In 'The Critic as Artist' Gilbert says: 'It is not the moment that makes the man, but the man who creates the age' (CW 1021), a claim which Wilde continued to make after his downfall. To create one's own age—to *invent* it—is to put one's own name over its threshold in the place of the conventional placard, 'Know thyself'. The self-description of the artist in this world, which is outwardly fictive but inwardly *sui generis*, puts him beyond any judgment (κριτικος, critic as judge) other than his own. 'Art finds her own perfection within, and not outside of, herself,' says Vivian. 'She is not to be judged by any external standard of resemblance. She is a veil, rather than a mirror.' (CW 982) From this he proceeds to the position that 'Life imitates art far more than Art imitates Life' (CW 983), because 'Art never expresses anything but itself. It has an independent life, just as Thought has, and develops purely on its own lines.' (CW 991)

This leads to an intensification of personality and of individualism, which gives the critic the ability to interpret the work of others, by means of which the critic can effect social change, making society 'absolutely modern' by intensifying 'the collective life of the race'. But the apostle of modernism, for Wilde as for Baudelaire, is the dandy: the artist poisoner Wainewright 'determined to startle the town as a dandy', and his style was recognised as 'signs of a new moment in literature'. The presence of the dandy as the fulcrum of *An Ideal Husband* is subjected to the condition that the future belongs to him—'the first well-dressed philosopher in the history of thought', he is the critic, the judge, of society, because, as Gilbert has said, 'it is to criticism that the future belongs' (CW 1054). When, therefore, Wilde tells us that Wainewright the dandy 'sought to be somebody', he was describing that most tragic of dilemmas simultaneously on both the personal and the political levels: that those who were lost in the maze of nineteenth-century society were those best fitted to give it a new direction; they suffered from the disability of not knowing who they were and were at the same time liberated by it because they were thus enabled to invent themselves. By defining themselves, however ficti- tiously, they defined the age. But because they lacked prove- nance and connection, society would reject them. The messiah would go unrecognised or, as Wilde put it in 'The Critic as Artist', 'A dreamer is one who can only find his way by moonlight, and his punishment is that he sees the dawn before the rest of the world.' (CW 1058)

The same argument permeates *The Soul of Man under Socialism*, a confused and confusing document which set out (perhaps at the unconscious prompting of G. B. Shaw)[44] to give authority to the fiction of individualism in an age which, as Wilde had said in reviewing Confucius, was 'rot- ten with its worship of success' and yet demanded uniformi- ty in the way in which that success was achieved.

'Socialism itself will be of value simply because it will lead to Individualism' (CW 1080): with this statement Wilde manifested his disinterest in socialism as a levelling force or as a means of achieving equality (echoes of John/Ernest's 'I don't see much fun in being christened along with other babies. It would be childish.' (CW 3470)) Instead and by contrast, 'Socialism would relieve us from that sordid necessity of living for others' (CW 1079)—a view which accords closely with Adam's *Axël*. One suspects that Wilde's motive in exposing this idiosyncratic credo is primarily artistic and not at all political, except for the fact that it embodies his violent dislike for philanthropy—that very walk of life which he had once made a serious effort to enter. But the statement 'Art is this intense form of individualism' (CW 1090) brings us back to the time when Wilde had admired Hellenism for its capacity to foster 'intense individualism' and thus suggests that, as with his article on Confucius, he was well aware that his propositions applied equally to both art and politics and indeed brought them into confluence. 'Art is Individualism, and Individualism is a disturbing and disintegrating force' (CW 1091)—thus Wilde announced the advent of a new republic. Like Lady Bracknell, he dispenses with property on account of its 'duties' (CW 1081), and as society is steadily deconstructed, marriage and other bourgeois mannerisms are relegated (CW 1086). 'No Authoritarian Socialism will do. . . . All association must be quite voluntary.' (CW 1082) Again Wilde's paranoia leads him to think that a model republic will dispense with precisely the social conventions— such as a house, a marriage, and 'family life' (CW 1086)— which he himself found problematic, in order to elevate those virtues of which he felt himself capable: 'Disobedience, in the eyes of any one who has read history, is man's original virtue. It is through disobedience that progress has been made.' (CW 1081) Here we see not only the influence of Thoreau in the political sense and of Whitman in the aesthetico-sexual dimension, but also of the spirit present in Poe's Raven and his own Sphinx—a speaker who occupies a corner of his life and of his conscience. 'Real men' are poets, philosophers, men of science, men of culture—the artists 'who have realised themselves' (*CW* 1080) in a manner which Wilde himself found almost impossible because he could not connect his daily persona with that haunting presence.

Politically, his essay predates the bizarre commentary on Marxism which took the form of Plekhanov's anarcho-syndicalism.[45] Aesthetically, it refers to Morris's Kelmscott works, Ricketts' and Shannon's book illustrations and, later, the Yeats sisters' Cuala Press. Socially, it relates to associations such as the 'Souls'.

'The important thing is to be.' (*CW* 1083) It was clear to Wilde that society, with its various hoops through which the courtier, no less than the entertainer, was obliged to jump, was a place of entrapment, and that he would not be permitted to 'be' Oscar Wilde the dramatist if it was once discovered to what extent the other Wilde, the debaucher of aristocratic and proletarian youth, the mocker of morals, and the subverter of values, had laid a careful scheme, a labyrinth which underlay the society which fed him. Yet the critic in Wilde knew that his real 'intention' was to be found out. He knew, for example, that the critic must play the Jamesian system at its own game; he would have derived a wry satisfaction from James's diary remark, 'Everything Oscar does is a deliberate trap for the literalist, and to see the literalist walk straight up to it, look straight at it, and step straight into it, makes one freshly avert a discouraged gaze from this unspeakable animal.'[46] The pattern would not be complete without discovery. When he wrote in 'De Profundis': 'People whose desire is solely for self-realisation never know where they are going' (*L* 488), he merely acknowledged that nemesis had been an inevitable part of his life-plan. As he had previously said that the time when aesthetics is superior to ethics is an impossible time, so in *The Soul of Man under Socialism* he accepted that the perfect man—'one who is not wounded, or worried, or maimed, or in danger'—is an impossible man. Ultimately Wilde's critical path came full circle in the last line of *The Soul of Man*: 'The new Individualism is the new Hellenism.' (*CW* 1104) It was both a defiant assertion of principle and a call to rebellion. Realistically, he knew that neither was feasible. But he knew that in his defeat lay his triumph.

Renan had said at the conclusion of his *Poetry of the Celtic Races* that 'At bottom philosophy is only a matter of poetry',[47] a proposition which Wilde would have borne in mind when he noted in his commonplace book that 'parodies of plays and legends' in pre-Aristophanic Athens were 'a rude form of criticism', while *The Frogs* was both a comedy and a development in literary criticism (*CPB* 113). The essential synoptic point made by Wilde in this note is that there can be no such concept as a discrete, hermetic art form, but that all art forms are reflections of one another and that what is art is also art criticism. His Irish background provided him with the tradition of Molyneux, Swift, Berkeley, Tone, Emmet, Mitchel and Parnell as 'a training in critical thought'.[48]

This philosophical approach to creativity was clearly derived from the notion of individual, rather than collective, reasoning, which resisted the normative social emphases and pursued instead the antinomian compulsions of what we must regard as the artist's imagination and conscience operating as one entity. Thus in 'The Critic as Artist' we find Wilde rejecting the Jamesian idea that a critic should be 'fair', 'rational' and 'sincere' (*CW* 1047–8) and elevating 'temperament', 'the cultivation of taste' and 'the creation of the critical spirit' (*CW* 1049–50).

All this points not to a libertinist interpretation, nor even to a subjective view, of art, because Wilde denied such values as objectivity and subjectivity and insisted on the self-regulatory morality of art. But it is a method which insists on the *intellect* as the proper sphere of art and of criticism simply because it is in the artist's own mind, from which he can never escape, that the image is formed: 'Every work of art is the conversion of an idea into an image.' (*L* 481) It would have been inconceivable to Wilde that the pop art and the images of the mass media in our own time should have capitulated to the larger forces of what Umberto Eco calls 'hyper-reality'.[49] 'Is it really all done by hand?' he inquired of Frith's painting 'Derby Day'. That Barthes should write that 'the petit-bourgeois is a man unable to imagine the Other'[50] or that 'the foundation of the bourgeois statement of fact is common sense'[51] may have been as accessible to Wilde as it was to James, but the extension of that idea in the development of mass taste dominated by the advertising power of the image would have been anathema to him. Wilde's Protestant Irishness would have reacted with horror to the depersonalisation alike of art and artist.

The identity of the 'third meaning' was essential to Wilde, because, as we have seen throughout this book, the between space, the space within two contradictories, which could be both beautiful and poisonous, between heaven and hell, was the only sphere where he could commemorate and renew his own soul. If the highest criticism is the record of one's own soul, then it can be nothing else. By writing it he may or may not rewrite history, but by making oneself the 'master of language' one repossesses words and refashions them. Language thus becomes entirely personal and, perhaps, 'more beautiful than she really is'.

In his dialogues 'The Decay of Lying' and 'The Critic as Artist' Wilde achieves this by creating a middle space between the dialogists, akin to the silences between the actors of his 'discussion play'. Cyril and Vivian, Ernest and Gilbert serve as players in a net-game where the real message resides in the net. Although in each case one is dominant—the master—and appears to shape the discussion, the other—the servant—also provides important pointers to the direction taken. Indeed, given the flatness of his stage characters, we might see these dialogues themselves as 'discussion plays', in the sense teased out by Shaw, that 'discussion [in the third act of a play] is the test of a playwright'.[52]

It is Ernest who says: 'The Greeks had no art-critics', which is equally as valid as Gilbert's retort: 'The Greeks

were a nation of art-critics.' (CW 1015) It is Ernest who, like
the 'feeder' in a comedy duo, supplies Gilbert with the
material on which to work his imagination: if it were not for
an exchange such as the following—

> ERNEST: Surely, the higher you place the creative artist,
> the lower must the critic rank.
> GILBERT: Why so?
> ERNEST: Because the best that he can give will be but an
> echo of rich music (CW 1026)

—Gilbert would not be able to develop the argument that
criticism is not only an art form, but the highest such. It is
essential that when Gilbert says: 'When people agree with
me, I always feel that I must be wrong,' Ernest is present to
reply: 'In that case I certainly won't tell you whether I agree
with you or not.' (CW 1054) And it is Ernest who detects the
significance of 'If' (CW 1010).

In most cases the natural empathy between master and servant leads to betrayal, and in this sense the critic is unfaithful
to both 'sides' of the argument. A literal reading of Wilde's
dialogues leaves one adrift because he appears to betray
both Cyril and Vivian, both Ernest and Gilbert. Although he
appears to convince us that temperament and taste are the
chief components of art, and that nature imitates life, we are
left with the suspicion that the author may also have been
sincere and fair, if not entirely rational, in reaching his conclusions—qualities which he has ostensibly rejected as too
restrictive. The need for betrayal is also the need for self-
betrayal in writing the autobiography which is to be the
supreme work of art; as Sartre says, 'To betray is to engender
a destiny by means of words.'[53]

Barthes' 'third meaning' comes after the first (communication) and the second (signification), like the third part of the
oracle—the hint. 'The obtuse meaning is a signifier without

a signified, hence the difficulty in naming it.'[54] It can perhaps be divined, but not defined. This is the essence of criticism or 'metalanguage',[55] which Barthes calls 'the epitome of a counter-narrative',[56] an act of subversion. Writing, he suggests in discussing Balzac's *Sarrasine*, is sexless: 'Writing is that neutral, composite, oblique space where our subject slips away, the negative where all identity is lost, starting with the very identity of the body writing.'[57] It thus becomes mythical, that is, it becomes 'a *value*' and 'truth is no guarantee for it'.[58] Reading any of Wilde's critical works, we recognise Barthes' statement that 'Myth is speech *stolen and restored.* . . . Myth is neither a lie nor a confession: it is an inflexion.'[59]

It is the purpose of the critical metalanguage to confront the 'problematics of language'.[60] Wilde would have applauded Barthes' statement in *Writing Degree Zero* that 'Placed at the centre of the problematics of language, which cannot exist prior to it, writing is thus essentially the morality of form, the choice of that social area within which the writer elects to situate the Nature of his language.'[61] Barthes implicitly acknowledges Wilde's socialism when he says: 'For [the writers of today] the search for a non-style or an oral style, for a zero level or a spoken level of writing, is . . . the anticipation of a homogeneous social state.'[62] 'Style', he states, 'is always a secret.'[63]

Vivian Mercier also addresses this issue in his discussion of 'macabre and grotesque humour in the Irish tradition'. He quotes Beckett: 'the mirthless laugh is the dianoetic laugh', which succeeds the 'ethical' laugh of satire and the 'hollow' laugh of irony.[64] Mirthlessness, like sexlessness, goes beyond satire and irony, and explores the place where there is no possibility of comical laughter, and Mercier suggests that 'there is a laugh . . . the aesthetic laugh . . . which laughs at whatever is not beautiful'.[65] Elsewhere he rehearses 'three archaic attitudes which have remained embedded in the popular beliefs of the Irish: first, that wisdom can be demonstrated by the propounding or answering of seemingly insoluble riddles; second, that the dexterous use of verbal ambiguity is inseparable from wit and wisdom; third, that truth can be arrived at by witty dialectic'.[66]

Taken together, these two observations by Mercier illustrate Wilde's point about *Salomé*—that it is only the shudder which counts—and the paradoxical use of humour in his dialogues to produce a particular kind of truth, one which takes the potentially witty conundrum and produces an answer which obeys the hint rather than the rational. And it shows that he might solve the insoluble riddle of the Sphinx in only one place: Ireland.

Part Three

7

The Parallel Decades

'IF one tells the truth,' Wilde said, 'one is sure, sooner or later, to be found out.' (CW 1205) He also said: 'I live in terror of not being misunderstood.' (CW 1016) Wilde lived in apprehension, somewhere between the two. In February 1895, having worn an open disguise for the past twenty years, he was acclaimed by royalty, aristocracy, bourgeoisie and the critics as the author of the two plays dominating London theatreland, *An Ideal Husband* and *The Importance of Being Earnest*. Two weeks later, the full extent of his anti-social misdemeanours at last revealed, he had fallen from his pedestal and was heading for denunciation as 'High Priest of the Decadents'.[1] Between the two positions was a complex set of negotiations by which he had made his way within London society as a fifth-columnist for a new republic in social, aesthetic and sexual terms. Between the two he had manipulated appearances, sometimes acting out the reality of his position, at others disguising his intentions by means of a fictional biography, giving a false appearance to each opus number. Thus while he had not entirely escaped detection, deliberately allowing certain clues—such as his early posturing with the lily and the elaborate dress, or the later Preface to *The Picture of Dorian Gray* and the curtain speech after the première of *Lady Windermere's Fan*—to fall into his critics' laps, other provocations (most notably his sexual proclivities) had been accidental, confirming the accusation by the Marquess of Queensberry that he was a 'posing somdomite [*sic*]'.[2] Yet while there were overt responses to his equally overt sexual and aesthetic behaviour, he was permitted to push towards extremes. It is as if there were a compact between society, its commentators, and Wilde himself (and, of course, other actors in this charade among artists, socialites and politicians) that nothing would be done until it needed to be done—at the point where the two cities met, where, one might say, sodomy was not only done, but seen to be done. Up to that point comment was not necessarily judgment. The essential meaning of *hypocrisy*, we must remember, is *acting*, and, in its response to Wilde's personal drama, England, 'the native land of the hypocrite', played its part.

Wilde had already established at an early stage that he regarded England not merely as Philistia—indifferent to culture—but actively detrimental to the artistic life. Prophesying his own 'Renaissance of Art' as the period when the Celtic imagination might take the initiative once more, Wilde would also postulate a change in social and political forms as a concomitant of aesthetic change. 'I am a thorough republican,' he said in America. 'No other form of government is so favourable to the growth of art.'[3] In 'Ave Imperatrix' he had prophesied that Milton's and Cromwell's England would be reborn as a republic; and much later he had demonstrated the Irishman's capacity to invert the relationship of subject and object when, on the issue of Home Rule, he said: 'My own idea is that Ireland should rule England.'[4]

In this chapter we shall discuss these three interrelated aspects of the manner in which Wilde lived both openly and covertly within English society—as an Irishman, in social contradistinction; as an artist, in aesthetic revolt; and as a homosexual, proposing the restoration of Greek attitudes to, and practices of, love. We shall see the same attempt which fired his critical work, to establish a middle place, a third meaning, where both the home truths of conformity and the away truths of rejection are superseded by a mutual recognition and appraisal.

While the three aspects were intricately linked—not least in Wilde's overt behaviour—it is important to recognise that each of them was—and is—separable from the others in terms of what Wilde set out to achieve and of what he in fact attained. Each, moreover, was addressed to a separate audience, and this in itself decreased the likelihood of detection.

* * *

Wilde's world was binomial: it obeyed two sets of laws, one of which was hermetic, so intensely personal that it was known only to himself, the other the code which governed appearances and his engagement with the world. But the world in which he lived—the social milieu of literary and theatrical London—was itself binomial, establishing one code to govern the great affairs of empire and another to dictate the niceties of the domestic hearth and its environs. In addition, we must recall that the acting profession constituted another secret society with its own vocabulary and persuasions. In such a complex situation it was possible for the lives of private citizens to remain covert and untouched by the wider world and for the great and famous to live according to both codes.

When Wilde wrote in 'De Profundis' that 'We think in Eternity but we move slowly through Time' (*L* 474), he was expressing this complexity: for the Irishman, eternity is but an instant of thought, yet each moment is a lifetime of endurance, a crude and onerous breaking-in upon the integrity of that longest of mental spaces. As we have noted in Wilde's remarks on the need for quiet and a place where the unseen could become visible, the Celtic imagination was capable of running back in time, but, more importantly, it demonstrated that different kinds of imagination proceed towards infinity at differing temporal speeds. Space and time, as Einstein was about to disclose, are unreal, because they are relative to what inheres in the location and mind of the subject. This is a truth of which the Irish mind had long been aware.[5]

As Wilde moved closer to the unknown, his tone became both more strident and more apprehensive. Towards the end of 1894 he wrote to Douglas of a visit to the theatre:

> The bows and salutations of the lower orders who thronged the stalls were so cold that I felt it my duty to sit in the Royal Box with the Ribblesdales, the Harry Whites, and the Home Secretary: this exasperated the wretches. How strange to live in a land where the worship of

> beauty and the passion of love are considered infa-
> mous. (*L* 377)

The remarks are ambiguous: who were 'the wretches'—the lower orders who saw Wilde seated with the courtiers, or the courtiers forced to associate with him? What did he mean by 'the worship of beauty'—his artistic crusade or his adoration for Lord Alfred? And was 'the passion of love' the name for that adoration or the more common practices which he pursued with the rent-boys? There is no doubt, however, as to Wilde's amusement at the illustrious company he was keeping: Lord Ribblesdale, a former Lord-in-Waiting to the Queen, was currently Master of Buckhounds; Sir Henry White was Private Solicitor to the Queen; and the Home Secretary was H. H. Asquith, who became Liberal Prime Minister in 1908—he had recently married Margot Tennant, a member of the 'Souls' and a model for the heroine of E. F. Benson's runaway success of the year, the novel *Dodo*.[6] The timbre of Wilde's letter is also ambiguous: knowing that he is running with the hare and hunting with the hounds, he is unsure where the greater danger lies. The fact that, when under pressure from Queensberry, he vacillated for so long before deciding to instigate proceedings highlights the vertiginous nature of his situation. He later described the excitement of living in the homosexual demi-monde: 'To have entertained at dinner the evil things of life ... was like feasting with panthers.'(*L* 492) Douglas himself was a kind of panther or—as Wilde put it—a lion-cub; referring once more to *Agamemnon*, he wrote in 'De Profundis': 'Aeschylus tells us of the great Lord who brings up in his house the lion-cub ... and loves it because it comes bright-eyed to his call and fawns on him for its food. ... And the thing grows up and shows the nature of its race ... and destroys the lord and his house and all that he possesses.' (*L* 431) Yet the politicians and the courtiers were themselves panthers, and Wilde, author of 'The Birthday of the Infanta' and 'The Young King', knew it, if only subconsciously and by inference.

Of course once I had put into motion the forces of Society, Society turned on me and said, 'Have you been living all this time in defiance of my laws, and do you now appeal to those laws for protection? You shall have those laws exercised to the full. You shall abide by what you have appealed to. (*L* 491–2)

The statement as a whole sits uneasily with Wilde's idea that under the influence of Douglas he threw caution to the winds, rejecting the advice of Sir George Lewis, the circumspect society solicitor who 'knows all about us' (*L* 92) and whose discretion and diplomacy made him, for so many, 'the one great safeguard of my life' (*L* 440). It is the ready admission of the player that he has played by double standards, but it is also the perception that the code itself is bifurcated, lending credence both to the law and to Wilde's defiance of it.

We could with facility substitute a political programme for Wilde's aesthetic pretensions: he is reported as saying that

Things are because we see them, and what we see, and how we see it, depends on the arts that have influenced us. To look at a thing is very different from seeing a thing. One does not see anything until one sees its beauty.[7]

The first statement—'Things are because we see them'—is pure Berkeley, and the second—'what we see, and how we see it'—adapts Berkeley to the extent that it politicises the theory of vision into a theory of partisan knowledge. If for the word 'arts' we substitute 'perception', the statement becomes a strategy whereby one acknowledges only what it is expedient to acknowledge, and, conversely, it permits another observer to continue seeing something 'other' in the same object. One may, indeed, see nothing at all unless the 'beauty', the inherent truth of the object, is apprehended. The 'beauty' of Wilde's own pose was that he was looked at, but not 'seen'.

A further passage from 'De Profundis' illuminates this:

> Modern life is complex and relative. Those are its two
> distinguishing notes. To render the first we require
> atmosphere with its subtlety of *nuances*, of suggestion,
> of strange perspectives: as for the second we require
> background. (*L* 460)

Such a statement not only explains Wilde's own critical path
but that of the dramatic characters onto whom he projected
so many of his preoccupations. Mrs Cheveley and Mrs
Erlynne, shadowy women whose goodness is in question
but who exercise a heady and threatening fascination for the
past and future of apparently strong men, represent this
'atmosphere'. But their 'background' is also crucial for an
understanding of how they have arrived at this critical junc-
ture where they exercise such power over so many lives. For
their author, the constant shift between the two, the dignity
of the artist and the respectability of the socialite, kept his
charisma vibrant and indefinable.

It is important for us to recognise that this was not a sudden revelation to Wilde, either on the eve of collapse or in
the course of his subsequent darkness. There is evidence
from his Oxford commonplace book that he appreciated not
only the simple division of the garden into good and evil but
also the complex conditions required for the balance between
different kinds of energy to be achieved:

> As far as the Renaissance is concerned what humanity
> demanded at that splendid crisis, when the world-spirit
> was in the throes of travail of things evil and good—
> was not new theories of conduct or even its practice—
> not order—not virtue even—but free scope for the
> intellect—the throwing off of authority to breathe again
> in the free frank air. . . . The Christian religion required as
> it's [*sic*] precursor no philosophy or art but an emotional
> and spiritual awakening. . . . Primitive religions contain
> the germ of philosophy and of physical science—
> unnatural children who seek to annihilate their mother

when they have attained to their maturity · yet the intellectual synthesis between religion and science … is nothing more than a monstrous Œdipodean vision of vigorous manhood with the effete mother who bore it—a union whose children must be wanderers and born to evil things. (*CPB* 77–83)

The scope and implications of this note are remarkable. Wilde at the time he wrote it was 'in the throes' of a 'splendid crisis' of faith, sexuality and affiliation, and he clearly saw the larger movements of religious and social evolution in terms of the personal. The relation of physical to ethical well-being, the birth and development of consciousness, and the fated discourse and *agon* within the 'tiny ivory cell', are related to the twin elements of background—the knowledge of origins—and of destiny. The fact that these two elements are coeval, that every cell carries within it the seeds of conscience and of ambition, provides the critical point with its drama. That Wilde's staged plays largely concentrate on the lost children of unhappy or unlucky unions is a further commentary on the 'atmosphere' and the 'background' which constitute so powerful a part of his cultural hinterland. As with his proclivity towards Greek love, this search for an end to wandering was another aspect of Wilde's 'love of the impossible'.

The popular press had lampooned Wilde since his first involvement with the aesthetic craze. In 1881, for example, du Maurier's aesthetic caricature 'Maudle', whom he had first penned for *Punch* the previous year, adopted some of Wilde's physical appearance and was presented as saying: 'How *consummately lovely* your son is, Mrs Brown'—to which the indignant mother replies: 'What? He's a *nice manly* boy, if you mean *that*, Mr Maudle.'[8]

Punch also referred directly to Wilde as a 'Mary-Ann', while a college contemporary, in a decidedly antagonistic account of Wilde's career at Oxford, described him in the *New York Times* in 1882 as 'epicene'.[9] On his return from America, *Truth* (edited by the Radical politician Henry Labouchere) said he had been perceived during his tour as 'an effeminate phrase-maker'.[10] Privately too his acquaintances expressed their awareness that Wilde was less 'manly', and more 'that', than might be desirable or advisable. 'What a mass of unmanly absurdity,' the mother of a college acquaintance noted,[11] while in America several commentators, although admiring his aesthetic arguments, resented his personal style and sexual ambiguity. Henry James, meeting him in New York, recorded his impression of 'an unclean beast . . . a fatuous cad',[12] a trait noted by Edmond de Goncourt in Paris the following year—'this person of ambiguous sex, the language of a ham-actor, and phony stories'.[13]

Occasionally, private conversation would be more explicit. Wilfrid Scawen Blunt recalled that in 1891 his Oxford contemporary George Curzon, then a Conservative member of parliament, had entertained members of the Crabbet Club, in Wilde's presence, with an account of his 'reputation for sodomy and his treatment of the subject in *Dorian Gray*'.[14] It was also possible that his manners were more subject to comment than his morals. Lady Emily Lutyens, daughter of Lord Lytton, the ambassador to Paris, recorded that in 1891 Wilde lunched at the embassy: 'We all thought him very amusing and not so odious as we expected (evidently, at the time I wrote, rumours had already begun to be rife about him, though I think, it was more of his egotism and extravagance than of anything else).'[15] It is possible that, despite his conversational ability to charm and captivate all kinds of acquaintances—including on one occasion Queensberry himself—Wilde's flamboyance and his domination of the table offended and alienated many others by its grossness.

As early as 1883 the *Illustrated Sporting and Dramatic News* had cartooned Wilde in convict dress—a most serious imputation since at that time, before the passing of the Criminal Law Amendment Act, 1885 (under which Wilde was eventually imprisoned), the only homosexual crime on the statute books was sodomy. Previously punishable by death, under the Offences Against the Person Act, 1861, the penalty became penal servitude for life. In early 1895 *Footlights* magazine portrayed him in drag, a chilling intimation of the disclosures which Queensberry's researches would shortly facilitate. In the years between these cartoons many references with varying degrees of suggestiveness had been made to Wilde's personal behaviour and the tendencies of his literary style.

In a direct reference to the 'Cleveland Street Scandal' of 1890 (when the Earl of Euston and Lord Arthur Somerset, son of the Duke of Beaufort, had fled the country after being implicated in the affairs of a male brothel), the *Scots Observer* in 1891 had characterised the author of *Dorian Gray* as writing 'for none but outlawed noblemen and perverted telegraph-boys'.[16] In the guarded language of Victorian Britain, this was the equivalent of his being 'outed'. Wilde, in a writing career which culminated in the production of *Earnest* and the appearance in book form of *The Soul of Man under Socialism* in May 1895, was revealed in the debauch of youth and the buggery of the social and political system.

There is a sense in which he could not have been anything else. The Irishman in London, unlike the American outsider (such as James, Harte, Whistler, Crane, Harland—and even for a time Twain), had a more extensive agenda. However deviant these Americans might be in sexual or artistic matters, they lived in London against the background of their century-old democratic independence in political matters which had already survived the acid test of civil war. Ireland in that period had seen four abortive uprisings and the crippling experience of the Famine; especially after the débâcles of the Pigott forgery and the O'Shea divorce cases in the years 1887–91, it still enjoyed the urgency of pursuing Home Rule. Irishmen in London were 'provincial', as Yeats said of both himself and Wilde,[17] and therefore dangerous.

Seamus Deane has suggested that 'the Parnell crisis ... became a symbol of the country's interpretation of its struggle to represent itself as unified in the midst of division'.[18] The celebration of failure embodied in the downfall of Parnell was, in Deane's words, both a 'sense of betrayal' and a 'sense of self-betrayal'.[19] It embraced the spirit of defiance, but hesitated in the face of rebellion. The Home Rule movement was at the forefront of the principle that the recently promulgated Victorian Empire was about to disintegrate with the fragmentation of its satellite colonies. 'Parnell's fate was a parable,' says Deane;[20] as a history lesson it was to be repeated, before the chapter was closed, in the tragedies of Casement, Childers and the 1916 Rising. The book of Wilde was less a parable than a legend of sexual and artistic emancipation which questioned the notions of censorship and social direction.

In 1891 Wilde had stood bail for his friend of at least eight years standing, the Scottish poet John Barlas, who had threatened to blow up the Houses of Parliament. The gesture was both one of compassion for a demented fellow-artist and one of identity with a potential regicide. 'Whatever I did was merely what you would have done for me or for any friend of yours you admired and appreciated. We poets and dreamers are brothers.' (*ML* 108) Justin McCarthy, a Home Rule member of parliament 1879–1900 (who had started professional life in 1848 as a journalist with the *Cork Examiner* during the trials in Clonmel of William Smith O'Brien and T. F. Meagher after the Ballingarry disturbances), claimed to have invented the term 'exile-world' to describe London, particularly in the 1860s, when it was home to political exiles such as Louis Blanc, Garibaldi, Herzen and Boulanger[21]—the background against which James wrote his novel of nihilism, *The Princess Casamassima*.

In one sense McCarthy thought 'the Irish did not count for very much in London society',[22] but in another they were of cardinal significance. In her *Social Studies* Lady Wilde had made the vigorous point that at a certain stage in the earlier part of the century all the leading women figures in London—Maria Edgeworth, Lady Morgan, Lady Blessington, Lady Dufferin, Mrs Norton ('of that wondrous Sheridan race'), the

Brontës, Mrs S. C. Hall—were Irish.[23] On the literary front, the Irish continued to be of substance. With a great deal of leadership from the youthful Yeats (championed in turn by Lady Wilde), the Irish created both an inner and an outer world: Yeats, with his proclivity for secrecy and enigma, which he had already tasted in his association with Rosicrucianism, took Wilde's own decade and created his personal version of it. Already in 1894 W. P. Ryan was able to give an extensive account of 'The Irish Literary Revival' which clearly had Yeats at its centre; both the Irish Literary Society (to which all three of the Wildes—Jane, Willie and Oscar—belonged) and the Rhymers' Club, with a joint membership revolving around John Todhunter, T. W. Rolleston, Katherine Tynan, Lionel Johnson and Douglas Hyde, and under the benevolent eye of Charles Gavan Duffy,[24] were influential societies. Another gathering which regularly featured Irish participation was that at the premises of the *Hobby Horse* magazine, where Rolleston, Wilde, Shaw, Yeats and (later) Augustus John would encounter Arthur Mackmurdo, John Gray, Herbert Horne, Selwyn Image, Walter Crane and Ernest Rhys.

Wilde's sense of this Irish presence in London was so strong that when Grant Allen published an article on 'The Celt in English Art' in the *Fortnightly Review* in 1891 Wilde proposed that 'All of us who are Celts, Welsh, Scotch and Irish, should inaugurate a Celtic Dinner and assert ourselves, and show these tedious Angles or Teutons what a race we are, and how proud we are to belong to that race.' (*L* 287)

Wilde's dual mission was to create a new civilisation and to conceal its true nature from those to whom he preached it; to realise and occupy the new society while appearing to live in the 'real' world. It was natural for any Irishman to do so, and it was particularly natural for an artist to feel that, as Parnell had held the balance of power in the mother of parliaments while changing the face of politics, so he too could become the arbiter of style and the master of the most powerful language and culture in the world, while adapting it to the needs of his own nationalism. Both politically up to 1890, and artistically up to 1895, London hung upon the words of Irishmen.

There is a very distinct sense in which Wilde carried a memory and a landscape within him; and there is a very natural chemistry by means of which memory and landscape come into use as weapons of critical intent once they become distant and at risk. The Irish past, and its survival in the concept of Tír na nÓg, were merged and equated in Wilde's imagination with the classical past and the contemplative life. They were incorporated into a body of work which had a hidden message in addition to its superficial wisdom. As Declan Kiberd observes, 'antithesis was the master key to the entire Victorian cast of mind',[25] and thus the feminine arts could be seen as the antithesis to materialism and imperialism and to the domination of women by men. By means of this polarisation, Wilde was able to let the subliminal message run its own course, slipping through the interstice between thesis and antithesis.

Much more so than in his own sexual behaviour, Wilde here demonstrated the principle of inversion as a critical strategy. Among his characters, Vera, Salomé, Lady Bracknell, Mrs Erlynne and her echo Mrs Cheveley are the figures of strength and will-power. With the exception of the dandy (Lord Goring), his principal male characters—Chiltern, Darlington, Windermere, Herod—are figures of indecision, men broken before their time of action. Women rise above fate, destiny and history; men sink beneath them. The dandy—a heraldic figure in the realm of manners, mind and morals[26]—is a third sex, androgynous, capable of moving within the codes of dress and speech which define opposite states, and thus creating an interior dialogue which, in 'The Critic as Artist' and 'The Decay of Lying', plays the masculine form against the feminine content—precisely the same tactics which made Parnell such a successful parliamentarian.

It is thus insufficient to say, as Ellmann does, that 'essentially Wilde was conducting, in the most civilized way, an anatomy of his society, and a radical reconsideration of its ethics'.[27] He certainly did so; but the further purpose of extolling and putting in place an alternative society which could rise above ethics meant that this was only a preparatory exercise to a much more radical purpose. In the long run-up to *The Soul of Man under Socialism*, he had announced as early as 1882 in Omaha: 'I want to make this artistic movement the basis for a new civilisation.'[28] This may be another meaning of his cryptic remark to Gide, that he had put his genius into his life and only his talent into his work—a remark which caused Verlaine, who overheard it, to say: 'This man is a true pagan ... he does not know penitence.'[29] Wilde knew that what he was doing was wrong, and that what he said in his writing was a permanent shadow of what he had achieved, merely by acting the role of himself, in his ephemeral farce of manners. This struck Yeats very forcibly, for, beyond the poseur who preached to him the necessity of masks, he saw the man of action.[30]

The publication in English translation of Max Nordau's *Degeneration*, containing a chapter on Wilde as an egomaniac, coincided exactly (March 1895) with Wilde's nemesis. Its definition of egomania, 'that the "I" has actually no knowledge of a "Not-I", of an external world',[31] stands at the epicentre of the parallel decades. Attacking the metaphysicians, including Berkeley, for refusing to answer the question, 'How the "I" conceives of the "Not-I"', Nordau, in identifying one of the maladies of the century—the danger of alienating mind from social purpose—perhaps unconsciously also exposed a deeper truth, that this alienation occurs throughout society and affects all minds. The egomaniac, according to Nordau, concludes that 'there is no external world', that it is 'a creation of our mind, and exists only in our thought ... but not outside our "I" as a reality'.[32] The argument that to lose reality is to lose relation, and thus to become potentially if not actually a criminal, is to plot a very narrow line indeed between permissible and impermissible behaviour, between saint and thief. In particular, it becomes difficult if not dangerous to conceive of social change or its vectors. In Wilde's case, the idea of a crusade becomes not merely a matter of framing the parameters of a new society but also a search for ways of doing so which will escape scrutiny yet find a persuasive voice. The binary opposition of 'soul' to materialism is articulated in terms of a renaissance, while the exact terms of socialism are muted if not suppressed and the notion of sexual inversion is completely disguised by means of the ironies and paradoxes which supply this complex system of signifiers with its maps and its scrambling devices.

As early as 1882 Wilde had been preaching the notion of a 'Renaissance in Art' under the rubric 'For most of us the real life is the life we do not lead.' This is a neat conflation of Rousseau's dual dictum that the 'manie commune' is 'de nier ce qui est, et d'expliquer ce qui n'est pas'.[33] When, in reply to criticism of *Dorian Gray*, Wilde said that 'Life by its realism is always spoiling the subject-matter of art. The supreme pleasure in literature is to realise the non-existent' (*L* 259), he had more than an artistic meaning in mind. It was part of a social and moral assertion that the unseen, or even the unimaginable, might change modern society.

In literal terms, the denial of reality in order to describe what does not exist is a point of utopian strategy; but in figurative terms, to replace the status quo with its opposite is to give a quite different impetus to imaginative thought. Wilde, of course, was a *flâneur*, but a *flâneur* with a serious purpose: to promulgate a 'Renaissance in Art' 'that might change—as indeed it has changed—the face of English art' (*Misc* 256) was a bold, feminine gesture. To suggest that the imagined change had already been achieved was in itself a trick of speech. To recolonise materialist England with a creed which was anathema to its prevailing orthodoxies would be a sweet revenge for the dreaming Celt. In doing so, Wilde can justifiably claim to have invented his age, the feminine, artistic and predominantly pagan and introspective decade running parallel to that in which the Jameson Raid, the Boxer Rebellion and Kitchener's initiative in the Sudan grasped the imperial outward-bound imagination.

They were not entirely unrelated in their tenor. The political momentum was melodramatic, a dying fall, while decadence and anti-decadence met often on the same platform. The age was one of curiosity based on self-consciousness: revolutionary, evolutionary, degenerate and regenerative in its dynamics. The 1890s as a decade might be characterised as a mixed metaphor trying to embrace its own reputation. Wilde's career is symbolic of that decade because the 1890s were concerned with the development of social life. Democratic, volatile, extrovert—social debate was concerned with everything: Morris's socialism and Shaw's; Wilde's anarchism and Kropotkin's. The decadence defined by Arthur Symons in 1893 as 'a moral and spiritual perversity... a new and beautiful and interesting disease'[34] was by 1899 in danger of having no more substance than 'unsatisfied virtue masquerading as uncomprehended vice'.[35] As Holbrook Jackson remarked—and this epitomises Wilde's approach to both criticism and drama—'the decadents were romantic in their antagonism to current forms, but they were classic in their insistence upon new'.[36] *The Yellow Book* (first issued in April 1894) demonstrated that the age was at a crossroads; together with Dowson, Le Gallienne, Beerbohm, Benson, Beardsley, Symons, Harland and Gosse (but not Wilde) were George Saintsbury, William Watson, Arthur Waugh, Frederick Leighton, Edward Garnett and J. T. Nettleship; halfway stood James and Bennett.

Few personalities or imaginations were capable of accommodating the two decades, although they saw each other every day—in clubland, at first nights and *vernissages*, in the park, at the Café Royal or the meetings of learned and literary societies—and, of course, in the cabinet room. During that decade the two Londons had coexisted. Not least, they met in the reading-rooms of gentlemen's clubs such as the St Stephen's, a Conservative club near the Houses of Parliament which Wilde had joined in 1877 while still at Oxford; the Albemarle, a mixed club founded in 1879, to which both Oscar and Constance Wilde belonged, and where Queensberry left his accusing card; the New Travellers', where Wilde was also a member; and the largely artistic Savile, which refused him membership in 1888 despite the fact that his candidature was supported by Henley (soon to become an arch-enemy), James, Gosse, Rider Haggard, Besant and J. K. Stephen. It was in the clubhouse that reprimands were administered: in *Dorian Gray* we are told that Dorian's grandfather had been ostracised for neglect of his daughter, and that members leave the room in a marked manner to indicate their disapproval of Dorian himself—a gesture repeated to Wilde himself when rumours of his behaviour with Douglas and less exalted associates became common gossip.

Something of Wilde's disregard for the establishment—or at least for its manners—may be understood from Aubrey de Vere's enigmatic statement that 'Society in this country [Ireland] is a great Fact for which it is hard to account'[37] and compounded by the fact that 'from the earliest times, the people of this country, though very reverential in disposition, have had no respect for the law of the land'.[38] De Vere, intent on explaining to England the qualitative difference between the two countries, adopts a tone which suggests to an English ear that Ireland is almost an imaginary country:

> There is an unwritten law as well as a written.... There are in Ireland social traditions ... which have been to us a substitute for law.... There is a moral sense, profound though perverted.... Society would seem to include permanently its imaginative element as well as its sensual and moral; and the first... is subject to strange aberrations.[39]

De Vere makes the neat distinction that

Sympathy with crime is a depravity common neither in Ireland nor elsewhere. Sympathy for the criminal, rather than for the law, is an hereditary disease.... The Englishman reveres the law because his liberty has been its creature, and his prosperity its ward. The Irish peasant has had liberty too: but for centuries it was the liberty of moonlight mountains and tufted bogs, that bewildered his pursuers.[40]

On a juridical and fiscal level, de Vere argued that 'Not only men's actions, but their words, their looks, and their thoughts, are depraved from their natural bent by habitual insecurity.'[41] But the aesthetic dimension of life is also reflected in that depravity. The distortion which Wilde brought to the aesthetic movement was a similar gambit—the need to compensate for insecurity by being different, in action (lectures), words (uranian verse), looks (extravagant dress) and thought (criticism). De Vere argued that the Irish as perceived by the English suffer from 'various infirmities which ... lead to a want of truth' and, ambiguously, that 'dishonesty is no Irish vice'.[42] He unwittingly established a template for Wilde's use of paradox as an Irish weapon when he characterised this perceived otherness as proceeding 'from an abuse of metaphor; ... from an extraordinary readiness and inaccuracy of thought; from vanity, and from sensitiveness'.[43] De Vere's 'letter' was one of the very few explicit statements by an Irishman of the reasons for England's curiosity about, and incomprehension of, Ireland. It was also an excursion, a stepping outside oneself in order to take the other point of view. De Vere gave a further impetus to Wilde when he said that 'It is the custom of effeminate men ... to aggravate their own sufferings by supposing them to be peculiar, if not unprecedented.'[44] Recognising feminine qualities both in himself and in Irish aesthetics, Wilde certainly elevated these Irish offences against English mores to the level of Christ.

(ii) AESTHETIC POLITICS

In dedicating *Degeneration* to Cesare Lombroso, the leading criminologist of the day, Nordau stated, it seems by way of apology:

> Degenerates are not always criminals, prostitutes, anarchists, and pronounced lunatics, they are often authors and artists. These, however, manifest the same mental characteristics, and for the most part the same somatic features.[45]

As will become clear, Nordau forges a connection between the artistic mind and the criminal mind wherever he detected an anti-moral intention, which he construed as egomania. The chief constituent of this mania was the relation of the ego to the rest of society, and especially to that part of the personality which should be socially oriented. The persistence of an introspective ego in the artistic world, in Nordau's view, gives rise to an unhealthy, anti-social work of art.

> Books and works of art exercise a powerful suggestion on the masses. It is from these productions that an age derives its ideals of morality and beauty. If they are absurd and anti-social, they exert a disturbing and corrupting influence on the views of a whole generation.[46]

Nordau, albeit unconsciously, may have been the first commentator to nod towards a concept of an 'absurd' theatre: certainly at the time when he wrote, the growing interest in the work of Ibsen, which was to influence 'a whole generation' of playwrights, if not of playgoers, could have been construed as 'absurd and anti-social', and Wilde's vivid anti-comedies may be regarded in the same vein. It was, however, in Wilde's dialogues that Nordau detected the chief evidence of his egomania. But if Wilde's capacity to corrupt the masses were to be measured by the impact of his texts or performances, he would hardly count as a major threat to society. His plays may have entertained the vast part of London's high society, but their inner meaning went largely undetected, while his other writings were read and discussed by only a small proportion of the population.

Regina Gagnier (1987) correctly sees Wilde's style as seductive and inverted, and identifies his 'special community' or 'audience' in the homosexual quarter of society, yet she allows his apart-ness to influence her too strongly in thinking that he therefore had no organic links or social affinities with the society to which he was opposed: 'Wilde was removed from life—as his British middle-class adversaries conceived of it—on several counts. By birth Irish, by education Oxonian, by inclination homosexual, he was an adjunct to Victorian imperial, commercial, and polite society.'[47] This view ignores the fact that, ostensibly and on one plane, Wilde was central to that society: he amused it, even though his plays were more serious than comic; he criticised it from within, even though the full impact of his commentary went unnoticed; he charmed its womenfolk and was on easy if bantering terms with its men, many of them in the front line of intellectual or political prominence. Gagnier is on safer ground when she says that 'perceiving a fallen art world and an unregenerate public, Wilde had two alternatives: to respond cynically or idealistically. He chose both alternatives and developed two distinct styles to represent them.'[48] The fact that in melodramas such as *An Ideal Husband* or in dialogues such as 'The Decay of Lying' he chose to effect the voices of both cynicism and idealism within the single text is not, however, evident to Gagnier.

On the relationship between master and servant—on which much of Wilde's binomial style and *double entendre* might be said to hinge—Gagnier says 'upper-class characters have masks because they do not need personalities; and their servants have them because they cannot afford to have personalities'.[49] But this overshadows the transitus of the mask between servant and master, the shifting relationship of the wise man and the fool, and thus obscures the question of what constitutes a personality, and what that personality, or persona, might mean. We have already noted the shift in significance between the manservant Phipps in *An Ideal Husband* and his successor, Lane, in *The Importance of Being Earnest*, and have commented on the extended role of servants and onlookers in *Salomé*. Here it is necessary to see, from the modernist perspective, the way in which intelligence, and with it significance, commutes between master and servant, in the most subtle and yet necessary form of play. The heightened domestic impact of a phrase or a gesture passing from one to the other, as in the transference of dialogue between the aristocracy and the plebs, the central and the peripheral (in *Vera*), or between the old world and the new (in *A Woman of No Importance*), or between debt-collector and spendthrift, city and suburb (in *Earnest*), or between statue and swallow (in 'The Happy Prince'), or fisherman and ondine (in 'The Fisherman and his Soul'), at one and the same time creates contrasts and dissolves them. Wilde was the master of this technique because it was to him less a technique of writing than a strategy of being, a necessary means of concealing what he intended behind what he said, even though what he said continued to express a diminished meaning within one acoustic and an amplified meaning within another.

Ernest Newman said that the author of the paradox 'can see round corners and the other side of things'.[50] This describes the Celtic ability to envisage the alternative, to create the oblique. And it is vital, in appreciating the transactions between the parallel decades, to realise that Wilde was able to see both sides of the corner at once. In this sense, he was the author of both, bringing them into existence only when it was necessary to unveil them in their mutual absurdity.

The contemporary debate of Wilde's morality or lack of it centred on the reaction to *The Picture of Dorian Gray* and to

what was veiled, and unveiled, therein. In response to the
accusations of decadence and filth levelled by such architects
of public opinion as the *Daily Chronicle*, the *Scots Observer* and
the *St James's Gazette* (to which Wilde himself was a major
contributor), Wilde appealed, mainly in a series of letters to
the *Gazette*, for readers to appreciate the deeply moral tone
of the book:

> All excess, as well as all renunciation, brings its own
> punishment. The painter, Basil Hallward, worshipping
> physical beauty far too much, as most painters do, dies
> by the hand of one in whose soul he has created a mon-
> strous and absurd vanity. Dorian Gray, having led a life
> of mere sensation and pleasure, tries to kill conscience,
> and at that moment kills himself. Lord Henry Wotton
> seeks to be merely the spectator of life. He finds that
> those who reject the battle are more deeply wounded
> than those who take part in it. Yes, there is a terrible
> moral in *Dorian Gray*—a moral which the prurient will
> not be able to find in it, but which will be revealed to
> all whose minds are healthy. (*L* 259)

Elsewhere Wilde said he was 'anxious to have it treated
purely from the art-standpoint: from the standpoint of style,
plot, construction, psychology' (*ML* 97). This response may
be judged to have been mere posturing by an iconoclast
whose intention had been exposed to ridicule and vilifica-
tion. But to the extent that Wilde himself at least posed as a
homosexual, his assumption of an air of immorality already
identified him as a potential threat to society. It was in the as
yet undetected transactions between himself and society
that the extent of his antinomianism was to be measured.
Dorian Gray represents three aspects of those transactions: it
was the place where, between the first and second editions,
Wilde amplified and made explicit, for those equipped to
recognise it, his adoration of Alfred Douglas; it was the
work in which he raised to the furthest extent the issue of art

in relation to society; and it was the occasion of a debate on the uses of morality and immorality which was seriously aired in only one other place, *An Ideal Husband*. *Dorian Gray* is thus the interstice between Wilde and society within which he negotiated the relationship of 'I' and 'Not-I'.

In Nordau's terms, the simplex division of 'I' and 'Not-I' occurs in the separation of subject-as-life in the biography of Dorian Gray himself from subject-as-object in the biography of the portrait. It is only at critical moments—the impact of which is lessened by the fact that the reader is almost pro-grammatically prepared to expect them—that picture and subject encounter and recognise one another. This can also be appraised at a more fertile and sinister level in terms of the boy's continuing awareness of the portrait as an affect. Where 'I' is a young man of astonishing and undiminished beauty, 'Not-I' contains more than the mere sum and mirror-image of Dorian's actual misdoings: the gloating, hideous creature has an atavistic function, relating somehow to Dorian's romantic and mysterious origins and representing a family history of terror and misgiving. Yet again, it can be read as a classic statement of the Rimbaudian *'je est un autre'*, the continual awareness of oneself as elsewhere, other, elu-sive and superior, without whom one can never be complete yet with whom one can never be at ease. In Wilde's case, this triple association of 'I' with 'Not-I' is evident firstly in his sit-uation as a writer in a personal relation with everything he wrote—particularly in his indignation at the reception of *Dorian Gray* and the deferral of *Salomé* as products of his pen which he had difficulty in seeing as having independent lives of their own; secondly, in his troubled critical relation-ship with his various audiences—both with his 'wise' readers who were attuned to his more, and less, subtle sexual and social nuances, and with the wider circle of literary and drama critics who interpreted his work to the public; and thirdly, in the broad sense of an artist who perceived society as part of, rather than distinct from, the artistic world.

* * *

In each of these roles, Wilde indeed typifies the 'conformist rebel' who both recognises and disregards the constraints on manners, mind and morals. He knows that the constraints are imposed by a concrete society of which, in one sense, he is a consenting member, and that they are unacceptable or irrelevant to him in the sense that he is a dissenting outsider representative, if at all, of a different, distant and more abstract society.

Wilde was certainly not the first Irishman to fill this role: in the field of political science Burke, quintessentially Irish yet commonly regarded as typically English in his thought; in that of metaphysics, Berkeley; in that of ethics, Swift; in the theatre, Sheridan—all preceded Wilde in the matter of re-presenting Ireland and thereby redefining English genres.

In particular, the subversion and leavening of English dramatic forms by Irish writers depended not only on the grander names of Sheridan, Congreve, Goldsmith and Farquhar, but also on minor writers like Charles Macklin (*c.* 1697–1797), Arthur Murphy (1727–1805), Hugh Kelly (1739–78) and John O'Keeffe (1747–1833). When Wilde and Shaw consciously formed the 'Celtic School' of drama (*L* 339), they adopted this traditional transitus between the two cultures. They contributed to the English stage a collected alternating *œuvre* which by 1895 consisted of: Opus 1, *Lady Windermere's Fan*; Opus 2, *Widower's Houses*; Opus 3, *A Woman of No Importance*; Opus 4, *The Philanderer*; Opus 5, *An Ideal Husband*. But they also, in Shaw's recollection, wrote, between them, 'all the long reviews of distinctly Irish quality during the 1885–8 period'.[51] They shared what Yeats called Wilde's 'extravagant Celtic crusade against Anglo-Saxon stupidity', recognising the value of 'the irresponsible Irishman ... in literature and in things of the mind'.[52]

Wilde's 'crusade' was certainly directed against Philistinism and brought into play the Celtic values associated with the soul. In 'De Profundis' he again identified himself with Christ, with specific reference to his perception of a new civilisation:

His chief war was against the Philistines. That is the war every child of light has to wage. Philistinism was the note of the age and community in which he lived. In their heavy inaccessibility to ideas, their dull respectability, their tedious orthodoxy, their worship of vulgar excess, their entire preoccupation with the gross materialistic side of life, and their ridiculous estimate of themselves and their importance, the Jew of Jerusalem in Christ's day was the exact counterpart of the British Philistine of our own. (*L* 485–6)

Wilde's unnecessary adjectives—*heavy...dull...tedious... vulgar...gross*—are an index to his discomfort in and with English society. *Vera* had been the first sign of his aesthetic, social and political revolt. Thereafter his tone became more assured as it became more calculating, outwardly charming and inwardly cynical as he brought mockery to the high point where it was most repaid by those whom it most mocked.

Katherine Worth draws attention to the fact that Wilde's crusade 'was a campaign of an Ibsenite kind'[53] which, as we have seen, utilised melodrama and similar strategies as vehicles of modernism. It is not difficult to see that Wilde was inspired by the same mindset which Ibsen brought to *A Doll's House*, *Hedda Gabler* or *Ghosts*, a determination to introduce new issues and make them futuristic while employing existing forms which made them accessible, at least in outline, to his audiences.

It was Shaw who, in 'The Sanity of Art', published a spirited rebuttal of Nordau. Where Nordau had been ponderously orthodox, Shaw was provocatively deviant, referring to 'the continual danger to liberty created by law',[54] and at the same time upheld both the value and the necessary irresponsibilty of art: 'What in the name of common-sense is the value of a theory which identifies Ibsen, Wagner, Tolstoy, Ruskin and Victor Hugo with the refuse of our prisons and lunatic asylums?' (the article appeared just after Wilde himself had been sent to prison)—immediately adding, as a brilliant paradox in its own right: 'Swift, though he afterwards died in a madhouse, was too sane to be the dupe of his own logic.'[55] Shaw's killing peroration was masterly:

> In a country where art was really known to the people, instead of being merely read about, it would not be necessary to spend three lines on such a book. But in England, where nothing but superstitious awe and self-mistrust prevents most men from thinking about art as Nordau boldly speaks about it; where to have a sense of art is to be one in a thousand, the other nine hundred and ninety-nine being either Philistine voluptuaries or Calvinistic anti-voluptuaries, it is useless to pretend that Nordau's errors will be self-evident.[56]

It was an argument previously rehearsed in *The Quintessence of Ibsenism* (1890–91), in which Shaw said that Ibsen's thesis was 'that the real slavery of today is slavery to ideals of goodness',[57] and that 'the main effect of his plays is to keep before the public the importance of being always prepared to act immorally'.[58] It was a bold statement in 1890. It was much bolder, and braver, after Wilde's imprisonment. Preceding the composition of *An Ideal Husband*, the original lecture on which Shaw's book was based contained a proposition which may well have influenced Wilde's play: '[Ibsen] reminds men that they ought to be as careful how they yield to a temptation to tell the truth as to a temptation to hold their tongues.'[59]

In rebutting Nordau, Shaw had said:

> Every step in morals is made by challenging the validity of the existing conception of perfect propriety of conduct; and when a man does that, he must look out for a very different reception from the ... composer who ends his symphony with an unresolved discord. Heterodoxy in art is at worst rated as eccentricity or folly: heterodoxy in morals is at once rated as scoundrelism, which

must, if successful, undermine society and bring us back to barbarism after a period of decadence like that which brought imperial Rome to its downfall.[60]

The Quintessence of Ibsenism was contemporaneous with Cesare Lombroso's *The Man of Genius*, Part Four of which is concerned with 'Characteristics of Insane Men of Genius' and contains the following observations, all of which have a distinct and quite possibly legitimate application to Wilde:

> Insane geniuses have scarcely any character. ... Genius is conscious of itself, appreciates itself. ... Instead of preferring the quiet seclusion of the study, they cannot rest in any place and have to be continually travelling. ... Sometimes they change their subject and course of study several times in succession.[61]

I have suggested that Wilde's letters betray a lack of substantive humour or innate character, and it may be that Lombroso's first statement applies to Wilde in the sense that the distinguishing mark of the genius, insane or otherwise, is not that he possesses an inherent persona but that he is grounded in difference, that his persona eludes us because it also eludes him. We have also noted the predisposition of the Celtic imagination towards a decadent introspection, and here too Lombroso's remark about self-consciousness is relevant: Wilde need not, because he is trying to find himself, necessarily disregard his inner being, and conversely we can regard his introspection as a vital element in the pursuit of self. The tendency to continual movement is another aspect of this pursuit which is also a flight towards the self: not only is it evident in the literal wandering and restlessness of the outcast which we can detect both in Wilde's early lecturing engagements and in the homelessness of his later exile, but it is also observable in the peregrine mind of Dorian Gray in his search for the pleasure and beauty 'that abideth for a moment' and in the dialogue of the wordy poet with the silent Sphinx. Lombroso's final observation, that geniuses frequently change their subject-matter, is applicable to Wilde's movement from poetry to the podium, from story-telling to polemics, from criticism to stagecraft, and his final return to the ballad.

Lombroso also alerts us to the condition of

> these energetic and terrible intellects ... regardless of danger, facing with eagerness the greatest difficulties—perhaps because it is these which best satisfy their morbid energy.[62]

This explains, perhaps, Wilde's follies and indiscretions, although for a fuller understanding of his inconsistency we should have to suppose that they had their converse in periods of caution or concealment, available to him as he adapted masks to suit the moment.

'These morbid geniuses', Lombroso tells us, 'have a style peculiar to themselves—passionate, palpitating, vividly coloured—which distinguishes them from all other writers',[63] and this accurately describes both the decoration of Wilde's vocabulary and syntax and the eager thrust of his thought. 'The principal trace of the delusion of great minds is found in the very construction of their works and speeches, in their illogical deductions, absurd contradictions, and grotesque and inhuman fantasies.'[64]

Of the capacity of genius for metaphor and paradox Lombroso says:

> They seize the strangest connections, the newest and most salient points.... Originality, carried to the point of absurdity, is the principal characteristic of insane poets and artists.[65]

Here, we might argue, the receptiveness of the Celtic mind to the unexpected and the irrational, like that of the Latin-American propensity for magical realism, approximates to the recipe for *Salomé* of 'genius wedded to insanity'.

Throughout this brief account of insane genius the most evident principle has been the constant danger of identification between different homologies. Wilde's dispute with the age which ran parallel to his own invisible age was, literally, an altercation during which what he said was variously seen as brilliant or absurd, a profound commentary or a monstrous aberration.

Ultimately Wilde's art offered him nothing more or less than the path by which he might, rather than being himself or knowing himself, simply *find* himself. It was in this sense that he wrote: 'I treated Art as the supreme reality, and life as a mere mode of fiction.' (*L* 466) To live with the knowledge that 'the final mystery is oneself' (*L* 488) is to recognise that within oneself are the mysteries of all the preceding generations of parents, artists and nations. It is both visionary and concrete, haunted and haunting, craving and bereft. (The genius, Lombroso says, is 'painfully preoccupied by religious doubts. ... All insane men of genius, moreover [like Nordau, he cites Whitman, Rousseau, Musset, Poe, Baudelaire, Nerval and Dostoyevsky], are much preoccupied with their own *Ego*.')[66] In order to inhabit himself, Wilde must turn his back on all forms and all modes, rejecting reason, morality and religion.

> When I think about Religion at all, I feel as if I would like to found an order for those who cannot believe: the Confraternity of the Fatherless one might call it, where on an altar, on which no taper burned, a priest, in whose heart peace had no dwelling, might celebrate with unblessed bread and a chalice empty of wine. Everything to be true must become a religion. And agnosticism should have its ritual no less than faith. It has sown its martyrs, it should reap its saints, and praise God daily for having hidden Himself from man. But whether it be faith or agnosticism, it must be noth-

ing external to me. Its symbols must be of my own creating. Only that is spiritual which makes its own form.
If I may not find its secret within myself, I shall never
find it. (*L* 468)

The *tabula rasa* of his own soul is a place where everything
is denied. Aesthetic politics thus becomes the most vicious
and demanding route to the truth which is the self. The idea
that 'people generally turn out to be someone else' is the chief
article of doubt in its canon. We encounter here a restatement of the legend of 'The Priest's Soul' where the ontology
of the self is called in question. For the artist, seeking to change
the way in which beauty is both perceived and achieved, the
most painful act is the denial of beauty itself in order to create
beauty. Just as Melmoth cannot live until he has destroyed the
picture of an antecedent Melmoth painted within himself,
on his conscience, so Dorian will know a moment's peace
only as he destroys his own image. These peripatetic icons of
pain are 'fatherless' because they practise autogenesis, calling themselves into tradition by virtue of a blank missal
wherein the book of his life is to be inscribed.

(iii) SEXUAL POLITICS

The fact that a large proportion of the male literary establishment was gay—including Gosse and James—was a matter
on which society kept silent. This was partly due to their
close association with members of the political establishment. Some figures such as Oscar Browning (himself dismissed from his mastership at Eton for alleged homosexual
behaviour) and George Curzon (the pupil with whom
Browning was obsessed at the time) provided the nexus
through which the two worlds communicated. The tacit
recognition of the two was also due to the fact that leading
political figures were also gay. At the height of his thunder-
ous denunciations Queensberry pointed to the Prime

Minister himself: he suspected Rosebery of homosexual relations with his eldest son, Lord Drumlanrig, and had pursued him to Homburg with a horsewhip—an action insufficient to prevent Drumlanrig's suicide. In a private letter he described Rosebery and similar figures as 'The Snob Queers',[67] and it was on their judgment that action, or inaction, depended. Wilde was eventually prosecuted not because he was associated with a younger Douglas son, but because it had become clear that the names of the Prime Minister himself and a relative of the Solicitor-General had been implicated in the scandal.

Oscar Browning was in many ways the key to homosexual behaviour in the intellectual world of art and politics, and the circle of friendships which he maintained during the last thirty years of the century was a network of those who admired—and practised—the pursuit of 'Greek love' or *paederastia*. In particular, his infatuation with his pupils George Curzon and Gerald Balfour (Chief Secretary for Ireland in 1895 and brother of the future Prime Minister), and his friendships with the painter Simeon Solomon, with Pater, A. C. Benson (son of the Archbishop of Canterbury, future Master of Magdalene College, Cambridge, and brother of E. F. Benson), J. A. Symonds and the expert in the literature of erotica, Lord Houghton, indicate the extent to which paedophilia and homosexuality had permeated English society. In a private undated letter (probably written in the 1920s) Browning, the presumed author of an anonymous pamphlet entitled *Paederastia Apologia*, said:

> Few people know that the aesthetic movement which had so much influence in England from Ruskin to Oscar Wilde had as one of its characteristics a passionate desire to restore 'Greek love' to the position which its votaries thought it ought to occupy. They believed that bisexual love was a sensual and debasing thing and the love of male for male was in every way higher and more elevating to the character.[68]

In the pamphlet itself he said:

> We are not ashamed to kiss each other: we glory in that
> long embrace in which the souls of the two lovers meet
> and unite on their lips, and seal the faith which these
> lips have vowed.[69]

It was a still covert expression of what Wilde had unequivocally stated in the first official 'outing' of homosexuality in
England when he stood in the dock in the Old Bailey. A long
way from the suspicions about 'mentally spooning the boy'
with which his sexual career had begun, it was greeted at the
time with admiration:

> 'The love that dare not speak its name' in this century
> is such a great affection of an older for a younger man as
> there was between David and Jonathan, such as Plato
> made the very basis of his philosophy, and such as you
> find in the sonnets of Michaelangelo and Shakespeare.
> It is that deep, spiritual affection that is as pure as it is
> perfect. It dictates and pervades great works of art. . . . It
> is in this century misunderstood, so much misunder-
> stood that it may be described as 'the love that dare not
> speak its name' and on account of it I am placed where
> I am now. It is beautiful, it is fine, it is the noblest form
> of affection. There is nothing unnatural about it. It is
> intellectual and it repeatedly exists between an elder
> and a younger man, when the elder has intellect, and
> the younger man has all the joy, hope, and glamour of
> life before him. That it should be so, the world does not
> understand. The world mocks at it, and sometimes
> puts one in the pillory for it.[70]

It was Wilde's greatest triumph, as a reformer, to have
been able to deliver such an *apologia*, but it was his greatest
misfortune to have done so in a forum where he was on trial
not for advocating 'Greek love' but for committing sexual

offences. However much he might have wished to practise 'the highest form of affection', however much he wished to both regale and reveal England's national poet as a paederast, he was sent to prison, as he had been rusticated from Oxford, for breaking commonly accepted, and commonly respected, rules of conduct.

There is a very concrete sense in which we can consider Wilde's triple view of himself in *Dorian Gray*. The 1890s saw a deepening and a widening of the scope of criminology, in works by Nordau and Lombroso. These to a certain extent assumed the role previously exercised by the popular press and performed a critical, definitive function, in which accusations of deviance could be levelled at specific types of social—or anti-social—behaviour. Thus what had been satirised in the popular press and imagination in the 1870s and 1880s, what was greeted by contempt or indignation by reviewers in the 1880s and 1890s, became the subject of a major scientific dissertation on the nature of literary evil. Nordau, in particular, is of relevance because, as we have seen, the third edition of *Degeneration* (1893), translated into English in 1895, contained a specific consideration of Wilde as a degenerate. Nordau defined degeneracy as 'deep-rooted cerebral disturbance' and the degenerate as knowing 'in his heart that his aberrations are morbid, immoral and anti-social'.[71] The question is not merely a clear-cut distinction between degenerate morbidity and society at large. Nordau distinctly refers to madness as a form of alienation. In attempting to define this form of deviance, which (with an unconcealed high moral tone of disapproval) he particularly noted in 'the Aesthetes', Nordau comes close to Wilde's own idea of the 'three souls'—one seen by the world, one known to the author but hidden from the world, and one, in a discrete zone beyond space and time, desired but unpossessed by him.

In Nordau's case, this separation of functions took two forms. The first occurs in his general discussion of degeneracy, in which Baudelaire emerges as the chief example of the anti-social egomaniac: 'For them there is neither virtue nor vice, but only the beautiful and the ugly, the rare and the commonplace.'[72] Secondly, Nordau pursued the legacy of Baudelaire, exploding its various manifestations into diabolism, necrophilia, sexual aberrations, glorification of crime, and mysticism, and attributing them to various successors, including Rollinat, Mendès, Verlaine, Swinburne, Villiers de l'Isle Adam and Barbey d'Aurevilly. In discussing Wilde, whom he identified as the chief of the English aesthetes, Nordau attributed most of these 'aberrations' to the author of *Intentions*, identifying his

> hysterical craving to be noticed, to occupy the attention of the world with himself, to get talked about...a purely antisocialistic, ego-maniacal recklessness and hysterical longing to make a sensation...a malevolent mania for contradiction. ... Wilde apparently admires immorality, sin and crime. ... The artist who complacently represents what is reprehensible, vicious, criminal, approves of it, perhaps glorifies it, differs not in kind but only in degree from the criminal who actively commits it.[73]

But behind Nordau's accusatory stance is a more perplexed attempt to understand Wilde's paradoxical manner. Himself the author of a volume entitled *Paradoxes*, Nordau devoted several pages of *Degeneration* to exploring and refuting the paradox, thus unwittingly lending some support to Wilde's statement that 'Society often forgives the criminal. It never forgives the dreamer.'

Wilde had been accused, in the public press and in the dock, of 'systematic corruption' of youth, and while it is clear that if this was in fact an official view it was misinformed, he himself did later admit:

> I used to be utterly reckless of young lives. I used to take up a boy, love him passionately—and then grow bored with him, and often take no notice of him.
>
> (*L* 616)

Pathologically, his sexual appetite, like his artistic temperament, hungered for new sensations. Under the increasingly transparent cloak of the 'High Priest of the Decadents' Wilde was able to indulge these appetites, while society accepted him as its court jester, the creator of charming, if ridiculous, comedies. But once he began to seduce the sons of the aristocracy and bourgeoisie, and to mock the double standards of their parents in his farces, tolerance decreased and police vigilance, particularly since the Cleveland Street male brothel scandal, increased.[74]

Labouchere, who framed the clause which became Section 11 of the Criminal Law Amendment Act, 1885, under which Wilde was convicted, expressed prevailing opinion, saying: 'In view of the mischief that such a man does, the sentence [two years with or without hard labour, at the discretion of the judge] compares but lightly with those almost every day awarded for infinitely less pernicious crimes.'[75]

Wilde's defeat meant that attitudes towards homosexuality hardened: frivolity, irresponsibility or disdain for convention became synonymous with immorality, the dandy became an ogre. Those such as Gosse, James and Symonds who had worked patiently and quietly for the cause of those whom Krafft-Ebing had called 'these step-children of nature'[76] were horrified. On the appearance of *Dorian Gray* Symonds, who found the book 'psychologically interesting', said: 'If the British public will stand this they can stand anything,' adding: 'I resent the unhealthy, scented, mystic, congested touch which a man of this sort has on moral problems.'[77]

The prevailing trend in the literary development of 'uranianism' had been in the expression of tenderness between an older and a younger man, based on the antique example of 'Greek love' or *paederastia*. Symonds's translation of

Michelangelo's sonnets in 1878 had given it a major impetus, as had the appearance of Pater's collected essays on the Renaissance in 1873. Visually, photographers such as Baron von Gloeden and artists like Henry Scott Tuke had also celebrated the beauty of youth in 'Greek poses', which Symonds eloquently expressed in his *Greek Poets* as early as 1873:

> If we in England seek some loving echo of this melody of curving lines, we must visit the fields where boys bathe in early morning, or the playgrounds of our public schools in summer or the banks of the Isis when the eights are on the water, or the riding-schools of young soldiers.[78]

With his increasing morbidity Wilde had abandoned the uranian cover of his early poetry and had introduced hermaphroditism into English literature (closely followed by Rachilde's *Monsieur Vénus*) forty years before the appearance of *Orlando* and the prosecution of *The Well of Loneliness*. Dorian Gray, Mr W.H., even the Sphinx, are hero-heroines, while Lady Bracknell's callous disregard for any niceties other than those of blatant profiteering make the men of *Earnest* merely wilting cissies: perhaps this is what Joyce meant when he identified a 'sexless instinct' as one of Wilde's distinctive qualities. Gender became unimportant to Wilde as he imagined an irresponsible socialist utopia based on the 'new Hellenism/hedonism', the 'higher philosophy'. Pater's *Marius* had suggested it in 1885; Forster's *Maurice* rediscovered it in the *Phaedrus* in 1913—'He saw there his malady described exquisitely, calmly, as a passion which we can direct, like any other, towards good or bad. Here was no invitation to licence ... ',[79] yet to explain his 'malady' he is forced to blurt out: 'I'm an unspeakable of the Oscar Wilde sort.'[80]

The question of the ethical code of Victorian society in relation to pathological egomania is central to Wilde's case. One of Wilde's bitchiest enemies, André Raffalovitch, rushed into print in 1895 with his account of *L'Affaire Oscar Wilde*, in which he announced:

When I say he was a criminal nature, I am not concerned with the sexual offences with which he has been charged, but with the role he has played, the influence he has exerted, with the young ideas he has mis-directed, the vices he has advocated: English society is equally to blame.[81]

Was this a 'systematic corruption of youth'? In a direct comparison with the Cleveland Street affair, Raffalovitch pointed out that in the earlier case the details

proved that private vice made use of a recognised system. . . . One cannot accuse society of unwarranted tolerance nor the guilty parties of wanting to practise sodomy openly. . . . Sodom exists, venal and menacing, the invisible city. But the 'Oscar Wilde tragedy' is of another kind. Oscar Wilde has been encouraged, tolerated by English society. He was regarded as an institution.[82]

Dorian Gray, *Intentions* (inscribed to Alfred Douglas 'in memory of the higher philosophy'), 'The Portrait of Mr W. H.', had all helped to establish a certain reputation against which the press had righteously fulminated, and it had been expected that any prosecution of Wilde as a poseur would be directed at his artistic reputation, as indeed his cross-examination by Carson had commenced. But because Wilde had exposed the hypocrisy of the 'invisible city', presenting the shocked bourgeoisie with the clearest evidence of a widespread culture of paederasty and homoerotism, society's reaction was to find a clinical explanation, as provided by Lombroso and Nordau: Wilde was criminally insane—a position he himself came to accept. Even his persecutor, the Marquess of Queensberry, said in *The Star* (before the trial came on):

Were I the authority that had to mete out to him his punishment I would treat him with all possible consideration as a sexual pervert of utterly diseased mind, not as a sane criminal. If it is sympathy Mr Wilde has it from me to this extent.[83]

It was the fact that Queensberry held similar views about the Prime Minister that made it necessary to confine the outbreak. Tim Healy, a friend of Wilde and later Governor-General of the Irish Free State, recorded in his memoirs that he had urged Lockwood, the Solicitor-General, 'not to put him "on his country" again' after the first trial, and was told: 'I would not, but for the abominable rumours against ———.'[84]

Just as Wilde came to acknowledge his indulgence in 'the most revolting passions' (*L* 402), Symonds too turned away from what he called the 'asiatic extravagance of pleasure'[85] and hoped that 'in future, sexual excess will surely be reckoned a form of madness'.[86] For Symonds, the ideal was close to that in which Wilde proposed to lead the contemplative life, a genderless state of innocence, epitomised by the Hermaphrodite: 'The union of athletic goodliness and consummate womanhood [Hermes and Aphrodite] produced a blending of two beauties forgotten by an oversight of nature.'[87] Wilde, echoing Symonds and Krafft-Ebing, said of himself and Douglas: 'Nature was a stepmother to each of us' (*L* 413).

The problem of the 'higher philosophy' in contrast to the baser passions was explained by Symonds:

> The one is mad for pleasure; the other loves beauty.
> The one is an involuntary sickness; the other a sought enthusiasm.[88]

Wilde had disaffected and alienated many homosexuals by indulging that sickness and thus devaluing the quest for beauty. Alfred Douglas had borrowed a phrase from Symonds for the closure of his poem 'Two Loves'—'I am the love that dare not speak its name'[89]—and had thus given Wilde the opportunity to 'come out' with his resounding 'speech from the dock' which had done much to redeem the bad odour which the revelation of his conduct had created for homosexuals. Symonds had said in 1883: 'No one dares speak of it; or if they do they bate their breath.... Those who read these lines will hardly doubt what passion it is that I am hinting at.... Surely it deserves a name.'[90] (Whitman too had hinted in *Leaves of Grass*: 'There is that in me...I do not know what it is....I do not know it....It is without name....It is a word unsaid / It is not in any dictionary or utterance or symbol.')[91]

Apart from Wilde's own impassioned defence of Greek love at his trial, serious work in the form of case studies was being carried out at precisely this time, and this more than anything was jeopardised by exactly the same set of circumstances by which he had popularised 'the noblest form of affection'. Symonds had collaborated with Havelock Ellis in the early research for *Sexual Inversion* (published in Germany in 1896 and in England in 1897). Ellis largely followed the work of Krafft-Ebing, whose *Psychopathia Sexualis* had appeared in 1886. Krafft-Ebing asserted that

> Inverted sexuality appears spontaneously, without external cause, with the development of sexual life...a congenital phenomenon; or it develops upon a sexuality, the beginning of which was normal, as a result of very definite injurious influences, and thus appears as an acquired anomaly.[92]

Artistic brilliance, he noted, was common in cases of effemination in the psychosexual hermaphrodite (congenital homosexual), while 'pathological emotional states, periodical insanity, paranoia' indicate 'insanity of a degenerative character'.[93]

In a later edition of *Sexual Inversion* (published as *Psychology of Sex*, 1936) Ellis, although wrongly believing that there was no early sign in Wilde of homosexual tendencies (thinking that this was ruled out by his having married and begotten children), said that nevertheless

We must hesitate to describe Wilde's homosexuality as acquired. If we consider his constitution and his history, it is not difficult to suppose that homosexual germs were present in a latent form from the first, and it may quite well be that Wilde's inversion was that kind which is now described as retarded, though still congenital.[94]

In the same volume he refers to a rare type of inversion, of which Wilde may be an example, 'in which a heterosexual person apparently becomes homosexual by the exercise of intellectual curiosity and aesthetic interest'.[95]

In his *Autobiography* Alfred Douglas tried to rationalise and at the same time diminish the nature of the problem identified by Symonds when he said:

> The sort of things that boys do at school and college, that Wilde and thousands of others go on doing all their lives, are contrary to Christian ethics but not to pagan ethics.[96]

It was an attempt to live in one country but by the rules of another. Wilde said after his release from prison: 'A patriot put in prison for loving his country continues to love his country; a poet put in prison for loving boys, goes on loving boys.'

As Shaw said, 'Guilty or not guilty is a question not of fact but of morals', and since Wilde believed in the nobility of his passion, he could 'plead not guilty with perfect sincerity, and indeed could not honestly put in any other plea'.[97] The court, we might observe, on the basis of its own subjective morality, could bring in no verdict other than guilty.

8
Yeats's Transitus

(i) MYTH

ON Christmas Day 1888 the twenty-three-year-old Yeats dined with the Wildes. Living in London with his parents and sisters for the past year, he had already been introduced by his father, the painter John Butler Yeats, to the idea that 'personality is neither right nor wrong... it transcends intellect and morality'.[1] Now, when he said to Wilde: 'I envy those men who become mythological while still living,' the older man replied: 'I think a man should invent his own myth.'[2] The comment was to direct Yeats towards the creation of a fictional personality and a corpus of literature unequalled in Ireland for its intensity and its intention. On that Christmas Day Wilde read to him the text of 'The Decay of Lying', which would appear in the following month's issue of *The Nineteenth Century*. It was a seminal moment in the history of Irish literature, since Wilde's arguments would impress Yeats with the need to create a personal myth. He would henceforth stand between the two islands, oscillating between the centre of the world and the edge of the world, between the last romantics and first modernists. In this chapter we shall examine Yeats's debt to Wilde—and to the mindset which reflected the nineteenth century and anticipated the twentieth—by reference to his use of myth, symbol and rhetoric.

W. J. McCormack writes: 'Nothing in nineteenth-century Irish writing predicts Yeats, and nothing in Yeats requires that body of work.... Yeats is the culmination of a mid- and late-Victorian rereading of the Irish eighteenth century.'[3] This would undoubtedly be true if it were also true of Wilde, but, as we have seen, Wilde drew sustenance not only from re-readings of intellectual history but also from re-creations of centuries much older than the eighteenth, continuing centuries which gave him his 'half-civilized blood'. Yeats's imagination was certainly grounded in the era of Swift, Berkeley and Burke, but—like Wilde's—it was also nurtured on the nationalism of Davis, Mangan and Ferguson and, indeed, on that of Sir William and Lady Wilde themselves. His quest for a 'Unity of Being' and a 'Unity of Culture' rested on a much broader base than that of a Protestant nation as revealed in the notion of ascendancy. However proprietorial and patronising his attitude to folklore may have been, it provided the vital link between his own people's past and the past of an 'other' people which was not ordinarily accessible to him, and which had been formed into a 'book' by the nineteenth-century Protestant conscience. In Ferguson's terms, he needed not merely to 'live back' in the eighteenth century but to re-enact the conflicts within a perennial culture and bring them to a resolution which would also determine the conflicts within himself, his 'antinomies'.

Like Wilde, Yeats embodied a series of tensions; in order to encounter them, he needed the shelter of a myth, a mask by means of which to deceive himself. His life story perhaps indicates how Wilde's own career might have developed had Wilde's gyre not widened so far. A controlling hand in the creation of a national theatre and of a drama which encoded the evolution of a nation, and membership of the Senate of the Irish Free State, where he represented the conscience of the Protestant nation, bestowed on Yeats the twin roles of thesis and antithesis, strophe and antistrophe, whereby he constructed and deconstructed reality and the ideas which lay behind it: Yeats was the Wilde who went home to face the consequences of the Protestant revival; it might have been Wilde who said:

> I carry from my mother's womb
> A fanatic heart.[4]

Yeats was consumed by the need to create a vision of a possible world in order to resolve the tensions of his antinomies. Where Wilde's antinomianism encouraged him to see himself pitched by nature against society, Yeats internalised the problem, seeing himself as the place of conflict. He thus impersonates in many senses the tensions of nineteenth-century Ireland.

> I am always, in all I do, driven to a moment which is the realisation of myself as unique and free, or to a moment which is the surrender to God of all that I am.... Could those two impulses ... be reconciled ... all life would cease.[5]

If there is a modern embarrassment between being and doing, it is rooted in the difficulties of self-knowledge and self-awareness faced by Irishmen in the long march towards freedom. 'Man may embody truth, but he cannot know it'[6] was Yeats's way of expressing it; the fact that he also personalised the difficulty—seeing himself as *the* man—enables us to see in the evolution of both his thought and his poetry a continual struggle for the equilibrium of rhetoric and poetry which gives his work its inner strength and dynamic. Wilde preceded Yeats in this dilemma, since he too divined within himself a 'truth' which was evident to his presiding *daimon* yet not disclosed to him: a secret history, a tragedy, which must be pursued in the anti-self.

Yeats's tensions are Irish tensions, expressed by Louis MacNeice in his brilliant study of his fellow-poet:

> The Irish are sentimental / the Irish are unsentimental;
> The Irish genius is personal / the Irish genius is impersonal;
> The Irish are formal / the Irish are slapdash;
> Ireland is a land of tradition / Ireland suffers from a lack of tradition.

Ultimately

It is easy to be Irish / it is difficult to be Irish.[7]

Here again the difficulty was Wilde's before it was Yeats's, a discomfort with being Irish in any place—at home or abroad. Shaw had seen it in Wilde and knew it in himself. Even Yeats encountered that difficulty with 'home' which saw him vacillating between Ireland and London, between Sligo and Dublin, between Berkeley and Cuchulain. Wilde (and his parents before him) provided Yeats with an anxious role-model of the Irish writer commuting between differing notions of Irishness and differing ways of exercising 'genius' and 'tradition'.

In Yeats's poetry in particular, these tensions emerge as violence/civilisation, brutality/heroism, words/action, the still point in time / history as movement in time, the library / the wilderness. The ultimate set of opposites was summed up in Yeats's succinct and pungent statement of the dichotomy between the inner self and the mundane self: 'We make of the struggle with others, rhetoric, of the struggle with ourselves, poetry.'[8] It will be my particular intention in this chapter to indicate that it was Wilde who, in his fictions and poetry, catalysed both heroism and brutality, violence and civilisation, and thus represented for Yeats a critic whose perceptions of self and anti-self were canonic in their attention to form, and yet atypical, heterodox, in their effect.

There was a strongly Irish basis to the writings of both men, and an equally strong cosmopolitan horizon. As Katherine Worth has demonstrated, the theatre of Maeterlinck was a starting-point for both. Wilde's imaginative journey began with an unfulfilled partnership with Whistler to reinvent Japan; Yeats's theatre culminated as he brought the Japanese dramatic genre to Ireland where he married it to a symbolism heavily influenced by Wilde. Thus the masks which underpin and front the hieratic commune of *The King of the Great Clock Tower* and *A Full Moon in March* are derived from the ritual of a country whose reality Wilde had doubted, yet it was also underpinned by the sense of mystery in the ritual of Ireland itself, in the way in which it set up tensions within dialogue.

Of his 'Plays for Dancers' Yeats said that he wished to create an artistic conflict which 'takes place in the depths of the soul' and which would represent 'the struggle of a dream with the world'.[9] Nothing could be more typical of the nineteenth-century consciousness which possessed, and was possessed by, spiritual and physical dimensions. There are five nodes of conflict: that between the inward-looking self and the outward-looking anti-self; that between self and the inner world; that between anti-self and the outer world; that between the private self and the public world; and that between the public self and the private world. This is a much more complex circumstance—and requires a much more complex system of thought—than anything emerging from Wilde's situation. But our reading of Wilde's poems and fictions will have indicated the extent to which Wilde was at least as conscious as Yeats of the depths to which antinomies could bring his 'soul'.

In many senses, Yeats was the successor to Wilde and thus acts as an extra conduit for Wilde's ideas and emotions to be translated into the rhythms of twentieth-century speech and thought. Firstly, and in particular, his statement (already noted) that 'we begin to live when we have conceived life as tragedy' is identical with Wilde's and his mother's own observation of life as tragedy. It was the natural condition for the mind of nineteenth-century Ireland, but, more importantly, it was re-validated as a motto for modernism: speaking of the renaissance of Irish culture and of the birth of a new theatre in particular, he said: 'Our literary movement would be worthless but for its defeat.'[10] Secondly, Yeats accepted, endorsed and, in his own mind, exercised the role of the wanderer. Of children he said:

When they imagine a country for themselves, it is always a country where one can wander without aim, and where one can never know from one place what another will be like.[11]

Heroes too 'live always as if they were playing a game', and Yeats himself aspired to a new childhood in 'a life without dates and without any settled abode'.[12] Clearly this accords to the Celtic notion of Tír na nÓg as closely as anything in Wilde—the mental image of a land where both time and space have been dismantled. The transitus between innocence and experience is made difficult, however, by the natural tendency of the hero to failure—and by the necessity of failure. Where Wilde elevated failure, Yeats seems to have preferred Lady Wilde's notion of despair as the principal fruit of the union:

> man's life is thought
> And he, despite his terror, cannot cease
> Ravening through century after century,
> Ravening, raging, and uprooting that he may come
> Into the desolation of reality.[13]

The points of contact between this fragment of Yeats's late, disillusioned poetry ('Meru') and the work of Wilde as a whole are many and remarkable. It takes up and intensifies Wilde's youthful notion (in 'The Rise of Historical Criticism') that all history must be surveyed if we are to understand any specific moment of history. It takes the central activity of the eighteenth century as perceived by Yeats, *thought*, and turns it loose on modern times. Yeats, after witnessing the première of Alfred Jarry's *Ubu Roi* in 1899, remarked: 'What more is possible? After us the Savage God.'[14]

Our first duty, then, is to examine the meaning of *myth* as promulgated by Wilde and adopted by Yeats. Firstly, myth as *muthos* represents a scheme or system, a legendary tale from within by which the man governs his life; it is opposed to *logos*, which is conduct handed down to him by tradition and government. When a man *invents* (or finds) his own myth, he creates a persona which becomes a template for his relations with others. By taking Wilde's advice and making his own life into a book, a work of art, Yeats expected to transcend the world. In this aspect of his development he went far beyond Wilde's text, constructing schemes for reconciling the life of the mind (poetry) with the life in the world (rhetoric) by means of texts such as *A Vision*, which are to the intellectual world what the inventions of Heath Robinson are to that of mechanics: a schematic pursuit of truth and the possible which always teetered on the brink of instability.

Within this myth, however, the contending voices (Wilde's 'heaven and hell') are to be heard, experienced and, if possible, reconciled. 'Body and soul', he writes, are 'estranged amid the strangeness of themselves'.[15] Like Wilde's fisherman, he separates body and soul in order to know more of both worlds and to join their independent minds once more in a brilliant synthesis. 'Ego Dominus Tuus' is the archetypal statement, in its dialogue of 'Hic' and 'Ille', of this bifurcated sensibility, a cruel commentary on the double life which must be lived if humankind is to be given more than desolation.

> I call to the mysterious one who yet
> Shall walk the wet sands by the edge of the stream
> And look most like me, being indeed my double,
> The most unlike, being my anti-self,
> And standing by these characters disclose
> All that I seek.[16]

In the combination and mutual traffic of like/unlike, such thought defeats the Aristotelian choice of 'either/or' and replaces it with a series of receding and contrasting masks leading to a distant unity. It was a 'consummation' which, even though he had identified the like/unlike divorce in his own nature, had eluded Wilde in his bewilderment at the presence of the double. Wilde was never more 'like' himself than when he was trying to be 'unlike'—a mistake which Yeats seems to have evaded.

But Yeats sought not only knowledge but also his self. He therefore stands beside the self, outside it, and from within sees himself doing so:

> *Ille*: By the help of an image
> I call to my own opposite, summon all
> That I have handled least, least looked upon.

To which 'Hic' ripostes:

> And I would find myself and not an image.

The two ambitions are not antithetical: 'Ille' replies: 'That is our modern hope', and yet there is a powerlessness as the mind finds itself an observer rather than a creator:

> We are but critics, or but half create,
> Timid, entangled, empty and abashed,
> Lacking the countenance of our friends.[17]

The pursuit of countenance is one aspect of history, the disclosure of images (or 'lineaments') which is imprescriptibly tragic, and happy only when tragedy can accommodate happiness. Of Keats 'Ille' says: 'His art is happy, but who knows his mind?' To Yeats, as to Wilde, it may have been obvious that, by definition, the 'love of the impossible'—whether in sexual or intellectual terms—cannot be achieved, but that did not obviate the necessity for testing the definition by which fate is sealed: we can 'recall a time when people were in love with a story, and gave themselves up to imagination as if to a lover',[18] but we may not live it.

The heaven and hell are both expressed by Yeats in his choice of motto when he joined the Order of the Golden Dawn: '*Demon est Deus Inversus* [The Demon is the Invert God]'. Before despair and desolation comes bewilderment: 'We sing amid our uncertainty.'[19] It gives rise to a classic division between two personae, 'Michael Robartes and Owen Aherne'—in his poetry, for example in 'Michael Robartes and the Dancer', and in his prose in 'Rosa Alchemica', 'Tables of the Law' and 'The Adoration of the Magi', and in Aherne's 'Preface' to *A Vision*. Nothing in Anglo-Irish literature would match such necessary invention until Brian O'Nolan's various autonomous personae in *At Swim-Two-Birds*. Each script has two authors. As Wilde's garden had two sides, sunlit and obscured, so Yeats writes in his early autobiography:

> A man walked as it were casting a shadow, and yet one could never say which was man and which was shadow, or how many the shadows that he cast.[20]

As Wilde thought that the 'panthers' might be his accomplices in the subversion of society, so Yeats looked for 'allies for my secret thought'[21] and, significantly, found them in another form of the secret society so accessible to the political and sexual deviant, that of 'psychical research and mystical philosophy'.[22]

Yeats and Wilde deliberately cast many shadows, of which the greatest is that which interrogates 'the dancer' present first in *Salomé* and then throughout Yeats's drama. 'I seek an image, not a book'[23] is the least equivocal, most aspirational of Yeats's theses, yet it is belied by the necessity of language, which subverts symbol into logical construct. Immediately after 'Ego Dominus Tuus' Yeats wrote, in 'The Phases of the Moon', that 'The soul begins to tremble into stillness,/To die into the labyrinth of itself!'—not, we note, to *live* within it. Thus, Robartes tells Aherne,

> All thought becomes an image and the soul
> Becomes a body.[24]

This accords closely to the schema of *A Vision*, where Yeats aphoristically quotes Heraclitus: 'Dying each other's life, living each other's death.'[25] This represented a philosophical means for Yeats to express his belief in the accessibility of the otherworld, and it also encapsulates the symbiotic relationship of poet and symbol, of signifier and signified. The 'images for the affection' which he had seen in Davis's tarot of 'Soldier, Orator, Patriot . . . ' were the same images which Wilde cast in his own mind when he spoke with reverence of Smith O'Brien and wrote so respectfully to Davitt, and which were also invoked by Yeats himself in his lament for John O'Leary and 'romantic Ireland'.

It is the measure of Yeats's achievement in reconciling antinomies, that he both separated them into their constituent parts yet continued to hold them in the same optic. 'No mind can engender till divided in two,' he said,[26] and elsewhere he acknowledged that destruction must precede creation: 'Nothing can be sole or whole / That has not been rent.'[27] His capacity for reconciliation is evident in the way he relished a remark by Synge:

> There are three things any two of which have often come together but never all three: ecstasy, asceticism, austerity; I wish to bring all three together.[28]

This encapsulates the way in which Yeats and Synge, together and individually, succeeded Wilde in illustrating the two sides of the garden, and in doing so resolved his dilemma by seeing the garden once again whole. 'Ecstasy' is the passionate standing-outside-oneself; 'asceticism', the discipline of oneself; and 'austerity', the severe denial of the luxuries proscribed by that discipline. Wilde, we recall, yearned for the recovery of his 'austere control', a quality which combines Synge's 'asceticism' and 'austerity'. To absorb discipline and self-denial, and to join them to ecstasy—it is clear why Yeats coveted the formula on foot of which Synge pursued his own drama. For Wilde, it represented the capacity 'to drift with every passion' while at the same time maintaining 'ancient wisdom' which would enable the poet to strike 'one clear chord' to 'reach the ears of God'. For Yeats, it meant the ability to live in both the world of images and the world of the book, to hold in equilibrium the perennial culture of

'Great Mind and Great Memory' which replicated Wilde's 'ancient wisdom'. For Synge, it represented a quantum leap in dramatic terms, by powering a metaphor by means of lies on both sides of the fulcrum.

It became an ambition of Yeats (as of Hyde) to follow the example of the Wildes, Ferguson and Petrie in unveiling the unwritten history of Ireland to all classes of folk. His prescription was that of Davis, and his essay 'Ireland and the Arts' of 1899[29] echoed Davis's aspiration of 1846, that artists should raise the taste and cultivate the nationality of Ireland.[30] Even here, however, Yeats bowed before the division of the artistic energy between 'love of country and love of the unseen life'[31]—one logocentric and concrete, the other mythopoeic and amorphous. The more that speech tended to express a universal truth, the more secret and arcane it became, the less amenable to reason and prose. Like Wilde's Sphinx, Yeats's 'secret thought' was located in an artificial destination, 'Byzantium', where it was enacted before a court and hierarchy of crafted icons. The meeting-point was achieved in both prose and verse: not only in the poem 'Meru' did Yeats say that

> Civilisation is hooped together, brought
> Under a rule, under the semblance of peace,
> By manifold illusion[32]

but also, and thirty years previously, in a diary of 1909 published under the title 'Estrangement', he wrote: 'All civilization is held together by the suggestions of an invisible hypnotist—by artificially created illusions. The knowledge of reality is always in some measure a secret knowledge. It is a kind of death.'[33]

The fact that Yeats found it necessary twice to express this bitter truth is indicative of the power which the figure of the grandfather-god exercised over his imagination, and of the reverence which this normally unaffected man clearly had in the face of a reserved presence. It is also intimately connected with the idea of autobiographical fiction, whereby a persona is created during the writing of a life which is yet to be lived, and it is in this sense that Yeats may have interpreted the ambiguity of Wilde's 'invent his own myth'—both to conjure up and discover, to find within oneself. As David G. Wright has persuasively argued,[34] Yeats negotiated a life which would enable him to build, as Wilde wished to build, a new society, but which would remain faithful, as Wilde in essence remained, to ancient truths. To write the book of Ireland became the imperative, and here the Wilde family offered Yeats a potent model.

Where Wilde took Irish folklore for the basis of parables and prose poems, Yeats saw in it the heart of dialogue, a place where soul and intellect could engage in an interrogation of the infinite and invisible. He believed, as Sir William and Lady Wilde had believed, that the Irish peasantry embodied in their foklore a living belief in an otherworld and that they represented it in their own lives. To be in communication with this otherworld marked them as different within modern Irish society, belonging to an age when such connection was regular and normal. 'None among people visiting Ireland, and few among the people living in Ireland, except peasants, understand that the peasants believe in the ancient gods, and that to them, as to their forebears, everything is inhabited and mysterious.[35] . . . Men who live primitive lives where instinct does the work of reason are fully conscious of many things that we cannot perceive at will.[36] . . . Tír na nÓg . . . is as near to the country people of to-day, as it was to Cuchulain and his companions.'[37]

Praising Lady Wilde's *Ancient Legends* for revealing 'the innermost heart of the Celt', Yeats prized the book because it gives us 'the Celt dreaming'.[38] Reviewing her second collection of Sir William's *disjecta*, *Ancient Cures, Charms, and Usages of Ireland*, Yeats titled his review 'Tales from the Twilight'. It was in this review that he penned the lapidary statement 'In Ireland this world and the other are not widely sundered,' continuing: 'Sometimes, indeed, it seems almost as if our earthly chattels are no more than the shadows of things beyond.'[39] It became the guiding motif of his *Celtic Twilight*.

Yeats, like Lady Wilde, was at pains to observe the disposition of the Celt to melancholy: 'The accidents of Nature supply a good store of it to all men, and in their hearts, too, there dwells a sadness still unfettered. Yet in the sadness'—Yeats tells us in an echo of Aubrey de Vere—'there is no gloom, no darkness, no love of the ugly, no moping. The sadness of a people who hold that "contention is better than loneliness", it is half a visionary fatalism.'[40]

Within the Celtic vision Yeats discovered 'a universe where all is large and intense enough to almost satisfy the emotions of man'.[41] Anticipating modernism, Yeats wrote that the folktale was not 'a criticism of life but rather an extension... an existence and not a thought'.[42] Yeats was anxious to emphasise that it was normal for an age of realism to look to folklore for a new reflection of the world—'a parable to show how man mounts to the infinite by the ladder of the impossible'.[43]

We will readily recognise in this 'infinite' the same imaginative realm sought—and plundered—by Wilde in his poetry, and the same resource from which his own 'fairy stories' had been drawn. But more than this, Yeats wanted to emphasise that the stories now quarried from the Gaelic peasantry and published in translation by Douglas Hyde (Alfred Nutt, the publisher of *Beside the Fire*, was also the publisher of Wilde's *The Happy Prince and other tales*) were a means of recouping an antecedent world of Homeric proportions and significance, 'one of the oldest worlds that man has imagined',[44] in which every man was an aristocrat:

> When one reads of the Fianna, or of Cuchulain, or of some great hero, one remembers that the fine life is always a part played finely before fine spectators....If we would create a great community...we must recreate the old foundations of life...as they must always exist when the finest minds and Ned the beggar and Seaghan the fool think about the same thing, although they may not think the same thought about it.[45]

To obey Yeats's injunction is to live one's art in such a way that art and artist mutually possess and consume one another, to 'live back' in a time when 'this' and 'other' were adjunctive and also to acknowledge the mythology and symbolism of that artistic life. 'Nations, races and individual men are unified by an image, or bundle of related images, symbolical or evocative of the state of mind which is...the most difficult to that man, race, or nation.'[46] The symbol is thus not a mere mask which conceals, but a statement—the signified—which embodies the signifier itself: man and symbol must be one, even though man may be embodied in many symbols, many masks.

(ii) SYMBOL

One of the most telling comments on Yeats's work is Richard Ellmann's: 'Each Yeats poem is likely to begin in decadence and end in renaissance.'[47] The passage from one side of the poet's experience to the other makes of his personality a vital membrane between opposing states, between rhetoric and poetry, between the nineteenth century and the twentieth.

For both Wilde and Yeats, the central artistic and critical activity was the establishment of metaphors in order to repossess 'ancient wisdom and austere control', to reach the wellsprings of antiquity, to reinvent an Ur-text of the emotions. For Wilde to say to Yeats:

> We Irish are too poetical to be poets; we are a nation of brilliant failures, but we are the greatest talkers since the Greeks[48]

was to point him towards three concurrent notions: that the mythopoeic faculty is not necessarily manifested in poetry; that thought is superior to action; and that the Greek mind could be reborn and metamorphosed in modern Ireland. Thus the idea that there was an aboriginal 'fixed type', as Yeats called it at the end of his life,[49] was, as Ellmann has shown,

derived through Wilde from Pater and ultimately Hegel.[50]
Yeats continued to emphasise that it was from the lives of the
peasantry that modern art would receive its vitality:

> Folk-art is ... the oldest of the aristocracies of thought ...
> and because it has gathered unto itself the simplest and
> most unforgettable thoughts of the generations, it is the
> soil where all great art is rooted.[51]

For this reason Yeats considered the only worthwhile pursuit
to be the 'dream of the noble and the beggar-man', either in
art or, as we might call the political dimension of his work,
applied art. Yeats in 'The Municipal Gallery Revisited' insisted on the validity of bringing the past into the future, and in
a certain way:

> John Synge, I and Augusta Gregory, thought
> All that we did, all that we said or sang
> Must come from contact with the soil, from that
> Contact everything Antaeus-like grew strong.
> We three alone in modern times had brought
> Everything down to that sole test again,
> Dream of the noble and the beggar-man.[52]

In an essay of 1898 entitled 'The Celtic Element in Literature'
Yeats insisted that Celtic lore was directly connected with 'the
ancient religion of the world'.[53] 'All the august sorrowful persons of literature, Cassandra and Helen and Brunhilde, and
Lear and Tristram, have come out of legends and are indeed
but the images of the primitive imagination mirrored in the little looking-glass of the modern and classic imagination.'[54] The
contemporary 'Celtic movement' represented a renaissance
of the ancient wellspring and was 'a new intoxication for the
imagination of the world'.[55] Like Shaw, Yeats saw excess as a
necessary element of progress.

We can thus see how Yeats easily made the connection
between Irish themes and decadent forms: 'The arts by brood-

ing upon their own intensity have become religious, and are seeking, as some French critic [Emile Verhaeren] has said, to create a sacred book. . . . The Irish legends . . . may well give the opening century its most memorable symbols.'[56] These were therefore to be found not only in 'the Savage God' of *Ubu Roi* but also in the Celtic flavour of *Axël*, of which Yeats wrote: 'Those strange sentences so much in the manner of my time—"as for Living? our servants will do that for us"— did not seem so important as the symbols.'[57] The symbolic role was that of noble and beggar-man, master and servant, wise man and fool, so thoroughly incarnate in the exchange and reversal of roles of *Purgatory*, *The Hour-Glass* and *The Cat and the Moon.*

Yeats and Wilde shared the fact that they saw life through eyes which were at once Irish and European. 'When the moon is full' is a superstitious rural observation which was Wilde's ('The Fisherman and his Soul', CW 253) before it was Yeats's; their understanding of '*fin de siècle*' was, as Austin Clarke observed, 'exotic. . . not quite English'.[58] Both understood what it means to serve a destructive passion, Wilde when he said: 'Each man kills the thing he loves', Yeats in saying: 'Love's pleasure drives his love away'[59] and again 'If I triumph I must make men mad';[60] and both knew that the only true poetry lay in the intellectual image: 'I call to the eye of the mind.'[61]

Yeats recalled Wilde telling him: 'Olive Schreiner is staying in the East End because that is the only place where people do not wear masks upon their faces, but I have told her that I live in the West End because nothing in life interests me but the mask.'[62] He learned from Wilde that he needed a mask both for himself and for his characters. The masked figures on his stage and the ambiguous, arcane visitors to his poetry sprang from his indecision between the classic antinomies of 'perfection of the work or of the life', of rhetoric and poetry, of 'love of country and love of the unseen life'. 'Every passionate man', he declared, 'is. . . linked with another age, historical or imaginary, where alone he finds images that rouse his energy.'[63] The mask is thus not merely a pretence, but the positive adoption of an identity. It is 'an emotional antithesis' of our internal nature,[64] an anti-self which is the mirror of the self, the image of the beloved—'for love also creates the Mask'.[65] For Yeats, this invention of the anti-self was an essential discipline, since 'all happiness depends on the energy to assume the mask of some other self; ... all joyous or creative life is a rebirth as something not oneself'.[66]

As George Steiner says, 'When it is torn loose from the moorings of myth, art tends towards anarchy. It becomes the outward leap of the impassioned but private imagination into a void of meaning.'[67] To submit to that discontinuity is to allow the erosion and wastage of the *anima mundi* which Ellmann has called 'a sublime lexicon of the imagination which stores old images and the potentialities of new ones' and which enabled Yeats 'to conceive of human destiny as a panorama of images and men'.[68] Yeats's instruction to Synge, to find himself, and to find a national epic, in the Aran Islands, was advice which Sir William or Lady Wilde might have given to Oscar. The proprietorial aspect of the mind which could colonise the west anew with mythological beings becomes, in the contemplation of those beings, submissive. To fashion and manipulate a puppet which contained all one's own soul was only half the struggle; the rest consisted in worship. In this Wilde and Yeats had profoundly classical imaginations. Wilde had written in 1892: 'The actor's aim is, or should be, to convert his own accidental personality into the real and essential personality of the character he is called upon to impersonate, whatever that character may be.' He went on to put an arrogant slant on a subject which would later occupy Yeats's profoundest attention:

> There are many advantages in puppets. They never argue. They have no crude views about art. They have no private lives. We are never bothered by accounts of their virtues, or bored by recitals of their vices... nor do they speak more than is set down for them. They recog-

nise the presiding intellect of the dramatist. ... They are remarkably docile, and have no personalities at all. (*L* 310)

Beneath the persiflage is the same seriousness of intent in relation to the nature of the stage as we find in Yeats's enthusiasm for the work of Gordon Craig (son of E. W. Godwin and Ellen Terry) in defining the mask and the screen. The importance of the puppet lay not in its inability to speak on its own behalf, but in the clarity and intensity of its function without extraneous considerations. The actor is metamorphosed into the role—the signified—just as in the Eucharist priest and communicant believe in the transubstantiation of bread and wine into flesh and blood.

In the figures of Salomé, Herod and Iokanaan we see the personae of that transitional world between pagan and Christian, we acknowledge the changing of that world. *Salomé*, from which Yeats borrowed extensively for *The King of the Great Clock Tower* and *A Full Moon in March*, is the aristocratic drama not because it treats of imperial affairs and is expressed in exotic language, but because its kings and gods, its moons and its blood-images, are primitive counters, original tropes of experience and meaning. For both Wilde and Yeats, the image, as an intellectual construct, was paramount. For Yeats, the possibility of the world depended on the affective presence of a tarot of psychological types, each bearing a distinct identity and embodying an accessible command. The opening setting of *Salomé*—

A great terrace in the Palace of Herod, set above the banqueting-hall ... a gigantic staircase ... an old cistern surrounded by a wall of green-bronze. Moonlight (*CW* 552)

—becomes, in Yeats's own plays, 'the King's Threshold, steps before the Palace of King Guaire at Gort',[69] 'The Hawk's Well [in] the Irish Heroic Age'.[70] In his poetry it becomes 'the holy city of Byzantium',[71] 'a starlit or a moonlit dome', 'the Emperor's pavement', 'the dancing floor'.[72] It is the same

Byzantium where, as Wilde had said, 'the two arts met—Greek art, with its intellectual sense of form, and its quiet sympathy with humanity; [and] Oriental art, with its gorgeous materialism, its frank rejection of imitation, its wonderful secrets . . . its splendid textures . . . its marvellous and priceless traditions' (*CPB* 150).

Tragedy—the fated destruction of doomed personalities and of their civilisations—was an expiation and transcendence of guilt. The dance of Salomé is the embodiment of transitus, the meeting-point of the ancient soul and the modern conscience. In suspending space and time during the action, Wilde makes the dancer at one with the dance and with the meaning of the dance. What is danced is tragedy and fulfilment, and this explains Salomé herself and the hatred and longing passing between Iokanaan and Salomé. After her dance everything is transformed: Herod and his world become absurd, their gestures and imprecations meaningless, because their meaning has been absorbed into, and rendered nil by, the acting out of the impossible—Salomé's dance for the death of both Iokanaan and herself.

As Katherine Worth has pointed out, in Herod's line 'It would be terrible if the dead came back' (*CW* 565) 'there is something that is not absurd'.[73] This is the point at which all the dead and all the living are gathered together on the top of a jewelled pin. 'At this point', says Worth, 'interesting connections between Wilde and Yeats begin to force themselves on our attention, the idea of masks enters the play, the notion of character as an inner drama with a perpetual pull between archetypal opposites.'[74] And it is in the dance in Yeats's plays—especially in *The King of the Great Clock Tower* and *A Full Moon in March*—that the world is transformed from the hemisphere of thought into that of sensuality, from clamour to silence, from fear to submission. Worth reports that Yeats, in attempting to produce an Irish Salomé, believed that 'it was an Irish tradition to describe the wind as "the dance of the daughter of Herodias"'.[75] In *The King of the Great Clock Tower*, as in *Salomé*, the severed head is no 'evidence of his death'[76] because it prefigures 'Crucifixion', 'Resurrection' and 'Purgatory'. Here too Yeats had learned from Wilde the power of the prose-poem such as 'The Crucifixion of the Outcast' or 'The Wisdom of the King' to provide a parabolic lesson for the aesthetic version of modern Ireland which he hoped to create.

There is, as Worth has noted, a close textual affinity between *Axël* and *The Shadowy Waters*, but the example which she gives us from the latter, Dectora's temptation of Forgael—'Bend lower, that I may cover you with my hair / For we will gaze upon this world no longer'[77]—also echoes both *Salomé* and 'La Sainte Courtisane'. It is striking how extensively the brief fragment of 'La Sainte Courtisane'—which Yeats would have known from its inclusion in the collected editions of both 1908 and 1909—impinges on the terrain of Yeats's plays, and thence on Beckett's. The 'broken rocks', the 'No-place' (as Worth calls it)[78] of *At the Hawk's Well*, *The Dreaming of the Bones* and *Endgame* constitute the same permanent threshold across which Wilde's saints and sinners have attempted to entice one another. It was as well suited to Yeats as it was to Wilde, the liminal point where self and anti-self address each other, making perennial statements about the perceived nature of good and evil. Yeats in fact carries this biblical theme to the ultimate level imagined but never enacted by Wilde, in the portrayal of Christ and Judas in the ribald anti-comedy of *Calvary*.

Nowhere is that transitus and transformation more subtly and imagistically explored than in the brief, unjustly neglected poem of 1927, 'Symbols', which acts as a commentary on a line quoted above, 'Timid, entangled, empty and abashed':

> A storm-beaten old watch-tower,
> A blind hermit rings the hour.
>
> All-destroying sword-blade still
> Carried by the wandering fool.
>
> Gold-sewn silk on the sword-blade,
> Beauty and fool together laid.[79]

It is the same theme which we find at the core of the contemporaneous 'Vacillation' and 'A Dialogue of Self and Soul'. In each couplet of 'Symbols' Yeats looks at one of his lifelong paradigms—wisdom, power, love. A blind hermit achieves wisdom, a wandering fool finds power in a sword, and love, instead of resolving antinomies, deepens them by uniting beauty and foolery, thus heightening the apparently ineradicable conflict which resides in all consciousness and thought.

But these six lines also provide absolute confirmation of Ellmann's argument. Not simply the poem itself, but each couplet, begins in decadence and ends in renaissance: the traditional symbol of the nineteenth-century melodrama, 'a storm-beaten old watch-tower', is juxtaposed with the sinister figure of the blind hermit; the symbol of power, the sword-blade, is put in the hands of a wandering fool; and the sensuality of the decoration on the sword, the 'gold-sewn silk', is put there to heighten our sense of brutal and stupid power residing within the sword. Even in Yeats's word-construction there are antinomies between the first and second line of each couplet: everything in the first lines is held together with hyphens: *storm-beaten . . . watch-tower . . . all-destroying . . . sword-blade . . . gold-sewn*. In the second lines individual words, left to their own devices, challenge the syntax as well as the surety of the prevailing aesthetic. With the exception of the sword-blade (although even here the concept of the sword in action is implicit) the hyphenated constructs unite physical properties with movement. If he had wanted to continue this nineteenth-century aesthetic into his second lines, Yeats could have done so: 'the sword-blade fool-carried'. But he chooses to move from decadence into renaissance, that is, to challenge the decadent, imagistic, complacent aesthetic which relies on a deep sense of interconnection, of order, with something renascent, menacing, singular, doubting, modern. He decides to populate the world not with gold-clad princes and warriors, but with blindness and madness, a wandering, hermetic life where the only roots are those leading deeply and sharply into one's own psyche, a world shorn of tradition. From his iconic 'images for the affection' he had passed to images for the intellect.

(iii) RHETORIC

'Culture is the sanctity of the intellect,' Yeats declared.[80] Typical of his widespread commentary on the artistic and creative role of criticism, it is an incisive contribution to the historical view of culture to which Wilde had given a hibernian slant in 'The Critic as Artist', 'The Truth of Masks' and 'The Decay of Lying'. With Yeats, criticism is the anti-self of poetry, the rhetoric through which he confronts and negotiates a relation with the world—'country', 'others', public images, history. It is a tool to be used and abused, to be placed at the service of poetry and ultimately, in his plays, to be reconciled with it. Like symbolism, it is a verb, gerundive, fecundating the noun in the mind.

If Yeats had been unfettered by home considerations, his 'heraldic universe' would have been built in the non-place, Byzantium. But, from the early novel *John Sherman* (1891), atmospheric and episodic like *Dorian Gray*, to the last plays, *Purgatory* and *The Death of Cuchulain*, he was summoned back to Ireland and the high ground of Sligo. More importantly for our purposes, as late as 1933 he was still writing passionately on Gaelic themes in critical articles which sustain the trenchant arguments he had put forward in the creation of the 'Celtic Twilight'.

The Celtic Twilight, first published in 1893, and Yeats's cognate writing on Irish legend and folklore, is a construction of belief as much as *A Vision*, and a fiction as much as his poems, but Yeats's attempt to find 'the innermost heart of the Celt' was also a struggle with the public world and constitutes some of its most charged rhetoric. The opening of 'Belief and Unbelief'—'there are some doubters even in the western villages'[81]—is a determined insistence on the reality of 'the unseen life' which thereby makes it visible and public.

For Yeats, the tension here was between leaving his country 'unborn' or bringing it, seen and unseen, into 'the opening century'. Even as Yeats wrote in *The Celtic Twilight* that 'I have desired, like any artist, to create a little world' he made it available to scholars and unbelievers. 'The things a man has heard and seen are threads of life, and if he pull them carefully from the confused distaff of memory, any who will can weave them into whatever garments of belief please them best.'[82] As the first paragraph of 'Belief and Unbelief' opens with doubt, so it ends with the assertion that the faeries 'stand to reason'.

Between doubt and inverted reason Yeats unfolds the otherworld. He encounters a visionary whose poems 'were all endeavours to capture some high, impalpable mood in a net of obscure images'.[83] This visionary, alive to the presence of 'some one who is dead or who has never lived',[84] has the capacity 'to persuade queer and conscience-stricken persons to deliver up the keeping of their troubles to his care'.[85] We might surmise that, taken together, the poems, the undead and the salving of conscience constitute the same medium by means of which Wilde made it possible to see, in other forms, beings which had not yet been born—which could not be otherwise uttered: his inscrutable, antagonistic Sphinx, his portrait of the beloved but mythological Mr W.H., his own childhood. Yeats adverts to such a condition when he writes of 'the threshold, between sleeping and waking, where Sphinxes and Chimeras sit open-eyed and where there are always murmurings and whisperings'.[86] He finds the *topos* of the artist's struggle, both with himself and with the world, in 'The Eaters of Precious Stones': 'One day I saw faintly an immense pit of blackness. . . . I knew that I saw my own Hell there, the Hell of the artist, and that all who sought after beautiful and wonderful things with too avid a thirst, lost peace and form.'[87]

Yeats in many ways offers us an insight into the way in which Wilde's career might have developed if it had not been cut short. Commuting between the now strange land of his birth and places where his restless imagination was more at home, his always exceptional character might have continued to provide a commentary on the 'evolution [of my own country] as a nation'. Given that he had foreseen the likelihood of a political career had he stayed in Ireland, there is also the possibility that had he made a return to Dublin after his imprisonment—or even, like his father after his own disgrace, to the west of Ireland—he might eventually have taken a hand in shaping the rhetoric of the new nation as it defined itself in terms of its own past and its continuing relationship with Britain and Europe. Wilde, unlike Yeats, would have displayed an openness to Catholic thought and mores, and at the same time would have represented the homosexual experience as both aesthete and convict, which might have mellowed the tone of both ultramontanism and ascendancy.

Furthermore, given Yeats's energetic direction of the Abbey Theatre, it is also possible that the elder playwright might have made common cause with the ambitions of a literary—a playwright's—theatre, pushing the aristocratic drama in the direction of Yeats's Cuchulain cycle and the 'Plays for Dancers' and introducing the influence of Ibsen and Maeterlinck to the Irish stage.

Through all this possibility runs the slogan, first Berkeley's, then Wilde's and Yeats's—'we Irish'. It employed the strategy of *assimilation* in creating a disingenuous bond among Irish peoples, and the strategy of *difference* in separating what was perceived as Irish from whatever was not. This paradigmatic exclusionism on the part of the seers of the new state—one which continued until after Yeats's death in a symbolic constitutional relationship with Britain—bore a striking resemblance to the thought of Wilde and Yeats in emphasising the solitary and unified activity of the artist—*sinn féin* [we ourselves] being the hallmark of their conscience and their behaviour.

* * *

The strongest indication of the connection between the minds of Wilde and Yeats lies in the fact that one of Wilde's last, and most disruptive, essays was *The Soul of Man under Socialism*, exploring man's relation to both freedom (self) and necessity (society), while Yeats continued to be fascinated with the relationship between this same soul of man, *anima hominis*, and the life of society, *anima mundi*. The idea that man had a self and a *daimon*, an anti-self in the supernatural, yet real, world, focuses our attention on Yeats's private and public worlds in the same way in which Wilde compels us to think of the real and unreal selves by means of the portrait in *Dorian Gray*. Himself the son of a portrait painter, Yeats would have known that a portrait—indeed, any image—contains both poetry and rhetoric, speaks both to itself and to the world, to sitter, painter and voyeur. Published in 1917, 'Anima Hominis', together with the poem 'Ego Dominus Tuus' (with the dialogue between 'Hic' and 'Ille'), made up the volume *Per Amica Silentia Lunae*, which, in turn, was collected with *The Celtic Twilight* (1893), *The Secret Rose* (1897) and *Rosa Alchemica* (1897) in *Mythologies*, published in 1925. The succession of titles reveals the cumulative method by which Yeats proceeded from chaos to form, towards a unity which might reconcile philosophy and passion.[88]

'I was full of thought, often abstract thought, longing all the while to be full of images,' he said, voicing a condition which we might readily detect in Wilde—wistfulness for the easier path of decadence. The 'double perspective' which constitutes Yeats's aesthetic[89] always ran from one side to the other of the antinomies. In purely aesthetic terms, the equation, hardly ever to be maintained, was a 'stylistic arrangement of experience';[90] in rhetorical terms, it was a political resolution of opposites—Catholic and Protestant, ancient and modern, bound and free. It was 'a dualistic mode of thinking' in pursuit of 'monistic aspirations'.[91]

It was, however, a problem which Wilde had recognised and avoided. His own 'third meaning' or third path took him into a purely personal world of poetry, of fiction, whereas

Yeats was permanently exercised by the problem of country and rhetoric. Where Wilde took the idea of a symbol as a personal challenge, making the relation between symbol and symbolism oblique, Yeats observed the need to make sense of it in every dimension. Yeats knew that he wanted to create a new society in Ireland, and he knew that it could not be Utopia. Whether he deserved it or not, he relished his 'reputation as an Irish rebel'.[92] He saw strife as the necessary precursor to restitution and wrote forcefully: 'The end of wisdom is sometimes the beginning of heroism.'[93] While he wanted to incorporate all its former greatness, to persuade its citizens to acknowledge the 'great tapestry' of the perennial culture, he also knew that 'the dream of my early manhood, that a modern nation can return to Unity of Culture, is false'.[94] He approached what Ellmann has called 'a *tertium quid*'[95] by avoiding thought whenever possible in favour of a 'stylistic arrangement' of thought which made it more like a book of images than the image of a book.

It is in his critical work, where he introduced poetry to rhetoric, that Yeats, like Wilde, established most effectively this *tertium quid*. As often as Wilde dogmatically declares: 'That is all,' Yeats goes to the other extreme, of vagueness, with his regular 'I do not know . . .'. At the instant when he asseverates truth, Yeats places it within the frame of myth.

> It is one of the ailments of our speculation that thought, when it is not the planning of something, or the doing of something or some memory of a plain circumstance, separates us from one another because it makes us always more unlike.[96]

It is useful here to refer to W. J. McCormack's discussion of the same subject in relation to Le Fanu: citing Yeats's distinction between 'the life' and 'the work', he observes that Le Fanu's life and work are linked in his narrative by 'the recurring revelation of the past in the present, the implicit declaration that what is happening in the immediate context of a scene has already happened'.[97] The declaratory act, which we have seen in the portraits revealed not only by Le Fanu but also by Maturin and Wilde, makes it inevitable that the painter or poet *must* carry over the image from one age to the next. Even though most of heroism and chivalry died— in Europe, on the field of Paschendaele[98] and in Ireland in the aftermath of the 1916 Rising—the resulting waste land saw the revival of tawdry heroes and bright young things. However debased—and this is also the message of 'De Profundis'—certain icons continue to reverberate within the modern imagination. The exchange—more a rhetorical debate than a poetical intercourse—between master and servant becomes the new tone of contemporary discourse.

Thus Yeats's treatment of the Cuchulain theme obliged him to worry and worry until he had made a satisfactory resolution on both the poetic and the rhetorical planes. Nowhere, in fact, is the question of symbolism as a verb more extraordinarily displayed than in three words at the close of Yeats's last play, *The Death of Cuchulain*:

> Who thought Cuchulain till it seemed
> He stood where they had stood?[99]

'*Who thought Cuchulain*' transmutes the summoning of Cuchulain to Pearse's side in the Post Office into a cerebral act of creation: it both elevates the hero and resurrects the collective unconscious; ancient Ireland leaps across the boundaries of time, death and history, to reinvent itself as its own metaphor, creating an epiphany yet never having been absent. It is the same act of summons by which Wilde repossessed Charmides or Hylas in his love-poems. Love or warfare, the motion is the same, and the action by which the hero is made present is the same intense act of intellectual symbolism. It is the gerund brought to the highest point.

9
The First Modernists

IN this final chapter I will indicate Wilde's lessons for, and involvement in, what may loosely be termed 'modernism': a phenomenon of all the arts which is descriptive both of the 'profound psychological change'[1] which has affected the Western mind since the middle of the nineteenth century and of the entropy occasioned by what Vaclav Havel calls 'the lack of metaphysical certainties'.[2] I shall do so firstly by reference to reflections of Wilde in Joyce, and then by exploring his relevance for the main thrust, or thrusts, of modernism, in particular in Borges and Barthes, and his affinities with Genet. My intention, here and in my Conclusion, is to establish how far Wilde's Irishness has become—however subliminally—a genre for our own time.

Modernism has been described as 'apocalyptic' and 'catastrophic',[3] but it can also be regarded as evolutionary, as being not only cata-strophic but also strophic in its own right. Barthes said that 'the whole of literature, from Flaubert to the present day, became the problematics of language',[4] and this judgment can be extended to the rhetoric and iconography of all art forms. If there was a crisis from which the modern world emerged, it existed in the watershed of political, scientific and artistic thought and behaviour from 1890 to 1920, of which the 1890s was the catalyst and the following two decades the equivalent of its nuclear fall-out.

The importance of modernism lies in its reaction to, and reformulation of, existing critical problems in thought and behaviour. To state that each vowel represents a separate colour, or that all art aspires to the condition of music, or that 'the truths of art are the truths of metaphysics', is to anticipate, and become the author of, developments in the study of relativity and psychology. It is to return contemporary thought to the condition of Greek drama. It may be apocalyptic in its description of cataclysmic events, but this is to be merely contemporary; in describing the fall of a *house*, however great, the apocalyptic writer already presages its renewal. It is in the perennity of its continual discovery of the *face* that art—*écriture*, the inscription of lineaments in all forms—is modernist.

Wilde lived at the epicentre of the period which gave rise to 'modernism'. Yet his claim to have invented his own age, however 'modernist' this may have been, was problematic in that the very success of the assertion separated and excluded him from that age. The role of Victorian Ireland in moulding first Ferguson's and Le Fanu's imagination and then that of Wilde, Moore, Yeats, Synge and Shaw can still be seen in the work of Joyce, Beckett, Orpen and Le Brocquy and a number of relatively neglected writers such as James Stephens, Brinsley MacNamara and Francis Stuart. To be both typical and exceptional, to revel in both anarchy and order, evolution and revolution, is the mark of the 'conformist rebel', the invert prone to orthodoxy. The gay imagination of our own age is an accumulated spirit of Restoration and baroque conceits, gothic wonder and romantic imagery atop a concrete base of doubt and disenchantment. 'I believe', said Wilde, 'that at the beginning God made a world for each separate man, and in that world which is within us one should seek to live' (*L* 512). That he said it at the point where, released from Reading, he recognised that he was 'merely passing from one prison into another' is indicative of man's need to liberate himself from the constraints of faith in order to more fully accept those constraints.

(i) JOYCE

Joyce's strategy of escape from the nets of nationality, language and religion[5] was permanently marked by the intention of seeking an accommodation with them, his *non serviam*[6] an acknowledgment as much as a rejection. His attempt to write the book of himself in *A Portrait of the Artist as a Young Man*, in *Ulysses* and in *Finnegans Wake* was also the creation of the book of Ireland, its iconoclastic method a working out of the need 'to forge in the smithy of my soul the uncreated conscience of my race'.[7] The weapons of 'silence, exile and cunning'[8] are placed at the service of a range of images all of which—conscience, shame, and ultimately 'soul'[9]—are images of Victorian interior dialogue. The keynote of *A Portrait* is 'One thing alone is needful, the salvation of one's soul'[10] because that soul is not only the *ipsissimus* of the individual man but also the cadaver of his father and the image of his nation. It breeds what Joyce calls 'the tragic emotion... a face looking two ways, towards terror and towards pity'.[11]

The transitus effected in Yeats's 'Symbols', which predicts the work of Beckett, swings around the figure of Joyce—a figure which we might see as unique, if it were not for his indebtedness to the same imagery and the same emotions as affected Wilde. The congruence of their vocabularies, the likeness of their cadences, the shared compulsion to pursue the nature of the soul as something both sacred and racial, mark Wilde and Joyce as epitomes of, on one side, the Protestant conscience in flight from the burden of its history and of its future, and, on the other side, the Catholic conscience. Portora and Clongowes, TCD and UCD, Mahaffy and Newman, frame Wilde and Joyce as the art school, the lecture room and the salon frame Wilde and Yeats. But where Yeats and Wilde shared a version of Pre-Raphaelitism, Wilde and Joyce are both contrasted and identified by their pursuit of the correct method of naming, of a knowledge of secrets, and above all of an intense awareness of the soul. Wilde was succeeded by Yeats as a mind in action, by Joyce as a mind in emotion.

Joyce's own relationship to English is embedded in the crucial passage in *A Portrait* where Stephen discovers the difference between his own use of the language and that of the Englishman, on whom it sits more naturally and comfortably:

> The language in which we are speaking is his before it is mine. . . . His language, so familiar and so foreign, will always be for me an acquired speech. I have not made or accepted its words. My voice holds them at bay. My soul frets in the shadow of his language.[12]

Like Wilde, who 'adapted and ennobled' the language of the Saxon, Joyce subverted and translated it into the new hybrid of *Finnegans Wake*. Joyce, whose *A Portrait* is a litany of doubts as to the ways of saving a soul, saw Wilde's deathbed reception into the Catholic Church as

> adding another facet to his public life by the repudiation of his wild doctrine. After having mocked the idols of the market place, he bent his knees, sad and repentant that he had once been the singer of the divinity of joy, and closed the book of his spirit's rebellion with an act of spiritual dedication.[13]

Approximating to the notion of 'Melmoth reconcilié à l'Église', this reading of Wilde's unconscious act seems a perversion of artistic freedom, until we realise firstly that Joyce 'hoped [Wilde] was not sincere'[14] and secondly that Joyce's own acts of defiance were equivocal, that he would never escape the nets unless he also acknowledged them, and could never encompass them except by leaving that difficult idea of 'home' and surrendering to another form of 'Christ'.[15] 'Man cannot reach the divine heart except through that sense of separation and loss called sin,' Joyce said apropos Wilde, thus adding another possible meaning to the sense of sin, and indeed to that of the fretting 'soul'.

* * *

In the third chapter of *A Portrait* Stephen Dedalus has a vision of 'his own soul going forth to experience, unfolding itself sin by sin'[16] which we might read as a neat paraphrase of 'Hélas!'. Later he determines that 'he would create proudly out of the freedom and power of his soul, as the great artificer whose name he bore, a living thing, new and soaring and beautiful, impalpable, imperishable'.[17] The soul's rebirth is thus simultaneously penitent and transcendent, as Wilde's would become in the metamorphosic experience of prison and *apologia*. Yet even his identity, depending on an interpretation of 'the fabulous artificer', is 'strange' and 'seemed to him a prophecy':[18] he is both rooted in the past—'himself, his name and where he was'[19]—and in the trajectory towards the future, thus mirroring the quandary of many characters in Wilde's plays and stories, the idea that in one's origins lies the secret of one's destiny. The hieratic nature of the journey is underlined by the way in which Joyce, like Wilde in his poems and parables, embraced the form if not the content of religion—'In vague sacrificial or sacramental acts alone his will seemed drawn to go forth to encounter reality.'[20]

Joyce's embarrassment, born of anxiety, is evident from the first page of *A Portrait*, in the child's placing of himself both in the world and in relation to himself. It proceeds through the family row on the death of Parnell, to his painful schooling where he appears to betray friends and faith in his search for autonomy, sense of purpose and meaning itself. 'What was the right answer to the question? . . . It pained him that he did not know well what politics meant and that he did not know where the universe ended.'[21] The longing for a place where poetry becomes the dominant sense of life is the driving force of all Joyce's work as it was of Wilde's: 'You could not have a green rose. But perhaps somewhere in the world you could.'[22]

Joyce is exercised by the dual danger that 'he . . . sought someone that eluded him'[23] and that 'another nature seemed to have been lent him',[24] thus necessitating a constant journey to and from the self; and equally that by means of dispossession of 'home' he must 'find in the outer world a trace of what he had deemed till then a brutish and individual malady of his own mind';[25] and that 'by this monstrous way of life he seemed to have put himself beyond the limits of reality'.[26] To unite himself with 'the real world' by finding 'an echo of the infuriated cries within him'[27] is the end of meaning, the way of overcoming the temptation (which besets Mr Duffy in 'A Painful Case') to think of oneself in the third person, which is the enemy of reason.

The epiphany, for Joyce, was 'a revelation of the whatness of a thing'.[28] When the epiphany is of oneself, and the 'whatness' or quiddity is rooted in difference and distance, one begins to doubt the viability of the self:

> He saw clearly, too, his own futile isolation. He had not gone one step nearer the lives he had sought to approach nor bridged the restless shame and rancour that had divided him from mother and brother and sister. He felt that he was hardly of the one blood with them but stood to them rather in the mystical kinship of fosterage, fosterchild and fosterbrother.[29]

This failure, or at least obfuscation, of relation bedevils the notion of kinship, of possession and belonging.

> He turned to appease the fierce longings of his heart before which everything else was idle and alien. He cared little that he was in mortal sin, that his life had grown to be a tissue of subterfuge and falsehood. Beside the savage desire within him to realize the enormities which he brooded on nothing was sacred.... By day and by night he moved among distorted images of the outer world.[30]

It is too seldom remarked that before he came to remake language, and therefore its rhythms, in *Ulysses* and *Finnegans Wake*, Joyce, in *Dubliners* and *A Portrait*, wrote with exquisite lyricism and elegiac grace. The revelations, or epiphanies, of his earlier work constitute a threnody for conscience, by means of which he both liberates and indelibly marks the soul. To state that 'nothing was sacred' is to write *'nihil'* across the book of experience in order to open a new book, which will be written only on one's own terms: 'His soul had arisen from the grave of boyhood, spurning her grave-clothes.'[31] Later, in conversation with Cranly, Stephen asks, in Yeatsian vein: 'What kind of liberation would that be to forsake an absurdity which is logical and coherent and to embrace one which is illogical and incoherent?'[32] (The choice is between remaining a Roman Catholic and becoming a Protestant.) The idea that there can be logical and coherent absurdities is not a clear-cut or comfortable one: there is no awareness here of what we have earlier seen as 'supralogical' possibilities. Stephen's Catholicism sits uneasily on him, and he lives in discomfort with it; yet it is preferable to endure whatever provides a precarious balance between sense and non-sense than to forsake it for whatever threatened that balance and put one back 'sprawling among the archetypes'.[33] Equally, Joyce is Wildean in his declaration of Irishness:

—This race and this country and this life produced me, he said. I shall express myself as I am.
—Try to be one of us, repeated Davin. In your heart you are an Irishman but your pride is too powerful.
—My ancestors threw off their language and took another, Stephen said. They allowed a handful of foreigners to subject them. Do you fancy I am going to pay in my own life and person debts they made? What for?[34]

Despite the nets which are flung at 'the soul of man',[35] Joyce will be Irish and not English—quite another thing. That this requires the permanent use of the mask is accepted as given:

—Did the idea ever occur to you, Cranly asked, that
Jesus was not what he pretended to be?
—The first person to whom that idea occurred, Stephen
answered, was Jesus himself.[36]

The Wildean identification with Christ as an Irish martyr—
which would later stain the history books with mystical
blood—is complete.

(ii) BORGES, BARTHES

In 1893 Hugo von Hofmannsthal expressed the fact that to
be modern meant to be both in the vanguard of one's age
and a danger to that age, by defining modernism in two
forms: as *analysis of life* and as *escape from life*. The former is
'the anatomy of the inner life of the mind', the latter an
'instinctive surrender to every revelation of beauty, to a glit-
tering metaphor, to a wonderful allegory'.[37] As such, it is, in
the terms which I have employed above, both decadent
(introspective) with an acute awareness of its relation with
the past, and forward-looking, redefining itself in terms of
that past and of its imagined future. One of our key readings
in Wilde in this respect is therefore 'The Critic as Artist',
which counterpoints the imaginative freedom of Gilbert's
rewriting of history with Ernest's insistence on the continuity of history. Gilbert is the flight from life, which returns to
refashion it by means of art, Ernest the analysis of life for the
purpose of deriving art.

It has become a commonplace that in the tension of this
bifurcation between 'analysis of life' and 'flight from life'
language has been the principal victim. Barthes not only
refers to literature as 'the problematics of language' but also
says that ultimately 'writing . . . is a blind alley . . . because
society itself is a blind alley'.[38] As I have demonstrated elsewhere,[39] the *difficulty* of writing becomes a parable for the
difficulty of living, the growing impossibility of ontology—

as a language-animal, man is both defined and condemned by the unique gift of speech. In his futile entreaties and injunctions to the Sphinx, Wilde demonstrates the overthrow of content—of what Mallarmé called 'la direction personelle enthousiaste de la phrase'[40]—by the form itself. In his puns—'I *mot* and you reap'—and in his prose-poems he was contributing to the formation of 'a modernly ironic aesthetic',[41] a freedom of form which would find its ultimate and most barren expression in Eliot's *The Waste Land*.

Literature in the 1890s found itself in new relationships with life—reflected, for example, in new magazines like *The Yellow Book*, *The Hobby Horse*, *The Savoy* and *New Age*, and new configurations of writers such as the Rhymers' Club and the Irish Literary Society. The language by means of which it was expressed, and the form in which it was expressed, were subject to violent and profound changes: George Moore's *The Untilled Field* (1903) was preceded by an Irish edition in 1902 as *An tÚr-Ghort*; *The Ballad of Reading Gaol* was first published over a convict's cell number and dedicated to the memory of an executed murderer; the Irishwoman Mary Chavelita Dunne, writing as 'George Egerton' in her *Keynotes* (1894), celebrated her artistic and personal freedom in terms which left no doubt about her love-affair with the Norwegian writer Knut Hamsun; Hopkins, dead since 1889, was discovered to have revolutionised the construction of verse; and Yeats began to cast his sacred drama in the form of the Japanese *nôh*.

Melodrama gave way to the sacred drama of symbolism, and this in turn became the open space of the absurd. The continuance of figures like Beckett's Clov and Hamm, Vladimir and Estragon, as dominant presences on the contemporary stage, is a reminder that the 'crucially aesthetic problems in the making of structures and the employment of language'[42] are problems about the structure and language of human life itself. From Wagner's *Tristan und Isolde* to Maeterlinck's *Les Aveugles* to Wilde's 'La Sainte Courtisane' to Yeats's *The Cat and the Moon* and Synge's *Well of the Saints* is but a short step in the history of imaginative entropy. That this short journey has been shadowed by the emergence of new ways of perceiving consciousness, in the work of Bergson, Freud, Groddeck and Jung, should not surprise us. Literature preceded science in discovering ways of looking within, because it had already evolved, in the Greek tragedies, the means of giving voice to the double.

The impetus to our understanding of what constitutes the human and distinguishes it from other species lies in the work of Lamarck, Darwin and Alfred Russel Wallace in anthropology, and was accompanied by the developments of archaeology and palaeontology, which prefigure the psychologists' digging into the substructure of the human mind. In literature, Pater in *Marius the Epicurean* (1885), Musil in *The Confusions of Young Törless* (1906) and Hesse in *Demian: A Story of Youth* (1919) frame Wilde's *Dorian Gray* in describing this evolutionary consciousness of man's aesthetic, psychological and historical origins and fate.

From this point onwards man became increasingly out of phase with himself, until Georg Groddeck could ask: 'Is the word "man" an answer to a question?'[43] Under the pressure of works like Newman's *Apologia Pro Vita Sua*, Smiles's *Self-Help* and Darwin's *Origin of Species*—disparate but essentially cognate texts—the nineteenth century found itself needing more accommodating means of translation in order to make sense of the competition between the contemporary spirit of the age and the perennial soul of man. Playwrights like Ibsen and Strindberg nudged the century into recognition of this traffic between *zeit* and *psyche*. The sensibility of the age came to recognise—but not to accept—the limits of rationality. As Borges says in *A Universal History of Infamy*, 'history . . . like certain film directors, proceeds by a series of abrupt images',[44] and thus, without benefit of consequential thought, mankind must devise new ways of connecting those images, a new storyline for the imagination, a new theory and practice of metaphor.

'The act of fictionality thus becomes the crucial act of imagining.'[45] In Törless, Demian and Stephen Dedalus, fiction traces a new route to the face of the unknown. Even at his most frivolous, Wilde displays his concern for the interior: his quip that 'a gentleman never looks out of the window' is a facetious way of excusing the almost complete lack of interest in, or attention to, external detail in scenery, dress or outlook. Following Wilde's, Maturin's and Le Fanu's search for the true icon, it seeks to dis-cover, to *invent*, a parallel text. Its voice is that of the intimate confession of the psychiatrist's couch, its imagery that of the labyrinth which appears to have neither beginning nor end. Only by a severe act of will—or creativity—can an origin or a terminus be created, a situation on which Lady Bracknell has poured a withering scorn: 'Is Miss Cardew at all connected with any of the larger railway stations in London? I merely desire information. Until yesterday I had no idea that there were any families or persons whose origin was a Terminus.' (*CW* 373)

In the year when *Dorian Gray* appeared, Hamsun was writing of 'the unconscious life of the mind' in terms which anticipated Pound's imagism: 'the incalculable chaos of impressions, the delicate life of the imagination seen under the magnifying glass; the random progress of these thoughts and feelings; untrodden, trackless journeyings by brain and heart, strange writings of the nerves'.[46] The balance between the impressionist moment—'they last a second, a minute, they come and go like a moving winking light'[47]—and life stretching between two infinite points is that between Wilde's 'Time' and 'Eternity'. Natalie Sarraute will call the former 'tropisms',[48] pinpricks of consciousness filtering onto the bed of memory; Beckett will say with epicurean disillusion: 'They give birth astride a grave, the light gleams an instant, then it's night once more.'[49] This is partly an attempt to organise contemporary thought for contemporary purposes under contemporary difficulties (which Eliot, speaking of *Ulysses*, called 'a way of controlling, of ordering, of giving a shape and a significance to the immense paradox of futility and anarchy which is contemporary history'),[50] but it is more importantly a recognition of the futility and anarchy of all history. Without tradition, the culturalists tell us, the individual imagination is nothing, but it still suffers the indignity of living. The pursuit of the dream is the attempt to connect the dream with the myth of history, and in that respect 'making sense' relates to life itself, not to the manner in which life is lived. Therefore the presiding deity of *Demian*, Abraxas, is both male and female, god and anti-god, allowing a commutation between home truths which would otherwise remain polarised opposites.

To develop this line of thought, we might say that the modernist reading of Wilde will include (with 'The Critic as Artist') *The Sphinx*, for its verbal significance; *The Picture of Dorian Gray*, for its development of the theme of the double; 'The Portrait of Mr W.H.', for its *mélange* of biography, autobiography and textual criticism; *Salomé* and 'La Sainte Courtisane' for their transformation of classical forms; and 'Pen, Pencil and Poison', for its treatment of art in relation to morality. By contrast, his social dramas/melodramas, even *The Importance of Being Earnest*, and his other works of conscience—the short stories, *The Ballad of Reading Gaol* and *The Soul of Man under Socialism*—are of lesser relevance.

But we must not overlook the fact that previous genres, not least the picaresque theatre of Calderón's *La Vida es Sueño* [Life is a Dream], and the baroque, typified by Diderot's *Jacques le Fataliste*, with its profound interplay of master and servant, are present in Wilde's work and in that of his contemporaries such as Strindberg, Hesse, Musil and Hamsun. We thus see Wilde simultaneously as part of a European tradition which has had its effect on modern Ireland and a figure in the Irish dramatic tradition which has intimate connections with the theatre of Europe.

This is particularly evident in the Janus-like dedication by Borges to two traditions, the ruminative historical-philosophical and the exploitative *romancier*. Borges, partly because he enjoyed a mixed cultural and genetic heritage

(Spanish-Argentinian, English and Jewish-Portugese) and partly because as a non-European he was commenting from a Latin-American viewpoint on that mixed heritage, was acutely situated in relation to the New World and the Old. His writing justifies the assertion that if the New World was brought into existence in order to redress the balance of the Old, then the literature of Latin-America, moving in parallel with its political evolution, is a rich vein of commentary upon, and amendment of, the tired and entropic literature of the European tradition. Borges was exceptionally aware of Irish writing and thought. It is natural that he should have been a devotee of Wilde and Joyce—he read *Ulysses* on publication and translated part of it in 1925—but he had been thoroughly familiar with Berkeley since the age of ten—'from that day forth, I realized that reality and fiction were betrothed to each other, that even our ideas are creative fictions'.[51] His passion for metaphysics led him further to read Eriugena and Toland, and in literature to pursue Wilde and Shaw, learning that Shaw 'held that all genuine creation stems from a metaphysical nothingness, which Erigena [*sic*] called the "Nihil" of God, which resided at the heart of our existence'.[52]

It is conceivable, but hardly possible, that Borges could have written the 'parable' 'Borges and I' without knowing the work of Wilde, whom he called 'a dandy who was also a poet . . . a gentleman dedicated to the paltry aim of startling people by his cravats and his metaphors'.[53] He saw Wilde as readers have seen Borges himself, as a constant provocation. And the provocation is irksome because 'Wilde is almost always right'.[54] Borges is brilliant in his definition of Wilde (and himself) as 'a man of the eighteenth century who sometimes condescended to play the game of symbolism'.[55] The definition is exactly apposite on one level because he brings into confluence the ideas of two centuries; but it becomes masterly on another level by his use of the words 'sometimes condescended' and his addition of the epithet 'negligent glee'. He makes Wilde into a master of ceremonies whose nonchalance stems from his innate sense of play; conversely, he says Wilde is 'a man who keeps an invulnerable innocence in spite of the habits of evil and misfortune',[56] thus depicting him as a child, unmoved in his core by tragedy.

Borges proves himself Wilde's sibling by the title of his first collection of stories, *A Universal History of Infamy* (1935). Just as language has been a casualty of the semantic disturbance, so Borges detaches his storyline from reality, making pictures which bear some relation to it but not enough for us to be convinced of their authenticity. They are distant, oblique and powered by a listless energy which has only just succeeded in turning its back on boredom. There is a ritualistic quality about Borges' stories which never makes it entirely clear whether the infamy is a quality of the stories themselves or merely of the bandits, pirates, thugs and frauds whom they contain and depict. These citizens of Borges' world are heroes by virtue of the immense care which their author takes in elevating their misdeeds to the status of a religion. Whether they perform in the swamps of Louisiana, the coast of China or the sewers of New York, they are universal in their acting out of a totemic relationship to life, morality and the pillage of life of which they thereby make an art. Their truest siblings are Wilde's Wainewright, Harland's Prospero and Beerbohm's Zuleika Dobson; 'the hoodlum', says Borges, 'aspires to refinement'.[57] The stories, he tells us, 'are not, they do not try to be, psychological',[58] and in the sense that they constitute 'no more than appearance, than a surface of images' this is true; but in their transmogrification of the original subject-matter—Billy the Kid, the Tichborne claimant, Widow Ching the Chinese pirate—the stories betray the fact that the hero is larger than life not merely by virtue of his exploits but also because he has risen from a position beneath the contempt of society in order to strike fear and admiration into those whom he now supplants.

The creatures of New York portrayed in 'Monk Eastman, Purveyor of Iniquities' are merely the denizens of Dorian Gray's London, animated and transported. 'The Dread Reducer, Lazarus Morell' is no more than Lord Henry Wotton

set in action as the altruistic builder of an empire of slaves
'great and blameworthy'[59] whose weakness is the preaching
of hypocritical but mordant sermons. Tom Castro, who nearly carried off the Tichborne inheritance, spent his last years,
as Wilde spent his apprenticeship, lecturing the length and
breadth of England on the nature and methods of deception—'modesty and ingratiation were so deep-seated in him
that many a night he would begin by exoneration and end
by confession';[60] the same pretender made no attempt to disguise the gross disparities between himself and the true
Tichborne heir—he 'steered clear of all likeness',[61] with the
result that his 'mother' recognised him as her own. In another story Hakim, 'The Masked Dyer', was acclaimed in one
voice as both 'Sorcerer' and 'Impostor'[62]—because, Borges
tells us, identities shift as in a masquerade 'in which one is
not quite certain who is who', since it is a mere supposition
that 'there is such a thing as a real name'.[63] Heroism on such
a scale is possible and necessary because 'the world we live
in is a mistake, a clumsy parody. Mirrors and fatherhood,
because they multiply and confirm the parody, are abomina-
tions. Revulsion is the cardinal virtue.'[64] This *apologia* might
find a home in Wilde's 'De Profundis', so anxious is it to dis-
parage and at the same time honour the deceptiveness of
both appearance and reality, of images and origins. In the
presence of Borges' rogues, we share the 'sacred terror'
experienced in the presence of Salomé which culminated in
the shudder—'Revulsion is the cardinal virtue.' Billy the
Kid, we learn, was, like Wainewright, 'a disinterested killer'.
Not only is the hero larger than life; the storyline is always
larger than the hero. Thus Billy the Kid, 'spawned by a tired-
out Irish womb but...brought up among Negroes...never
completely matched his legend, but he kept getting closer
and closer to it.... For seven desperate years he practised the
extravagance of utter recklessness'[65]—again the comparison
with Wilde's own biography is compelling.

André Maurois has commented on Borges' affinity with
the worlds of Swift—'gravity amid the absurd'—and of

Berkeley—'where only inner life exists'.[66] The affinity might be extended to Wilde, since Borges explores the same bitter-sweet which shares the breath of ecstasy with revulsion, of being locked into a universal library with the one other reader of the book of oneself. Indeed, Borges' assertion that there are four literary devices—the work within the work, the contamination of reality by dream, the voyage in time, and the double[67]—might be Wilde's description of, respectively, 'The Portrait of Mr W.H.', his folk-tales, 'The Rise of Historical Criticism' and *The Picture of Dorian Gray*. We might add to these the capacity to entertain, with passion and commitment, truths which we know to be less than immemorially posited and which depend on a non-truth for their justification. Borges invented 'Pierre Menard, Author of the *Quixote*', which is a document cognate with his unwritten 'Oscar Wilde, Author of the *Sonnets*'; but it is his 'Borges and I', which is neither story nor essay but a prose-poem of Wildean subtlety and elusiveness, which encapsulates all the dualism in Wilde's concern for not being understood. A single page in length, it enacts Borges' four themes and adds to them the ability to see oneself as totally other, so much so that it can end: 'I do not know which of us has written this.'[68] There is a cartoon by Beerbohm which indicates how very closely Willie Wilde and Oscar Wilde resembled one another, and the comment 'a veritable tragedy of family likeness'.[69] One wonders if somehow Willie—the elder brother, of course—was not an invention of Oscar's imagination. All these notions were rehearsed by writers previous to Wilde—Cervantes, Kleist, Hogg, for example—but it is only in the age when the need to *see* the soul is paramount that the capacity of the traditional storyteller for meeting that need has been recognised.

Barthes writes with a uranian wit. How many have read *A Lover's Discourse* without discovering that the author's gay—and often morose—temper was in fact homosexual?

The book is a series of meditations on the *solitude* of the modern lover and on his (or her) attempts to define the absence at the heart of being. 'Severed not only from authority but also from the mechanisms of authority', he tells us that the lover's exile and unreality must become 'the site, however exiguous, of an *affirmation*'.[70] Like Borges' pictures of infamous heroes, the book, Barthes insists, is 'a portrait—but not a psychological portrait'.[71] But how, when it is to be 'the site of someone speaking within himself, *amorously*, confronting the other (the loved object), who does not speak',[72] could it be anything other than psychological? It is probably the most successful psychology since *Die Leiden des jungen Werthers*, but it is, in addition, indicative of the sea-change which the lover has undergone in the intervening two centuries, whereby he is thrust in upon himself: those centuries saw the extermination of amorous, external love, and the implosion of the hero.

In the solitude of masturbation Barthes will 'oblige the other ... to enter into the interplay of meaning'. Life, and particularly love, has been reduced to a system of secret codes; physicality has been replaced by semiology:

> I am about *to make the other speak*. In the lover's realm, there is no *acting out*: no propulsion, perhaps even no pleasure—nothing but signs, a frenzied activity of language... a kind of festival not of the senses but of meaning.[73] [*Barthes' emphasis*]

There is no movement outward: *acting out* becomes an inverted motion, an inner embrace of the stranger who takes the place of the beloved. The instrument which is made to speak is within oneself, upon oneself. *Hélas!*

'Always the voice,'[74] says the haunted Barthes. He imagines that madness consists not in *'Je est un autre'*, as 'an experience of depersonalization', but in 'being unable to keep myself from...becoming a subject. ... I *am not someone else*: that is what I realize with horror.'[75] The madness of ecstasy is, literally, the delirium of standing outside oneself; for Barthes, it is the prison of *enstasis*, of standing within himself. Thus it is not the standing-outside-oneself which maddens (that would be too easy, too accessible), but the fact that, even when standing within oneself, one cannot inhabit, seize upon and possess this sense of strangeness: 'Here then, at last, is the definition of the image, of any image: that from which I am excluded.'[76]

Consciousness of oneself as self (rather than as other) is at the heart of this madness, and at the heart of the consciousness is *paradox*:

> What is heavy is the silent knowledge: I know that you know that I know: this is the general formula of embarrassment, a frozen, white modesty which takes the insignificance (of remarks) as its insignia. Paradox: the unspoken as the symptom... of the *conscious*.[77] [*Barthes' ellipsis*]

But where there is paradox there is also a shared meaning which Barthes seems reluctant to name: *irony*. The 'I know that you know that I know' is an admission that the beloved thus addressed is of the same essential nature, shares the confidences and the ambitions of the lover, and is thus a fragment of the totality of the self. 'Not extraneous, but self,' as Beckett will later say[78] in explicating the significance of *esse est percipi*. Barthes' lover calls his beloved into existence by perceiving him—just as Basil Hallward supplied Dorian with his lifelong passion by painting his portrait: 'hypocrite lecteur, mon semblable, mon frère'.[79]

Yet Barthes complains that

> The other is impenetrable, intractable, not to be found; I cannot open up the other, trace back the other's origins, solve the riddle. Where does the other come from? Who is the other? I wear myself out, I shall never know.[80]

We have, of course, encountered this riddle briefly in the biographies of Bethel Ormsby, John Melmoth and Silas Ruthyn. It is not the riddle of 'Where does the other come from?' but of 'Where do I come from?' or, in Jack Worthing's earnest entreaty, 'Would you kindly inform me who I am?' The search for the identity of the lover is the search for self, because ultimately it is only to the self that we can be faithful, only the self whom we can truly betray. It is this which terrifies Barthes in his vertigo, at once energising and enervating him.

'The lover's anxiety', he says, 'is the fear of a mourning which has already occurred, at the very origin of love.'[81] The intense frustration of the quest for the place before the first place derives from the fact that 'the very origin of love' can never be reclaimed because it is the moment before the conception of the lover himself. A kiss can never be re-created. 'The ego discourses only when it is hurt';[82] thus the search for love is both subject and object of such hurt—the permanent injury to the psyche of modern man.

In such circumstances, Barthes surmises, '*I-love-you* is without nuance. . . . *I-love-you* has no "elsewhere". . . . *I-love-you* is not a sentence: it does not transmit a meaning.'[83] In Wilde's plays the expression of love is gauche, uninspired, sentimental. There is a stronger passion between Goring and Phipps, between Algernon and Lane, than there is between Goring and Mabel, Algernon and Cecily. 'I-love-you', on Barthes' terms, is meaningful only when it can be addressed to the self. He brings an intellectual excitement and reassurance to the semantic disturbance when he says: 'It is not that I keep the other from speaking; but I know how to *make the pronouns skid*'[84] [*Barthes' emphasis*]. Thus he rearranges subject and object in order to relocate the image of the beloved within his heart, not in the mirror of his heart.

'Only the Other could write my love story, my novel.'[85] With this recognition Barthes clarifies the role of Wilde as both lover and writer, as Irishman and homosexual. If the novel is the history of an unknown love, if the history book is a fiction of that love, if the love story is a chronicle of absence and betrayal, then the Irishman must turn to England, the man to the woman, for the genre and syntax by which to read his own past, and the Englishman must accept that his history will be rewritten in the manner of an Irish vision. The symbiosis is, ultimately, not the joint captivity of opposite poles, but the mutual recognition of life as elsewhere within a single house.

(iii) GENET

Jean Genet typifies modernism. He is an orphan, a rebel, an autarch, a poet. He is, in Sartre's words, both saint and thief, dignifying his society and his culture with the very gestures by which he rejects and spits on it. Genet is also the orphan child of Oscar Wilde. As Wilde knows that he is the orphan of Sir William and Lady Wilde, scholar and poet, so Genet knows that his traits are those of the most famous homosexual of the nineteenth century and its most successful playwright and hoaxer.

Many of Genet's autobiographical statements replicate either those of Wilde himself—'If I cannot have the most brilliant destiny, I want the most wretched'[86]—or those of his characters. 'My being a foundling entailed a lonely youth and childhood,' he tells us, immediately justifying his existence with the statement 'Being a thief led me to believe in the singularity of thieving.'[87] Is Jack/Ernest Worthing a thief of confidence? Is theft simply the appropriation of a more acceptable storyline, a more accommodating biography than that given at birth? Genet, like Wilde, is certain that he is an exception and builds his career around that central fact of absence. 'I know nothing of her who abandoned me in the cradle';[88] instead he must create his own legend, a fiction which will be more truthful to life than the truth can be. 'Betrayal, theft and homosexuality are the basic subjects of this book,' he says of *The Thief's Journal*. 'There is a relationship among them which, though not always apparent, at least, so it seems to me, recognizes a kind of vascular exchange between my taste for betrayal and theft and my loves.'[89] His membership of the Confraternity of the Fatherless (and motherless) is such that he becomes a thief because life has been stolen from him. 'She who abandoned me' is the thief; it remains to him to compensate for this lifelong absence by stealing life from others, by appropriating a persona which can be both the spectator and the author of another life. 'I used to be present at my nativity';[90] he imagines himself as a god—'The uncertainty of my origin allowed me to interpret it.'[91] He embraces a career as a prostitute and a thief because 'it is the abandoned urchin's amorous imagining of royal magnificence that enables me to gild my shame, to carve it, to work over it like a goldsmith, until, through usage perhaps and the wearing away of the words veiling it, humility emerges from it'.[92] Like Wilde, Genet achieves a humility not before other men or their gods but before the lover who is the mirror-image of himself, before himself as his own god. And here we have the commentary which explains the directness, the emphasis on the writer's personality, which pervades 'De Profundis'—'the wearing away of the words'. Before Wilde's trials, and even during them, life was described and transformed by means of words 'covered with jewels'; after them, by the terse statement of the new reality.

'My life must be a legend, in other words, legible, and the reading of it must give birth to a certain new emotion which I call poetry. I am no longer anything, only a pretext.'[93] Thus Genet equates himself, the orphan deprived of reality, of memory and meaning, with a unique method of creating meaning. 'I was writing for myself a secret history.'[94] His life, in order to signify, must be both signifier and signified, it must become a book and must be legible. Thus fiction supplants, and improves on, reality, makes it spurious. Language thus receives the burden of the orphan and exile. It has always been the medium of betrayal and transition, but now it serves the extraterritorial who is simultaneously outside house, country and sex. In gothic temper, Genet says: 'My quintessence has taken refuge in the deepest and most secret retreat,'[95] but he has severed the umbilical cord by which previous novelists, such as Sterne, had repossessed their first light. The book is not 'my life' but 'the interpretation of it'.[96] This is a new linguistic construct, since Genet asks it to inter-pret—to excuse—a *status quo ante* which, like Barthes, he has already denied and removed from the book. It is the discovery of the rules of the game of book-writing which becomes the act of writing itself. 'My book, which has become my Genesis,' he writes on the last page of his *Journal*, 'contains... the com-mandments which I cannot transgress.'[97] The absence of a home truth also makes all away truths impossible. To be faithful to oneself means to create oneself in opposition to any truths which might have been home to the orphaned, forgotten self.

As Wilde spent a year on the road at the outset of his career as the thief of reason, so Genet's earliest experiences were those of a vagabond existence in search of 'another country' where he might re-make himself:

> The crossing of borders and the excitement it arouses in one were to enable me to apprehend directly the essence of the nation I was entering. I would penetrate less into a country than to the interior of an image.[98]

This transference and the seizing of the image is both a knowledge of the other country and a redefinition of self. If, in Steiner's words, 'every act of communication between human beings takes on the shape of an act of translation' and 'all dialogue is a proffer of mutual cognizance and a strategic redefinition of self',[99] then this silent operation substitutes a physical for a linguistic *peripatos*. It is an undercover activity, for Genet says: 'For the foreigner, there are no other means than espionage.... Espionage is a practice of which states are so ashamed that they ennoble it for its being shameful.'[100] His speech throughout his journal is allusive and uranian when addressed to strangers, even including himself.

Genet tells us that 'I had to hollow out, to drill through, a mass of language in which my mind could be at ease.'[101] But what is he describing? The path by which a child makes sense of his patrimony, negotiates the world of others, and finds himself; the historical path by which a nation possesses its own culture. But for the fatherless, for the stateless nation, there is both the helplessness and the signlessness which places one permanently at the frontier of the waste land. There is fear, despair and guilt in Genet's expression 'Perhaps I wanted to accuse myself in my own language.'[102] Just as Borges called the Irish outcast, Billy the Kid, 'a disinterested killer', so Genet says:

> Theft . . . had become a disinterested undertaking, a kind of active and deliberate work of art which could be achieved only with the help of language, my language, and which would be confronted with the laws springing from this same language.[103]

The thefts or acts of espionage which he performs are attempts to compensate himself for the fact that his orphaned state leaves him outside history, needing both heroes and mythologies. Genet expresses all extraterritorial homeless longing when he says:

> Michaelis loved me. Perhaps the painful position he knew I was in transformed this love into a kind of pity. Mythologies are full of heroes who are changed into servants.[104]

Here is the vivid explanation of Quixote and Pancha, of Jacques and his master, of all 'devoted friends' who become the traitor, accuser or executioner of their partner. The transitus between master and servant illustrates the symbiotic commerce between being and doing which is at the heart of the thief's dilemma.

He is the thief of reason, the thief of language, but he must also be the thief of life itself, because it is his loss of an original, personal life which has robbed *him* of meaning. When Sartre says that post-Holocaust man must derive a new existence *ex nihilo*,[105] when Steiner posits a 'lost centre', the lack of an 'inner history',[106] as the starting-point of modernism, we recognise the opportunity for the homeless, genderless intellect to star in any new system of encoding and decoding which may be devised for our feeble messages. Genet's existence reminds us that Wilde continues to fascinate us because his gay temper bridges the gulf between being and doing which is so problematic for less commodious minds.

Conclusion

MAN searches for a face whereby he may learn a fundamental truth: will it be the face of himself or of another? All sexual curiosity and all metaphysical speculation[1] leads to the discovery of the face. 'The book of man', says Derrida, 'is a book of question.'[2] All the men discussed in this book—whether real or imagined—have searched for this highest of truths. All the women have known and possessed it, because they are the home-place of secrets.

This book has discussed Wilde as a conduit between the thought of the nineteenth century and that of the twentieth; between pagan, folkloric Ireland and modern Ireland; and between the masculine and feminine intellects. The heroism of epic poetry, and its failure, is replicated in today's blood-sacrifice and the symbolic *agon* of Gaelic games—a fact which suggests that the lessons of history have yet to be learned, that Ireland is still in pursuit of a vision as yet unseen: are Ireland's heroes her natural enemies?[3]

In concluding this discussion, I shall examine Wilde's continuing relevance for Ireland and the post-colonial world, as an intellectual whose search for freedom and meaning conveys a signal for people who have difficulty in finding an authentic voice for their energies and anxieties.

Why does Wilde himself continue to fascinate people of the stage? Is his drama so archetypal of dramatic conventions that it remains a template for later generations, so powerful as a role-model for those whose burning need is to metamorphose themselves within the shelter of the theatre? Certainly it seems possible that *Salomé* and *The Importance of*

Being Earnest can each be reinterpreted in the light of changes in our social and aesthetic perspectives. But Wilde's own life, and the thought imprisoned within it, continues to attract playwrights wishing to find there a route into deviance and the nature of play. John Osborne reverently dramatised *The Picture of Dorian Gray* in 1972, and more recently two plays in particular, Terry Eagleton's *Saint Oscar* (with its echo of 'Saint Genet') and Frank McGuinness's *The Beautiful Lie: The Lives of Oscar Wilde*, return persistently to Wilde's childhood as the seedbed of his later experiments with, and antagonism to, society.

But running throughout contemporary Irish drama—a drama which, it can be claimed, is one of the most vigorous on the world stage—is the continuous presence of Wilde as a divided self. A pivotal work for this drama was Brian Friel's *Philadelphia, Here I Come!*, produced in Dublin in 1964 and subsequently on Broadway, which marked a sea-change in the representation of the rural experience. Friel is one writer who has taken a new route to the dilemma of communication by adopting the Wildean proposal that one's first duty to history is to rewrite it. It is not the place here to rehearse the extent to which he has undertaken this, but we should advert to his plays concerning the extinction of Gaelic culture by the logocentric force of empire in *Translations* (1980) and *Making History* (1988), the latter striking a particularly poignant note in relation to the hero's commutation between his native Ulster, with the grim realities of feudalism, and the court of Elizabeth with its constantly jewelled and highly literate halberd at the throat of ignorance and darkness.

Here, however, it is important to note the division of the principal character of *Philadelphia*, Gareth O'Donnell, into two personae, Private Gar and Public Gar. While this was not entirely original (Ubu, for example, was attended by an unwelcome and troublesome 'Conscience', and, nearer home, Lennox Robinson's *Church Street* (1934) split the main character into 'Hugh' and 'Evoked Hugh'),[4] the division, as a method of displaying the commerce between 'the Gar that people see, talk to, talk about' and 'the unseen man, the man within, the conscience, the *alter ego*, the secret thoughts, the id', identified the fact that 'one cannot look at one's *alter ego*'.[5] In two of Friel's plays, *Philadelphia* and *Translations*, the lines 'Isn't this your job?—to translate?'[6] and 'Do your job. Translate'[7] insist on the need to carry meaning across from one deep structure to another. It might seem from the discrepancy between the circumstances of the two plays that the translation in question belongs to two different orders—one the mediation by the church between God and man, the other the scout simultaneously translating and betraying two cultures—but the similarity of the experience is stronger than the differences: Robert Welch says it 'conveys the difficulty of communication by underlining the normality of failure rather than the failure of normality'.[8] The two dilemmas, the barrier between things and people seen and unseen, that of the past at the cutting-edge of the present, are notably Wilde's dilemmas, which neither he, nor Ibsen, nor Jarry, nor Yeats, nor Shaw had succeeded in resolving. The failure is a continual reprimand to modernism, because it undermines the novelty of modernism itself.

'Irish literature', Denis Donoghue wrote in 1972, 'is a story of fracture ... the divergence of one Irishman from another.' It would be difficult to contradict that judgment, or to refute his expectation that 'an Irish writer might find the situation rich in artistic possibilities, even if he found it distressing in other respects'.[9] At the moment he wrote, Ireland had just experienced the phenomenon of 'Bloody Sunday', which gave immediate rise to Friel's only explicit treatment of the modern Ulster troubles, *The Freedom of the City*. But since then many other 'artistic possibilities' have been found, not only in those troubles but also in the wider context of a divided society, one which is bedevilled by obstacles to intercourse, to commerce, to the open display of passion, to the unfettered expression of opinion or allegiance. It is possible that its ancient anxieties—the role of the hero and the fate of language—continue to dominate the imagination to the vir-

408 The Thief of Reason

tual exclusion of more recent troubles, to the extent that the
most compelling examples of contemporary drama in Ireland
today, besides those already referred to, are Tom Murphy's
Bailegangaire (1985) and *The Gigli Concert* (1983), Thomas
Kilroy's *Double Cross* (1986), Frank McGuinness's *Observe the
Sons of Ulster Marching towards the Somme* (1985) and Friel's
Dancing at Lughnasa (1990) and *Wonderful Tennessee* (1993).
Only McGuinness's *Carthaginians* (1988) is set in the same
time and the same territory as Friel's *The Freedom of the City*.

In 1972 Donoghue said: 'The best writers in Ireland are
those who remember most. I do not mean the oldest writers,
necessarily. I mean those who feel immediate experience not
merely in itself but in relation to a long perspective, mythological and historical, pagan and Christian.'[10] Such writers
today would include Dermot Healy and John Banville, John
McGahern and William Trevor, as surely as Wilde, Yeats and
Synge, and before them Ferguson and Mangan, all transla-
tors of their past into their future, all observers of the contrast between myth and history, of the fatal but fruitful
proximity of *traduttore* and *traditore*, and between different
modes of faith, ways of seeing. Above all, they have been
remembrancers, faced with the difficulty of paying due regard
to an unknown memory which still colonises the mind.

W. J. McCormack suggests that we may have to cross
'seismic lines' to connect the Irish literature of the early nineteenth century with that of the twentieth.[11] Yet the qualitative
similarities are often as great as the differences. If Aubrey de
Vere's *English Misrule and Irish Misdeeds* (1848) was responsible for nothing else, it is remarkable for its statement that
there are 'two Englands',[12] a prediction of the basis on which
Albert Memmi would posit the symbiotic relationship of
coloniser and colonised,[13] and a prediction also of Tom Paulin's
Ireland and the English Crisis.[14] 'Ireland is certainly very unlike
England,' wrote de Vere. 'Perhaps we cannot approve our
own opposites without being untrue to ourselves.'[15] Gavan
Duffy thought that 'the history of Ireland . . . had the unity
and purpose of an epic poem',[16] an ambition which many

contemporary poets are still attempting to realise, while David Lloyd asks: 'If the function of literature is to form and unite a people not yet in existence, how will a writer of sufficient stature arise, given that it is from the people he must arise, if he is to express the spirit of the nation?'[17] Are Ireland's poets her natural historians?

Whether he was Irish or homosexual or modernist, Wilde stood outside the mainstream because he epitomised the fact that that mainstream was no longer the way in which progress was to be measured. It is the fascination of his extraterritoriality which leads us into a confusion between *defining* Wilde and *divining* him—divining being the compelling exercise for the modern, and post-modern, world. Moreover, it is in the exercise of *naming* that this becomes most explicit, and I turn now to three examples, beginning with *The Importance of Being Earnest* and then moving on to two masterpieces of contemporary literature, Friel's *Translations* and André Brink's novel *An Instant in the Wind* to indicate the extent to which Wilde remains an author of modern significance.

In *Earnest* an exasperated Algernon remonstrates with Jack/Ernest:

> ALGERNON: Your name isn't Jack at all; it is Ernest.
> JACK: It isn't Ernest; it's Jack.
> ALGERNON: You have always told me it was Ernest. I have introduced you to every one as Ernest. You answer to the name of Ernest. You look as if your name was Ernest. . . . It is perfectly absurd your saying that your name isn't Ernest . . .
> JACK: Well, my name is Ernest in town and Jack in the country. (*CW* 325)

Perfectly absurd it may be, but the dual life of Mr Worthing, depending on where he is, and to whom he is talking and relating, is a fact which remains so until it is eventually revealed that he is, actually, both.

In *Translations* the son of the O'Donnell household returns, bringing with him the soldiers who now employ him as a scout in the mapping exercise of the Ordnance Survey. Known at home as Owen, he has for some inexplicable reason become 'Roland' to the soldiers:

> OWEN (*explodes*): George! For God's sake! *My name is not Roland!*
> YOLLAND: What?
> OWEN (*softly*): My name is Owen. (*Pause*)
> YOLLAND: Not Roland?
> OWEN: Owen.
> YOLLAND: You mean to say—?
> OWEN: Owen.
> YOLLAND: But I've been—
> OWEN: O – w – e – n.
> YOLLAND: Where did Roland come from?
> OWEN: I don't know.
> YOLLAND: It was never Roland?
> OWEN: Never.
> YOLLAND: O my God!
> (*Pause. They stare at one another. Then the absurdity of the situation strikes them suddenly. They explode with laughter.*)
> . . .
> MANUS: What's the celebration?
> OWEN: A christening!
> YOLLAND: A baptism![18]

Once more, absurdity, once more a potential baptism. The added factor here is the suggestion that 'never' is a negotiable term, since it has proved perfectly feasible for 'Owen' to be called, and to pass as, 'Roland'. He has been 'Roland' in town, but now, in the country, he reverts to 'Owen'.

My third example is André Brink's parable of South Africa set, like *Translations*, in an historical epoch where its vectors can be examined outside the rubric of contemporary conflict.

Elisabeth and the black slave, the only survivors of a map-making expedition into the interior—how unconsciously congruent the themes!—become lovers, but even at the height of intimacy there is between them the problem of naming:

> 'Adam?' she whispers.
> 'Why do you call me Adam?'
> 'It's your name.'
> 'My name is Aob.'
> 'For me you're Adam. That's how I learnt to know you. If I called you Aob it would change you into someone else, a stranger.'
> 'But it's my own name.'
> 'When you're inside me, sometimes, quite suddenly, yes, then I can call you Aob. But mostly you're Adam.'
> 'I'm Adam for the Cape.'
> With a shy, shivery smile, her eyes unnaturally bright and her cheeks flushed, she moistens a finger in the slit of her sex and touches him on his forehead, between his eyes. 'I'm baptising you again,' she says. 'Now your name is Adam. For me.'[19]

Where the connection between *Earnest* and *Translations* was 'absurdity', here we have a third baptism. But the casualty in each case is language, and with it identity, since in the irony of Elisabeth stepping outside her tribe to encompass Aob, she gives his city name to his country persona, thereby emasculating the man who brings her to life with his heart of darkness.

The distinction between what we call ourselves in town and what we are called in the country is one with which Wilde was thoroughly familiar. It is intimately concerned with what Denis Donoghue calls 'the complex fate of being Irish ... exacerbated by the fact that division in a country so small seems perverse'.[20] To return the discussion to a period and an occasion within Wilde's direct experience, we might cite the fact that every year until 1959 in the village of Asdee, in the north of Kerry, the parish priest would celebrate a memorial mass for Frank and Jesse James, whose ancestors were from that parish.[21] The bandits, whose fall-out Wilde had seen at first hand (*L* 113–15), continued to be heroes in the land they had abandoned. It casts a challenging light on another double-edged comment by Vivian Mercier: 'Irish writers of international reputation never cut much ice at home until they become as localized as our saints.'[22] The 'complex fate' consists primarily in knowing how to be oneself in two places and at the same time of how to be someone else. It is the fivefold problem which I identified in discussing the tension between Yeats's self and anti-self.

But it also marks the recurrence of phenomena and the phenomenon of recurrence. Wilde expected, after his release from prison, to return as 'an unwelcome visitant to the world that does not want me; a revenant' (*L* 413), imagining himself as Melmoth *redivivus*. On his release, Ada Leverson recalled that 'he came in with the dignity of a king returning from exile' (*L* 563), but this was already a dead man, one for whom *le monde visible* had almost totally ceased to exist. It suggests that the 'myth of eternal return' discussed extensively by Mircea Eliade[23] is a condition experienced previously by the Irish mind in relation to situations where 'this world and the other are not widely sundered': the transitus between the two enables epiphanies of former gods and heroes to occur before ordinary folk, and for ordinary folk to make excursions into the unreal world in order to hold discussions with gods.

Like the attraction of the James gang, the Wilde gang continues to fascinate because what is beyond and above the law, or considers itself to be so, attracts those of us who live within and beneath the law. Those who live lives of obscurity will find their appetites for glamour fed by Hollywood, their imaginations temporarily raised to a new plane where they can identify with the rich and famous, the outcast and the anti-hero. Novels, films, fantasies all supply us with a confirmation that, hyperbole aside, there is a world parallel to our own world, and one where the eternal values are verified and augmented. Drama, especially, is the place where we may experience, as was said of Yeats's theatre, 'the evocation of a sacred presence'[24] or, as Edmund Husserl saw it, relocate the primary point of contact between man and the world.[25]

In this world where play, politics and philosophy are, at every moment, re-creating reality, the outsider knows that he has no proper place except elsewhere. But the writer craves the landscape which he sees as his own. Protestant, Unionist Ferguson's plight is no greater than Catholic, Nationalist Heaney's:

> My *patria*, my deep design
> To be at home
> In my own place and dwell within
> Its proper name.[26]

Even if one lives abroad, one's imagination revisits home, or the idea of home, in strophic rhythms, and the country itself revisits the artist in cata-strophic rhythms:

> The whole imagined country mourns
> Its lost, erotic
>
> Aisling life.[27]

In Heaney's *Station Island* the penitential circular motion of the pilgrimage reinforces that of Wilde's prison yard, its centripetal force confirming the centrality, as much as the exile, of the deviant.

This suggests that the site of writing, the place of imagination and commitment, can be separate from the state which it describes only at the risk of a complete crisis of ontology. It suggests that we must examine, in the modernist and post-modernist perspective, the question: Is Ireland a real country or a state of mind?[28]

Crucial to the answer will be an agreement on whether the site of writing, and the matter, intention and audience of writing, must necessarily be congruent for the action to have any valid or meaningful effect. If the identification of writing with its purpose can be thus assured, then the writing will be discrete, cellular and, most importantly, continuous. Otherwise—and it is very much a case of *other*-wise—every writing is a new beginning, a new discontinuity, setting out on the path to a new society. Something of this is captured by Tom Stoppard in *Travesties*, which implausibly has Lenin, Joyce and Tzara in Zurich, each contemplating a new beginning in art or politics, set against the background of a rehearsal of Wilde's *The Importance of Being Earnest*.

I have already drawn a parallel between Wilde's Salomé and Sophocles' Antigone. It remains to point out that Wilde himself continues to command attention because he too embodies the five nodal points of rebellion, the critical indices to tension—and exchange—between men and women, old and young, the individual and society, the living and the dead, and between men and gods. He did so firstly in his own life and secondly in his writing; but if we recall that in his mind he lived in oblique relation to his 'real' life, and if we accept for a moment that he saw his own work as a commentary upon each of those lives—that indeed his writing *was* the imagined life lived in public—then we can see that Wilde represents these tensions and exchanges both in the physical and in the metaphysical senses. As both man and woman, there was a constant internal intercourse in his own imagination which is also shadowed in his writing, between the androgynous personae of his poems and stories, and between the curiously affected lovers of his plays. But he also lived out this tension in his appearance as a man in the Victorian world, as heterosexual and homosexual lover, as a man in a man's world lampooned for being less manly than was normal and ultimately revealed as being neither man nor woman. In his own social performance he was a young upstart in an age of elder statesmen, yet in private he was the patron of catamites and the mentor of much younger men, creating a new taste and timbre for the age, a role played out in his writing by the search for Mr W.H. and the education of Dorian by Lord Henry Wotton. His socialism and his anarchism are evident both in his private sexual defiance of social mores and in *The Soul of Man under Socialism* where he creates a profoundly anti-social Utopia. In prison he was forced to come to terms with the way in which his conduct had soiled the reputation of his parents and, beyond them, the evolving generations of Irish culture who had been evoked in their work and the work of Ferguson. Acknowledging the *bean sídhe* [banshee] as the herald of death, he was reproached by the dead for having failed Ireland. And in his continual renegotiation of his relations with Protestantism and Catholicism, but much more profoundly so with the pagan cultures of Greece and Ireland, he epitomised in his private conscience the public route taken by Salomé in her advance towards, and retreat from, the Baptist.

This in itself would allow us to regard Wilde in the same curious light which Mario Praz shed on the psychosexual preoccupations of the 'romantic agony'. But it is also cardinally modern in the signpost which it turns towards the development of Irish drama and of the modern novel. It allows us to understand how Wilde could say of himself: 'I am not, happily I think, an ordinarily constituted being'[29] and how Gide could call him 'that terrifying man, the most dangerous product of modern civilisation'.[30]

Throughout this book we have seen the interchangeability of homosexuality and Irishness as ways of seeing and thinking and ways of being seen and being described. Behind this mutual reference has been the third issue, of the identity—or lack of it—of individuals and societies in a post-colonial world which has largely lost its signposts in the act of birth. *Salomé*, like *Antigone*, is a crucial moment in western thought, but equally seminal as a means of bringing east and west into a closer understanding and reinterpretation of each other. As its creator, Wilde acts as a catalyst in encouraging Yeats to bring the eastern drama onto the western stage; his example may also have persuaded Yeats to turn Synge away from that type of rapprochement and instead to lie down in the manger of Aran and thus to bring to the Dublin audience not the ancient wisdom of the east but that of its own western island. The tension which flowed from that release of energies is still a point of discussion today, and one which has had repercussions in the incipient study of the folk-drama of India. That same power can be found in the bare landscapes and barren interiors of Beckett's drama, as strongly influenced, and punished, by Irish considerations, as by those in the absurd theatre of elsewhere. And even in the myth- and ritual-ridden plays of Friel—*Dancing at Lughnasa* and *Wonderful Tennessee*—we see a questing mind turning to the forces of paganism and suggesting that the feral and the chthonic are as potent today as they were for a handful of Homeric or Sophoclean households.

In the wider literary context, the way in which Borges took the play of ideas into his bloodstream and married it to the magical realism of Latin-America is a beacon illuminating a new territory of fiction, of which *Midnight's Children* and *Shame* are one aspect. The marriage of history, fantasy and psychology in the manipulation of personalities, the permutation of possibilities and the prescriptions of fate is a union of elements which, in the preceding fiction of Pater, Wilde and Jarry, had provided a bridging passage between the gothic and the modern imaginations. Today's novel, of which Mario Vargas Llosa's *The Real Life of Alexandro Mayta* is a supreme example, combines the antigonal oppositions in such a way that the reader of Llosa, as of Wilde, is left wondering which is real, which imagined? what has been told, a life or an idea, a biography or an autobiography, an argument for insurrection or for homosexuality?

We see here—in the treatment of post-colonial India and Latin-America—new ways of perceiving what had previously been occluded and suppressed, and we also recognise that the intensely personal and the supremely public are hardly separated. Manlio Argueta's *One Day of Life* portrays all the aspirations for freedom and communication purely in terms of the everyday life of ordinary peasants, which Pater and Wilde had so studiously neglected. But it *is* an inversion, rather than a reversal: the ideas themselves are those which have been stolen and placed in the crib with the orphaned child—the dispossessed. Mythology, which is present in every new child, whatever his origins and his circumstances, requires heroes; history requires that it is interpreted by fathers. In Wilde and Genet, one high-born and one a bastard, we see a pair of foster-brothers, doomed to meet at the point where each devises his own mythology and his own paternity. In Llosa's Mayta and Beckett's Lucky we see the same inexorable groping towards a statement which unites meaning in the present with its antecedent past. It is tragic only because modern life is tragic in its incapacity for self-fulfilment. And again the centuries speak to one another: Mangan wrote: 'According to Vallencey every Irishman is an Arab';[31] Derrida (it might almost be Edward Said) asks: 'Are we Jews? Are we Greeks?...We live in and of difference, that is, in *hypocrisy*....And what is the legitimacy, what is the meaning of the *copula* in this proposition from perhaps the most Hegelian of modern novelists: "Jewgreek is greekjew. Extremes meet"?'[32]

I end this Conclusion by reference to the 1993 Reith Lectures given by Edward Said. An academic and polemicist of distinction, who has played an important role in the intellectual evolution of the Palestinian people, he has also commented incisively on Irish affairs.[33] In his lectures Said referred to Wilde and Joyce as intellectuals-in-opposition. For Said, a 'real' intellectual is one whose 'powerful personality' is 'in a state of almost permanent opposition to the status quo', 'a being set apart'.[34] Especially noted for their experience of exile,[35] intellectuals are 'the nay-sayers, the individuals at odds with their society.... Exile for the intellectual in this metaphysical sense is restlessness, movement, constantly being unsettled, and unsettling others.'[36] The voices of 'all those people and issues who are routinely forgotten or swept under the carpet', they are 'representative not just of some subterranean or large social movement, but of a quite peculiar, even abrasive, style of life and social performance that is uniquely theirs'.[37] Endowed with a 'passion for thinking',[38] the intellectual is engaged in a 'culture of critical discourse',[39] which makes his exile into 'a median state, neither completely at one with the new setting, nor fully disencumbered of the old'.[40] To be thus a metaphor in oneself is the most painful of conditions, a membrane between two cultures, belonging to neither, often castigated and rejected by both. Said calls this displaced individual 'someone whose whole being is staked in a critical sense.[41] ... The intellectual in exile is necessarily ironic, sceptical, even playful—not cynical.'[42] But this is to forget Wilde. Despite his famous disclaimer—'A cynic [is] someone who knows the price of everything and the value of nothing' (*CW* 418)—Wilde was supremely cynical in his reckless theft of youth, in his caustic criticism of social hypocrisy. Yet it is in the *play* of irony that he most exemplifies this exile; as Yeats put it in *The Tragic Generation*, 'he was meditating upon possible disaster, but one took all his words for play'.[43]

Using Bazarov, the catalyst of Turgenev's *Fathers and Sons*, as a yardstick, Said observes that 'the intellectual is not only a being set apart from parents and children, but ... his modes of life, his procedures of engaging with it are necessarily allusive, and can only be represented realistically as a series of discontinuous performances'.[44] While we may agree that the intellectual-in-opposition will live in a discontinuous state and that he will therefore be necessarily allusive—the structures of both *Dubliners* and *Ulysses* bear this out—Said's further point is distinctly arguable, that 'by virtue of living a life according to different norms, the intellectual does not have a story, but only a sort of destabilising effect.... He can neither be explained away by his background nor his friends.'[45] The point in relation to Wilde and Joyce is that they do indeed have a story—one which is inscribed severely on their own conscience and which they spend their careers in translating into this critical discourse. It is a measure of the extent to which that story disturbs and destabilises the society to which they live in oblique relation which constitutes the critical position by which they are judged: we continually return to Wilde, Yeats and Joyce precisely because we are troubled by the fact that each of them had a personal story which we need to apprehend and interpret for our own discourse. 'Exile', says Said, 'means that you are always going to be marginal, and that what you do has to be made up because you cannot follow a prescribed path.'[46] Wilde was marginal in the sense that he stood voluntarily outside the norms of society, yet central to that society in the sense that he invaded and plundered it. The thief—particularly the recidivist—is as important to society as Bazarov is central, while he lives, to the Kirsanov family, because he has captured its attention in the form of its presiding reason. Temporarily in possession of its *raison d'être* and residing at its core, he becomes the vulnerable and pathetic metaphor by means of which each society gains a limited view of the otherworld. Theodor Adorno said that 'for a man who no longer has a homeland, writing becomes a place to live';[47] although Wilde may have seen his disconnected life as a greater place than his writing in which to live, it is only in his writing that his mind and his life can meet and engage with us in this critical discourse.

Notes and References

Introduction: The Irishman as Outsider (pp 1–18)

1. J. Joyce, 'Oscar Wilde: the Poet of *Salomé*' (originally published as 'Oscar Wilde: Il Poeta di *Salomé*' in *Il Piccolo della Sera*, 24 Mar. 1909), reprinted in *Critical Writings of James Joyce*, ed. E. Mason and R. Ellmann (New York: Viking Press, 1959), p. 203.
2. R. H. Sherard, *The Real Oscar Wilde* (London: Werner Laurie, 1917) p. 200.
3. L. Housman, *Echo de Paris* (London: Cape, 1923): a composite conversational portrait of Wilde in his final years in Paris; while the atmosphere of Wilde's table-talk is authentic, no single remark is necessarily verifiable.
4. B. Brasol, *Oscar Wilde* (London: Williams & Norgate, 1938) p. 31.
5. A. Bird, *The Plays of Oscar Wilde* (London: Vision Press, 1977).
6. K. Worth, *Oscar Wilde* (Houndmills: Macmillan, 1983).
7. N. Kohl, *Oscar Wilde: Das Literarische Werk zwischen Provokation und Anpassung* (Heidelberg: Carl Winter Universitätsverlag, 1980).
8. N. Kohl, *Oscar Wilde: the works of a conformist rebel*, trans. D. H. Wilson (Cambridge: Cambridge University Press, 1989). (All subsequent citations are from this translation.)
9. I. Small, *Oscar Wilde Revalued: an essay on new materials and methods of research* (Greensboro, NC: ELT Press, 1993).
10. Kohl, op. cit., pp 1, 2.
11. Ibid., p. 6.
12. Ibid., p. 252.
13. V. Mercier, *The Irish Comic Tradition* (Oxford: Clarendon Press, 1962).
14. R. McHugh and M. Harmon, *A Short History of Anglo-Irish Literature* (Dublin: Wolfhound, 1982) p. 145.
15. A. Warner, *A Guide to Anglo-Irish Literature* (Dublin: Gill & Macmillan, 1981), pp 5, 106.
16. Ibid., p. 9.
17. Kohl, op. cit., p. 253.
18. Ibid., p. 5, quoting R. Merle, *Oscar Wilde* (Paris: Hachette, 1948), p. 490.
19. Ibid., pp 11–12; P. Cohen, *The Moral Vision of Oscar Wilde* (London: Associated University Presses, 1978), p. 11, refers to Wilde's work as 'a single, unified record of ontogenesis'.
20. Kohl, op. cit., p. 1.

21. The term is discussed by G. Steiner, *Extraterritorial: papers on literature and the language revolution* (Harmondsworth: Penguin, 1975).

22. T. Eagleton, *Saint Oscar* (Derry: Field Day Publications, 1989), p. viii.

23. Kohl, op. cit., p. 131.

24. Ibid., p. 20.

25. Ibid., p. 318.

26. Ibid., p. 325.

27. R. Ellmann, *Oscar Wilde* (London: Hamish Hamilton, 1987).

28. R. Ellmann, *Oscar Wilde at Oxford* (Washington: Library of Congress, 1984).

29. R. Ellmann, 'Oscar and Oisin' in *Eminent Domain* (London: Oxford University Press, 1967), pp 9–28.

30. R. Ellmann, 'Corydon and Ménalque' in *Golden Codgers: biographical speculations* (London: Oxford University Press, 1973), pp 81–100.

31. R. Ellmann, 'Overtures to *Salome*' in *Golden Codgers*, pp 39–59.

32. R. Ellmann, 'The Critic as Artist as Wilde' in *Golden Codgers*, pp 60–80; originally published as introduction to *The Artist as Critic: critical writings of Oscar Wilde* (London: W. H. Allen, 1970).

33. Kohl, op. cit., Conclusion, pp 318–26. Kohl hinted (p. 11) at Wilde's revelation of the triple portrait in *Dorian Gray*; later he amplified this: 'His literary *œuvre* is as two-headed as Janus: it looks backward to Victorian and late romantic traditions, with its nineteenth-century exoticism, and its good or fallen women, dandies and *doppelgänger*; and it looks forwards as it sows the seed of modernism with its growing gulf between individual and society, its scepticism towards linguistic communication, its crises of identity and its artistic autonomy.' (p. 318)

34. J. Joyce, *Finnegans Wake* (London: Faber & Faber, 1939), p. 583.

35. A. de Vere, *English Misrule and Irish Misdeeds* (London: Murray, 1848), p. 49.

36. Quoted in Ellmann, *Oscar Wilde*, p. 322.

37. Hegel's *Lectures on the Philosophy of Religion*, quoted by G. Steiner, *Antigones* (Oxford: Clarendon Press, 1986), p. 21.

38. *Daily Examiner* (San Francisco), 27 Mar. 1882.

39. A. Raffalovich, *L'Affaire Oscar Wilde* (Lyon: Storck, 1895).

40. Quoted by H. M. Hyde, *Oscar Wilde* (London: Eyre Methuen, 1976), p. 37.

41. V. Mercier, *Modern Irish Literature: sources and founders* (Oxford: Clarendon Press, 1994), p. 110.

42. W. Ward, 'Oscar Wilde: An Oxford Reminiscence' in Vyvyan Holland, *Son of Oscar Wilde* (Harmondsworth: Penguin, 1957), p. 220.

43. E. Jepson, *Memoirs of a Victorian* (London: Gollancz, 1933), i, 120.

44. Lord A. Douglas, *Without Apology* (London: Martin Secker, 1938), p. 75.

45. Douglas to his mother, 6 Jan. 1894, quoted in R. Croft-Cooke, *Bosie* (London: W. H. Allen, 1963), p. 93.
46. *Pall Mall Budget*, 30 June 1892.
47. M. J. O'Neill, 'Irish Poets of the Nineteenth Century: Unpublished Lecture Notes of Oscar Wilde', *University Review*, i, no. 4 (spring 1955).
48. Ellmann, *Oscar Wilde*, p. 95.
49. *National Observer*, 6 Apr. 1895.
50. J. M. Cahalan, *Great Hatred, Little Room: the Irish historical novel* (Dublin: Gill & Macmillan, 1983); J. M. Cahalan, *The Irish Novel: a critical history* (Dublin: Gill & Macmillan, 1988); R. Fallis, *The Irish Renaissance: an introduction to Anglo-Irish literature* (Dublin: Gill & Macmillan, 1978); W. E. Hall, *Shadowy Heroes: Irish literature of the 1890s* (Syracuse, NY: Syracuse University Press, 1980); J. W. Foster, *Fictions of the Irish Literary Revival: A Changeling Art* (Syracuse, NY: Syracuse University Press, 1987).
51. Ellmann, *Oscar Wilde*, p. 95.
52. Ibid., p. 185.
53. L. Daudet, *Memoirs*, trans. A. K. Griggs (London: Constable, 1926), p. 200; cf. an anonymous account of Wilde in Reading Prison by a warder: 'He was so unlike other men. Just a bundle of brains.' ('In the Depths', *Evening News and Mail*, 1 Mar. 1905)
54. Ellmann, *Oscar Wilde*, p. 356.
55. In his obituary of Wilde (*Saturday Review*, 8 Dec. 1900) Beerbohm said: 'His writing seemed always to be an overflow of intellectual and temperamental energy than an inevitable absorbing function. That he never concentrated himself on any one form of literature is a proof that the art of writing never really took hold of him.' Cf. also A. Symons, *A Study of Oscar Wilde* (London: Sawyer, 1930), p. 47: 'The whole man was not so much a personality as an attitude. Without being a sage, he maintained the attitude of a sage; without being a poet, he maintained the attitude of a poet; without being a poet, he maintained the attitude of a poet; without being an artist, he maintained the attitude of an artist. And it was precisely in his attitudes that he was most sincere.'

Chapter 1: 'Quite Another Thing': Nineteenth-Century Irishness (pp 21–46)

1. W. B. Yeats, *Autobiographies* (London: Macmillan, 1955), p. 189.
2. Small, *Oscar Wilde Revalued*, pp 2, 17.
3. Ibid., pp 2, 3.
4. Ibid., p. 2.
5. Ibid., p. 4.
6. Ellmann, *Oscar Wilde*, p. 406.
7. Ibid., p. 293.
8. See H. Bracken, 'George Berkeley: The Irish Cartesian' in R. Kearney (ed.), *The Irish Mind: exploring intellectual traditions* (Dublin: Wolfhound, 1985), pp 107–18.

9. A. C. Fraser, *The Life and Letters of George Berkeley* (Oxford: Clarendon Press, 1871), pp 500–01.

10. *The Senate Speeches of W. B. Yeats*, ed. D. R. Pearce (London: Faber & Faber, 1961), p. 72.

11. Ibid.

12. W. B. Yeats, *Explorations* (London: Macmillan, 1962) p. 333.

13. W. B. Yeats, *Autobiography* (1965), quoted in Ellmann, *Eminent Domain*, p. 14.

14. 'The Statues' in W. B. Yeats, *The Poems*, ed. R. Finneran (London: Macmillan, 1983), p. 337.

15. D. Donoghue, *We Irish: essays on Irish literature and society* (London: University of California Press, 1986), p. 8.

16. W. B. Yeats, *Senate Speeches*, p. 172.

17. W. B. Yeats, *Essays and Introductions* (London: Macmillan, 1961), p. 28.

18. See T. Ó Cathasaigh, 'The Concept of the Hero in Irish Mythology' in Kearney (ed.), *The Irish Mind*, pp 79–90.

19. The concept of the hero was addressed in the production of the five Cuchulain plays in the inaugural International Yeats Theatre Festival (Director, Professor James Flannery), Abbey Theatre, Dublin, 1989.

20. J. Genet, *The Thief's Journal*, trans. B. Frechtman (London: Penguin, 1967), p. 173.

21. In a notebook in the Berg Collection, New York Public Library, quoted in Ellmann, *Oscar Wilde*, p. 467.

22. Ibid.

23. W. Pater, *The Renaissance: studies in art and poetry* (London: Macmillan, 1873), p. 253.

24. L. Durrell, *Caesar's Vast Ghost* (London: Faber & Faber, 1990), pp 143, 61, 22–3.

25. M. Arnold, *On the Study of Celtic Literature* (London: Smith, Elder, 1867), p. 100.

26. See R. Pine, 'The Children of the Waste Land, 1920–1930' in *The Dandy and the Herald: manners, mind and morals from Brummell to Durrell* (Houndmills: Macmillan, 1988), pp 124–37.

27. E. Renan, *The Poetry of the Celtic Races* (London: Scott, 1896), p. 8.

28. D. Cairns and S. Richards, '"Woman"—the Discourse of Celticism' in B. Bramsbäck and M. Croghan (eds), *Anglo-Irish and Irish Literature: aspects of language and culture* (Stockholm: Almqvist & Wiksell, 1988), ii, 31–43.

29. J. Marshall in *The Independent* (undated cutting), c. November 1993.

30. Arnold, op. cit., p. 15.

31. Ibid.

32. Ibid., p. 84.

33. R. Kearney, 'An Irish Intellectual Tradition?', introduction to *The Irish Mind*, p. 8.

34. Arnold, op. cit., pp 100–01.
35. Ibid., p. 102; cf. Wilde: the English 'are always degrading the truth into facts. When a truth becomes a fact, it loses all its intellectual value' (quoted in D. Coakley, *Oscar Wilde: The Importance of Being Irish* (Dublin: Town House, 1994), p. 46). Wilde said of *The Picture of Dorian Gray* that 'it reacts against the crude brutality of plain realism' (*L* 264).
36. Arnold, op. cit, p. 144.
37. Ibid., p. 158.
38. Ibid., pp 102–3.
39. Ibid., p. 104.
40. Ibid., p. 108.
41. Ibid., p. 109.
42. Ibid., p. 259.
43. Ellmann, *Oscar Wilde*, p. 186.
44. Renan, op. cit., pp 50, 53.
45. Ibid., p. 53.
46. Ibid.
47. Ibid., p. 9.
48. B. Kennelly, 'Modern Irish Poets and the Irish Epic' (unpublished Ph.D. thesis, Trinity College, Dublin, 1966), p. 5.
49. Ibid., p. 6.
50. Ibid., p. 15.
51. Ibid., p. 19.
52. Ibid., p. 20.
53. Ibid.
54. Ibid., pp. 31–2.
55. Ibid., p. 243.
56. E. Goffmann, *Stigma: notes on the management of spoiled identity* (Englewood Cliffs, NJ: Prentice–Hall, 1963), p. 3.
57. Ibid.
58. Ibid., p. 10.
59. Ibid., p. 56.
60. Renan, op. cit., p. 2.
61. Ibid.
62. Ibid., p. 7.
63. See Goffmann, op. cit., p. 13.
64. Lady Wilde, *Social Studies* (London: Ward & Downey, 1893), p. 134.
65. Ibid., pp 134–5.
66. Goffmann, op. cit., p. 100.
67. Ibid., pp 48–9.
68. Wordsworth: 'Every great and original writer, in proportion as he is great and original, must himself create the taste by which he is to be relished.' (letter of 21 May 1807) Cf. Wilde: 'No artist requires any standard of beauty but that which is suggested by his own temperament.' (*L* 302)

69. W. Archer, 'Mr Oscar Wilde's New Play', *Black and White*, 11 May 1893. Cf. A. de Brémont, *Oscar Wilde and his Mother* (London: Everett, 1911, pp 15–16): 'Oscar Wilde possessed the feminine soul. This was the ghost that haunted his house of life... the secret influence that weighed down his manhood and enervated his hope: the knowledge that...he was a slave to the capricious, critical, feminine temperament, the feminine vanity and feminine weakness to temptation; the feminine instinct of adaptibility; the feminine impulse of the wanton's soul.'

70. A. Gide, *Oscar Wilde: a study*, trans. S. Mason (Oxford: Holywell Press, 1905), p. 16.

71. Lady Wilde, *Ancient Legends, Mystic Charms and Superstitions of Ireland* (London: Ward & Downey, 1888), pp xi–xii.

72. Renan, op. cit., p. 8.

73. Wilde to Christian Krohg, Paris, 22 June 1897 (published in *New Age*, 10 Dec. 1908).

74. F. O'Connor, *The Backward Look* (London: Macmillan, 1967), p. 5.

75. See S. Ó Tuama and T. Kinsella (eds), *An Duanaire, 1600–1800: poems of the dispossessed* (Mountrath: Dolmen Press, 1981).

76. See S. Heaney, *Sweeney Astray: a version from the Irish [Buile Suibhne]* (Derry: Field Day Publications, 1983).

77. See Sean O'Faolain, *The Great O'Neill* (London: Longman, Green, 1942); Thomas Kilroy, *The O'Neill*, play performed at the Peacock Theatre, Dublin 1969 (unpublished); Brian Friel, *Making History* (London: Faber & Faber, 1989).

78. Yeats, *Essays and Introductions*, pp 312–13.

79. 'Every portrait that is painted with feeling is a portrait of the artist, not of the sitter.' (*PDG* 5)

80. D. Kiberd, 'Inventing Irelands' in 'Ireland: Dependence and Independence', *The Crane Bag*, viii, no. 1 (1984), p. 18.

81. Cf. R. Kearney's discussion of Seamus Deane's 'The Literary Myths of the Revival' in his introduction to *The Irish Mind*, p. 32.

82. S. Deane, 'Remembering the Irish Future', *The Crane Bag*, viii, no. 1 (1984), p. 90.

83. 'A Nation Once Again': the title (and refrain) of one of Thomas Davis's most popular ballads, still representative of republican and integrative aspirations.

84. Yeats, 'A Dialogue of Self and Soul', *Poems*, p. 234.

85. See R. Kearney in *The Irish Mind*, pp 9, 312, where he discusses the principle of 'excluded middle'.

86. M. P. Hederman, 'The "Mind" of Joyce: From Paternalism to Paternity' in Kearney (ed.) *The Irish Mind*, p. 264.

87. J. Keats, 'Ode on a Grecian Urn'.

88. Epigrams in the collection of Mrs M. Hyde, quoted in Ellmann, *Oscar Wilde*, p. 23.

89. *St Paul Globe*, 18 June 1882.

90. Hyde collection, quoted in Ellmann, *Oscar Wilde*, p. 285.
91. E. Newman, 'Oscar Wilde: A Literary Appreciation', *Free Review*, 1 June 1895.
92. W. Wilde, *Irish Popular Superstitions* (Dublin: McGlashan, 1852), pp 79, 80, 81.
93. Ellmann, *Oscar Wilde*, p. 96.
94. E. G. Carillo, *Obras Completas*, xvi, 190, quoted in Ellmann, *Oscar Wilde*, p. 324.
95. Quoted ibid., p. 530.
96. Yeats, 'Lapis Lazuli', *Poems*, pp 294–5.

Chapter 2: A 'Regal Republic': Cultural Nationalism in the Mid-Century (pp 47–106)

1. Hyde collection, quoted in Ellmann, *Oscar Wilde*, p. 60.
2. N. Frye, *The Anatomy of Criticism* (New York: Cornell University Press, 1957) p. 187.
3. Terence Brown, 'Cultural Nationalism, 1880–1930' in *Field Day anthology*, ii, 516–20.
4. The text of Davis's address to the Trinity College Historical Society in 1839 was reprinted in *The Nation*, vi, nos 277–8 (22, 29 Jan. 1848).
5. Renan, *The Poetry of the Celtic Races*, pp 74, 75.
6. See Maurice Colgan, 'Young Ireland in Literature and Nationalism' in F. Barker *et al.* (eds), *1848: The Sociology of Literature* [proceedings of the Essex Conference on the Sociology of Literature, July 1977] (University of Essex: 1978); see also N. Mansergh, *The Irish Question* (London: Allen & Unwin, 1975), pp 95–7. See also *Nation*, 18 Mar. 1843, which reported that Ireland, with 32,201 geo. sq. miles, was larger than Portugal; Bavaria and Saxony; Naples and Sicily; Greece and Switzerland; Holland and Belgium; but, in 'New Duties for the New Year' (8 Jan. 1848), 'plainly we have no hope of any conclusive political achievements for Ireland for 1848. . . . From Constantinople to Washington we are known not as a vital nation, but as a beggared community.'
7. See W. J. McCormack, *Ascendancy and Tradition in Anglo-Irish Literary History from 1789 to 1939* (Oxford: Clarendon Press, 1985).
8. R. B. McDowell, *Irish Public Opinion, 1750–1800* (London: Faber & Faber, 1944); R. B. McDowell, *Public Opinion and Government Policy in Ireland, 1801–1846* (London: Faber & Faber, 1952).
9. See W. J. McCormack, 'Isaac Butt (1813–79) and the Inner Failure of Protestant Home Rule' in C. Brady (ed.), *Worsted in the Game: losers in Irish history* (Dublin: Lilliput, 1989).
10. Quoted in J. Sheehy, *The Rediscovery of Ireland's Past: the Celtic revival, 1830–1930* (London: Thames & Hudson, 1980), p. 15.

11. Ibid.; see also R. Pine, *Oscar Wilde* (Dublin: Gill & Macmillan, 1983), pp 8–9.
12. Quoted in O'Connor, *The Backward Look*, p. 150.
13. McCormack, *Ascendancy and Tradition*, p. 248.
14. See D. Lloyd, *Nationalism and Minor Literature: James Clarence Mangan and the Emergence of Irish Cultural Nationalism* (Berkeley: University of California Press, 1987), p. 50.
15. M. Brown, *The Politics of Irish Literature: from Thomas Davis to W. B. Yeats* (London: Allen & Unwin, 1972), p. 65.
16. W. J. McCormack, 'J. Sheridan Le Fanu's "Richard Marston" (1848): the history of an Anglo-Irish text' in Barker *et al.* (eds), op. cit., p. 111.
17. Lady Morgan [Sydney Owenson], *The Wild Irish Girl* (London: Pandora, 1986), p. 7.
18. Ibid., p. 37.
19. Ibid., p. 41.
20. Ibid. p. 82.
21. Ibid., p. 7.
22. W. Scott, postscript to *Waverley* (Edinburgh: A. & C. Black, 1877), ii, 420.
23. J. Joyce, *Ulysses* (London: Penguin, 1968), p. 27.
24. Mercier, *Irish Comic Tradition*, p. 84.
25. See Renan, op. cit., p. 43: 'We know the use that Ireland has made of this theme [of heroism *versus* the feminine spirit] in the dialogues which she loves to imagine between the representatives of her profane and religious life, Ossian and St Patrick.'
26. Voltaire: 'Le secret de s'ennuyer est de tout dire [The secret of being a bore is to tell everything]' (*Sept Discours en Vers sur l'Homme*, VI: 'Sur la Nature de l'Homme', V, 174–5); Lafourge: 'Ah, que la vie est quotidienne' (*Complaints sur Certains Ennuis*, 1885).
27. M. Edgeworth, *Ennui* (London: Penguin, 1992), p. 143; cf. E. Lytton, *Pelham* (*Collected Works* (London: Routledge, 1873–7), p. 132): 'We pass our lives…in conjugating the verb *je m'ennuie*'.
28. *Ennui*, p. 291.
29. Ibid., p. 273.
30. Ibid., p. 144.
31. Ibid., p. 323.
32. Introduction to *Castle Rackrent* and *The Absentee* (London: Dent, 1910), p. 83.
33. Ibid., p. 203.
34. Ibid.
35. Ibid., p. 154; cf. *Ennui*, p. 320: 'What a horrid thing it will be to hear my girl called Mrs O'Donoghoe! Only conceive the sounds of—"Mrs O'Donoghoe's carriage there!"'; cf. also *The Absentee*, p. 99: '"Indeed, then, she's a sweet girl"…cried Lady Clonbrony, in an undisguised Irish accent, and with her natural warm manner. But, a moment afterwards, her features and whole form resumed

their constrained stillness and stiffness, and in her English accent she continued . . . '; cf. B. Friel, *The London Vertigo* (Lough Crew: Gallery Press, 1990), *passim*.

36. A remark which I have heard attributed to the literary historian Geoffrey Tillotson.
37. *Dublin University Magazine*, xxxi (June 1848), p. 741.
38. W. J. McCormack, *Sheridan Le Fanu and Victorian Ireland* (Oxford: Clarendon Press, 1980), p. 154.
39. Mercier, *Modern Irish Literature* , p. 190.
40. McCormack, *Sheridan Le Fanu*, pp 260, 263.
41. Ibid., p. 186.
42. S. Le Fanu, *Uncle Silas* (London: Macmillan, 1899), p. xviii.
43. Ibid., pp xvii–xviii.
44. Ibid., p. 9.
45. Ibid., p. 11.
46. Ibid., p. 105.
47. Ibid., p. 191.
48. Ibid., p. 159.
49. Ibid., p. 436
50. McCormack, Sheridan Le Fanu, p. 200.
51. P. Denman, *Samuel Ferguson: the literary achievement* (Gerrards Cross: Colin Smythe, 1990), p. 1.
52. Ibid.
53. Quoted ibid., p. 172.
54. Kennelly, 'Modern Irish Poets and the Irish Epic', pp 3, 4.
55. W. B. Yeats in *Bookman*, May 1896, p. 50.
56. Kennelly, op. cit., p. 69.
57. Ibid., p. 125.
58. Ibid., p. 124.
59. Ibid., p. 135.
60. Sir Samuel Ferguson, *Poems* (Dublin: W. McGee, 1880), p. 42.
61. Kennelly, op. cit., p. 124.
62. R. Barthes, *Image, Music, Text* (London: Fontana, 1977), p. 79.
63. Ibid., p. 80.
64. Anonymous introduction [by R. Ross and More Adey] to C. R. Maturin, *Melmoth the Wanderer*, 3 vols (London: Bentley, 1892).
65. A. Hayter, introduction to *Melmoth the Wanderer* (Harmondsworth: Penguin, 1977), p. 19.
66. *Melmoth*, p. 54.
67. Ibid., p. 57.
68. Ibid., p. 58.
69. Ibid., p. 61.
70. Ibid., p. 62.
71. Balzac, quoted in the preliminary matter to the 1892 edition of *Melmoth*.
72. *Melmoth*, p. 67.
73. Ibid., p. 87.

74. Ibid., p. 105.
75. Ibid., p. 106.
76. Ibid., p. 697.
77. C. R. Maturin, *The Wild Irish Boy*, 3 vols (London: Longman Hurst, 1805), i, 22–3.
78. *'His Sensations and Ideas'* was the subtitle of Pater's *Marius the Epicurean* (London: Macmillan, 1885).
79. *Wild Irish Boy*, i, 26.
80. Ibid., pp 34, 49.
81. Ibid., pp 78, 99.
82. Ibid., p. 101.
83. Ibid., pp 102–4.
84. Ibid., p. 111.
85. Ibid., ii, 14.
86. Ibid., p. 262.
87. C. R. Maturin, introduction to *Women, or Pour et Contre*, 3 vols, (Edinburgh: Constable, 1818).
88. Introduction to *Melmoth* (1892), pp li, lvi.
89. Ibid.
90. The masthead of *The Nation* quoted Chief Baron Wolfe: 'to create and to foster public opinion in Ireland—to make it racy of the soil'.
91. *Nation*, 15 Jan. 1842 (vol. i, no. 1).
92. Reprinted in *Nation*, 1 Jan. 1848.
93. Ibid.
94. Ibid., 19 Nov. 1842.
95. Ibid., 26 Feb. 1848.
96. Ibid.
97. Ibid.
98. Ibid., 17 Dec. 1842.
99. Ibid., 8 Jan. 1848.
100. Ibid., 15 Jan. 1848.
101. Ibid., 1 Jan. 1848.
102. Ibid., 8 Jan. 1848.
103. Ibid., 22 Jan. 1848.
104. Ibid., 1 Apr. 1848.
105. Ibid., 22 July 1848.
106. Ibid.
107. Ibid., 29 July 1848.
108. Ibid., 26 Nov. 1842.
109. *Dublin University Magazine*, ii (Nov. 1833), pp 586–9.
110. The later consequences of this are discussed in detail by T. Brown, *Ireland: A Social and Cultural History, 1922–1979* (London: Fontana, 1981), especially pp 109–37.
111. *Dublin University Magazine*, ix (Mar. 1837), p. 369.
112. Ibid., xxi (June 1848), pp 787–8.
113. Ibid., xxiii (June 1849), p. 796.

114. Ibid., i (Jan. 1833), pp 87–90.
115. Ibid.
116. Ibid., i (May 1833), pp 471–83.
117. Ibid., ii (July 1833), preface.
118. Ibid., v (Apr. 1835), pp 470–90.
119. Ibid., vi (Sept. 1835), pp 313–31.
120. Ibid., vii (Jan. 1836), pp 75–95.
121. Ibid., xxxiii (June 1849), p. 774.
122. Ibid., vi (Nov. 1838), pp 552–68.
123. Ibid., xxxiii, (Jan. 1849), pp 60–62.
124. Quoted in Ellmann, *Oscar Wilde*, p. 556.
125. *Nation*, 18 Mar. 1848.
126. Quoted in R. O'Driscoll, *An Ascendancy of the Heart: Ferguson and the beginnings of modern Irish literature in English* (Dublin: Dolmen, 1976), p. 15.
127. *Dublin Unversity Magazine*, v (Apr. 1835), p. 451.
128. Ibid.
129. Lady Wilde, *Ancient Legends, Mystic Charms and Superstitions of Ireland* (London: Ward & Downey, 1888), p. 346.
130. W. Wilde, *Irish Popular Superstitions* (Dublin: McGlashan, 1852), p. 122.
131. Ibid., p. 120.
132. Sir Peter Froggatt, quoted in J. B. Lyons, 'Sir William Wilde, 1815–76' in *What Did I Die Of? The deaths of Parnell, Wilde, Synge and other literary pathologies* (Dublin: Lilliput, 1991), p. 65.
133. Quoted in Pine, *Oscar Wilde*, p. 151.
134. *The Census of Ireland for 1851; Reports of Commissioners*, xii, 'Report, Tables of Pestilences, &c.' [C 2087–I], H.C. 1856, xxix, 526.
135. Ibid.
136. Ibid., p. 243.
137. Ibid.
138. W. Wilde, *Irish Popular Superstitions*, p. 9.
139. Ibid., p. 10.
140. Ibid., p. 11.
141. Ibid., p. 20.
142. Ibid., pp 18, 26, 72, 73.
143. Ibid., p. 74.
144. W. Wilde, *Lough Corrib* (Dublin: McGlashan & Gill, 1867), p.v.
145. Ibid., pp 1, 2.
146. Ibid., p. 1; cf. Lady Wilde, *Ancient Legends*, p. 132: 'There is a poetry in the scenery that touches the heart of the people'; p. 144: 'Ireland is a land of mists and mystic shadows; of cloud-wraiths on the purple mountains.' Yeats was in particular anxious to assert that the twilight zone, lying between two qualities of light, was the site of the supernatural: see his poem 'Into the Twilight', *Poems*, p. 59; 'those long, blue, ragged hills' (preface to Lady Gregory, *Cuchulain of Muirthemne* (London: Murray, 1902).

147. See W. Wilde, *Lough Corrib*, pp 1, 2, 3.
148. Ibid., p. 158.
149. Ibid., p. 196.
150. Ibid., p. 186.
151. Ibid., p. 187.
152. M. Haverty, 'The Aran Isles: or a Report of the Excursion of the Ethnological Section of the British Association from Dublin to the Western Islands of Aran in September 1857' (1859), reprinted in B. and R. Ó hEithir (eds), *An Aran Reader* (Dublin: Lilliput, 1991), p. 44.
153. Ibid., p. 46.
154. Ibid., p. 45.
155. W. Wilde, *Ireland Past and Present* (Dublin: McGlashan & Gill, 1864), p. 3.
156. Ibid., p. 4.
157. Ibid., p. 23.
158. Ibid., p. 25.
159. Ibid.
160. Ibid., p. 27.
161. Ibid., p. 39.
162. Ibid., pp 39–40.
163. Ibid., p. 43.
164. Ibid., p. 51.
165. Ibid., p. 50.
166. Quoted in H. Wyndham, *Speranza: a biography of Lady Wilde* (London: Boardman, 1951), pp 144–5, and previously in T. F. O'Sullivan, *Young Irelanders* (Tralee: Kerryman, 1941), pp 107–8.
167. *Irish People*, 25 Feb. 1865, quoted in O'Sullivan, *Young Irelanders*, pp 110–11.
168. Quoted in T. de V. White, *The Parents of Oscar Wilde* (London: Hodder & Stoughton, 1967), p. 123.
169. S. Deane, 'Poetry and Song, 1800–1890' in *Field Day anthology*, ii, 1–9, 76–7, discusses Davis, Ferguson, Mangan, Yeats, Moore, Lady Dufferin, George Darley, William Allingham and others, to the (pointed?) exclusion of Speranza.
170. See O'Sullivan, *Young Irelanders*, pp 115–30, for the careers of 'Mary' [Ellen Mary Patrick Downing], 'Eva' [Mary Eva Kelly], 'Finola' [Elizabeth Willoughby Treacy] and 'Ethne' [Marie M. Thompson].
171. *Poems by Speranza* (Dublin: Duffy, 1864), p. iii.
172. Ibid., p. 4: 'The Brothers': 'Those pale lips yet implore us, from their graves— / To strive for our birthright as God's creatures, / Or die, if we can but live as slaves.'
173. Ibid., p. 5.
174. Ibid., pp 8, 9.
175. Ibid., pp 14–15.

176. Ibid., p. 26.
177. Ibid., pp 27–9.
178. Ibid., p. 51.
179. Ibid., p. 55.
180. Lady Wilde, *Ancient Legends*, p. xi.
181. Ibid., p.xii.
182. Ibid., p. 1; see also ibid., p. 4: 'Philologists also affirm that the Irish language is nearer to Sanskrit than any other of the living and spoken languages of Europe; while the legends and myths of Ireland can be readily traced to the far East.'
183. Ibid., p. 4; see also ibid., p. 126: 'The migration of races can be clearly traced by their superstitions. . . . Persia, Egypt, India, the Teuton and the Celt, have all the same primal ideas in their mythology.' The thesis has more recently been explored by filmmaker Bob Quinn in a series tracing the migration of Celtic peoples from Egypt: *Atlantean*, transmitted by Radio Telefís Éireann, 19, 26 Mar., 2 Apr. 1984.
184. Ibid., p. 7.
185. Ibid., pp 276, 278.
186. Ibid., pp 38, 49, 256.
187. Ibid., p. 275.
188. Ibid., p. 122.
189. Lady Wilde, *Men, Women and Books* (London: Ward & Downey, 1891) p. 221.
190. Ibid., p. 186.
191. Ibid.
192. Lady Wilde, *Social Studies* (London: Ward & Downey, 1893), p. 283.
193. Ibid., p. 272.
194. Ibid., p. 226.
195. Ibid., pp 269–70.
196. Ibid., p. 272.
197. Ibid.
198. Ibid., p. 1.
199. Ibid., pp 15, 18.
200. E. Said, 'Representations of the Intellectual', pt 2, 30 June 1993, BBC Radio 4, summarised in *The Independent*, 1 July 1993.
201. Lady Wilde, *Social Studies*, p. 229.
202. Ibid., pp 233–4.
203. Ibid., p. 247.
204. Robert Yelverton Tyrrell, quoted in White, op. cit., p. 154.
205. Lady Wilde, *Social Studies*, p. 248.
206. Ibid., pp 78, 81–2.
207. Ibid., pp 80–81.

Chapter 3: A Secret and Selected Life (pp 107–158)

1. Renan, *The Poetry of the Celtic Races*, p. 20.
2. Ellmann, *Oscar Wilde*, p. 121; A. Nicoll, *A History of Late Nineteenth-Century Drama, 1850–1900* (Cambridge: Cambridge University Press, 1946) lists W. C. K. Wilde as having authored an 'Extravaganza', *The Dark Princess*, produced at Boscombe House, West Kensington, on 17 January 1894, while James Woodfield, *English Theatre in Transition, 1881–1914* (London: Croom Helm, 1984) p. 46, records that in 1891 the Independent Theatre's production of *Ghosts* announced forthcoming plays by, among others, Willie Wilde.
3. See Ellmann, *Oscar Wilde*, p. 24.
4. Yeats, *Poems*, p. 73.
5. Edmond de Goncourt, journal entry for 5 May 1883, published in part in 1892 as the sixth volume of the Goncourt diary—cf. *L* 303–4.
6. Gide, *Oscar Wilde*, p. 1.
7. Ellmann, 'The Critic as Artist as Wilde' in *Golden Codgers*, p. 62.
8. Croft-Cooke, *Bosie*, p. 93.
9. Gide, op. cit., pp 17, 49.
10. Ibid., p. 51.
11. 'Jacta Alea Est', *Nation*, 29 July 1848.
12. J.-P. Sartre, *Saint Genet, Actor and Martyr*, trans. B. Frechtman (New York: Braziller, 1963), pp 1, 2.
13. The 'third meaning': see Barthes, *Image, Music, Text*, pp 52–68.
14. 'Jacta Alea Est', loc. cit.
15. 'The Butterfly's Boswell', *Court and Society Review*, 20 Apr. 1887.
16. Quoted in V. O'Sullivan, *Aspects of Wilde* (London: Constable, 1936), p. 65: the remark is said to have been made to Arthur Balfour.
17. Quoted in White, *Parents of Oscar Wilde*, p. 123.
18. Quoted in Kathleen Everett, *Bricks and Flowers* (London: Constable, 1949), p. 258.
19. *Letters of John Stuart Blackie to his Wife*...ed. A. S. Walker (Edinburgh: Blackwood, 1909), p. 227.
20. H. Furniss, *Some Victorian Women* (London: John Lane, 1923), p. 1.
21. M. J. O'Neill, 'Irish Poets of the Nineteenth Century: Unpublished Lecture Notes of Oscar Wilde', *University Review*, i, no. 4 (spring 1955).
22. W. R. Rodgers (ed.), *Irish Literary Portraits* (London: BBC, 1972), p. 99.
23. Mercier, *Irish Comic Tradition*, p. 238.
24. Ibid., p. 242.
25. Letter quoted in L. Broad, *The Friendships and Follies of Oscar Wilde* (London: Hutchinson, 1954), p. 23.
26. Lady Wilde, *Ancient Legends*, pp 84–5.
27. Joyce, 'Oscar Wilde', reprinted in *Critical Writings of James Joyce*, ed. Mason and Ellmann, p. 204. On 'Osgar' see W. B. Yeats, preface

to Lady Gregory, *Gods and Fighting Men* (London: John Murray, 1904).

28. Letter, 22 Nov. 1854 (Reading University), quoted in Ellmann, *Oscar Wilde*, p. 20.
29. Letter, 6 May 1875 (National Library of Ireland), quoted ibid., p. 23.
30. Letter, 27 Apr. 1883 (Clark Collection), quoted ibid., p. 234.
31. White, op. cit., p. 241.
32. Letter, 1874 (National Library of Ireland), quoted in Ellmann, *Oscar Wilde*, p. 34.
33. Yeats, *Autobiographies*, p. 138.
34. Lady Wilde, *Men, Women and Books*, p. 182.
35. White, op. cit., p. 235.
36. O'Sullivan, op. cit., p. 76.
37. Rather than reproducing this line as it is quoted in Hyde, *Oscar Wilde*, p. 107, and Holland, *Son of Oscar Wilde*, p. 45, I prefer to quote it as spoken to me by the late Brian Tobin, who heard it from Vyvyan Holland and wrote it for me in the Connacht Irish which Wilde would most likely have heard in Leenane or Cong.
38. W. Wilde, *Irish Popular Superstitions*, p. 76.
39. Letter, 28 May 1879, quoted in Ellmann, *Oscar Wilde*, p. 101.
40. Ellmann, *Oscar Wilde*, p. 29; cf. Lloyd, *Nationalism and Minor Literature*, p. 130: 'The enormous popularity of German plays in Dublin at the turn of the century was quite explicitly seen to relate to the spirit of the United Irishmen of 1798 and of 1803.'
41. E. Saltus, *Oscar Wilde: An Idler's Impression* (Chicago: Brothers of the Book, 1917), p. 20.
42. W. Wilde, *The Beauties of the Boyne and its tributary the Blackwater* (Dublin: McGlashan & Gill, 1849), p. 161.
43. Ibid., pp 176, 183.
44. Ibid., pp 159, 186.
45. J. P. Mahaffy, *Principles of the Art of Conversation* (London: Macmillan, 1887), pp 1, 3.
46. Ibid., pp 84–5.
47. Ellmann, *Oscar Wilde*, p. 30.
48. J. P. Mahaffy, *Social Life in Greece from Homer to Menander* (London: Macmillan, 1874), p. viii.
49. Ibid., p. 305.
50. Ibid., p. 1.
51. Ibid., p. 2.
52. Ibid., 2nd ed. (1875), pp ix–x: 'In one direction . . . this edition is partially rewritten. There were certain phases in Greek morals, which had hitherto not been fairly discussed and had been consequently misunderstood, and upon these I wrote freely what I thought due to the Greeks and to their culture. I see no reason to retract one word of what I have written.'

53. Quoted in W. B. Stanford, *Ireland and the Classical Tradition* (Dublin: Figgis, 1976), p. 92.
54. W. B. Yeats, *Pages from a Diary* (Dublin: Cuala Press, 1944), p. 36.
55. Maturin, *Wild Irish Boy*, i, 112, 113, 115.
56. *Nation*, 22 Jan. 1848.
57. Stanford, op. cit., p. 177.
58. A. J. Balfour, *Decadence* (Cambridge: Cambridge University Press, 1908), pp 50, 58.
59. Rev. L. C. Prideaux Fox, 'People I Have Met', *Donohoe's Magazine* (Boston), liii, no. 4 (Apr. 1905).
60. Quoted in P. N. Furbank, review of Norman White, *Hopkins: a literary biography* (1992), in *Times Literary Supplement*, 27 Mar. 1992.
61. Ellmann, *Oscar Wilde*, p. 58.
62. W. Ward, 'Oscar Wilde: An Oxford Reminiscence' in Holland op. cit., p. 220.
63. Joyce, 'Oscar Wilde'.
64. P. E. Smith and M. S. Helfand (eds), *Oscar Wilde's Oxford Notebooks: a portrait of mind in the making* (Oxford: Oxford University Press, 1989), p. 33.
65. Ibid., p. 8.
66. F. M. Turner, *The Greek Heritage in Victorian Britain* (London: Yale University Press, 1981), p. xii.
67. J. A. Symonds, *A Problem in Greek Ethics* (privately printed edition of 10 copies, 1883); J. A. Symonds, *A Problem in Modern Ethics* (privately printed edition of 100 copies, 1896): both texts had the same subtitle: *'being an enquiry into the phenomenon of sexual inversion addressed explicitly to medical psychologists and jurists'*.
68. Ellmann, *Oscar Wilde*, p. 442.
69. J. Ruskin, *Modern Painters*, iii, in *Collected Works* (London: George Allen, 1903–12), v, 353.
70. J. A. Symonds, *Studies of the Greek Poets*, second series, (London: Smith, Elder, 1876), pp 154, 358–9.
71. Smith and Helfand, op. cit., suggest Herbert Spencer's *Study of Sociology* as a possible source (*CPB* 177).
72. Ibid., p. 66.
73. Yeats, *Autobiographies*, p. 135.
74. Ibid., p. 132.
75. A. J. A. Symons, *Essays and Biographies*, ed. J. Symons (London: Cassell, 1969), p. 162.
76. R. Barthes, *A Lover's Discourse*, pp 93, 98.
77. Ibid., p. 3.
78. Ibid., p. 5.
79. Ibid., p. 7.
80. Ibid., p. 13.
81. Ibid., p. 135.

82. Ibid., p. 134.
83. Ibid., p. 35.
84. A. Rimbaud, 'L'Epax Infernel et la Vierge Folle', quoted in E. Starkie, *Arthur Rimbaud* (London: Faber & Faber, 1961), p. 187.
85. Barthes, op. cit., p. 229.
86. H. Pearson, *Oscar Wilde* (London: Methuen, 1954), p. 111.
87. Ibid.
88. Holland, *Son of Oscar Wilde*, pp 44–5.
89. Quoted in Ellmann, *Oscar Wilde*, p. 268.
90. Croft-Cooke, *Bosie*, p. 44.
91. In an editorial comment in *Letters of Oscar Wilde*, p. 281.
92. Fr Sebastian Bowden, letter of 15 Apr. 1878 (Clark Collection).
93. 'When a young man says not in polished banter, but in sober earnestness that he finds it difficult to live up to the level of his blue china, there has crept into these cloistered shades a form of heathenism which it is our bounden duty to fight against and to crush out, if possible': sermon by Dean Burgen, printed in *New York Tribune*, 8 Jan. 1882, during Wilde's American tour.
94. W. Hamilton, *The Aesthetic Movement in England* (London: Beeves & Turner, 1882), p. 97.
95. Ibid., p. 100.
96. Ibid., p. 99.
97. Ibid., p. 105.
98. Ibid., p. 108.
99. Ibid., p. 111.
100. Ibid.
101. Ibid., p. 123.
102. Ibid., p. 124.
103. Yeats, *Autobiographies*, p. 138.
104. Ibid., p. 139.
105. Gide, *Oscar Wilde*, p. 45.
106. Gide, *Si le grain ne meurt* (*If It Die*, trans. D. Bussy, Harmondsworth: Penguin, 1977), p. 274.
107. Ibid., p. 279.
108. Gide, *Les nourritures terrestres* (*Fruits of the Earth*, London: Penguin, 1970), p. 24.
109. Ibid., p. 57.
110. Ibid., pp 18, 80.
111. Ibid., pp 56, 22.
112. *Pall Mall Gazette*, 4 Jan. 1893.
113. See R. Pine, 'The Children of the Waste Land, 1920–30' in *The Dandy and the Herald*, pp 124–65.
114. W. B. Yeats, 'Away', *Fortnightly Review*, Apr. 1902; cf. Ada Leverson's account of Wilde's appearance on the morning of his release from Reading: 'He came in with the dignity of a king returning from exile. . . . His first words were, "Sphinx [Leverson's

nickname], how marvellous of you to know exactly the right hat to wear at seven o'clock in the morning to meet a friend who has been away!"' (*Letters to the Sphinx*, London: Duckworth, 1930, p. 45).

115. Goffmann, *Stigma*, p. 62.
116. A. Symons, 'Villiers de l'Isle Adam', *The Woman's World*, ii, no. 24 (Oct. 1889), pp 657–60.

Chapter 4: Fictions (pp 161–235)

1. Gide, *Oscar Wilde*, p. 38.
2. Ibid., pp 23–4.
3. Ibid., pp 27–8.
4. Charles Baudelaire, *Poems in Prose*, trans. by Arthur Symons (London: Elkin Mathews, 1905), p. 59.
5. Mercier, *Irish Comic Tradition*, p. 1.
6. Ibid.
7. E. San Juan, *The Art of Oscar Wilde* (Princeton, NJ: Princeton University Press, 1967), p. 12.
8. See the anonymous reviews of *A House of Pomegranates* in *Pall Mall Gazette* (30 Nov. 1891), *Saturday Review* (6 Feb. 1892) and *Athenaeum* (6 Feb. 1892).
9. Yeats, *Autobiographies*, p. 135.
10. W. B. Yeats, 'Irish Folk Tales', *National Observer*, 28 Feb. 1891.
11. Ibid.
12. A. Symons, review of *Intentions*, *Speaker*, iv, no. 24 (4 July 1891).
13. W. Stevens, 'A High-Toned Old Christian Woman' in *Collected Poems of Wallace Stevens* (London: Faber & Faber, 1955), p. 59.
14. W. B. Yeats, introduction to *Representative Irish Tales* (London: Putnam, 1891), p. 25.
15. Quoted in Sartre, *Saint Genet*, p. 135.
16. Cahalan, *The Irish Novel*, p. 15.
17. Cahalan, *Great Hatred, Little Room*, p. 15.
18. Fallis, *The Irish Renaissance*, p. 156.
19. Foster, *Fictions of the Irish Literary Revival*, p. xiv.
20. McCormack, *Ascendancy and Tradition*, p. 1.
21. Goffmann, *Stigma*, p. 65.
22. Ibid., p. 74.
23. Genet, *The Thief's Journal*, p. 89.
24. Quoted in Ellmann, *Oscar Wilde*, p. 532.
25. I am indebted to Margaret MacCurtain, in the course of a lecture on 'The Mystic, the Artist and the Pursuit of Enlightenment' delivered at the Peacock Theatre, Dublin, on 2 September 1993, for this observation.
26. Gide, op. cit., pp 28–9.
27. W. B. Yeats, 'Ireland Bewitched', *Contemporary Review*, Sept. 1899.

28. W. B. Yeats, *Collected Plays* (London: Macmillan, 1952), p. 88.
29. Goffmann, op. cit., p. 110.
30. Kohl, *Oscar Wilde*, p. 60.
31. On Wilde's sources see Cohen, *Moral Vision of Oscar Wilde*, pp 96–102.
32. Lady Wilde, *Ancient Legends*, pp 87–8.
33. Lady Wilde, *Poems*, pp 186–7.
34. Ibid., pp 182–3. Gary Schmidgall, *The Stranger Wilde: Interpreting Oscar* (New York: Dutton, 1994), p. 163, confirms my point about the secrecy of the sexual deviant with his remark *re* 'The Fisherman and his Soul': 'It is not stretching credulity, I think, to imagine the story's Sea-folk as representative of homosexuals.'
35. Donoghue, *We Irish*, p. 22.
36. Quoted by Augustine Martin in his introduction to J. Stephens, *The Charwoman's Daughter* (Dublin: Gill & Macmillan, 1972), p. 4.
37. Gide, op. cit.
38. Stephens, *The Charwoman's Daughter*, p. 50.
39. Ibid., p. 87.
40. Stephens, *The Demi-Gods* (Dublin: Butler Sims, 1982), pp 46–7.
41. Ibid., p. 78.
42. In error, I stated in *Oscar Wilde* (1983) that this reading took place after the première of *Lady Windermere's Fan* in 1892.
43. 'Cheiro' [Count Louis Hamon], *Memoirs* (London: Rider, 1912), p. 57.
44. Kohl, op. cit., p. 91.
45. Ibid., p. 31.
46. Donoghue, op.cit., pp 142–3.
47. But Isobel Murray in her edition of *PDG* (pp 243–4) discusses the claims of other works to provide this model.
48. S. Beckett, interview with Tom Driver, *Columbia University Forum*, 1961, quoted in Kearney (ed.), *The Irish Mind*, p. 288.
49. *Daily Chronicle*, 30 June 1890.
50. Cf. Lloyd, *Nationalism and Minor Literature*, p. x: 'The power of nationalism lies in its countering of an imperial model of identity, for which the colonized represents a primitive stage in a universal history of civilization whose apex is the colonizing power, with another, formally similar model that seeks to forge an oppositional identity from within.'
51. 'The Woman On Whom God Laid His Hand' in P. Ó Conaire, *The Woman at the Window and other stories* (Dublin: Talbot Press, n.d. [1921]), p. 126.
52. See Ellmann, *Oscar Wilde*, p. 132.
53. San Juan, op. cit., pp 24–5.
54. Ibid., p. 48.
55. Cohen, op. cit., p. 11.
56. D. Bush, *Mythology and the Romantic Tradition in English Poetry* (New York: Norton, 1963), p. 418; see also *CPB* 35.

57. W. H. Auden, 'Lullaby', *Collected Poems* (London: Faber & Faber 1976), p. 131.
58. T. d'Arch Smith, *Love in Earnest* (London: Routledge, Kegan Paul, 1970), p. 31.
59. A. Raffalovich, *Tuberose and Meadowsweet* (London: Bogue, 1885), p. 119.
60. John Gray, the title of his poem, derived from 2 Samuel, describing the love of David and Jonathan, quoted in d'Arch Smith, op. cit., p. 187.
61. Ibid., pp 163–96.
62. Ibid. p. 50.
63. Steiner, *Extraterritorial*, p. 16.
64. P. F. Behrendt, *Oscar Wilde: Eros and Aesthetics* (Houndmills: Macmillan, 1991), p. 23.
65. *Le captif amoureux*: the title of Genet's later autobiography, published in English as *The Prisoner of Love*.
66. Yeats, *Collected Plays*, p. 281.
67. Coakley, *Oscar Wilde: The Importance of Being Irish*, pp 210–11, draws attention to the possible influence of Denis Florence McCarthy's 'A New Year's Song' on *The Ballad of Reading Gaol* and develops the notion of Wilde's place in Irish 'prison literature', which includes Mitchel's *Jail Journal* and Behan's *The Quare Fellow* (ibid., p. 212).
68. E. A. Poe, *The Raven* (London: Redway, 1885), p. 17.
69. Lady Wilde, *Ancient Legends*, pp 151, 157.
70. Yeats, *Mythologies*, p. 336.
71. Ibid., pp 365–6.
72. Sartre, op. cit., p. 276.
73. M. Praz, *The Romantic Agony* (Oxford: Oxford University Press, 1933/1951/1970).
74. The term used by homosexuals for 'normal' persons whose 'special situation has made them privy to the secret life of the stigmatised individual and sympathetic with it' and to respect their 'moral career' (Goffman, op. cit., p. 86).

Chapter 5: Dramas (pp 236–281)
1. We should be conscious of Mercier's admonition in *Modern Irish Literature*, p. 86: 'If the term "Revival" or "Renaissance" is to have any validity as a metaphor, those who accept and use it need first of all to be convinced that what is revived or reborn did once enjoy an independent existence of significant dimensions.'
2. Sartre, *Saint Genet*, p. 124.
3. G. Steiner, *Antigones* (Oxford: Clarendon Press, 1986), p. 234.
4. See A. Ganz, 'The Dandiacal Drama: A Study of the Plays of Oscar Wilde' (unpublished Ph.D. thesis, Columbia University, 1957), discussed in Kohl, *Oscar Wilde*, p. 206.

5. L. G. Zatlin, *Aubrey Beardsley and Victorian Sexual Politics* (Oxford: Clarendon Press, 1991), p. 151.
6. H. James, *The Princess Casamassima* (Harmondsworth: Penguin, 1977), p. 319.
7. M. Ó hAodha, *Theatre in Ireland* (Oxford: Blackwell, 1974), p. 74: he is specifically discussing the drama of T. C. Murray, 'the first realistic dramatist to write tragedies of rural life from the inside'.
8. Worth, *Oscar Wilde*, p. 155.
9. See M. Meisel, *Shaw and the Nineteenth-Century Theater* (Princeton, NJ: Princeton University Press, 1968), p. 13.
10. See ibid., p. 184.
11. Ibid., p. 431.
12. Ellmann, *Oscar Wilde*, p. 117.
13. See Bird, *Plays of Oscar Wilde*, p. 20.
14. W. H. Auden, quoted in Worth, op. cit., p. 181.
15. Archer wrote (in defence of *Salomé*) of Wilde's 'unique' talent (*Pall Mall Gazette*, 1 July 1892); Shaw, writing of *An Ideal Husband*, declared Wilde's plays are 'unique' (*Saturday Review*, 12 Jan. 1895).
16. W. Archer on *A Woman of No Importance*, *World*, 26 Apr. 1893.
17. Worth, op. cit., p. 54.
18. K. Worth, *The Irish Drama of Europe from Yeats to Beckett* (London: Athlone Press, 1978), chs 3 and 6 *passim*.
19. See Bird, op. cit., p. 186.
20. Worth, *Oscar Wilde*, p. 14.
21. Meisel, op. cit., pp 397, 414–15.
22. R. D. Laing, *The Politics of Experience* (Harmondsworth: Penguin, 1967), p. 95.
23. This source was first identified by David Krause in his introduction to *The Dolmen Boucicault* (Dublin: Dolmen Press, 1964).
24. Morgan, *Wild Irish Girl*, p. 230.
25. A. B. Walkley, review of *The Importance of Being Earnest*, *Speaker*, 23 Feb. 1895.
26. Ibid.
27. In his preface to *A Short History of Irish Literature* (London: Hutchinson, 1986) Seamus Deane refers to 'the enabling fictions which win for [the Irish experience] the necessary degree of acceptance' (p. 7).
28. Walkley, loc. cit.
29. *Saturday Review*, 12 Jan. 1895.
30. D. Boucicault, *A Lover by Proxy: a comedietta in one act* (London: Webster, n.d. [1842]), p. 13.
31. Quoted in Worth, *Irish Drama of Europe*, p. 81.
32. Deane, *Short History of Irish Literature*, p. 7.
33. Ibid., p. 8.
34. Lady Wilde, *Ancient Legends*, pp 205–6.
35. Deane, op. cit., p. 130.

36. Meisel, op. cit., p. 177.
37. H. A. Jones, *The Renascence of the English Drama* (London: Macmillan, 1895), p. 24.
38. Quoted in L. Edel, *Henry James: The Conquest of London, 1870–1881* (London: Hart-Davis, 1962).
39. H. James, *Letters*, ed. L. Edel (Cambridge, Mass.: Harvard University Press, 1974), i, 233.
40. Quoted in Bird, op. cit., p. 164.
41. *Phoenician Women*, trans. E. Wyckoff, in *Complete Greek Tragedies*, ed. D. Grene and R. Lattimore (Chicago: University of Chicago Press [1992 reprint]), iv, 524–5.
42. Bird, op. cit., p. 149.
43. San Juan, *The Art of Oscar Wilde*, p. 143.
44. Bird, op. cit., p. 123.
45. Interview with Gilbert Burgess, *Sketch*, 9 Jan. 1895.
46. Ibid.
47. Ibid.
48. Pearson, *Oscar Wilde*, p. 252.
49. R. B. Sheridan, *The Rivals*, Act 1, scene 1, line 54.
50. Ibid., Act 1, scene 2, line 206.
51. Ibid., Act 4, scene 2, lines 135–7.
52. Ibid., line 105.
53. Ibid., lines 94–8.
54. R. B. Sheridan, *The School for Scandal*, Act 1, scene 1, line 23.
55. Ibid., Act 2, scene 2, lines 24–5.
56. Ibid., Act 1, scene 1, lines 150–54.
57. Quoted by S. Deane, 'Remembering the Irish Future', *The Crane Bag*, viii, no. 1 (1984), p. 90. In 'Envoi', his introduction to Rennell Rodd's *Rose Leaf and Apple Leaf* (New York: Stoddart, 1982), Wilde spoke of 'the metaphysical mind of Asia'.
58. Lady Wilde, *Social Studies*, p. 1.
59. W. B. Yeats in *Bookman*, Mar. 1896.
60. Meisel, op. cit., p. 3.
61. Ibid., p. 290.
62. T. Kilroy, 'Theatrical Text and Literary Text' in A. Peacock (ed.), *The Achievement of Brian Friel* (Gerrards Cross: Colin Smythe, 1993), p. 91.
63. Ibid.
64. As Steiner calls man in an essay of that title included in *Extraterritorial* (pp 66–109).
65. Steiner, *Antigones*, pp 231–2.
66. Cf. ibid, p. 69: 'The very act of translation is a crucial moment in a larger design. The ideal is that of fusion, of a homecoming (tragically frustrated) to oneness between consciousness and the world.'
67. Ibid., p. 235.

68. *Agamemnon*, trans. R. Lattimore, *Complete Greek Tragedies*, i, line 16.
69. Ibid., line 502.
70. Ibid., line 1378.
71. *Herakles*, trans. W. Arrowsmith, *Complete Greek Tragedies*, iii, line 1405.
72. *Phoenician Women*, line 626.
73. Ibid., line 406.
74. See *Agamemnon*, line 535.
75. See *Herakles*, introduction by W. Arrowsmith, op. cit., p. 271.
76. Ibid., p. 274.
77. Ibid., pp 275–6.
78. *Herakles*, line 318.
79. Ibid., line 1027.
80. W. B. Yeats, *Letters*, (London: Hart–Davis, 1954), p. 562.
81. 'Michael Field', *Works and Days*, quoted in Worth, *Irish Drama of Europe*, p. 39.
82. J. C. Mangan, 'My Bugle and How I Blow It', *Belfast Vindicator*, 27 Mar. 1841, quoted in Lloyd, *Nationalism and Minor Literature*, p. 196.
83. Quoted in Lloyd, op. cit., p. 203.
84. H. G. Zagona, *The Legend of Salome and the Principle of Art for Art's Sake* (Geneva: Droz, 1960).
85. Worth, *Irish Drama of Europe*, p. 113.
86. Sartre, op. cit., p. 236.
87. *L'homme dominé*, title by Albert Memmi (Paris: Gallimard, 1968).
88. *Punch*, 24 Nov. 1894.
89. W. Archer, 'Mr Oscar Wilde's New Play', *Black and White*, 11 May 1893.
90. Saltus, *Oscar Wilde: An Idler's Impression*, p. 20.
91. K. Powell's article was originally published in *English Literature in Transition* (vol. xxviii, no. 3, 1985) and enlarged and reprinted in K. Powell, *Oscar Wilde and the Theatre of the 1890s* (Cambridge: Cambridge University Press, 1990); I have quoted from the original article, p. 230.
92. Ibid.
93. *Times*, 23 Feb. 1893.
94. Quoted in Pearson, op. cit., p. 238.
95. San Juan, op. cit., p. 76.
96. Worth, *Irish Drama of Europe*, p. 10.

Chapter 6: The Third Meaning (pp 282–312)
1. *Spectator*, 7 Feb. 1891.
2. Barthes, *Image, Music, Text*, pp 52–68.
3. *Hellenism* (Edinburgh: Tragara Press, 1979), p. 5.
4. Ibid, p. 7.

5. Ibid.
6. Ibid., p. 12.
7. Ibid., p. 8.
8. Ibid.
9. Steiner, *Antigones*, p. 133.
10. G. Steiner, *After Babel: aspects of language and translation* (Oxford: Oxford University Press, 1975), p. 454.
11. G. Steiner, *Real Presences* (London: Faber & Faber, 1989).
12. Steiner, *Antigones*, p. 135.
13. Pater, *The Renaissance*, p. 253: 'for art comes to you proposing frankly to give nothing but the highest quality to your moments as they pass, and simply for those moments' sake'.
14. Quoted in Ellmann, *Oscar Wilde*, p. 164.
15. *Woman's World*, i, no. 1 (Nov. 1887), pp 7–10.
16. Lady Wilde, 'Historic Women', ibid, i, no. 3 (Jan. 1888); 'Irish Peasant Tales', ibid, ii, no. 13 (Nov. 1888).
17. M. G. Fawcett, 'Women's Suffrage', ibid., ii, no. 13 (Nov. 1888).
18. Theresa Shrewsbury, 'Our Girl Workers', ibid., i, no. 4 (Feb. 1888).
19. Julia, Lady Jersey, 'Sybil's Dilemma', ibid., i, no. 6 (Apr. 1888).
20. Lady Dorothy Nevill, 'Some Recollections of Cobden', ibid., i, no. 8 (June 1888).
21. Countess of Cork and Orrery, 'The King of the Birds' [the wren], ibid., ii, no. 20 (June 1889).
22. Lady Munster, 'A "Mauvais Quart d'Heure"', ibid., ii, no. 20 (June 1889).
23. Viscountess Herberton, 'Mourning Clothes and Customs', ibid., ii, no. 20 (June 1889).
24. Carmen Sylva, 'A Queen's Thoughts', ibid., i, no. 11 (Sept. 1888); 'Furnica, or, The Queen of the Ants: A Legend of the Carpathians', ibid., ii, no. 15 (Jan. 1889).
25. Mrs Craik on Mary Anderson's performance in *The Winter's Tale*, ibid., i, no. 2 (Dec. 1887).
26. Ouida, 'Dinner-giving', ibid., i, no. 5 (Mar. 1888); 'The Streets of London', ibid., i, no. 11 (Sept. 1888); 'War', ibid., ii, no. 16 (Feb. 1889); 'Field-Work for Women', ibid., ii, no. 19 (May 1889).
27. O. Schreiner, 'The Lost' (short story), ibid., i, no. 4 (Feb. 1888); short story (untitled), ibid., ii, no. 13 (Nov. 1888); 'Life's Gifts' (parable), ibid., ii, no. 20 (June 1889).
28. V. Fane, 'The Stuart Dynasty', ibid., i, no. 7 (May 1888).
29. M. Corelli, 'Shakespeare's Mother', ibid., ii, no. 20 (June 1889).
30. A. Symons, 'Charity' (poem), ibid., ii, no. 11 (Sept. 1888).
31. O. Browning, 'Bournemouth' (poem), ibid., ii, no. 16 (Feb. 1889).
32. B. Roosevelt, 'Guy de Maupassant', ibid., ii, no. 13 (Nov. 1888).
33. G. Sarrazin, review of Georges Ohnet, ibid., ii, no. 16 (Feb. 1889).
34. Mme Cadiot de Praz, 'Pierre Loti and his Works', ibid., ii, no. 21 (July 1889).

35. J. S. Campbell, 'The Woodland Gods', ibid., i, no. 1 (Nov. 1887).
36. J. E. Harrison, 'The Pictures of Sappho', ibid., i, no. 6 (Apr. 1888).
37. Emily Crawford, 'Women Wearers of Men's Clothes', ibid., ii, no. 18 (Apr. 1889).
38. *Pall Mall Gazette*, 17 Feb. 1887.
39. Ibid.
40. H. Thoreau, 'On Civil Disobedience' in *Essays and other writings* (London: Scott, 1893), p. 86.
41. Cf. Lawrence Durrell, *Key to Modern British Poetry* (London: Nevill, 1952), pp 28–9: 'Einstein's time was not a past–present–future object. . . . It was a sort of time which contained all time in every moment of time.'
42. D. Kiberd, report (*Irish Times*, 29 June 1993) of a lecture delivered to the Synge Summer School; discussed more fully in D. Kiberd, 'The Fall of the Stage Irishman' in R. Scheifer (ed.), *Genres of the Irish Literary Revival* (Dublin: Wolfhound, 1980).
43. Steiner, *Antigones*, p. 104.
44. Shaw's likely influence on the genesis of *The Soul of Man under Socialism* has been documented: as early as 1888 it was noted by *The Star* (7 July 1888) that Wilde and Shaw attended a lecture by Walter Crane on 'The Prospects of Art under Socialism' at which both Irishmen spoke. Shaw later recalled: 'Robert Ross surprised me greatly by telling me, long after Oscar's death, that it was this address of mine that moved Oscar to try his hand at a similar feat by writing "The Soul of Man under Socialism"' ('My Memories of Oscar Wilde', published as a separately paginated appendix to Frank Harris, *Oscar Wilde: his life and confessions* (New York: published by author, 1918), ii, 10–11).
45. See G. V. Plekhanov, *Anarchism and Socialism*, trans. E. M. Aveling (London: Twentieth Century Press, 1906).
46. Quoted in Edel, *Henry James: The Conquest of London, 1870–1881*, p. 39.
47. Renan, *Poetry of the Celtic Races*, p. 60.
48. Christine, Lady Longford, *Mr Jiggins of Jigginstown*, quoted in A. Martin, 'Anglo-Irish Literature' in M. Hurley (ed.), *Irish Anglicanism, 1869–1969* (Dublin: Figgis, 1970), p. 124.
49. 'Hyper-reality': Umberto Eco's *Faith in Fakes* (London: Secker, 1986) was originally published as *Travels in Hyper-Reality*.
50. R. Barthes, *Mythologies* (London: Cape, 1972), p. 151.
51. Ibid., p. 155.
52. Meisel, *Shaw and the Nineteenth-Century Theater*, p. 291.
53. Sartre, *Saint Genet*, p. 181.
54. Barthes, *Image, Music, Text*, p. 61.
55. Ibid., pp 33, 61.
56. Ibid., p. 63.
57. Ibid., p. 142.

58. Barthes, *Mythologies*, p. 123.
59. Ibid., pp 125, 129.
60. R. Barthes, *Writing Degree Zero* (London: Cape, 1967), p. 24.
61. Ibid., p. 16.
62. Ibid., p. 72.
63. Ibid., p. 13.
64. Mercier, *Irish Comic Tradition*, p. 47.
65. Ibid., p. 48.
66. Ibid., p. 86.

Chapter 7: The Parallel Decades (pp 315–353)

1. *National Observer*, 6 Apr. 1895.
2. *somdomite*: this word was inadvertently corrected in my *Oscar Wilde* (1983) to read '"sodomite" [sic]'. Richard Ellmann states somewhat cryptically (*Oscar Wilde*, p. xii) that 'R. E. Alton deciphered for the first time the message on Queensberry's visiting card which set off the libel suit', but the correct reading first appeared in print in John Stokes, *Oscar Wilde* (London: British Council, 1978). Although the card was reproduced in H. M. Hyde, *The Trials of Oscar Wilde* (Harmondsworth: Penguin, 1962) and on the endpapers of Hyde's *Oscar Wilde* (1976), Hyde himself misquotes it in both books (p. 46 and p. 196 respectively); Mary Hyde (*Bernard Shaw and Alfred Douglas: A Correspondence* (London: John Murray, 1982), p. xiv) asserts that Queensberry took legal advice before using this form of words.
3. Quoted in Ellmann, *Oscar Wilde*, p. 186.
4. Quoted ibid., p. 378. Likewise, most probably in imitation of Wilde, Shaw said: 'England had conquered Ireland; so there was nothing for it but to come over and conquer England' (in a letter to St John Ervine, quoted in M. Holroyd, *Bernard Shaw* (London: Chatto & Windus, 1988), i, 60); cf. also W. B. Yeats: 'Berkeley, Swift ... Goldsmith ... Burke ... found in England the opposite that stung their own thought into expression and made it lucid.' (*Essays and Introductions*, p. 402)
5. See R. Pine, 'Ireland as a State of Mind' in *Lawrence Durrell: The Mindscape* (Houndmills: Macmillan, 1994), pp 274–91.
6. See Pine, *The Dandy and the Herald*, pp 142–6.
7. Housman, *Echo de Paris*, p. 22.
8. *Punch*, 12 Feb. 1881. In the same year (2 May 1881) *Punch* stated, as directly as was possible at that time, that 'there are reasons for believing that an eminent physician, a leading QC, MP... and the genial and deservedly popular Head Master of one of our most ancient scholastic establishments will retire immediately from the labours of their professions': this must represent one of the earliest forms of 'outing'.
9. Article by Courtenay Bodley, *New York Times*, 21 Jan. 1882.

10. *Truth*, 19 July 1883.
11. Quoted in Ellmann, *Oscar Wilde*, p. 169.
12. Edel, *Life of Henry James*, i, 649.
13. Edmond de Goncourt, journal entry for 5 May 1883.
14. Quoted in Elizabeth Longford, *A Pilgrimage of Passion: the life of Wilfrid Scawen Blunt* (London: Weidenfeld & Nicolson, 1979), pp 290–91; see Pine, *Oscar Wilde*, pp 80–81, for Beerbohm's gossip in letters to Reginald Turner and in his satiric memoir *A Peep into the Past*.
15. *Adam International Review*, xxii, nos 241–3 (1954), pp vii–viii.
16. *Scots Observer*, 5 July 1890. Schmidgall, *The Stranger Wilde*, p. 91, quotes Constance Wilde: 'Since Oscar wrote *Dorian Gray*, no one will speak to us.'
17. W. B. Yeats, *Prefaces and Introductions* (London: Macmillan, 1989), p. 150.
18. S. Deane, 'Political Writings and Speeches, 1850–1918' in *Field Day anthology*, ii, 209–14.
19. Ibid., 210.
20. Ibid., p. 214. Wilde attended the sessions of the Parnell Commission and had several volumes of the proceedings in his library.
21. J. McCarthy, *Reminiscences* (London: Chatto & Windus, 1899), i, ch. 8: 'The Exile-World of London', pp 117–62.
22. Ibid., p. 125.
23. Lady Wilde, *Social Studies*, pp 59–60.
24. W. P. Ryan, *The Irish Literary Revival: its history, pioneers and possibilities* (London: published by the author, 1894), pp 119–20.
25. D. Kiberd, 'The London Exiles: Wilde and Shaw' in *Field Day anthology*, ii, 372–91.
26. See Pine, *The Dandy and the Herald*.
27. Ellmann, *Oscar Wilde*, p. xiv.
28. *Omaha Weekly Herald*, 24 Mar. 1882.
29. Quoted in Ellmann, *Oscar Wilde*, p. 322.
30. 'I remember that I spoke that night of Wilde's kindness to myself, said I did not believe him guilty... described Wilde's hard brilliance, his dominating self-possession. I considered him essentially a man of action, that he was a writer by perversity and accident, and would have been more important as soldier or politician; and I was certain that, guilty or not guilty, he would prove himself a man.' (*Autobiographies*, p. 285)
31. M. Nordau, *Degeneration* (London: Heinemann, 1895), p. 245.
32. Ibid.
33. Lytton, *Pelham*, p. 94.
34. A. Symons, 'The Decadent Movement in Literature', *Harper's Monthly*, Nov. 1893.
35. A. Symons, *The Symbolist Movement in Literature* (London: Heinemann, 1899), p. 8; his reference (p. 6) to symbolism as 'a

literature in which the visible world is no longer a reality and the unseen world no longer a dream', contemporaneous with (and highly influenced by) Yeats's aesthetic views, is distinguished as a significant midway point between Wilde's lecture on 'The English Renaissance in Art' and twentieth-century literary applications of symbolism.

36. H. Jackson, *The Eighteen Nineties* (London: Grant Richards, 1913), p. 57.
37. De Vere, *English Misrule and Irish Misdeeds*, pp 50–51.
38. Ibid.
39. Ibid., pp 51–2.
40. Ibid., p. 52; cf. a telling perception of Shaw as having 'the face of an outlaw, of one at war with life, customs...full of protest: wild and determined, a very brigand of a face' (quoted in Holroyd, op. cit., p. 94).
41. De Vere, op. cit., p. 152.
42. Ibid., p. 209.
43. Ibid.
44. Ibid., p. 5.
45. Nordau, op. cit., p. vii.
46. Ibid., p. viii.
47. R. Gagnier, *Idylls of the Marketplace: Oscar Wilde and the Victorian public* (London: Scolar Press, 1987), p. 7.
48. Ibid., p. 19.
49. Ibid., p. 129.
50. E. Newman, 'Oscar Wilde: A Literary Appreciation', *Free Review*, 1 June 1895.
51. G. B. Shaw, *Collected Letters, 1874–1897*, ed. D. Laurence (London: Reinhardt, 1965), p. 210.
52. W. B. Yeats, 'Oscar Wilde's Last Book', *United Irishman*, 26 Sept. 1891.
53. Worth, *Oscar Wilde*, p. 20.
54. G. B. Shaw, 'The Sanity of Art' in *Collected Works* (London: Constable, 1930), xix, 320.
55. Ibid., pp 339–40. Shaw echoed the twin statements by Wilde with which this chapter commenced: 'I found that I had only to say with perfect simplicity what I seriously meant just as it struck me, to make everybody laugh. My method is to take the utmost trouble to find the right thing to say, and then to say it with the utmost levity. And all the time the real joke is that I am in earnest.' (Quoted in Holroyd, op. cit., p. 133)
56. Ibid., p. 346.
57. G. B. Shaw, 'The Quintessence of Ibsenism' in *Collected Works*, xix, 125.
58. Ibid., p. 130.
59. Ibid.
60. Shaw, 'Sanity of Art', p. 314.

61. C. Lombroso, *The Man of Genius* (London: Contemporary Science Series, 1891), pp 314–17.
62. Ibid., p. 317.
63. Ibid., p. 318.
64. Ibid., p. 322.
65. Ibid., p. 317.
66. Ibid., p. 319.
67. Quoted in Ellmann, *Oscar Wilde*, p. 402.
68. O. Browning: letter quoted in Ian Anstruther, *Oscar Browning: a biography* (London: Murray, 1983), p. 59.
69. O. Browning, *Paederastia Apologia*, quoted ibid., p. 60.
70. Hyde, *Trials of Oscar Wilde*, p. 201.
71. Nordau, op. cit., p. 295.
72. Ibid., p. 18.
73. Ibid., p. 320.
74. See H. M. Hyde, *The Cleveland Street Scandal* (London: W. H. Allen, 1976).
75. H. Pearson, *Labby: the life of Henry Labouchere* (London: Hamish Hamilton, 1936), p. 76.
76. 'Step-children of nature': Krafft-Ebing, *Psychopathia Sexualis*, 12th ed. (New York: Paperback Library, 1965), p. 383.
77. J. A. Symonds to Horatio Brown, 22 July 1890 (*Letters and Papers of John Addington Symonds* (London: John Murray, 1923), p. 240).
78. J. A. Symonds, *Studies of the Greek Poets* [first series], (London: Smith, Elder, 1873), p. 408.
79. E. M. Forster, *Maurice* (Harmondsworth: Penguin, 1971), p. 67.
80. Ibid., p. 139.
81. Raffalovich, *L'Affaire Oscar Wilde*. The Archbishop of Canterbury was very disturbed by his son's involvement with the Wilde circle and sought a safe way of removing him from Wilde's influence, hoping he might become a clergyman or a solicitor (evidence in a letter to M. R. James, Cambridge University Library, MS Add. 7481/B171); it is thus not entirely accurate to state, as Brian Masters does in his *Life of E. F. Benson* (London: Chatto & Windus, 1991, p. 114), that 'there is no evidence whatever that the scandal which consumed Oscar Wilde and Fred's friend Lord Alfred Douglas in 1895 reverberated within the walls of Lambeth Palace, although it would be impossible to believe that they [Benson's parents] never discussed it'.
82. Raffalovich, op. cit.
83. Queensberry, letter to *The Star*, 25 Apr. 1895.
84. T. M. Healy, *Letters and Leaders of My Day* (London: Butterworth, 1928), ii, 416–17; see Pine, *Oscar Wilde*, pp 107–8.
85. Symonds, *Greek Poets* [first series], p. 419.
86. Symonds, *Greek Poets*, second series, p. 419.
87. Symonds, *Greek Poets*, [first series], p. 410.

88. Symonds, *A Problem in Greek Ethics*.
89. *The Chameleon*, Dec. 1894.
90. Symonds, *A Problem in Greek Ethics*.
91. W. Whitman, 'Song of Myself', stanza 50, in *Leaves of Grass* (Harmondsworth: Penguin, 1976), p. 84.
92. Krafft-Ebing, op. cit., pp 187–8.
93. Ibid., pp 221–3.
94. H. Ellis, *Studies in the Psychology of Sex* (London: Heinemann, 1936), i, pt 4, p. 49.
95. Ibid.
96. Lord A. Douglas, *Autobiography* (London: Secker, 1929), p. 28.
97. Mary Hyde (ed.), *Bernard Shaw and Alfred Douglas: A Correspondence*, p. 80.

Chapter 8: Yeats's Transitus (pp 354–380)
1. J. B. Yeats, *Letters to his son W. B. Yeats and others, 1869–1922* (New York: Dutton, 1946), p. 150.
2. Unpublished draft of *Autobiography*, quoted in Ellmann, *Eminent Domain*, pp 12–13.
3. McCormack, *Ascendancy and Tradition*, pp 324, 364.
4. Yeats, *Poems*, p. 255.
5. Yeats's diary of 1930, quoted in Donoghue, *We Irish*, p. 77.
6. Yeats to Lady Elizabeth Pelham, 4 Jan. 1939 (*Letters of W. B. Yeats* (London: Hart-Davis, 1954) p. 922).
7. L. McNeice, *The Poetry of W. B. Yeats* (London: Faber & Faber, 1967), p. 51.
8. Yeats, *Mythologies*, p. 331.
9. Curtis Bradford, *Yeats at Work* (Carbondale, Ill.: Southern Illinois University Press, 1965), p. 215.
10. I have been unable to trace the origin of this remark, which I heard in quotation at a lecture at the Yeats Summer School, Sligo.
11. Yeats, preface to Lady Gregory, *Gods and Fighting Men* (London: Murray, 1904).
12. Yeats, *Letters*, p. 551.
13. Yeats, *Poems*, p. 289.
14. Yeats, *Autobiographies*, p. 349.
15. Yeats, *Poems*, 000
16. Yeats, *Poems*, pp 160–63.
17. Ibid.
18. Yeats, preface to Lady Gregory, *Cuchulain of Muirthemne* (London: Murray, 1902).
19. Yeats, *Mythologies*, p. 331.
20. Yeats, *Autobiographies*, p. 263.
21. Ibid., p. 89.
22. Ibid.

23. Yeats, *Poems*, p. 162.
24. Ibid., p. 164.
25. W. B. Yeats, *A Vision* (London: Macmillan, 1961), p. 68.
26. Yeats, *Autobiographies*, p. 345.
27. Yeats, 'Crazy Jane Talks with the Bishop', *Poems*, pp 259–60.
28. Yeats, *Autobiographies*, p. 346.
29. W. B. Yeats, 'Ireland and the Arts', originally published in the *United Irishman*, 31 Aug. 1901, and reprinted in *Ideas of Good and Evil* (London: Bullen, 1903).
30. T. Davis, *Literary and Historical Essays* (Dublin: Duffy, 1846), p. 163.
31. Yeats, *Essays and Introductions*, p. 204.
32. Yeats, *Poems*, p. 289.
33. Yeats, *Autobiographies*, p. 482.
34. D. G. Wright, *Yeats's Myth of Self: a study of the autobiographical prose* (Dublin: Gill & Macmillan, 1987), pp 2, 6, 7.
35. W. B. Yeats, 'The Prisoners of the Gods', *Nineteenth Century*, Jan. 1898.
36. Yeats, preface to Gregory, *Gods and Fighting Men*.
37. Yeats, preface to Gregory, *Cuchulain of Muirthemne*.
38. W. B. Yeats, introduction to *Fairy and Folk Tales of the Irish Peasantry* (London: Camelot Classics, 1888).
39. W. B. Yeats, 'Tales from the Twilight', *Scots Observer*, 1 Mar. 1890; the expression recurs in *The Celtic Twilight* (London: Lawrence & Bullen, 1893).
40. Ibid.
41. W. B. Yeats, 'Irish Folk Tales', *National Observer*, 28 Feb. 1891.
42. Ibid.
43. Ibid. Yeats's affinity with Wilde's achievement in his folk-tales and fairy stories becomes further evident in his statement 'All the great masters have understood that there cannot be great art without the little limited life of the fable.' (*Essays and Introductions*, p. 216)
44. Yeats, preface to Gregory, *Gods and Fighting Men*.
45. Ibid.
46. Yeats, *Autobiographies*, pp 194–5.
47. Ellmann, *The Uses of Decadence: Wilde, Yeats, Joyce* (Bennington, Vermont: Bennington College, 1983), pp 19–20.
48. W. B. Yeats, *Autobiography* (1965), quoted in Ellmann, *Eminent Domain*, p. 14.
49. W. B. Yeats, *On the Boiler* (Dublin: Cuala, 1937), p. 37.
50. See Ellmann, *Eminent Domain*, pp 20, 130.
51. *An Claideamh Soluis*, 13 July 1901.
52. Yeats, *Poems*, p. 321.
53. W. B. Yeats, 'The Celtic Element in Literature', *Cosmopolis*, June 1898.
54. Ibid.

55. Ibid.
56. Ibid.
57. Yeats, preface to Villiers de l'Isle Adam, *Axël*, trans. M. G. Rose (Dublin: Dolmen, 1970), p. xiii.
58. A. Clarke, *The Celtic Twilight and the Nineties* (Dublin: Dolmen, 1970), p. 9.
59. Yeats, 'Two Songs from a Play', *Poems*, p. 213.
60. Yeats, 'The Tower', *Poems*, p. 196.
61. Yeats, 'At the Hawk's Well', *Collected Plays*, p. 200.
62. Yeats, *Autobiographies*, p. 165.
63. Ibid., p. 152.
64. Ibid., p. 189.
65. Ibid., p. 464.
66. Ibid., p. 503.
67. G. Steiner, *The Death of Tragedy* (London: Faber & Faber, 1961), p. 321.
68. Ellmann, *Eminent Domain*, p. 21.
69. Yeats, *Collected Plays*, p. 107.
70. Ibid., p. 207.
71. Yeats, *Poems*, p. 193.
72. Ibid., pp 248–9.
73. Worth, *Irish Drama of Europe*, p. 106.
74. Ibid.
75. Ibid., p. 112.
76. Yeats, *Collected Plays*, p. 638.
77. Ibid., p. 167; see Worth, *Irish Drama of Europe*, p. 16.
78. Worth, *Irish Drama of Europe*, p. 159.
79. Yeats, *Poems*, p. 239.
80. Yeats, *Autobiographies*, p. 489.
81. Yeats, 'Belief and Unbelief' in *Celtic Twilight*.
82. Yeats, 'This Country', introduction to *Celtic Twilight*.
83. Yeats, 'An Irish Visionary', *National Observer*, 3 Oct. 1891.
84. Ibid.
85. Ibid. The ambiguous territory between 'queerness' and the Celtic 'otherworld' is further suggested in Yeats's previously quoted essay 'Away', (*Fortnightly Review*, Apr. 1902), where he refers simultaneously to '"the others", or "the fairies", or "the sidhe", or "the forgetful people", as they call the dead and the lesser gods' (loc. cit.).
86. W. B. Yeats, 'New Chapters of the Celtic Twilight', *Speaker*, 15 Mar. 1902.
87. W. B. Yeats, 'The Eaters of Precious Stones' in *Celtic Twilight*.
88. See Yeats, *Autobiographies*, p. 195.
89. See Okifumi Komesu, *The Double Perspective of Yeats's Aesthetics* (Gerrards Cross: Colin Smythe, 1984).
90. Yeats, *A Vision*, p. 25.

91. Komesu, op. cit., p. 8.
92. Yeats, *Autobiographies*, p. 324.
93. W. B. Yeats, 'A Canonical Book', *Bookman*, May 1903.
94. Yeats, *Autobiographies*, p. 295.
95. Ellmann, *Eminent Domain*, p. 18.
96. Yeats, preface to Gregory, *Gods and Fighting Men*.
97. McCormack, *Sheridan Le Fanu*, p. 145.
98. See Pine, *The Dandy and the Herald*, pp 6, 55.
99. Yeats, *Collected Plays*, p. 705.

Chapter 9: The First Modernists (pp 381–404)
1. H. S. Hughes, *Consciousness and Society: the reorientation of European social thought, 1890–1930* (Brighton: Harvester, 1979), p. 34.
2. V. Havel, *Disturbing the Peace* (London: Faber & Faber, 1990), p. 10.
3. M. Bradbury and J. McFarlane, 'The Name and Nature of Modernism' in Bradbury and McFarlane (eds), *Modernism, 1890–1930* (Harmondsworth: Penguin, 1976), p. 20.
4. Barthes, *Writing Degree Zero*, p. 9.
5. See J. Joyce, *A Portrait of the Artist as a Young Man* in H. Levin (ed.), *The Essential James Joyce* (Harmondsworth: Penguin, 1963), p. 211.
6. Ibid., pp 142, 247.
7. Ibid., p. 252.
8. Ibid., p. 247.
9. Ibid., p. 212.
10. Ibid., p. 136.
11. Ibid., p. 213.
12. Ibid., p. 200.
13. Joyce, 'Oscar Wilde', reprinted in *Critical Writings of James Joyce*, ed. Mason and Ellmann.
14. Quoted in R. Ellmann, *James Joyce* (Oxford: Oxford University Press, 1982), p. 102.
15. See R. Ellmann, 'Joyce and Yeats', *Kenyon Review*, xii (1950).
16. Joyce, *A Portrait*, p. 131.
17. Ibid., p. 185.
18. Ibid., p. 184.
19. Ibid., p. 59.
20. Ibid., p. 176.
21. Ibid., pp 59, 61.
22. Ibid., p. 57.
23. Ibid., p. 101.
24. Ibid., p. 116.
25. Ibid., p. 120.
26. Ibid., p. 122.
27. Ibid.

28. Ellmann, *James Joyce*, p. 83; cf. Wilde's statement that 'Every single work of art is the fulfilment of a prophecy. For every work of art is the conversion of an idea into an image' (*L* 481) which underlines his role as a nexus between the imagery of Irish folklore and the Imagism expressed by Pound.
29. Joyce, *A Portrait*, p. 127.
30. Ibid.
31. Ibid., p. 185.
32. Ibid., pp 244–5.
33. L. Durrell, *Tunc* (London: Faber & Faber, 1968), p. 17.
34. Joyce, *A Portrait*, p. 211.
35. Ibid.
36. Ibid., p. 243.
37. Quoted in J. McFarlane, 'The Mind of Modernism' in Bradbury and McFarlane (eds), *Modernism*, p. 71.
38. Barthes, *Writing Degree Zero*, p. 63.
39. See R. Pine, 'The Unreadable Book' and 'Why? The Question of Writing' in *Lawrence Durrell: The Mindscape*, pp 325–75.
40. Quoted in C. Scott, 'Symbolism, Decadence and Impressionism' in Bradbury and McFarlane (eds), *Modernism*, p. 207.
41. Ibid., p. 206.
42. Bradbury and McFarlane, 'Name and Nature of Modernism', p. 49.
43. G. Groddeck, *The Book of the It* (London: Vision Press reprint, 1949), p. 191.
44. J. L. Borges, *A Universal History of Infamy* (Harmondsworth: Penguin, 1990), p. 63.
45. Ibid., p. 50.
46. Quoted in McFarlane, 'Mind of Modernism', pp 81–2.
47. Ibid.
48. N. Sarraute, *Tropisms* (London: Calder, 1963).
49. S. Beckett, *Waiting for Godot* (London: Faber & Faber, 1956), p. 89.
50. T. S. Eliot, '*Ulysses*, Order and Myth', *Dial*, no. 75, (1923).
51. Seamus Heaney and Richard Kearney, 'Borges and the World of Fiction', *The Crane Bag*, vi, no. 2 (1982), p. 75.
52. Ibid., pp 75–6.
53. J. L. Borges, 'About Oscar Wilde' in *Other Inquisitions, 1937–1952* (Austin, Tex.: University of Texas Press, 1964), p. 83.
54. Ibid.
55. Ibid.
56. Ibid.
57. Borges, *Universal History of Infamy*, p. 12.
58. Ibid., p. 15.
59. Ibid., p. 39.
60. Ibid., p. 35.
61. Ibid., p. 81.

62. Ibid., p. 53.
63. Ibid., p. 83.
64. Ibid., p. 62.
65. Ibid., p. 66.
66. A. Maurois, preface to J. L. Borges, *Labyrinths* (Harmondsworth: Penguin, 1970), p. 13.
67. J. E. Irby, introduction, ibid., p. 18.
68. Ibid., p. 282.
69. Quoted in Lord D. Cecil, *Max* (London: Constable, 1964), p. 85.
70. R. Barthes, *A Lover's Discourse* (London: Penguin, 1990), p. 1.
71. Ibid., p. 3.
72. Ibid.
73. Ibid., pp 68, 67.
74. Ibid., p. 71.
75. Ibid., p. 121.
76. Ibid., p. 132.
77. Ibid., p. 122.
78. S. Beckett, 'Film' in *Collected Shorter Plays* (London: Faber & Faber, 1984), p. 161.
79. '*Hypocrite lecteur*' (in the preface to Baudelaire's *Les Fleurs du mal*).
80. Barthes, *Lover's Discourse*, p. 134.
81. Ibid., p. 30.
82. Ibid., p. 55.
83. Ibid., p. 148.
84. Ibid., p. 166.
85. Ibid., p. 93.
86. J. Genet, *The Thief's Journal*, trans. B. Frechtman (London: Penguin, 1967), p. 203.
87. Ibid.
88. Ibid., pp 14–15.
89. Ibid., p. 141.
90. Ibid., p. 63.
91. Ibid., p. 71.
92. Ibid., p. 73.
93. Ibid., p. 98.
94. Ibid., p. 82.
95. Ibid., p. 171.
96. Ibid., p. 170.
97. Ibid., p. 224.
98. Ibid., p. 39.
99. Steiner, *Extraterritorial*, pp 26–7, 72.
100. Genet, op. cit., pp 39, 40.
101. Ibid., p. 94.
102. Ibid.
103. Ibid., pp 94–5.

104. Ibid., p. 89.
105. See R. Kearney, *Modern Movements* (Manchester: Manchester University Press, 1986), p. 52.
106. Steiner, *Extraterritorial*, pp 10, 14.

Conclusion (pp 405–419)

 1. 'Sexual curiosity and metaphysical speculation': L. Durrell, *The Dark Labyrinth* (London: Faber & Faber, 1961), p. 59.
 2. J. Derrida, *Writing and Difference* (Chicago: University of Chicago Press, 1978), p. 67.
 3. This was the title of a seminar held during the inaugural Yeats International Festival at the Peacock Theatre, Dublin, in 1989; the plays performed during the festival were the five based on the Cuchulain legends.
 4. See R. Pine, *Brian Friel and Ireland's Drama* (London: Routledge, 1990), p. 233.
 5. B. Friel, *Selected Plays* (London: Faber & Faber, 1984), p. 27. The division is reminiscent not only of Rimbaud's '*je est un autre*' but also of Wilde's reflection on Lord Illingworth in *A Woman of No Importance*: 'He is a figure of art . . . he is my self.' (quoted in H. Pearson, *Beerbohm Tree: His Life and Laughter* (London: Methuen, 1956), p. 65)
 6. Friel, *Selected Plays*, p. 88.
 7. Ibid., p. 439.
 8. R. Welch, '"Isn't This Your Job? To Translate?": Brian Friel's *Languages*' in A. Peacock (ed.), *The Achievement of Brian Friel* (Gerrards Cross: Colin Smythe, 1993), p. 318.
 9. D. Donoghue, 'Another Complex Fate' in *We Irish*, pp 145–6.
10. Ibid., pp 146–7.
11. McCormack, *Ascendancy and Tradition*, p. 241.
12. De Vere, *English Misrule and Irish Misdeeds*, pp 3ff.
13. A. Memmi, *The Coloniser and the Colonised* (London: Souvenir Press, 1974).
14. T. Paulin, *Ireland and the English Crisis* (Newcastle-upon-Tyne: Bloodaxe, 1984).
15. De Vere, op. cit., p. 31.
16. C. G. Duffy, *Young Ireland: a fragment of Irish history, 1840–1850* (London: Cassell, 1880), p. 153.
17. Lloyd, *Nationalism and Minor Literature*, p. 73.
18. Friel, *Selected Plays*, pp 421–2.
19. A. Brink, *An Instant in the Wind* (London: W. H. Allen, 1976), p. 177.
20. Donoghue, op. cit., pp 8, 16.
21. F. O'Toole, *A Mass for Jesse James: a journey through 1980s Ireland* (Dublin: Raven Arts, 1990), pp 82–3.

22. Mercier, *Modern Irish Literature*, p. 327.
23. M. Eliade, *Le Mythe de l'Eternel Retour* (Paris: Gallimard, 1949).
24. T. Parkinson, 'The Later Plays of W. B. Yeats' in T. Bogard and W. I. Oliver (eds), *Modern Drama: essays in criticism* (New York: Oxford University Press, 1965), p. 388.
25. See Kearney, *Modern Movements*, p. 13.
26. S. Heaney, *An Open Letter*, Field Day Pamphlet no. 2 (Derry: Field Day Theatre Company, 1983), p. 10.
27. Ibid.
28. See Pine, 'Ireland as a State of Mind' in *Lawrence Durrell: The Mindscape*, pp 274–91.
29. Hyde (ed.), *Trials of Oscar Wilde*, p. 202.
30. J. Delay, *The Youth of André Gide* (London: University of Chicago Press, 1963), p. 391.
31. J. C. Mangan, 'Literae Orientales', quoted in Lloyd, op. cit., p. 123.
32. Derrida, *Writing and Difference*, p. 153.
33. E. Said, *Nationalism, Colonialism and Literature: Yeats and decolonization*, Field Day Pamphlet no. 15 (Derry: Field Day Theatre Company, 1988).
34. E. Said, 'Representations of the Intellectual', first Reith Lecture, *The Independent*, 24 June 1993.
35. E. Said, third Reith Lecture, ibid., 8 July 1993.
36. Ibid.
37. Said, ibid., 24 June 1993.
38. Ibid.; he is quoting Seamus Deane on *A Portrait of the Artist as a Young Man* in *Celtic Revivals: essays in modern Irish literature, 1880–1980* (London: Faber & Faber, 1985), p. 75.
39. Ibid.
40. Said, *The Independent*, 8 July 1993.
41. Said, ibid., 24 June 1993.
42. Said, ibid., 8 July 1993.
43. Yeats, *Autobiographies*, p. 285.
44. Said, *The Independent*, 8 July 1993.
45. Ibid.
46. Ibid.
47. Ibid.; Adorno's observation is from *Minima Moralia* (London: Verso, 1978), no. 18.

Select Bibliography

1. Works by the Wilde Family

(a) WILLIAM WILDE

The Beauties of the Boyne and its tributary the Blackwater (Dublin: McGlashan & Gill) 1849

Irish Popular Superstitions (Dublin: McGlashan) 1852

The Census of Ireland for 1851 ... containing the Report, Tables of Pestilences, & an Historical Account ... Signed by William Donnelly and Sir William Robert Wills Wilde [C 2087–I], H.C. 1856, xxix

Ireland Past and Present; the Land and the People (Dublin: McGlashan & Gill) 1864

Lough Corrib, its shores and islands (Dublin: McGlashan & Gill) 1867

(b) JANE WILDE

Poems by Speranza (Dublin: Duffy) 1864

Ancient Legends, Mystic Charms and Superstitions of Ireland (London: Ward & Downey) 1888

Men, Women and Books: Selected Essays, first series (London: Ward & Downey) 1891

Social Studies (London: Ward & Downey) 1893

(c) OSCAR WILDE

Collected Works, edited by Robert Ross: published 1908 by Methuen (London) in three instalments: February, [i] *The Duchess of Padua*; [ii] *Salome, A Florentine Tragedy, Vera*; [iii] *Lady Windermere's Fan*; [iv] *A Woman of No Importance*; [v] *An Ideal Husband*; [vi] *The Importance of Being Earnest*. March: [vii] *Lord Arthur Savile's Crime and other prose pieces*; [viii] *Intentions, The Soul of Man*; [ix] *Poems*; [x] *A House of Pomegranates, The Happy Prince and other tales*; [xi] *De Profundis*. October: [xii] *The Picture of Dorian Gray*; [xiii] *Reviews*; [xiv] *Miscellanies*.

Collected Works, edited by Robert Ross: published 1909 by Methuen (London) as follows: [i] *Lord Arthur Savile's Crime, The Portrait of Mr W.H.*; [ii] *The Duchess of Padua*; [iii] *Poems*; [iv] *Lady Windermere's Fan*; [v] *A Woman of No Importance*; [vi] *An Ideal Husband*; [vii] *The Importance of Being Earnest*; [viii] *A House of Pomegranates*; [ix] *Intentions*; [x] *De Profundis*; [xi] *Essays and Lectures*; [xii] *Salome*. Uniform with this edition were subsequently published *The Picture of Dorian Gray* (1910) and *The Critic in Pall Mall* (1914)

The Works of Oscar Wilde, ed. G. F. Maine (London: Collins) 1948

The Letters of Oscar Wilde, ed. Rupert Hart-Davis (London: Hart-Davis) 1962

More Letters of Oscar Wilde, ed. Rupert Hart-Davis, (London: John Murray) 1985

Oscar Wilde's Oxford Notebooks: a portrait of mind in the making, ed. by Philip E. Smith and Michael S. Helfand, (Oxford: Oxford University Press) 1989

The Picture of Dorian Gray, ed. by Isobel Murray (London: Oxford University Press) 1974

2. Bibliographies of Oscar Wilde

Mason, Stuart [C. S. Millard], *Bibliography of Oscar Wilde* (London: Werner Laurie) 1914

Fletcher, Ian, and Stokes, John, 'Oscar Wilde' in Richard Finneran (ed.), *Anglo-Irish Literature: a review of research* (New York: Modern Languages Association of America) 1976

—— 'Oscar Wilde' in Richard Finneran (ed.), *Recent Research on Anglo-Irish Writers: a review of research* (New York: Modern Languages Association of America) 1983

Mikhail, E. H., *Oscar Wilde: an annotated bibliography of criticism* (London: Macmillan) 1978

Small, Ian, *Oscar Wilde Revalued: an essay on new materials and methods of research* (Greensboro, NC: ELT Press) 1993

3. Biographies of the Wildes

Coakley, Davis, *Oscar Wilde: The Importance of Being Irish* (Dublin: Town House) 1994

Ellmann, Richard, *Oscar Wilde* (London: Hamish Hamilton) 1987

Hyde, Harford Montgomery, *Oscar Wilde* (London: Eyre Methuen) 1976

Pearson, Hesketh, *Oscar Wilde* (London: Methuen) 1946

Pine, Richard, *Oscar Wilde* (Dublin: Gill & Macmillan) 1983

Symons, A. J. A., *Essays and Speculations*, ed. J. Symons (London: Cassell) 1969

White, Terence de Vere, *The Parents of Oscar Wilde* (London: Hodder & Stoughton) 1967

4. Literary Studies

Bird, Alan, *The Plays of Oscar Wilde* (London: Vision Press) 1977

Cohen, Philip, *The Moral Vision of Oscar Wilde* (London: Associated University Presses) 1978.

Ellmann, Richard, *Eminent Domain: Yeats among Wilde, Joyce, Pound, Eliot and Auden* (Oxford: Oxford University Press) 1967

——, *Golden Codgers: biographical speculations* (London: Oxford University Press) 1973

Gide, André, *Oscar Wilde: a study*, trans. with introduction by Stuart Mason [Christopher Millard] (Oxford: Holywell Press) 1905

Kohl, Norbert, *Oscar Wilde: the works of a conformist rebel* (Cambridge: Cambridge University Press) 1989

San Juan, Epifanio, *The Art of Oscar Wilde* (Princeton, NJ: Princeton University Press) 1967

Worth, Katherine, *Oscar Wilde* (Houndmills: Macmillan) 1983

5. Works by W. B. Yeats

Fairy and Folk Tales of the Irish Peasantry (London: Scott) 1888

Autobiographies (London: Macmillan) 1955

Mythologies (London: Macmillan) 1959

Writings on Irish Folklore, Legend and Myth, ed. R. Welch (London: Penguin) 1993

6. The Book of Ireland

Arnold, Matthew, *On the Study of Celtic Literature* (London: Smith, Elder) 1867

de Vere, Aubrey, *English Misrule and Irish Misdeeds: four letters from Ireland addressed to an English member of parliament* (London: Murray) 1848

Edgeworth, Maria, *Castle Rackrent* and *The Absentee* (London: Dent) 1910

Le Fanu, Sheridan, *Uncle Silas: a tale of Bartram-Haugh* (London: Macmillan) 1899

Maturin, Charles, *Melmoth the Wanderer*, ed. and introd. A. Hayter (Harmondsworth: Penguin) 1977

——, *The Wild Irish Boy* (London: Longman, Hurst Rees & Orme, 1808)

Owenson, Sydney (Lady Morgan), *The Wild Irish Girl* (London: Pandora) 1986

Renan, Ernest, *The Poetry of the Celtic Races and other studies* (London: Scott) 1896

7. Studies on Irish Literature

Denman, Peter, *Samuel Ferguson: the literary achievement* (Gerrards Cross: Colin Smythe) 1990

Donoghue, Denis, *We Irish: essays on Irish literature and society* (London: University of California Press) 1986

Holroyd, Michael, *Bernard Shaw*, vol. 1: *The Search for Love, 1856–1898*; vol. 2: *The Pursuit of Power, 1898–1918*; vol. 3: *The Lure of Fantasy, 1918–1950* (London: Chatto & Windus) 1988, 1989, 1991

Kearney, Richard (ed.), *The Irish Mind: exploring intellectual traditions* (Dublin: Wolfhound) 1985

Kiberd, Declan, 'The London Exiles: Wilde and Shaw' in *Field Day anthology*, ii, 372–76

Lloyd, David, *Nationalism and Minor Literature: James Clarence Mangan and the emergence of Irish cultural nationalism* (Berkeley: University of California Press) 1987

McCormack, W. J., *Sheridan Le Fanu and Victorian Ireland* (Oxford: Clarendon Press) 1980

——, *Ascendancy and Tradition in Anglo-Irish Literary History from 1789 to 1939* (Oxford: Clarendon Press) 1985

Meisel, Martin, *Shaw and the Nineteenth-Century Theater* (Princeton, NJ: Princeton University Press) 1963

Mercier, Vivian, *The Irish Comic Tradition* (Oxford: Oxford University Press) 1962

——, *Modern Irish Literature: sources and founders* (Oxford: Oxford University Press) 1994

Woodfield, James, *English Theatre in Transition, 1881–1914* (London: Croom Helm) 1984

8. Ana

Barthes, Roland, *Writing Degree Zero*, trans. A. Lavers and C. Smith, (London: Cape) 1984

——, *Image, Music, Text*, trans. S. Heath (London: Fontana) 1977

——, *Mythologies*, trans. A. Lavers (London: Paladin) 1973

——, *A Lover's Discourse*, trans. R. Howard (London: Penguin) 1990

Borges, Jorge Luis, *Labyrinths*, ed. D. Yates and J. Irby (Harmondsworth: Penguin) 1970

Derrida, Jacques, *Writing and Difference*, trans. A. Bass (Chicago: University of Chicago Press) 1978

Genet, Jean, *The Thief's Journal*, trans. B. Frechtman (London: Penguin) 1967

Goffmann, Irving, *Stigma: notes on the management of spoiled identity* (Englewood Cliffs, NJ: Prentice–Hall) 1963

Paglia, Camille, *Sexual Personae: Art and Decadence from Nefertiti to Emily Dickinson* (London: Yale University Press) 1990

Sartre, Jean-Paul, *Saint Genet, Actor and Martyr*, trans. B. Frechtman (New York: Braziller) 1963

Schmidgall, Gary, *The Stranger Wilde: Interpreting Oscar* (New York: Dutton) 1994

Sinfield, Alan, *The Wilde Century: Effeminacy, Oscar Wilde and the Queer Moment* (London: Cassell) 1994

Steiner, George, *Antigones* (Oxford: Clarendon Press) 1986

——, *Extraterritorial: papers on literature and the language revolution* (London: Faber & Faber) 1972

Index

Abbey Theatre (Dublin), 377, 423, 455
'absurd' theatre, 332, 389
Act of Union (1800), 49, 50, 56, 72–3, 80–81, 246
Adam, Villiers de l'Isle. *see* l'Isle Adam
Adey, More, 70
Adorno, Theodor, 419
Aeschylus, 115; *Agamemnon*, OW's knowledge of, 115, 166, 275, 318
aestheticism, aesthetics, 23, 166, 202, 247, chapter 6 *passim*, 331, 389; and ethics, 10, 32, 151, 170, 210, 332ff; M. Nordau on, 346–7; at Oxford, 129–30; OW and, 32, 83, 316ff
Ainslie, Douglas, 142
Albermarle Club (London), OW member of, 330
Alexander, George, 250–51, 283
Allen, Grant, 325
American Irish, 104–5, 296
anarchism, 329
Andersen, H. C., 181, 221; 'The Little Mermaid', 180
Anglo-Irish literature, 7, 9, 13, 14, 49, 64, 71, 77, 140, 169–70, 362
Anglo-Irish relations, 111–12, 337; difference in temperament, 232, 247, 400; and J. Joyce, 56, 384, 387; and C. R. Maturin, 66–7; and G. B. Shaw, 445; OW on, 296, 316, 328–9

Antigone, 106, 272ff, 295, 414–16
Antoine, André, 257
Aran Islands, 91–2, 416
Archer, William, on *Salomé*, 37, 244, 278, 279, 440n
Ardilaun, Lady, 113–14
Argueta, Manlio, *One Day of Life*, 417
Aristophanes, 308
Aristotle, 42, 47, 247, 294, 300, 360
Arnold, Matthew, on Celtic literature, 28ff, 37, 47, 111, 227, 255, 285, 302–3; as a critic, 210; OW on, 295
'ascendancy, Protestant', 50
Asquith, H. H., 128; and OW, 317–18
Auden, W. H., 202, 210; on *The Importance of Being Earnest*, 242
Austen, Jane, 53–4
Australia, OW's attitude to, 104

Balcombe, Florence, 138
Balfour, A. J., 128, 344; on decadence, 128
Balfour, Gerald, 344
Balzac, Honoré de, 65; *Sarrasine*, 311
Banim, John, 126
Banville, John, 408
Barbey d'Aurevilly, Jules, 277, 347
Baring, Maurice, 128
Barlas, John, 324
baroque, 382
Barrie, J. M., 28, 154

Barthes, Roland, 64, 139–41, 309, 310ff, 381, 388ff; *A Lover's Discourse*, 141, 396–7; *Writing Degree Zero*, 311

Baudelaire, Charles, 163, 231, 244, 305, 342, 347, 398

Beardsley, Aubrey, 112; illustrations for *Salomé*, 255; OW on, 276; and *The Yellow Book*, 329

Beaufort, Duke of, 323

Beckett, Samuel, 29, 162, 194, 250, 261, 301, 311, 382, 383, 391, 398, 416; *Endgame*, 280, 373, 389; *Waiting for Godot*, 389, 417

Beerbohm, Max, and OW, 142; on OW, 446; cartoon of OW and Willie W, 196; obituary of OW, 422; and *The Yellow Book*, 329; *Zuleika Dobson*, 394

Beerbohm Tree, Herbert, 280

Behrendt, Patricia Flanagan, 208–10

Bennett, Arnold, 329

Benson, A. C., 344

Benson, F. R., 142, 329, 344, 448; *Dodo*, 318

Bergson, Henri, 390

Berkeley, Bishop George, 17, 24–5, 40, 60, 162, 308, 319, 327, 337, 355, 357, 377, 393, 396

Bernhardt, Sarah, 293; and OW, 142; and *Salomé*, 276–7

Besant, Walter, 330

Best, Richard, 117

bimetallism, 239

Bird, Alan, 3, 261

Blackie, J. S., 114

Blake, William, 25

Blanc, Louis, 324

Blessington, Lady, 324

Blunt, Wilfrid Scawen, OW on, 295–6; on OW, 322

Bodley, Courtenay, 321–2

Borges, Jorge Luis, 381, 388ff, 416; interest in Irish literature, 393; on OW, 393; 'Borges and I', 393; *Universal History of Infamy*, 390, 394

Boucicault, Dion 241, 258; and OW, 116; *A Lover by Proxy*, 246, 248–9, 263; *Arrah-na-Pogue*, 241; *The Colleen Bawn*, 241; *The Corsican Brothers*, 241–2, 246; *The Shaughraun*, 241

Boulanger, General G., 324

Bourget, Paul, 71

Bowden, Fr Sebastian, and OW, 149–50, 216

Boxer Rebellion, 329

Boyne, Battle of, 40, 268

Brendan, St, 31

Brink, André, *An Instant in the Wind*, 409–11

Brontë family, 325

Brooke, Charlotte, *Reliques of Irish Poetry*, 135

Brown, Terence, 48

Browning, Elisabeth Barrett, 295

Browning, Oscar, 293, 343ff; *Paederastia Apologia*, 344–5

Browning, Robert, 216–17, 294

Brummell, 'Beau', 154

Bunbury, 239–40

Burke, Edmund, 24–5, 54, 126, 252, 337, 355

Burton, Frederick William, 92

Bush, Douglas, 201

Butt, Isaac, 35, 76, 80

Byron, George (Lord), 211

Café Royal (London), 329

Cahalan, J. M., 14, 168

Cairns, David, and Richards, Shaun, 29

Calderón, Pedro, *La Vida es Sueño*, 392

Carleton, William, 51, 78, 79

Carlyle, Thomas, 295
'Carmen Sylva', 292
'Carroll, Lewis', 28, 154
Carson, Edward, and OW, 117, 350
Casement, Sir Roger, 324
Catholic Emancipation (1829), 48, 50, 77
Celtic literature and mythology. *see* Ireland
Cervantes, Miguel de, 396
Chamberlin, J. E., x
Chekhov, Anton, 251, 299–300
Childers, Erskine, 324
Christ, OW's identification with, 143–4, 223, 228, 231–2, 331, 388
Clare, John, 210
Clarke, Austin, 369
Cleveland Street scandal, 323, 348, 350
Clifford, W. K., 27, 136
Coakley, Davis, xii, 424, 439
Cohen, Philip, x, 4, 180, 420
College Historical Society (TCD), 124, 127
Collins, Mr Justice Henn, 117
Confucius, OW on, 296–7, 305–6
Congreve, William, 3, 249
Connemara, and Wilde family, 90
Conrad, Joseph, 10
Corelli, Marie, 292; *The Sorrows of Satan*, 81
Cork and Orrery, Countess of, 292
Court and Society Review, OW contributes to, 291
Crabbet Club, OW at, 322
Craig, Gordon, 371
Craik, Mrs, 292
Crane, Stephen, 323
Crane, Walter, 325
Criminal Law Amendment Act (1885), 322–3, 348
Croft-Cooke, Rupert, x
Cuala Press, 307
Cuchulain, 25, 26, 33, 357, 365, 366. *see also* hero

culture and politics 10, 48, 83, 151, 332ff. *see also* aesthetics
Curzon, George, OW admires, 128–9; on OW, 322; and O. Browning, 343–4

Daily Chronicle on *PDG*, 195, 335
dandy, 239, 277, 305, 348; Christ as, 231; and Confucius, 297; in OW's plays, 242–3, 252–3, 269; OW as, 10–11, 393
d'Arch Smith, Timothy, 204
Darley, George, 126
Darwin, Charles, 390; *Origin of Species*, 390
Daudet, Leon, 15
Davis, Thomas, 39, 40–41, 49, 53, 63–4, 73, 82, 96, 103, 127, 355, 363–4
Davitt, Michael, OW writes to, 117, 363
Deane, Seamus, 97, 252, 256, 323–4
decadence, 281, 288, 329; A. J. Balfour on, 128; in Celtic thought, 340; in drama, 43, 128, 158; in Irish literature, 57, 65, 67; in OW's work, 169, 201, 202, 224, 236, 256, 271, 272, 335, 367–8, 378; OW as 'High Priest of the Decadents', 315
Denman, Peter, 62
Derrida, Jacques, 300, 405, 417
Derry, city, 40, 80; 'Bloody Sunday', 407
Desart, Lady, 142
de Valera, Eamon, 105
de Vere, Aubrey, 7, 330–31, 366, 408–9
deviance, 9, 10, 34, 35–6, 136, 166, 323, 346–7, 362. *see also* homosexuality
dialogue, and J. Genet, 220; in Celtic literature, 56, 365; in S. Ferguson's work, 62, 76;

in OW's work, 14, 254–5,
266, 301ff, 326; G. Steiner
on, 272; in W. B. Yeats, 42,
56, 62, 76, 220, 254–5, 266,
274, 301ff, 326, 332–4, 358,
359–61, 365ff
Dickens, Charles, 294
Diderot, Denis, *Jacques le Fataliste*,
392
Disraeli, Benjamin, 154
Donoghue, Denis, 25, 184, 193,
407–8, 411
Donoghue, John, 117
Dostoyevsky, F. M., 342; *The
Double*, 173; *The Insulted
and the Injured*, 294–5;
Douglas, Lord Alfred, 12, 15, 109,
141–3, 145–8, 165, 220, 226,
228, 232, 263, 296, 317–19,
330, 335, 344, 350, 351;
Autobiography, 353; 'Two
Loves', 351–2
Dowden, Edward, 124, 127
Dowson, Ernest, 329
Doyle, A. Conan, 117, 175
Dramatic Review, 291
Dreyfus, Alfred, 10, 45
dromomania, 27
Drumlanrig, Lord, 344
Dublin, 51, 241–2; Alexandra
College, 293; Dublin
Castle, 293; Gaiety Theatre,
242; Theatre Royal, 241–2
*Dublin Quarterly Journal of
Medical Science*, edited by
Sir William W, 86
Dublin University Magazine, 49,
50, 53, 73ff; Lady W and,
81–2, 99; Sir Willaim W
and, 127; OW contributes
to, 166, 291
Dufferin, Lady, 324
Duffy, Charles Gavan, 72–3, 75,
408–9; and Irish Literary
Society, 325; and OW,
116–17

du Maurier, George, 321
Dunn, James Nichol, OW writes
to, 207
Dunne, Fr Cuthbert, and OW, 117
Durrell, Lawrence, 27, 405, 444

Eagleton, Terry xi, 4; *Saint Oscar*,
406
'earnest', 239
Easter Rising (1916), 40, 75, 324,
380
Eco, Umberto, 309
Edgeworth, Maria, 49, 51, 53,
55ff, 77–8, 169, 324; *The
Absentee*, 56ff, 74; *Castle
Rackrent*, 56; *Ennui*, 56ff
Egerton, George, *Keynotes*, 389
egomania, 327ff
Einstein, Albert, 11, 301, 317
Elgee, Charles (OW's
grandfather), 96
Elgee, Jane. *see* Wilde, Jane
Eliade, Mircea, 412
Eliot, T. S., 154, 391; *The Waste
Land*, 389
Ellis, Havelock, *Psychology of Sex*,
352–3; *Sexual Inversion*, 352
Ellmann, Richard, x, 6, 21, 109,
156, 367–8, 370, 374–5, 379;
James Joyce, 5; *Oscar Wilde*,
x–xi, 5–6, 13, 14–15, 22, 23,
45, 124, 133, 326–7, 445
Emerson, R. W., 149
Emmet, Robert, 47, 51, 73, 308
epiphany. *see* image
Eriugena, John Scotus, 17, 393
Esterhazy, Commandant M-C. F.,
OW on, 45
Euripides, OW's interest in, 115;
Herakles, compared with
Salomé, 275; *Ion*, as
forerunner of *The Importance
of Being Earnest*, 265; *The
Phoenician Women*, echoed
in *An Ideal Husband*, 260;
OW's knowledge of, 275

Euston, Earl of, 323
Everett, Katherine, on OW's
parents, 113
extraterritorial, 15, 250, 270, 340,
409, 418–19

Fallis, Richard, 14, 168
Famine (Ireland), 48, 49, 77, 80, 85,
89, 94, 134, 178, 242, 323
Fane, Violet, 292
Farquhar, George, 247, 261
Fawcett, Millicent Garrett, 292
Ferguson, Sir Samuel, 7–8, 13, 38,
49, 52, 62ff, 76, 79, 82ff, 89,
92, 98, 135, 355, 364, 382,
408, 413, 415; 'Dialogue
between the Head and
Heart', 76–7
Fido, Martin, x
Flannery, James W., 423
Flaubert, Gustave, 381
Fletcher, Ian, 21–2
folklore, folktales, 16, 51, 56–7,
61, 175ff
Footlights, caricatures OW, 323
Forster, E. M., *Maurice*, 349
Fortnightly Review, 325; OW
contributes to, 282, 291
Foster, John Wilson, 14, 168
Fox, Rev. L. C. Prideaux, baptises
OW and Willie W, 129
Freud, Sigmund, 11, 390
Friel, Brian, *Dancing at Lughnasa*,
251, 408, 416; *The Freedom of
the City*, 407–8; *The London
Vertigo*, 17, 259; *Making
History*, 406; *Philadelphia,
Here I Come!*, 406–7;
Translations, 406–7, 409–10;
Wonderful Tennessee, 408, 416
Froude, J. A., 135, 295; *The Two
Chiefs of Dunboy*, OW on,
296
Frye, Northrop, 48
Furniss, Harry, caricatures Lady
W, 114

Gaelic Society (Dublin), 51
Gagnier, Regina, 333–4
Garibaldi, Giuseppe, 324
Garnett, Edward, 329
gay temper, 6–7, 12, 30, 35, 38ff,
61, 261, 278, 343, 382, 404.
see also homosexuality
Genet, Jean, xi, 26, 110, 168, 173,
213, 220, 381, 400ff, 417; *The
Thief's Journal*, 400–41
Gide, André, and OW, 22,
109–10, 142, 161, 162, 185,
327; on OW, 38, 108, 415;
preserves OW's parables,
175; *Si le grain ne meurt*,
OW in, 153; *Les nourritures
terrestres*, OW in, 153;
L'Immoraliste, OW in, 153
Gilbert, John, 92
Gilbert, W. S., 243; and Sullivan, Sir
A.; *The Gondoliers*, 245;
Iolanthe, 245; *Utopia, Limited*,
245
Gill, Charles, 117
Gladstone, W. E., OW writes to, 207
Glendalough (Ireland), 293
Godwin, E. W., 142, 225, 293, 371
Goethe, J. W. von, 233; *Die Leiden
des jungen Werthers*, 397
Goffmann, Erving, 33, 35–6,
155–6, 170–71, 180
Goldsmith, Oliver, 1, 4, 24–5; *She
Stoops to Conquer*, 242
Goncourt, Edmond de, on OW,
108, 322
Gosse, Sir Edmund,
homosexuality of, 343; and
OW, 330; on *PDG*, 348; and
The Yellow Book, 329
Grattan, Henry, 73
Graves, A. P., 127
Gray, John, 142, 204, 325
Greek love. *see paederastia*
Greek thought and literature, 51,
55, 94, 124–5, 167–8, 197,
237, 274–5, 279, 283–5,

301–2, 309–10, 382, 390, 415.
see also Hellenism
Gregory, Augusta, Lady, 89, 292,
368
Grein, J. T., 257
Grimm, J. and W., 180, 221
Groddeck, Georg, 390

Haggard, H. Rider, 330
Hall, Radclyffe. *see Well of
Loneliness*
Hall, Mrs S. C., 325
Hall, W. E., 14
Hamilton, Walter, on OW, 150–52
Hamilton, Sir William Rowan, 96,
113, 118
Hamon, Count Louis, on OW,
155, 187
Hamsun, Knut, 198, 389, 391–2
Hardiman, James, *Irish Minstrelsy*,
79
Harland, Henry, 10, 323, 329; *My
Friend Prospero*, 394
Harris, Frank, 10, 239, 291
Hart-Davis, Sir Rupert, 138, 145–6
Harte, Bret, 323
Havel, Vaclav, 381
Hawthorne, Nathaniel, 157
Hayter, Alethea, 64–5
Healy, Dermot, 408
Healy, Tim, on OW, 351
Heaney, Seamus, 413
Hederman, M. P., 42
Hegel, G. W., 8, 238, 368
Hellenism, 125, 165, 194, 201,
283–4, 306–8
Henley, W. E., attacks OW, 13; OW
writes to, 193; and OW, 330
Heraclitus, 362
Herberton, Viscountess, 292
hero, 26, 32ff, 48, 83, 103, 135,
275, 407, 423
Herodotus, OW's interest in, 115
Herzen, Alexander, 324
Hesse, Hermann, *Demian*, 174,
390, 392

Hobby Horse, 325, 389
Hogg, John, 396
Holland, Vyvyan. *see* Wilde,
Vyvyan
Home Government Association,
90
Homer, 286, 416
Home Rule movement, chapter 7
passim
homosexuality, ix, 124–6, 129–30,
202, 239, 267, 304, 316,
343ff, 396–7, 415. *see also
paederastia*; uranianism
Hopkins, Gerard Manley, 129–30,
389
Horne, Herbert, 325
Houghton, Lord, 344
Housman, Laurence, and OW,
228, 420
Hugo, Victor, 231, 338
Humphreys, Sir Travers, 155
Hunter Blair, Rev. D., on OW,
129–30
Husserl, Edmund, 413
Hyde, Douglas, 59, 325, 364, 366
Hyde, H. Montgomery, x–xi, 156,
445
hypocrisia, 253, 316, 350, 417
Huysmans, J.-K., ix; *À Rebours*,
57, 194, 196

Ibsen, Henryk, 243ff, 251, 257, 269,
278, 299–300, 332, 338, 377,
407; *A Doll's House*, 279, 338;
An Enemy of the People, 251,
279; *Ghosts*, 251, 279, 338;
Hedda Gabler, 338, and OW
on 279; *The Master Builder*,
279; *The Pillars of Society*,
279; *Rosmersholm*, 279
Illaunroe (Connemara), OW at,
ix, 116, 120–21
*Illustrated Sporting and Dramatic
News*, caricatures OW, 322–3
image, 40–41, 59ff, 63ff, 94, 131–3,
190ff, 201, 210, 237, 264,

image (*contd*)
    286, 308–9, 336, 359, 361,
    367, 369, 374–6, 386, 391,
    396–8, 402
imagism, 391
Image, Selwyn, 325
inversion, 129, 240ff, 304, 326ff,
    352, 361, 376, 417
Ireland: Celtic and Gaelic culture,
    13, 28ff, 51, 62–3, 135, 225,
    275, 286, 302–3, 316;
    contemporary drama, 406ff;
    folktales and folklore, 38, 51,
    89, 100ff, 118, 165, 180–81,
    365ff; historiography, 285; in
    nineteenth century, chapters
    1–2 *passim*; idea of a 'nation',
    22ff, 29, 42, 49, 64, 72ff, 85,
    89, 103, 113, 283, 296, 367,
    403; Irish anguage, 89–91,
    94, 100; Literary
    Renaissance, 48, 89, 236, 325,
    358; Protestants in, chapter 2
    passim, 118; state of mind/
    imagination, 1, 2, 7, 21ff, 40,
    53, 66, 196, 237, 300, 317, 334,
    340–41, 367, Conclusion
    passim; Tír na nÓg, 23, 31,
    100, 110, 163, 326, 359, 365.
    see also Davis; Famine;
    Ferguson; hero; Home Rule;
    Nation; Parnell
Irish Literary Society (London),
    and W family, 325
Irish Monthly, OW contributes to,
    206–7
irony, 25, 33, 49, 85, 164–5, 253,
    261, 266, 311, 328, 398, 411,
    418. *see also* paradox
Irvine, St John, x
Ismay's Children, OW reviews, 293

Jackson, Holbrook, 329
James, Henry, 4, 10, 22, 258, 307,
    323, 329–30, 343, 348; on
    OW, 322; *Guy Domville*, 258;

The Princess Casamassima,
    193, 239, 324; *The Turn of
    the Screw*, 65
James, Frank and Jesse, 411–12
Jameson Raid, 329
Jarry, Alfred, 154, 407, 416; *Ubu
    Roi*, 359, 369, 406
Jersey, Lady, 292
Joan of Arc, 293
John, Augustus, 325
Johnson, Lionel, and OW, 117, 325
Jones, H. A., 243, 257
Jowett, Benjamin, 129, 133
Joyce, James, 1, 6, 7, 13, 40, 41, 62,
    118, 201, 250, 414;
    relationship to work of OW,
    381ff; on OW, 119, 130, 384;
    idea of 'soul', 383; *Dubliners*,
    386, 418; 'A Painful Case',
    386; *Finnegans Wake*, 383–4;
    *A Portrait of the Artist as a
    Young Man*, 56, 168, 383ff;
    Ulysses, 56, 384, 391, 393, 418
Jullian, Philippe, x–xi
Jung, C. G., 390

Kalevala (Finland), 51
Keats, John, 42, 207, 211, 215, 289,
    361
Kelly, Hugh, 249, 337
Kennelly, Brendan, 32ff, 62ff
Kiberd, Declan, 41, 301, 326
Kilroy, Thomas, 271; *Double
    Cross*, 17, 408
Kingsley, Charles, *The Water-
    Babies*, 183
Kipling, Rudyard, 4, 144
Kleist, Heinrich von, 396
Klimt, Gustav, 264
Kohl, Norbert, 3ff, 22, 180, 189, 421
Komesu, Okifumi, 378
Kottabos (TCD), OW contributes
    to, 127, 203
Krafft-Ebing, R. von, 348;
    Psychopathia Sexualis, 351–2
Kropotkin, Prince P. A., 329

Labouchere, Henry, 322, 348
Laforgue, Jules, 57, 277
Laing, R. D., 245
Lamarck, Jean de, 390
Lampedusa, Giuseppe di, 'The
    Professor and the Siren', 180
Lang, Andrew, OW on, 295
Langtry, Lillie, 42, 142
language, 13, 29, 47–9, 78, 84,
    120–21, 226, 250, 251, 259,
    272–4, 287, 309ff, chapter 9
    passim; Conclusion *passim*.
    see also translation
Lavery, Hazel, Lady, 40
Le Brocquy, Louis, 382
Le Fanu, Sheridan, 13, 49, 58ff,
    64, 76–7, 110, 162, 169,
    379–80, 382, 391; *Uncle
    Silas*, 59ff, 278, 399
Le Gallienne, Richard, and OW,
    142, 225–6, 329
Leighton, Frederick Lord, 329
Lenin, V. I., 414
Lever, Charles, 76, 79
Leverson, Ada, 175, 412
Lewis, Sir George, 319
Lippincott's, PDG published in, 175
l'Isle Adam, Villiers de, 156–8, 293,
    347; *Axël*, 271–2, 306, 369,
    373; *Contes Cruels*, 157
Llosa, Mario Vargas, *The Real Life
    of Alexandro Mayta*, 416–17
Lloyd, Constance. *see* Wilde,
    Constance
Lloyd, David, 409
Lockwood, Sir Francis, 351
Lombroso, Cesare, *The Man of
    Genius*, 340ff, 346, 350
London Irish, 323–5
Lonnrött, Elias, 51
Lonsdale, Countess of, 142
Loti, Pierre, 293
Louÿs, Pierre, 226
Lover, Samuel, 76, 78, 79
Lutyens, Lady Emily, on OW, 322
Lytton, Edward Lord, 322

McCarthy, Justin, 324; and OW,
    117
McCormack, W. J., 52–3, 59, 61–2,
    169, 354–5, 379–80, 408
MacCurtain, Margaret, 437
McGahern, John, 408
McGlashan, James, 76
McGuinness, Frank, 251; *The
    Beautiful Lie*, 406; *Cartha-
    ginians*, 408; *Observe the
    Sons of Ulster . . .*, 408
McHugh, R., and Harmon, M., 3–4
Macklin, Charles, 249, 337; *The
    True-Born Irishman*, 259
Mackmurdo, Arthur, 325
MacNamara, Brinsley, 198, 382
MacNeice, Louis, 356–7
Maeterlinck, Maurice, 251, 257,
    280, 357, 377; *Les Aveugles*,
    280, 389; *Princesse Maleine*,
    244
magical realism, 341
Mahaffy, J. P., and classical studies,
    132; and TCD, 127;
    relevance to OW, 4; and
    OW, 55, 123–6, 142, 383;
    Social Life in Greece, 133, and
    OW's assistance in, 125
Mallarmé, Stéphane, 389
Mangan, James Clarence, 81, 355,
    408, 417; 'The Man in the
    Cloak', 81, 277
Manning, Cardinal Henry, 48
Marillier, Harry, ix , 142, 149
Martin, Henri, 30
Marxism, 307
mask, 81, 253, 261, 277, 387–8;
    and Lord Alfred Douglas,
    232; and OW, 16, 17, 130,
    151, 170, 222, 246, 259, 282,
    298–9; and W. B. Yeats, 137,
    327, chapter 8 *passim*
Mason, Stuart, 108
master–servant relationship,
    172–4, 179–80, 257, 333–4;
    in J. Genet, 403; in OW's

master–servant (*contd*)
plays, 253–5, 278; in OW's
dialogues, 309–10; in W. B.
Yeats, 369, 399
Maturin, C. R., 49, 52, 58, 64ff,
115, 126–7, 162, 380, 391;
relation to Jane Wilde and
OW, 64, 68, 95, 223; *Melmoth
the Wanderer*, 64ff, 149, 204,
343, 384, 399, 412; *The Wild
Irish Boy*, 64ff, 196, 399
Maupassant, Guy de, 293
Maurois, André, 395–6
Mazzini, Giuseppe, 50
Meagher, Thomas, 75, 77, 324
Meisel, Martin, 242, 245, 257, 270
Melmoth the Wanderer. see Maturin,
C. R.
melodrama, 45, 236ff, 283, 333,
374, 389
Melville, Harry, 142, 230
Memmi, Albert, 408
Mendès, Catulle, 347
Mercier, Vivian, xii; *Irish Comic
Tradition*, 3, 117–18, 163,
189, 311–12; *Modern Irish
Literature*, 11, 412, 439
Meredith, George, 128, 295
Merle, Robert, 4
Michaelangelo (Buonarotti), OW
on, 345–6
Miles, Frank, 142
Mitchel, John, 53, 74, 308
modernism, chapter 9 *passim*
Modjeska, Helena, 142
Molyneux, William, 308
Moore, George, 10, 71, 126, 382;
An tÚr-Ghort (*The Untilled
Field*), 389
Moore, Thomas, 78
Moreau, Gustave, 264
Morgan, Lady (Sydney Owenson),
23, 40, 324; *The Wild Irish
Girl*, 54ff, 67, 70, 82, 246
Morley, Sheridan, x
Morris, William, 48, 128, 210, 211,
307, 329

Moytura, and W family, 120
Munster, Countess of, 292
Murphy, Arthur, 249, 337
Murphy, Tom, 251; *Bailegangaire*,
408; *The Gigli Concert*, 408
Murray, Isobel, 145–6
Musil, Robert, 390, 392
Musset, Alfred de, 342

Nabokov, Vladimir, *Despair*, 174
Nassaar, C. S., x
nation. *see* Ireland
Nation, The, 49, 50, 71ff, 84, 99,
429; and Lady W, 85
National Observer, 13
Nettleship, J. T., 329
Nerval, Gerard de, 342
Nevill, Lady Dorothy, 292
New Age, 389
Newman, Cardinal J. H., 48,
129–30, 132–3, 383; *Apologia
Pro Vita Sua*, 390
Newman, Ernest, 44, 334
New Travellers' Club (London),
OW a member, 330
New York Times, 322
Nineteenth Century, The, OW
contributes to, 291, 298, 354
Nordau, Max, 229; on OW, 346ff;
Degeneration, 327ff, 346ff;
Paradoxes, 347
Norton, Caroline, 324
Nutt, Alfred, 366

O'Brien, William Smith, 75, 77,
116, 324, 363
O'Casey, Sean, 241
O'Connell, Daniel, 50, 102, 120
O'Connor, Frank, 39
Ó Conaire, Pádraic, 198
O'Croly, Rev. D., 80
O'Curry, Eugene, 62–3, 83, 91–2
O'Donovan, John, 91
Offences Against the Person Act
(1861), 323
O'Grady, Standish, 127

Ohnet, Georges, 293
O'Keeffe, John, 337
O'Leary, John, 363
O'Neill, Hugh, 40, 74
O'Nolan, Brian, *At Swim-Two-Birds*, 362
Ordnance Survey (Ireland), 52, 63, 80, 86–7, 89, 91, 410
O'Reilly, John Boyle, 116
Orlando (V. Woolf), 349
Orpen, Sir William, 264, 382
Osborne, John, 406
Osborne, Walter, 293
Oscar, 118–19
Ossian, 118–19
O'Sullivan, Samuel, 79
'Ouida', 292
Owenson, Sydney. see Morgan, Lady
oxymoron, 7, 8, 42, 55, 85, 187, 205, 217, 223, 231, 234, 258, 277, 287

paederastia, 316, 321, 344, 348–50, 352
Paglia, Camille, xi
Pall Mall Gazette, 291, 293
paradox, 6, 8, 9, 25–6, 29, 44, 57, 62, 122, 130, 141, 149, 163, 167, 171–3, 240, 263, 266, 298, 312, 328, 331, 334, 341, 347, 398. see also irony
Parnell, Charles Stewart, and politics, 10, 22, 83, 308; fall of, 35, 36, 48, 207, 302, 323–4; in J. Joyce 385; relevance to OW, 4; OW's interest in, 446
Pater, Walter, ix, 301; homosexuality, 209, 344; in Oxford, 129; and OW, 27, 142, 166–7, 283; OW on, 295, 368, 417; *Gaston de Latour*, 196; *Marius the Epicurean*, 57, 196, 349, 390;

The Renaissance, 196, 285, 289, 349
Patti, Adelina, 293
Pearse, Patrick, 48
Pearson, Hesketh, x–xi, 156, 262
Petrie, George, 51–2, 83, 91, 364
Phaedra/Phèdre, 243, 278, 295
Phoenix Park murders, 36, 242
Pinero, A. W. 243; *The Profligate*, 257
Plato, *Phaedrus*, 349; *Republic*, OW on, 303
Plekhanov, G. V., 307
Poe, E. A., 64, 157, 342; 'The Raven' (influence on *The Sphinx*), 217–18, 306; 'William Wilson', 65, 173–4
politics. see culture and politics
portrait. see image
Portsmouth, Countess of, 291
post-colonial society, 9, 10, Conclusion *passim*
Pound, Ezra, 391
Powell, Kerry, 279
Praz, Mario, 225, 415
Pre-Raphaelitism, 289, 383
'Protestant ascendancy', 50
Proust, Marcel, 209
'psychological', 130, 186, 196, 262, 284, 294, 295, 335, 348, 390, 397. see also homosexuality
Punch, caricatures OW, 321–2, 445
Purser, Louis Claude, 123, 127

Queensberry, Marquess of, 109, 117, 315, 318, 322–3, 330, 343–4, 350–51, 445
Quinn, Bob, 432

'Rachilde', *Monsieur Vénus*, 349
Racine, Jean, 278
Raffalovich, André, 204; *L'Affaire Oscar Wilde*, 349–50
Renan, Ernest, *Poetry of the Celtic Races*, 28ff, 39, 49, 107, 109, 111, 285, 308

Repeal Association, 50, 72, 90
Restoration drama, 237, 246, 261,
    263, 382
rhetoric, in W. B. Yeats, 355ff
Rhymers' Club, 325, 389
Rhys, Ernest, 325
Ribblesdale, Lord, OW meets,
    317–18
Ricketts, Charles, and OW, 142,
    175, 307
Ridgeway, William, 127
Rimbaud, Arthur, 139, 141, 336
Robinson, Lennox, *Church Street*,
    406
Robinson, Mrs (soothsayer), on
    OW, 187
Rodd, Rennell, 129
Rolleston, T. W., 127, 325
Rollinat, Maurice, 347
Roosevelt, Blanche, 187, 293
Rosebery, Earl of, 343–4, 351
Ross, Robert, ix, 70, 117, 142,
    143–5, 146, 148, 149, 230,
    232, 263
Rossetti, D. G., 211, 289
Rousseau, J.-J., 342
Rushdie, Salman, *Midnight's
    Children*, 416; *Shame*, 416
Ruskin, John, 128, 129, 206, 210,
    289, 295, 338; *Modern
    Painters*, 133
Ryan, W. P., 325

Said, Edward, 104, 417ff
St James's Gazette, on *PDG*, 226,
    335; OW contributes to, 335
Saintsbury, George, 329
St Stephen's Club (London), OW
    a member of, 329–30
Saix, Guillot de, 175
Salisbury, Marchioness of, 292
Saltus, Edgar, 8; on *Salomé*, 122,
    278
San Juan, Epifanio, x, 164, 200, 280
Sappho, 293
Sargent, J. S., 264

Sarraute, Natalie, 391
Sarrazin, Gabriel, 293
Sartre, J.-P., xi, 110, 237, 278, 310,
    400, 404
Savile Club (London), OW
    rejected by, 330
Savoy, The, 389
schizophrenia, 34, 245
Schmidgall, Gary, xii, 438
Schreiner, Olive, 292; OW on, 369
Scots Observer, 207; on *PDG*, 323,
    335
Scott, Sir Walter, 53, 56
Shakespeare, William, 174, 262,
    278; OW, on 207, 345–6. *see
    also* 'Portrait of Mr W. H.'
Shannon, Charles, 307
Shaw, G. B., 128, 241–3, 247, 368,
    407, 447; in London, 325; as
    a critic, 270; relevance to
    Anglo-Irish drama, 1, 4,
    247, 258, 261; and
    melodrama, 241–2, 257;
    and *The Yellow Book*, 10; on
    OW, 11, 128, 243, 248, 259,
    329, 353, 357, 368, 407; and
    Greek themes, 126; and
    Victorian Ireland, 382;
    Borges' interest in, 393;
    influence on OW's *The Soul
    of Man under Socialism*, 305,
    444n; and OW's 'Celtic
    School', 337; *Back to
    Methuselah*, 245; *The Devil's
    Disciple*, 251; *Fanny's First
    Play*, 270; *John Bull's Other
    Island*, 17; *The Philanderer*,
    337; *The Quintessence of
    Ibsenism*, 339–40; 'Sanity of
    Art', 338–9; *Widower's
    Houses*, 337
Sherard, Robert, 142
Sheridan, R. B., 1, 3, 244, 256, 261,
    262, 263, 269, 337; *The
    Rivals*, 17, 263; *The School
    for Scandal*, 249, 263

Shewan, Rodney, x
Shrewsbury, Countess of, 292
Sinfield, Alan, xi
Small, Ian, 3, 21–2
Smiles, Samuel, *Self-Help*, 390
Smith, P. E. and Helfand, M. S., 131–2, 136
Smith, Sydney, 112
Solomon, Simeon, 344
Somerset, Lord Arthur, 323
Somerville, E. Œ., and Ross, M., 58
Sophocles, 273, 414, 416. *see also* Antigone
soul, 30, 38, 39, 42, 81–2, 101, 132–3, 171, 196–7, 210, 297, 328, 343, 346, 365, 370
'Souls', 128–9, 307, 318
Speaker, OW contributes to, 296
Spectator, The, on *The Soul of Man under Socialism*, 282
'Speranza'. *see* Wilde, Jane
Spirit Lamp, The, OW contributes to, 226
Stanford, Charles, 78
Stanford, W. B., 126
Stead, W. T., 145
Steiner, George, 208, 238, 250, 272–4, 302, 370, 402, 404; *Antigones*, 286–7
Stephen, J. K., 330
Stephens, James, 184–6, 382; *The Charwoman's Daughter*, 185; *The Demi-Gods*, 185, 286
Sterne, Laurence, 402
Stevens, Wallace, 166
Stevenson, R. L., 145, 295; *Dr Jekyll and Mr Hyde*, 174
Stoker, Bram, 138; *Dracula*, 163
Stokes, J., 21–2, 445
Stoppard, Tom, 248; *Travesties*, 414
Strauss, Richard, 241, 244
Strindberg, August, 251, 392
Stuart, Francis, 382
Sullivan, Sir Edward, 124
Swedenborg, E., 61
Sweeney, King, 40, 41–2

Swift, Jonathan, 24–5, 158, 308, 337, 339, 355, 395–6
Swinburne, C. A., 8, 211, 289, 294, 347
Summers, Montague, 204
symbolism, 375, 389, 393, 446–7; in OW's plays 271ff; in W. B. Yeats, 367ff
Symonds, J. A., 132, 344, 348, 351; on *The Picture of Dorian Gray*, 348; translations of Michaelangelo, 349; *A Problem in Greek Ethics*, 133; *A Problem in Modern Ethics*, 133; *Studies of the Greek Poets*, 133; and homosexuality, 349; OW reads, 124
Symons, A. J. A., xi, 156
Symons, Arthur, 156–8, 293, 329
Synge, John Millington, 66, 117, 126, 241, 363–4, 368, 370, 382, 408, 416; *The Playboy of the Western World*, 301; *The Well of the Saints*, 179, 240, 389

Teleny, 171
Tennant, Margot, 128, 318
Tennyson, Alfred, 294
Terry, Ellen, 142, 371
'third meaning', 7, 26–7, 42, 49, 82ff, 111, 219, 238, 276, chapter 6 *passim*, 316, 326, 335–6, 378–9, 392
Thoreau, H. D., 35, 134, 306; 'Civil Disobedience', 297–8
Thucydides, 285–6
Times, on *Salomé*, 279
Tír na nÓg. *see* Ireland
Todhunter, John, 127, 325
Toland, John, 393
Tolstoy, Leo, 338
Tone, Theobald Wolfe, 73, 308
Toynbee, Arnold, 129
tragedy, 8, 26, 57, 58, 112, 166, 257, 275, 355ff, 372, 417
translation, 48, 55, 61, 83ff, 120, 208, 209, 272–3, 402ff

Travers, Mary, 88, 93, 114–15
Tree, H. Beerbohm. *see* Beerbohm Tree
Trevor, William, 408
Trinity College, Dublin, 49; OW at, 123–4
tropisms, 391
Truth, 322
Tuke, Henry Scott, 349
Turgenev, Ivan, *Fathers and Sons*, 418–19
Turner, F. M., 132
Twain, Mark, 323
Tynan, Katherine, 325
Tyrrell, R. Y., 127
Tzara, Tristan, 414

United Irishman, 74–5
United Irishmen, x
University Philosophical Society (TCD), 124
uranianism, 226, 299, 331, 348–9, 396–7; in Genet, 402–3; in OW's poetry, 202ff; in OW's prose, 293–4

Verdi, Giuseppe, 242
Verhaeren, Emile, 369
Verlaine, Paul, 327, 347
Verne, Jules, 144
Victoria, Queen, 292
Voltaire, 57
von Gloeden, Baron, 349

Wagner, Richard, 241, 338; *Tristan und Isolde*, 389
Wainewright, Thomas Griffith, 190, 305
Walkley, A. B., 247, 248, 270
Wallace, Alfred Russel, 390
Warner, Alan, 4
Watson, Sir William, 112, 329
Waugh, Arthur, 329
Welch, Robert, 407
Well of Loneliness, The (Radclyffe Hall), 349
Wells, H. G., 154

Whistler, James McN., 10, 112, 128, 323, 357
White, Sir Henry, OW meets, 317–18
Whitman, Walt, 35, 124, 290, 297, 306, 342; *Leaves of Grass*, 352
Wilde, Constance (wife), 119, 137, 143–5, 225, 230, 263, 330
Wilde, Cyril (son), 115, 137, 144, 148, 303
Wilde, Isola Francesca (sister), 107–8, 114
Wilde, Jane (mother), 2, 4, 26, 35, 49, 70, 82, 85ff, 107ff, 129, 143–4, 233, 241, 325, 358; influence on W. B. Yeats, 355, 359; family connections, 95; feminist essays, 105–6, 291–2; and Irish nationalism, 96, 178; translations, 122, 162; writes as 'Speranza', 96, and as 'John Fanshawe Ellis', 96; contributes to *The Woman's World*, 292; *Ancient Cures . . .* , 365–6; *Ancient Legends . . .* , 96, 100, 119, 180, 218, 255, 365; *Men, Women and Books*, 101ff; *Poems*, 55, 73, 96ff, 182; *Social Studies*, 101ff, 324; 'Australia', 104; 'The Bondage of Women', 104, 270; 'The Dead Soldier', 181–2; 'The Hour of Destiny', 75; 'Jacta Alea Est', 75, 81–2, 85, 96; 'The Priest's Soul', 38, 81, 180, 183–4, 343; 'Ruins', 81–2, 99
Wilde, Oscar:
  character: antinomianism, 2, 137, 154, 234, 239, 294, 308, 317, 335, 355, and ethics, 32, 307; critic, 16, 38, 83, 115, 128, 131–5, chapter 6 *passim*; dandy 222; and decadence, 42–3;

degenerate, 327ff, 346ff;
effeminacy, 321–2, 346;
search for identity, 35, 109;
intellectual, 16, 143;
paederasty, 36, 347–8, 352,
418; paradoxical, 12, 222;
and religion 129–30; as
seanchaí, 161; idea of the
soul, 39, 116, 132, 136, 171,
226, 268, 299, 302, 309;
searching for Tír na nÓg,
Utopia, 31; sense of tragedy,
21–2, 166, 216, 224, 230, 232;
sense of translation, 115.
see also gay temper;
decadence; egomania
Irishness, 2, 3, 11, 12, 112–13,
116–22, 140, 177ff, 210, 222,
230, 231–2, 267, 300–301,
308– 9, 316, 324–5, 377,
chapter 9 *passim*,
Conclusion *passim*
life, chapter 3 *passim*;
adolescence, 2, 35, 155,
241–2; early schooling, 123;
at TCD, 1, 13, 120, 123–4;
study of Greek tragedies
and poetry, 115, 123, 125,
253, 258; at Oxford, 1, 13,
27, 83–4, 115, 129–34, 150,
236, 282–7, 322, 330, 346; in
America, 14, 31, 43, 116, 151,
287–8, 316, 322, 327, 412; in
London, 35, 115–17, 142,
chapter 7 *passim*; aesthetic
crusade, 128, 150, 282ff,
316ff, 337ff; lectures, 287ff,
395, 402; marriage, 137,
143–4, 263; children, 144–5;
in Paris, 1–2, 116, 117, 143,
149, 220, 230, 322; trials,
148, 236, 345, 350–52; in
prison, 9, 216, 415;
petitions for release, 229–30;
after prison, 65, 353, 382,
412; and pornography, 171;

pseudonyms, 'C.3.3.', 45,
156, and 'Sebastian
Melmoth', 45, 156; as
'Ménalque' in Gide's work,
153; as 'Woman in the
Moon' (Beardsley); possible
career, 127–8, 375–6; relation
to parents, 15, 112–13, 115,
118–21, 140, 223, 370; edits
The Woman's World, 104,
105, 291ff, and includes
Irish topics in, 293; as a
scholar, 282ff; common-
place book, 6, 27–8, 127,
131–5, 320–21, 372
stories, 16, 101, chapter 4
passim; 'The Birthday of the
Infanta', 173, 175, 179–80,
318; 'The Canterville
Ghost', 174–5, 189, 224;
'The Devoted Friend',
172–3, 175; 'The Fisherman
and his Soul', 38, 81, 175,
177, 180, 183–4, 193, 194,
197, 235, 334, 369; 'The
Happy Prince', 162, 168;
'Lord Arthur Savile's
Crime', 174, 179, 186–8,
224; 'The Model
Millionaire', 175, 188–9;
'The Nightingale and the
Rose', 175; 'Pen, Pencil and
Poison', 174, 175, 190–91,
301, 304, 392, 394; *The
Picture of Dorian Gray*, 8, 16,
23, 29, 41, 42, 65–6, 71, 115,
127, 136, 143, 145, 161–3,
171, 173, 174, 175, 176, 183,
186, 193ff, 201, 225, 266,
277, 282, 315, 322–3, 330,
343, 346, 375, 378, 391–2,
396, 406, 415; revised
edition, 145–6, 175; criticism
of and OW's defence of,
226–7, 328, 334–6, 348, 350;
'Portrait of Mr W. H.',

Wilde, Oscar (*contd*)
  56, 131–2, 149, 174, 175,
  190–91, 349–50, 376, 392,
  396, 415; revised edition,
  175; 'The Remarkable
  Rocket', 50, 175, 191; 'The
  Selfish Giant', 144, 167, 175;
  'The Sphinx Without a
  Secret', 175; 'The Star-
  Child', 167, 175, 177, 191,
  256; 'The Young King', 162,
  175, 177, 318; publication:
  *The Happy Prince and other
  tales*, 175, 366; *A House of
  Pomegranates*, 175, 184; *Lord
  Arthur Savile's Crime and
  other stories*, 175
prose-poems/parables, 167–8,
  175ff, 288, 385, 389; 'The
  Artist', 162, 224; 'The
  Disciple', 176; 'The Doer of
  Good', 175; 'The House of
  Judgment', 176, 180; 'The
  Master', 176
plays, 16, chapter 5 *passim*; *An
  Ideal Husband*, 45, 106, 110,
  139, 154, 171, 173, 238, 240,
  242–3, 245, 250, 252–3,
  258ff, 269, 295, 305, 315,
  320, 326, 333–4, 337, 339,
  399; *A Woman of No
  Importance*, 106, 111, 187, 238,
  239, 250, 256–7, 261, 263,
  266–7, 277, 295, 326, 334, 337;
  A Woman's Tragedy, 239; *The
  Cardinal of Avignon*, 239;
  *Constance [Mr and Mrs
  Daventry]*, 238–9; *The
  Duchess of Padua*, 106,
  110–11, 224, 236, 238, 240,
  241, 244, 264, 266–7, 274, 280,
  283; *A Florentine Tragedy/
  *'Love and Death', 238, 242,
  280–81; *Lady Windermere's
  Fan*, 106, 110, 238ff, 283, 315,
  320, 326, 337; *The Importance
  of Being Earnest*, 58, 110, 169,
  173, 236, 238ff, 297, 306, 315,
  323, 326, 334, 349, 391–2, 399,
  405–6, 409, 414; 'The
  Pharaoh', 244; 'La Sainte
  Courtisane'/'The Woman
  Covered with Jewels', 238,
  240, 274, 277, 280–81, 373,
  389, 392; *Salomé*, 12, 37, 43,
  45, 106, 122, 137, 162, 169,
  173, 219, 224, 225–6, 236–7,
  238, 240, 244, 247, 251, 253–5,
  257, 264, 267, 272ff, 298–9,
  312, 326, 336, 341, 362, 371,
  373, 392, 395, 405–6, 414–16;
  Vera, or The Nihilists, 106,
  111, 236–7, 238, 240, 241,
  242–3, 247, 250, 252, 257, 264,
  283, 326, 334, 338
essays, lectures and dialogues, 16;
  'The Critic as Artist', 37, 38,
  56, 124–5, 135–6, 196, 272,
  286, 298–9, 301ff, 326, 375,
  388, 392; 'The Decay of
  Lying', 8, 37, 43, 54, 56,
  302–3, 309–10, 326, 333,
  375, read to Yeats, 354; 'The
  Decorative Arts', 287;
  'Dress Reform', 287; 'The
  English Renaissance in
  Art', 287–8, 328–9;
  'Hellenism', 283–4; 'The
  House Beautiful', 287;
  'Impressions of America',
  287; *Intentions*, 175, 298,
  301, 347, 350; 'The Poets
  and the People', 293–4, 303;
  'The Rise of Historical
  Criticism', 131–4, 198,
  283–5, 294, 295, 359, 396;
  *The Soul of Man under
  Socialism*, 5, 212, 252, 282,
  284, 288, 297–8, 305ff, 323,
  327, 378, 392, 415, and
  Yeats's 'Anima Hominis',
  378; 'The Truth of Masks',

301, 375; 'The Value of Art in Modern Life', 287
poems, 16, 55, 63, 199ff, 237, 358, 385; *Poems*, 207; 'Apologia', 212–13; 'Artist's Dream', 214; 'Ave Imperatrix', 150–51, 206, 209, 316; *The Ballad of Reading Gaol*, 45, 117, 212, 215–16, 228–9, 389, 392; 'The Burden of Itys', 205; 'By the Arno', 214; 'Charmides', 172, 202–3, 216; 'Endymion', 202; 'E Tenebris', 99; 'Flower of Love', 205–6; 'The Garden of Eros', 211; 'The Grave of Keats', 207; 'The Harlot's House', 132, 170–72, 213–14, 216, 226, 277; 'Hélas!', 199–201, 205, 208–9, 213, 217, 268, 385; 'Humanitad', 99, 212, 216; 'Impression du Matin', 215; 'Libertatis Sacra Fames', 207; 'Panthea', 212; 'Requiescat', 108; 'San Miniato', 204; 'Santa Decca', 211; 'Sonnet to Liberty', 207; *The Sphinx*, 106, 111, 132, 170–72, 192, 208, 217–20, 225, 276, 277–8, 306, 312, 349, 364, 376, 389, 392; 'Taedium Vitae', 213; 'Theoretikos', 99, 207, 211; 'To Milton', 206; 'Wasted Days'/ 'Madonna Mia', 203.
letters, 220; 'De Profundis', 98, 112, 141, 143–4, 149, 154–5, 185, 199, 220–22, 230–35, 236, 245, 258, 270, 294, 296, 307, 317–20, 337–8, 380, 395, 401
Wilde, Rev. Ralph (uncle), 88
Wilde, Vyvyan (son), x, 115, 121, 137, 303, 434; *Son of Oscar Wilde*, 137, 144

Wilde, Sir William (father), 2, 4, 9, 38, 49, 52, 76, 83, 85ff, 105, 107ff, 120, 124, 129; influence on W. B. Yeats, 355; founds Royal Victoria Eye and Ear Hospital, 86; edits *Dublin Quarterly Journal of Medical Science*, 86; Medical Census Commissioner, 86–7, 178; houses in Connemara, 90–92; visit to Aran Islands, 91–2, 104; 'On the Ancient Races of Ireland', 84; 'Ireland Past and Present', 94–5; *The Beauties of the Boyne*, 123; *Irish Popular Superstitions*, 44, 85, 88, 121; *Lough Corrib*, 88, 90–91; *Practical Observations in Aural Surgery*, 86
Wilde, William (brother), 36, 97, 107, 115, 119, 123–4, 127, 129, 325, 396, 433
Williams, T. J., *Who is Who*, 242
Wilson, Henry (OW's half-brother), 88, 116
Woman's World, The, 104, 105, 145, 156–8, 291ff
Wooldridge, Charles, 216
Woolf, Virginia. *see Orlando*
Wordsworth, William, 424
Worth, Katherine, 3, 241, 244, 245, 338, 357, 372
Wright, David G., 364

Yeats, Elizabeth and Lily, 307
Yeats, John Butler, 354
Yeats, W. B., 10, 13, 14, 24, 26, 30, 38, 39, 40–41, 42, 46, 59, 63, 66, 83, 89, 100, 108, 117, 118, 120, 126, 137, 154–5, 162, 165, 167, 169, 177, 193, 201, 210, 258, 268, 325, 382, 407–8, 413, 416; relationship with OW, chapter 8 *passim*;

Yeats, W. B. (*contd*)
  on OW, 152, 270, 276, 323,
    327, 337, 418, 446; reviewed
    by OW, 293; and antinomies,
    355ff, 412; theory of mask,
    355ff; interest in Japanese
    nôh, 389; on tragedy, 21
  prose works: 'Anima Hominis',
    219–20, 378; 'The Celtic
    Element in Literature', 368;
    The Celtic Twilight, 37, 366,
    375–6, 378; 'The Crucifixion
    of the Outcast', 373;
    'Estrangement', 364; *Fairy
    and Folk Tales of the Irish
    Peasantry*, 180; 'Ireland and
    the Arts', 364; *John Sherman*,
    375; *Mythologies*, 378; *Per
    Amica Silentia Lunae*, 378;
    'The Phases of the Moon',
    362; *Rosa Alchemica*, 378; *The
    Secret Rose*, 378; 'The Soul
    Cages', 182–3; *A Vision*,
    360, 375; 'The Wisdom of
    the King', 373
  poems: 'Byzantium', 364, 371–2;
    'A Dialogue of Self and
    Soul', 374; 'Ego Dominus
    Tuus', 360, 378; 'Meru', 359,
    364; 'The Municipal Gallery
    Revisited', 368; 'Symbols',
    373–5, 383; 'Vacillation', 374
  plays: *At the Hawk's Well*, 373;
    Calvary, 373; *The Cat and the
    Moon*, 369, 389; *Cathleen ni
    Houlihan*, 178; *The Countess
    Cathleen*, 184; 'Crucifixion',
    373; Cuchulain cycle, 377,
    423, 455; *The Death of
    Cuchulain*, 375, 380; *The
    Dreaming of the Bones*, 373;
    A Full Moon in March,
    357–8, 371–2; *The King of
    the Great Clock Tower*, 357–8,
    371–3; 'Plays for Dancers',
    358, 377; 'Resurrection', 373;
    The Shadowy Waters, 373; *The
    Hour-Glass*, 183, 369; *The
    Only Jealousy of Emer*, 215;
    Purgatory, 57, 369, 373,
    375; International Festival
    (Dublin), 423, 455
Yellow Book, The, 10, 329, 389
Youghal (Ireland), 293
Young Ireland, 39, 77, 90, 97

Zagona, Helen Grace, 277
Zatlin, Linda Gertner, 239–40